BUSINESS DATA PROCESSING

Elias M. Awad
Rochester Institute of Technology

PRENTICE-HALL, INC.
Englewood Cliffs, New Jersey

Library of Congress Catalog Card No.: 65–13576

Printed in the United States of America, C-09379

Current printing (last digit):

13 12 11 10 9 8 7 6 5 4

PRENTICE-HALL INTERNATIONAL, INC., *London*
PRENTICE-HALL OF AUSTRALIA, PTY., LTD., *Sydney*
PRENTICE-HALL OF CANADA, LTD., *Toronto*
PRENTICE-HALL OF INDIA (PRIVATE) LTD., *New Delhi*
PRENTICE-HALL OF JAPAN, INC., *Tokyo*

Preface

For several years, the School of Business Administration at the Rochester Institute of Technology has been offering to freshmen an introductory course in Electronic Data Processing with emphasis upon business aspects and the relationship of data processing to the various areas in a business enterprise. Available texts, it was found, were either too technical in approach for the average freshman business student, because the language was geared to the level of the advanced undergraduate and, in many cases, to the graduate student, or included higher mathematics at a level too challenging for the beginner.

Consequently, the instructor had to resort to pamphlets which the IBM Educational Center generously and willingly supplied, and to a small booklet entitled "Introduction to Data Processing," published and supplied by the public accounting firm of Haskins and Sells. The objective of these materials was primarily "acquaintanceship." Later, IBM manuals were introduced to add depth, but it was soon found that both the language and approach of the manuals, although seemingly elementary, were still too technical. Material in these manuals was not meant to be presented or taught to students who had no direct access to the equipment discussed, nor to those who were expected to learn it from a non-operational standpoint, unless they had acquired previous experience and basic knowledge of the machine(s) in question.

At this point, the School of Business Administration became convinced that data processing was acceptable as a required course and that it should be taught at the first- or second-year level, provided that a book could be found which would present in nontechnical language the ideas in data processing related to and commonly used in the business world. Because the texts purporting to do this do not do the job we think should be done, it has been decided to write a book that, in our estimation, will more nearly meet the goals set up for an introductory course.

This text is designed for a basic course in data processing, for first- or second-year students in schools or colleges of Business Administration, and in Departments of Economics, and/or Economics and Business Administration, in Liberal Arts colleges or Technological institutions. It can be used either as a quarter or as a semester course of three sessions per week. The materials were developed and tested as a result of the author's five years of teaching experience in this field and are based on his intensive research into the basic principles of data processing applicable to business situations.

The objective of the book is to provide the student of business administration with a basic and thorough understanding of data-processing principles, to acquaint him with the equipment, and to analyze and describe the impact of these principles on the business environment. Included are principles related to both punched-card and electronic data-processing equipment. Stress is laid upon the "what" and the "why" of the various components used and their capabilities, and not upon the "how" of these components, such as console operation, wiring techniques, and so forth. In other words, descriptions of "how to do it" are used only insofar as they are valuable in explaining *what* is done and *why* it is done.

The book does not require prior background in machine operation or in mathematics beyond the usual competence in basic algebra attained in high school. Neither does it require the purchase or rental of any equipment for an understanding of the materials presented. However, a live demonstration on a desk machine, such as the Minivac, or a film showing the components as a system in operation, is always helpful.

I am indebted to innumerable persons who directly and indirectly contributed to the preparation of the manuscript. I especially thank Dr. Ralston D. Scott, Chairman of the Faculty of Business Administration, Southern Illinois University, Edwardsville Campus, for his sustained interest and support and for the many helpful suggestions offered throughout the writing of the text.

Gratitude is expressed to Miss Marion L'Amoreaux, Assistant Director, Reading Laboratory, for her assistance in indexing and proofreading the text. I express my appreciation, too, to Miss Edwina B. Hogadone, Dean, College of Business, and to the faculty of the School of Business Administration, Rochester Institute of Technology, many of whom have offered literature and articles in the area of business data processing. Among others who read and/or commented upon the various versions of the manuscript, the following colleagues were especially helpful: Arden Travis, who read Part I of the manuscript and offered helpful comments; Miss Mary Burnet, who edited Chapter 8 and provided pertinent materials in data processing; John Hartley and John Cook, who teach Business Data Processing in the School of Business and who have made suggestions which were helpful in improving parts of the manuscript; William Fleming, William E. Beatty, Dorothy Brooks, and Agnes Putney, who provided me with many pieces of pertinent literature in the data-processing field; and to Houston (Tex) Elam, Bernard Baruch School of Business, City College of New York, who has been instrumental in preparing basic materials in business data processing and with whom I have had the pleasure of teaching the first two-week course in this area.

I thank also Robert Hill, Supervisor, David Hampson, Assistant Supervisor, and Joe Zaia, IBM Programmer, Data Processing Department, Lincoln Rochester Trust Company, for their time in reviewing the two banking applications presented in Chapters 10 and 20. Untold classes of students contributed significantly by comments, questions, criticisms, and suggestions that have served to test and improve these materials. Gratitude is expressed to Miss Elizabeth Klett and Miss Jean Benham for typing the rough draft of Parts I and II of the text.

I am especially indebted to the International Business Machines Corporation for the privilege of attending their educational centers at Endicott, Buffalo, and Syracuse, New York, for the interest and cooperation received from their competent instructors, and for permission to use and adapt the copyrighted photographs of the machines presented in this text. My thanks to Professors Louis J. Gentile, Chairman, Business Education Division, Chaffey College, Alta Loma, California; Laurence E. Harvey, Director of Data Processing, Foothill College, Los Altos Hills, California; Frank M. Rachel, School of Business Administration, North Texas State University, Denton, Texas; and Gilbert D. Saunders, Director, Business Data Processing, Orange Coast College, Costa Mesa, California, for their perceptive, encouraging, and critical reviews. Frederic K. Easter, Jr., Editor of Business Books, Prentice-Hall, Inc., deserves special mention for his enthusiastic interest and helpful comments on parts of this manuscript, as does the Prentice-Hall editorial staff for their general assistance.

ELIAS M. AWAD

Table of Contents

PART 1 WHAT IS DATA PROCESSING?

PART 1

WHAT IS DATA PROCESSING?

Chapter 1

Introduction

Why Data Processing?

By general definition, business data processing consists of recording and reporting business information through the use of either punched-card or electronic data-processing equipment. Everybody must process data, whether performing a decision-making function as an individual, a head of a family, a student, a leader of a social or political organization, or an owner of a business—large or small. In most cases, pencil and paper as manual aids have been and still are used in solving problems and processing data. Great interest has been shown in developments in data processing because businessmen strive constantly toward the attainment of their goals in an efficient way with whatever equipment is available, and they become intimately concerned when the need for developing equipment that will do a better job becomes apparent. In the distant past, under a barter system, a businessman was able to perform all of his necessary calculations mentally, without the aid of machines. His needs and demands, his environment and community, did not require any evidence of his work or any elaboration on his mental performance. Later, as communities expanded and as people began to veer away from the barter system, replacing it with more impersonal business relationships through the use of a monetary unit in their daily business routine, it became necessary for them to put down in writing (to record) their business activities in order to produce records which could be used for present and future analysis of these activities.

The problem

At this stage, human effort of a higher level of competence was considered more necessary than previously. Information related to business required all the presently known steps of recording, classifying, calculating, and summarizing. Much of the routine work necessitated specific processing methods which started with the manual method (for example, the use of a bookkeeper), evolving into mechanical (for example, the use of a cash register), and presently the electronic state (for example, the use of computers). Man, of necessity, has faced the problem of considering how to get more time for creative thinking in his decision making rather than spending most of his working hours in the mere processing of routine data. A consideration of this problem involves a recognition of (1) the physical factors that create large masses of data, (2) the costs involved, (3) the number of people available, (4) the necessity to reduce errors, and (5) the need for speed in preparing reports.

The physical factors

Pressures exerted from without and from within business firms make the job of data processing a "must." External factors include the following, among others: Some customers purchase merchandise for cash; others purchase on account. For the latter, billing is required at the end of a specific period after factors such as adjustments, returned items, and discounts are taken into consideration. Suppliers, too, ship merchandise to the seller on account, creating momentarily a liability on the books of the seller until the merchandise is paid for. Once received, items have to be counted and recorded. They have to be listed and checked (that is, inventoried). The supplier has to be paid, after allowance for returned or defective merchandise (if any) and cash or quantity discounts are taken into consideration. Owners (stockholders, single proprietors, or partners), on the other hand, require periodic reports of the current status and business activities of their firms. They want to know whether or not they are making a profit; whether they should keep the business, invest more money in it, or sell out.

In addition to these types of records, the government requires a multitude of reports from business firms. Taxes have to be paid and supporting statements produced concerning realized net income, the specific tax-deductible expenses incurred, and the periodic report of Social Security payments withheld. Many other statements are also required for presentation to various government agencies.

Internal factors, too, create the need for a host of records. Pressures within the firm necessitate the processing of all types of expenses and revenues in a predetermined order. For example, payroll and payroll taxes, revenue from sales, the updating of inventory, and the handling of receivables and payables all need processing. These and many other activities require building a data-processing system efficient enough to present all necessary reports accurately and economically with as little waste of time as possible.

The cost factor

The time element and timing are important, for our present business firms no longer practice the technique of price competition as much as they practice cost competition. A business firm can compete more successfully by practicing efficiency through reducing its operating costs than through merely reducing the retail price. In other words, firms that are "low-cost" firms and produce a quality product are those that are likely to dominate the markets for particular products. Further, factors such as technological change, innovation, and growth in size and complexity justify the need for and the importance of cost control in business. Business data processing can play a major role in this respect by reducing the amount of time taken to produce necessary records and reports accurately and quickly.

The labor factor

In the past 45 years, there has been a tremendous increase in the number of clerical helpers in business in the United States. This increase has been more than four times the increase in factory help, and has been due to the fact that, as data have increased, more clerical workers have been required because of the use of manual methods in analyzing these data. At this rate, in 50 to 100 years, securing enough people to do necessary clerical work would be a difficult, if not impossible, job. This, as well as the increase in the volume of data and the emphasis upon accuracy and economy, has prompted the search for methods other than manual ones for the processing of data.

The error factor

Once learned, most of the steps followed in analyzing any transaction become basically routine and consequently require comparatively little creative thinking. However, because it seems to be man's nature to think and make decisions upon each step, regardless of the necessity for it, there is a wide margin for error, especially if the steps involve some exceptions. For example, in computing the total pay of each full-time salesman working for a manufacturing concern, a payroll clerk will have to look up the salesman's base pay and add to it any commission based on a percentage of the value of items which he has sold to date. After a while, this job becomes routine and the steps seem mechanical and dull. Consequently, errors occur and perhaps multiply with prolonged work on the same application, because of carelessness, boredom, and environmental conditions, such as pressure for deadlines, and so forth.

The speed factor

Modern data-processing systems attempt to communicate current knowledge as it is needed, for without this kind of communication, such knowledge has little practical use in the making of day-to-day, "on the spot" business decisions. The business environment in the United States is one that stresses time and its cost very heavily. People tend to eat fast, walk fast, and work fast and, in this way, to achieve their primary and other related goals within the schedules they assign to themselves. With all other factors being equal, it takes a European more time to accomplish the many jobs that Americans do, simply because of the European's tendency to relax more and perhaps enjoy his work at a slower rate of speed. One of the things that makes this country and its people a leading power, and a wealthy nation, is the ability and willingness of the people to find ways and means of using time efficiently. We have gotten used to getting more done within a limited period of time than have the people of any other existing nation. We try to work fast *without loss of efficiency or quality*. As a result, competition is becoming more intense because of the tendency and aim of most companies to produce more and more efficiently. Business firms have become very cost-conscious as a result of their interest in mass-producing quality products at the lowest price possible.

Importance of rapid decisions

Because of the foregoing factors, decisions have to be made fairly rapidly and on as sound a basis as possible. Many "split-second" decisions are required daily of executives. These decisions require reliable and accurate financial information. Further, this information must be presented, at the time it is needed, in the form of clear reports, if it is to be useful. Because the slower manual approach is no longer considered satisfactory in meeting this demand, machines that can do significant repetitive jobs fast with a high degree of accuracy obviously are needed. Once this is understood, the role of data processing in business becomes clear.

The solution

Business data-processing systems are capable of performing and repeating the same step for the hundredth time as accurately and quickly as for the first time, no matter how routine or boring it may be. Speed and accuracy are important characteristics to be considered in designing the equipment used. Provided the source data are prepared correctly, processing of them by a computer can be performed very fast and with a degree of accuracy close to perfection. If source data are not prepared in an accurate form, however, the result is, of course, inaccurate. The machine comes up with inaccurate results just as easily as it does with correct ones, because it can be no more accurate than the person who prepares the data for its use. The advanced preparation of instructions for use by the machine is called *programming*. People who do it, called *programmers,* must be trained especially for the job.

Fields of Data Processing

There are two clearly defined fields of data processing: that is, punched card and electronic. Although the principles of operation used in each field are essentially the same, electronic is not only faster than punched card, but differs in the method of handling data. Although certain equipment is commonly used by both, each uses certain other equipment peculiar to its own needs. Considerations of economy and space usually govern the choice of which to install.

Punched-Card Data Processing

Punched-card data processing is the technique of preparing business reports following a routine which begins with the recording of source documents, such as sales reports and other similar types of reports, in a coded form in punched cards. The cards are then fed through equipment capable of detecting and interpreting the holes punched in them. The holes represent information about transactions and are punched in the cards in accordance with a predetermined code. The cards must be of a standard size so that they can be accommodated by the machines.

Necessity for punching information on cards

In its initial stages, information is usually written on paper of *any* size. If these different-size reports were to be used directly in machines, it would require the development of a machine flexible enough to adjust automatically to receiving and reading the desired information on the various-size reports. Such a machine would be too complex in mechanical design to prove satisfactory from the cost standpoint. Also, the likelihood that more than one transaction will be shown on each report would make the job of processing the data in such a machine very difficult if not impossible. For example, on a sales slip, a salesman may record the sales of different items to a certain customer. The items can be anything from furniture and rugs to tweezers and rubber bands. It is an easy task, of course, to figure out the total over-all sales made by that particular salesman, because each of his reports is a complete document and his total sales is the grand total of his reports. But, in figuring out his total sales of each different item sold during the week, each sales report would have to be analyzed individually. The situation becomes more complex if several salesmen in different districts, or several branches in each district, are involved. The processing of such data manually, and the preparation of the desired report, is highly expensive, owing to the time involved in completing the job.

Transactions with different prices and quantity, and other related information, are frequently handwritten. This method is the one used by an order department when dealing with customers who order merchandise by mail, by salesmen who take orders on the sales floor, and by the credit department in taking down information about a customer desiring to open a credit account. Handwriting differs from one person to another. To date, no machine has been developed commercially that can deal with such handwritten reports.* If a machine is to process data for the purpose of producing meaningful reports, it must be able to *read* and *interpret* accurately what it reads. Because machines cannot "read" handwriting or printed words, another solution had to be found before they could be used to process data. Thus, variations in the sizes of documents, recording of unrelated transactions on those documents, and the fact that they are handwritten or printed present a complex situation for the processor. It seems apparent, then, that in order to work out the above problem—or, in fact, any other similar problem in using business records—a standard method of recording facts becomes necessary. This is attained through the use of punched cards, which are then fed into punched-card machines for processing.

---

* Some progress has been made in developing machines to read handwriting in experimental form. They are very promising and will probably be available commercially soon.

Problems with manual handling

Manually, the problem can be solved without much difficulty, if expense is not a factor. A few clerks handle the reports, one at a time. They analyze each and every report, select the desired information from them, and record it on a report form for the person requesting the formal report. However, the manual approach is slow, because the clerks need to analyze each report in order to find the desired transaction in it, make a decision on it, and copy it on a separate page. Then they verify and double-check to see that no transaction is overlooked. The individual clerk is also slowed down by lack of clarity of reports as well as by lack of clarity of the handwriting used in preparing them. If the job is to be speeded up, a few more clerks can be added to work on the report. However, this procedure costs the company probably twice as much to get the job done, because the addition of one or more clerks, although saving time, would tend to increase errors. Hence, the inefficiency inherent in the manual system would be increased rather than lessened.

Standardization of recording a "must"

Punched-card machines can perform work on data and produce reports much faster, more accurately, and more efficiently than can be done manually if the data are standardized in the initial stages. In the case of the salesman's reports, each of the items he sold would be recorded by punching holes on separate cards. Thus, homogeneous, or like, items can be grouped together very easily. The cards become permanent records and can be used indefinitely for future processing.

The unit record principle

Standardization of recording is achieved through using punched cards based on the *Unit Record Principle*. This means the punching of a single complete transaction on a standard-size card. If more data flow in for the purpose of updating a specific transaction, the new data must be punched on a second card and an updated result, after processing, would then be punched on a third card. For example, suppose that on January 1 customer *A* purchases a suit from a retailing firm for $100 on account. Terms of payment: two equal installments of $50, the first due within 15 days, the second at the end of the month. The procedure followed on January 1 is as follows: General information, such as the customer's number, name and address, and so forth, in addition to the amount of $100, is initially punched in a card to record the necessary data for reference. Next, the card is fed through an accounting machine which is designed to handle punched cards. The machine reads and interprets the holes in the card and, on a statement form, prints the account number, name, and address of the customer, the item purchased, and its amount. This statement is mailed to the customer following his purchase of the item. On January 15, the customer pays his first installment of $50. Upon the receipt of the check by the firm, the name, address, and account number, along with the amount of $50, are punched in a card called the "payment card." The initial card containing the $100 is merged with the payment card for the purpose of calculating the balance due on the customer's account. The calculator first reads the initial card containing $100 and next the payment card containing the first installment of $50. On the payment card, it subtracts and punches the remainder (the balance of $50), along with the other necessary information, and the payment card becomes the customer's updated record. On January 31, when the second installment is paid, a new card is punched to record all the necessary information and the final payment of $50. It is then merged with the updated record of January 15 and the $50 payment is subtracted from the $50 balance to show that the account has a zero balance.

This simple transaction, multiplied many times during the week, requires a host of punched cards and punched-card machines set up to work as a team in processing the desired data and preparing needed reports.

Electronic Data Processing

In the early 1920's, the word *robot* was introduced by Czech author Karel Capek in his play *R.U.R.* (*Rossum's Universal Robots*). The word denotes a machine that, under human control, can do intelligent routine manual work for human beings. Since its introduction, the word has gained recognition in describing modern computers which can do such work automatically.

Since the 1940's, we have been hearing through many media of communication, for example, radio, television, newspapers, magazines, and national conferences, of the impressive functions of the "robots," or electronic computers; that is, their role in rocketry, in guiding missiles, in maneuvering a satellite in orbit, in controlling many sequential steps in an assembly line, and in performing a number of routine operations while virtually unattended. The average person is often overimpressed, and at times frightened, by these components, which are in reality relatively simple. It will take time before a majority of people understand, clearly and meaningfully, the capabilities and impact of the computer. Whether we like it or not, we have already entered the age of so-called "thinking" machines. These machines, made of metal and glass, properly set up by a human being, perform mechanical, repetitive activities that once required hours of routine work by a human being. They can be programmed to perform involved, as well as routine, numerical calculations by receiving and following instructions accurately. They have a "memory" unit that can store data or pieces of information for future need. Computers can also be programmed to compare two factors and choose the proper course of action among several alternatives. For these reasons, it is tempting to believe that these electronic "brains" are almost capable of thought because of the way they are programmed by man to behave. "Programming" is similar to giving a set of instructions orally or in writing to live workers. To the uninitiated, these machines become more and more awesome as manufacturers narrow the gap between the clerical capabilities of the machines and those of man. No one can tell with any degree of certainty that a computer will not some day be programmed to participate in a world-championship game of chess, and no one would doubt fully that it can be programmed to paint reproductions of pictures equal in technical detail at least to a Michelangelo, Da Vinci, or Rembrandt now hanging in one of the halls of art. Understandably enough, research has a long way to go before any such achievement by a computer can be realized, but, in view of the trend of progress in this area, the pace seems unusually fast.

Nature of the work performed by computers

Generally speaking, there are two types of human thinking: creative and routine. Creative thinking demands imagination and insight by a composer when he composes a symphony or by a mathematician when he develops a new formula or theory. There is no definite set of rules for attaining such results. Routine thinking, on the other hand, is the habitual, perfunctory approach to performing work based on a definite set of rules which requires essentially little talent other than that involved in following instructions accurately. Any person can figure out the sum of two one-digit numbers, or translate into English a simple paragraph in Spanish. Most of our daily work involves routine thinking which takes a lot of time because of the repetitive detail making it up. The computer is primarily designed to do the routine "thinking" in order to save human time and energy for more creative thinking and to present us with more accurate results. It can be programmed to serve in the capacity of a record keeper, a clerk, and/or an office worker. One of its most significant applications is in keeping track of inventories in a store and updating them every time new supplies are received or a certain quantity is sold.

Capabilities of computers

Computers have a built-in self-control. Once they are fed the desired instructions, they can process information in such a way that human attendance or supervision is no longer necessary. We should remember that, initially, a human being, called a "programmer," makes all the required decisions and converts those decisions into instructions for the computer. The computer, in this respect, is like a person learning to drive an automobile for the first time. The instructor sitting beside the student tells him what to do first, and how, when, and why he needs to operate which controls. He tells the student driver when and how to start up in first gear, how to shift into second, and what to do next. He instructs him further in the proper method of slowing down by applying his brakes and taking his foot off the gas pedal, and in shifting into a lower gear when approaching a red traffic light or a stop sign. Under such conditions, we may say that the instructor is in command of the automobile. He is making all the decisions. The student driver is merely obediently following and executing the instructions like a robot. He does not control the automobile until he drives alone and has to make all the necessary decisions regarding operation and manipulation of the automobile in traffic. A computer works primarily *like the student driver*, receiving instructions and executing them as directed.

Classification of computers

Computers fall into two classifications: that is, digital and analog. The latter *measures,* whereas the former *counts*. In a digital computer, all arithmetic computations depend eventually on counting, in the same manner as an abacus depends on the counting of beads for similar functions. By contrast, there is no counting of unrelated or discrete quantities in an analog computer.

The digital computer

In the digital computer, for example, addition of 115 and 352 is performed by the use of an adder, which consists of two counters. The first counter stores the 352. The second amount (115) is added through the utilization of a second counter, which now works simultaneously with the first. The sum of 467 is shown in counter 1 only after counter 2 holds 115. Mechanically speaking, counter 1 is increased by 1 every time counter 2 is increased by 1 also. That is, counter 2 drags with it counter 1 as 115 is being registered in it, thus causing addition to take place and the correct answer to be shown in counter 1. Subtraction is performed by adding the second quantity in reverse. For example, when a 20-cent item is purchased and a 25-cent coin is offered by the customer, the clerk hands back the difference of 5 cents as follows: Counting begins at 20 to account for the price of the item, and addition in change begins until 25 is reached. That is, *21, 22, 23, 24, 25;* or 5 cents in change.

Multiplication is performed by repetitive addition. For instance, 4×6 means that 4 is added to itself six times; that is, $4 + 4 + 4 + 4 + 4 +$

4 = 24, or that 6 is added to itself four times; that is, 6 + 6 + 6 + 6 = 24. Division is accomplished by repetitive subtraction. For example, in dividing 15 by 3, the following substractions are made:

	Number of Subtractions	
15 − 3 = 12	1	
12 − 3 = 9	1	
9 − 3 = 6	1	
6 − 3 = 3	1	
3 − 3 = 0	1	
Total Number of Subtractions	5,	or quotient.

The analog computer

In an analog computer, numbers are represented by physical quantities. In a multiplication problem, for instance, the numbers to be multiplied are represented by two voltages. They are applied to two sets of input terminals of an electric circuit. The circuit is so designed that the magnitude of the output voltage corresponds to the two numbers.

The idea of an analog computer was seriously considered by V. Bush, of the Massachusetts Institute of Technology, who was the first to build such a machine. It was called the *differential analyzer*. In general, analog computers perform addition, subtraction, multiplication, division, differentiation, and integration and solve differential equations. They are not considered as accurate as digital computers. They are characterized by continuous operations, in sharp contrast with the unrelated operations of the digital computers.

An analog computer is a mathematical instrument, an example of which is the slide rule. In fact, two rulers can act in the same capacity as an analog computer, Figure 1-1. For instance, in adding 6 + 3, first place ruler *A* on top of ruler *B*. Move ruler *A* to the right until its left edge is on top of number 3 on ruler *B*. The sum 9 is now displayed immediately under number 6 of ruler *A*. Try different examples and see how simple it is.

In Figure 1-1, a physical quantity was used to represent a number. In fact, we represented each of the two numbers by a length on a ruler. The sum was obtained simply by adding the length.

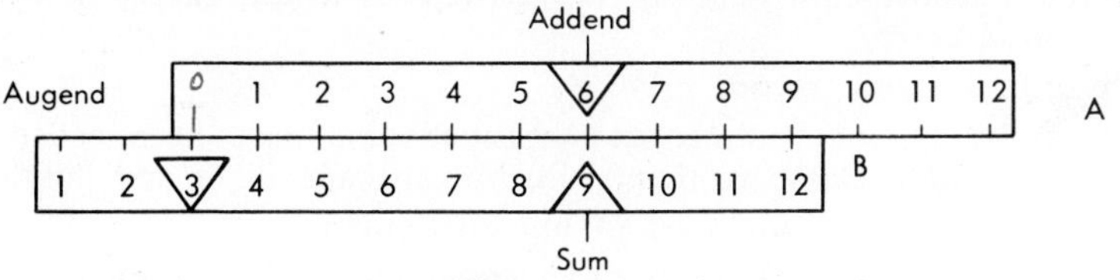

Figure 1-1

Nature of computers

Computers are, thus, tools. They function like any other tool in getting a job done. An axe, for example, is an extension of the hand; it increases the force of the hand in order to break a log. A telescope is an extension of the eye, for it, too, increases the magnitude of sight of the eye to identify faraway objects. A telephone is an extension of the ear; the bicycle, an extension of the leg. Therefore, it can be reasoned, likewise, that a computer is *an extension of the human brain.*

Computer designers and users of digital computers borrow terms from the fields of engineering, mathematics, and psychology in order to describe the component parts and the functions of these machines. For instance, they speak of machine "memory," machine "language," machine "logic," and even machine "intelligence." Because the adoption of such terms is meant for the use of trained computer people, they may lead to mental confusion, and hence misunderstanding, on the part of the layman. On the other hand, when properly explained, these terms tend to be much easier to use in describing the components of computers and their functions than serial numbers or more technical names.

REVIEW QUESTIONS

1. What is business data processing? Why did it come into being?
2. What factors are involved in the consideration of the processing of routine data?
3. What factors in business firms make the role of data processing necessary? Give examples.
4. Discuss "low-cost" firms and their functioning in regard to business data processing.
5. What is the main reason for human errors in the processing of data? Can electronic systems control such errors? Why?
6. Why is speed important in the processing of data?
7. How important is source data in the preparation of processing data?
8. What is programming? How important is this function to the processing of data?
9. Name and compare the two fields of data processing.
10. Define punched-card data processing. Why is it necessary to punch information in cards?
11. Describe the unit record principle.
12. Electronic systems with robot-like functioning have been called "thinking" machines. Compare them with human capabilities and limitations.
13. Name and discuss two types of human thinking.
14. What are the two classifications of computers? Describe their functions.

Chapter 2

Historical Background

Early Methods of Calculation

Until the nineteenth century, people found business calculations a very complex job, because they had to be done "in the head." This was so primarily because writing materials were very scarce and, therefore, too expensive to use for ordinary purposes. Paper was probably made by the Chinese before the time of Christ, but it was not until the fourteenth century A.D. that the science of paper making spread into Europe. Paper made from pulp was an invention of the nineteenth century. Thus, it was not until comparatively recent times that paper has been available on a mass-production basis.

Finger counting

The lack of paper caused people to do most of their calculations mentally, with the aid of their fingers. Simple additions were carried out by finger tallying. For example, to add five and two, one holds up two fingers, then five more fingers, and counts the total number of upraised fingers to get the result of seven. When more complex forms of calculation were devised, they were initially performed by the use of fingers. Finger training was so important that it was taught in Roman schools, and various methods were devised to do "advanced" operations such as multiplication and division. For instance, the student was required to learn the multiplication table up to 5 × 5 only. His fingers took over in figuring out the product of any numbers between 5 and 10. Suppose we wish to multiply 9 × 7. In order to do that, we would raise four fingers on one hand, representing 6, 7, 8, and 9, and two fingers on the other hand, representing 6 and 7—that is, the numbers over 5. The product is obtained as follows: The sum of the fingers raised (that is, 4 + 2 = 6) determines the value of the tens position, and the product of the fingers not raised (1 × 3 = 3) determines the value of the units position: thus, 63. Try this method, using different numbers between 5 and 10, and see how easy it is to multiply. Also, try to visualize how long it would take, using this method, to figure out bills for the average firm today to send to its customers at the end of the month.

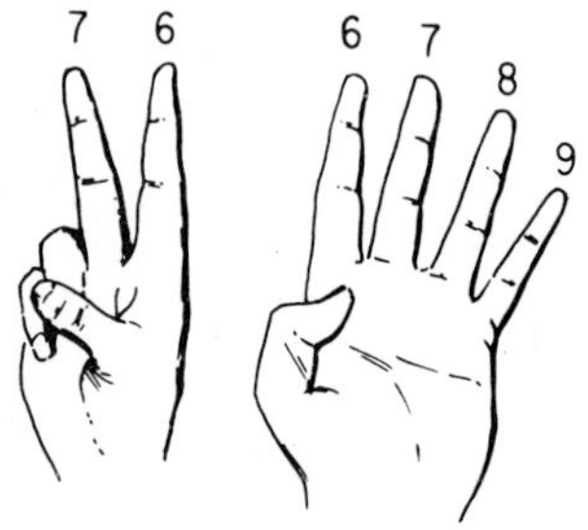

The abacus

The verb *calculate* is derived from the Latin *calculus,* which means "pebble" or "a small piece of marble." The experienced calculators of early times performed their calculations by the use of a device containing pebbles or beads strung on a string called an *abacus,* or a counting frame. The beads are strung on strings in the form of rows. Each row contains 10 beads. In Figure 2-1, beads in row A have a value of 1 each, representing the units position; beads in row B have a value of 10 each, representing the tens position; and beads in row C have a value of 100 each, representing the hundreds position; and so forth. All beads must start in the left part of the device.

To get number 436, as shown in Figure 2-2, first move six beads to the right in row A to represent the units position, which is 6. Second, move three beads in row B to the right to denote 3, the tens position, which is

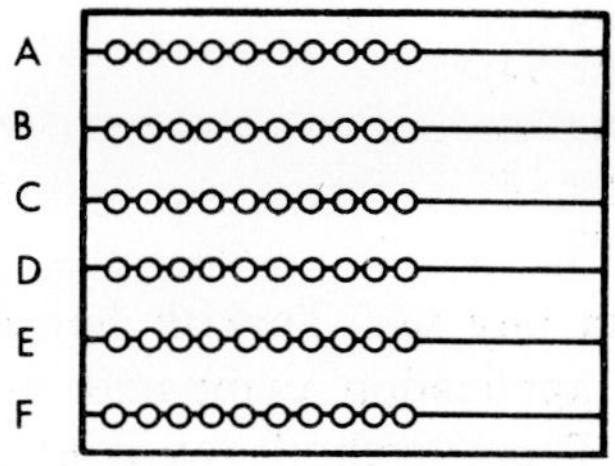

Figure 2-1. An Abacus

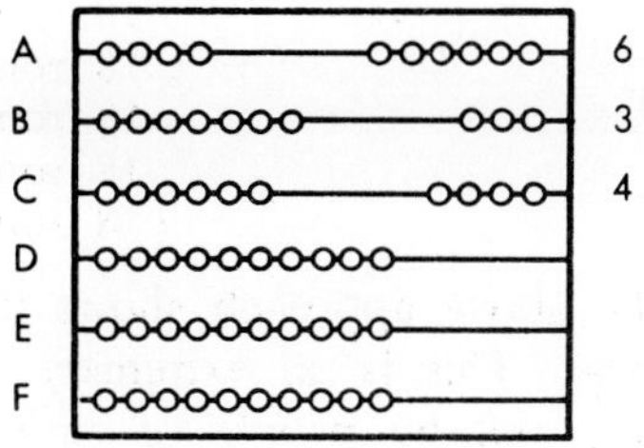

Figure 2-2. The number 436 on an Abacus

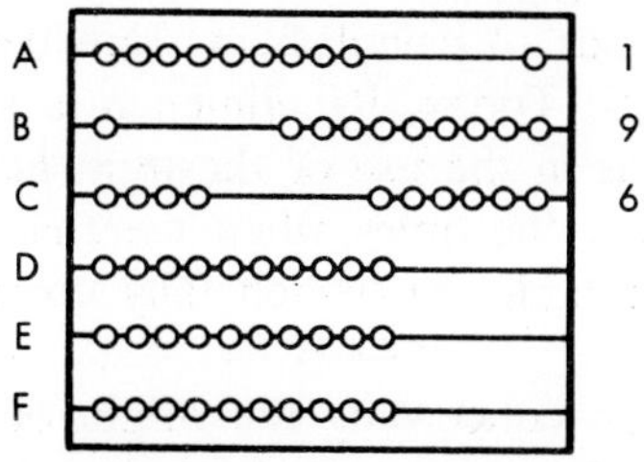

Figure 2-3. The number 691 on an Abacus

3; and last, move four beads in row C to the right to denote the hundreds position, which is 4.

If we wish to add, let us say, 255 to the above number (436), we would do the following: Move 5 beads in row A to the right. Because we have only four beads left in that row, addition of 5 + 6 is accomplished by moving five beads in row A to the left and moving one bead from row B to the right instead, as shown in Figure 2-3. In regular addition, 5 + 6 = 1 and carry one. Next, move five beads from row B to the right and two beads from row C to the right. Now add the beads in each row to get the answer; that is, in row A, the total is 1, the units position; in row B, it is 9, the tens position; and in row C, 6, the hundreds position: 691.

The abacus was used efficiently in addition and subtraction. However, even when it came to multiplication or division, limited historical data show that many people have used the abacus for these purposes, too. Multiplication was done by repeated addition, and division was done by repeated subtraction: a method which is at present performed by digital computers. For example, if seven Turkish horses cost eighteen liras each, the total value of seven horses would be obtained by the sum of 18 + 18 + 18 + 18 + 18 + 18 + 18. Likewise, if we wanted to know how many Turkish horses could be bought with ninety liras (approximately $15), we would take:

18 from 90, leaving 72;
18 from 72; leaving 54;
18 from 54; leaving 36;
18 from 36; leaving 18;
18 from 18; leaving 0.

The above approach shows that we can buy five Turkish horses with 90 liras. This is an extremely simplified application compared to those worked out by people of earlier times. Their methods were extremely complex, because they had to be practical. The abacus has been used until comparatively recent times, partly because of the scarcity of writing materials and partly owing to the lack of a practical numbers method. Even after written methods of calculations were devised, the influence of the abacus still remained. Today, its influence is seen in the use of the word *calculate,* as well as in the use of the term *buying over the counter*. The latter is derived from the times when merchants in the Middle Ages used boards or counting tables on which they computed their customer's account.

There is some question concerning the origin of the abacus. Although several nations claim to have originated it, the idea probably developed in many nations and was later carried into other parts of the world by merchants and travelers. Its original home is believed to have been Egypt or Babylon. The ancient Hindus used one type of abacus called the *sand-tray* or *dust-board,* which was also common in both the Roman and Greek civilizations. Some scholars trace the origin of the term *abacus* to the Semitic *Abai,* meaning "dust." However, others are of the belief that the Greek *abax,* which means "tablet," is a more likely origin. Other types of abaci include the Chinese Suan-pan, the Japanese Soroban, the Russian S'choty, the Armenian Choreb, and the Turkish Coulba.

The Development of Manual Aids in Written Calculations

The "grating" method

Arab, Hindu, and European calculators were the first to develop techniques of written calculations. The Arabs originated a "grating" method which was used by the Hindus in multiplication. This method involved a tablet consisting of a number of squares with diagonals. The idea was to place the multiplier on the top of the tablet with its high-order position on the top left column. The multiplicand was placed to the left side of the tablet with its high-order position in the top left corner also (Figure 2-4). The squares hold the product of the two digits opposite it. For example, assume the multiplication of 217 × 14. The number 217 is placed on top of the tablet: the 2 is on the left corner, 1 on top of the middle column, and 7 on top of the right column. The number 14 (the multiplicand) is placed on the left side of the tablet with 1 (highest power) to the side of the top left corner.

The lower halves of the upper three squares show the product of multiplying 217 × 1. The bottom three squares display the product of multiply-

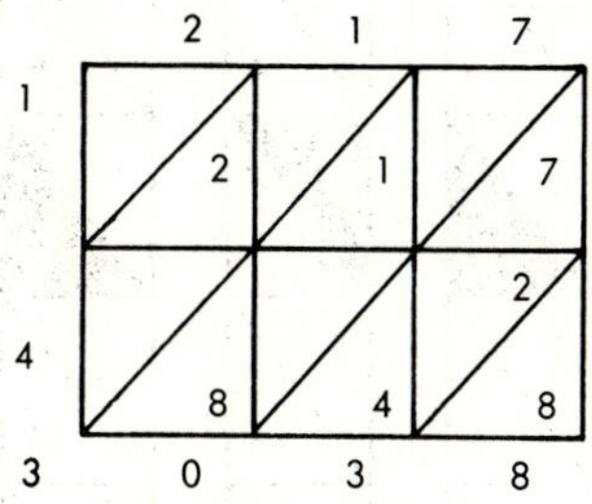

Figure 2-4

ing 217 × 4. Notice that the carry of 2 in 28 (product of 7 × 4) is displayed in the upper half of the square which shows 28. The product of 217 × 14 is attained by adding diagonally, as shown in Figure 2-4.

The "bones" method

The above technique was used later in 1617 in Napier's "bones." John Napier, of Merchiston, Scotland, attempted to reduce tedious calculations involving large numbers. His "bones," or rods, made a great impression on the Europeans and Chinese. To explain: each rod is divided into nine squares, each of which is divided diagonally. The top square holds a number (1-9). The remaining eight squares in the rod hold the product of multiplying that number by 2, 3, 4, 5, 6, 7, 8, and 9. The rods for multiplying 1, 3, 7, and 4 are shown in Figure 2-5. Once it is set up, it is easy to obtain the product of 2 × 374 or 5 × 374 or any other numbers from the top squares and the left rod, because the numbers in the middle are used to obtain the product only. For example, in order to get the product of 3 × 374, we add diagonally the numbers on the same level of 3 from right to left. See Figure 2-5.

The "sluggard" method

The Arabs and the Hindus rarely used any multiplication tables. But when written calculations became more and more common, calculators in the sixteenth century introduced a written method which, when used, would obtain the product of numbers up to 10 × 10, similar to the Roman approach using the fingers. The multiplication table of 5 × 5 had to be learned. The method was called the "sluggard's method." For ex-

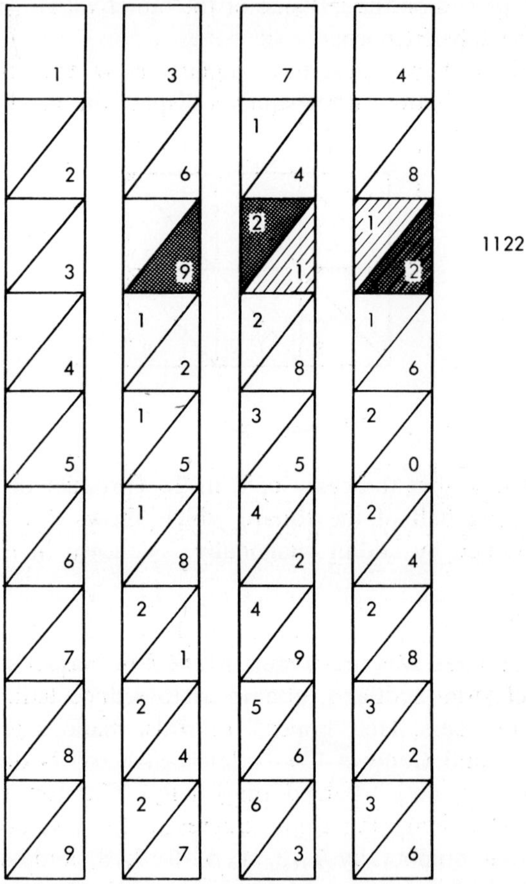

<u>Step 1.</u> Add the contents of the first diagonal column.

Answer is (2) (Units position)

<u>Step 2.</u> Add the contents od the second diagonal column.

Answer is (1+1)=(2) (Tens positions)

<u>Step 3.</u> Add the contents of the third diagonal column.

Answer is (2+9)=(1) and carry (1) (Hundreds position)

Therefore, the product is 1 1 2 2

Figure 2-5. Napier's bones

ample, assume the multiplication of 8 × 6. The numbers 6 and 8 are recorded in the manner shown in Figure 2-6. Opposite these two digits, their differences from 10 are written. The product, then, is obtained as follows:

The tens position of the product is obtained either by subtracting 2 from 6 or 4 from 8 (that is, 4).

The units position of the product is obtained by multiplying the 4 and 2 (that is, 8). So, the product of 6 x 8 is 48.

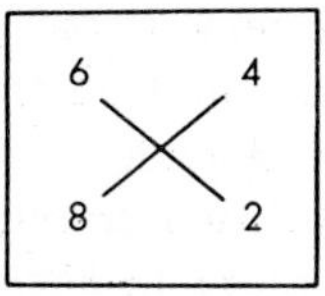

Figure 2-6

The "Arabic Numerals" system

The history of our number system is of Hindu origin, based on the use of ten fingers. The system was brought to Spain by the Moors in the ninth century as a result of the expansion of the Moslem Empire at that time. Later it was introduced into Europe. The number system was modified in India into what we now call the "Arabic Numerals." Actually, true Arabic numerals are still in use in the Middle and Near East. Figure 2-7 is an example of the Arabic numerals and their translation into the currently used English numerical symbols.

٠	١	٢	٣	٤	٥	٦	٧	٨	٩
0	1	2	3	4	5	6	7	8	9

Figure 2-7. Arabic numerals

The Development of Mechanical Aids to Written Calculations

Numerical wheel calculator

Because of the widespread use and knowledge of the Arabic system of numeration in Christian Europe about the thirteenth century, mathematicians began to develop computing devices to calculate at a much higher level than that of the abacus. The first of such devices was the numerical wheel calculator (the world's first adding machine), made around 1642 by Blaise Pascal of Paris at the age of 18. He was interested in building it because he wanted to aid his father, who at that time was the superintendent of taxes. His calculator was capable of registering decimal value by the rotation of the wheel by one to nine steps, with a carry lever to operate the next higher digit wheel as a given wheel exceeded 10 units of registration. It is considered the first real calculating machine to be developed.

"Four-function" machines

In 1673, Gottfried Wilhelm von Leibnitz, a philosopher and mathematician, showed how a mechanical multiplier could be made. He felt that multiplication could be treated like addition. For example, multiplying 5 × 4 means 5 added to itself four times or 4 added to itself five times. In this case, two counters would be needed: One to perform the addition and the other to show when addition should stop. Division was looked upon as the reverse of multiplication, and subtraction was adding the second quantity in reverse. Thus, these four basic arithmetic operations were based on counting. Leibnitz built his "Stepped-wheel" machine when he was about 25 years old. It was later manufactured in 1694. However, this machine, as well as that of Pascal, was not considered dependable in its operation.

One of the more dependable and successful calculating machines was developed in 1820 by Charles Xavier Thomas, of Colmar, France. It performed all the four functions of arithmetic. In 1872, Frank Stephen Baldwin, of the United States, introduced a different principle in his calculating machine from that on which the Thomas machine was based. He began building his machine a year later, thus marking the beginning of the calculating-machine industry in the United States.

The Development of Automatic Mechanical Aids to Calculation

Origin of the digital computer

Automatic computation began in 1812 with Charles P. Babbage, an English mathematician who mastered thoroughly the basic fundamentals of digital computers, to the marvel of those associated with him. His dreams and ideas were not fully appreciated, however, until the last decade of his century.

Born in 1792 in Devonshire, England, Babbage became wealthy when his father (a banker) died leaving him a sizable inheritance. He received a formal education interrupted by many personal factors. He taught himself enough mathematics to find out later at Cambridge University that what he already knew was far beyond the background of his teacher. At that time, he became interested in investigating applications of mathematics to practical projects, such as machine tools, and in a revival of the study of mathematics. Up to that time, universities such as Cambridge were still dominated by the theories of Newton. With two of his friends, George Peacock and John Herschel, whose father discovered the planet

Uranus and who himself later became a noted astronomer, he formed the Analytical Society. In 1828, with no scholarly distinction, Babbage was elected to the Lucasian Chair of Mathematics (Newton's Chair) and held it for 11 years, an unprecedented event in view of the fact that he had not delivered even one lecture at the University.

One of the better-known contributions of Babbage was the "Difference Engine." In 1812, while in the Analytical Society quarters looking at a table of logarithms full of mistakes, he began to think in terms of the use of a machine capable of computing mathematical tables. The French Government had already used several computers which could add and subtract only. The job performed on the tables was initially divided into simple operations, each of which was assigned to a separate computer. Babbage firmly believed that he could develop a special-purpose machine capable of doing the computations automatically. Figure 2-8 presents the main idea of computing tables. It is centered around the fact that the level difference between values computed for a formula remains the same. Once achieved, the subsequent values themselves can be produced by addition only. The table in Figure 2-8 shows the level difference between A^3 in the formula $B = A^3$.

When A is		B would be =	1st. diff. D 1	2nd. diff. D 2	3rd. diff. D 3
0	then	0			
			1		
1		1		6	
			7		6
2		8		12	
			19		6
3		27		18	
			37		6
4		64		24	
			61		6
5		125		30	
			91		6
6		216		36	
			127		
7		343			

Figure 2-8

The third-level difference corresponds to the third power of A in $B = A^3$ and is constant. If we wish to compute any other value of A, it can be done by addition alone. For example, in computing the value of $A = 8$, we would add $6 + 36 + 127 + 343$ to give us the sum of 512. Additional numbers in D2 can be found by simple addition, that is, 42, 48, 54, 60, and so forth. From these numbers, the numbers of the second column (D1), and ultimately of the first column, can be found.

The foregoing idea was demonstrated in a model of the Difference

Engine which Babbage made in 1822. It was received with such great interest and enthusiasm that the Royal Society promised to subsidize Babbage's project for developing a larger machine, after an interview with the Chancellor of the Exchequer. The British Government built a workshop for him, as well as a special fireproof vault to safeguard the blueprints of his engine. However, it took Babbage more time than anticipated to complete his model. This was because he became interested in a new idea involving a machine of fantastic capabilities which he wanted to build instead. This "defection" led, in 1842, to the official withdrawal of the government from any further support for the project, which forced Babbage to give up its construction. A model of the Difference Engine built in 1859 for the Registrar General was adopted four years later by life insurance companies and for several years was used to compute life tables.

In 1833, while the Difference Engine project was suspended for a year, Babbage conceived the idea of building an Analytical Engine which would be capable of performing any calculation. It was to be the first general digital computer. Babbage worked on it for the remaining years of his life and financed it completely from his own funds. He died in 1871 with the job undone, a disappointed man, although he left thousands of drawings which outline the details of building the engine. Later his son, Major General H. P. Babbage, took up his father's project and succeeded in completing part of the arithmetic unit.

Babbage's plan to build what seemed to his colleagues to be a fantastically large engine, at a time when such a machine was beyond the grasp and comprehension of the majority of mathematicians, probably hampered the serious development of his ideas for over 100 years. Once he developed the idea of the Analytical Engine, he virtually abandoned the rather simple and useful Difference Engine. The Analytical Engine was to contain a storage capacity for 1,000 members, of 50 digits each. He designed the machine to accept input from cards invented by a Frenchman named Joseph Marie Jacquard for the control of looms. The engine fascinated Babbage during the major part of his life. However, his failure to express himself adequately, because of his impatience with people who were slow-thinking as far as mathematics and mechanics were concerned, made him a poor salesman of his ideas. He tried to solve his problems independently with his own means—problems which eventually occupied the efforts and talents of two generations of engineers. Because of this, he became a frustrated and unhappy man, and once told a friend that he could not remember a single completely happy day in his life. He seemed to feel that mankind in general was against him, and especially the English people and the British Government. Despite this failure to "sell" his ideas, it would not be improper to think of Babbage as one of the great pioneers in the field of computation. He was a philosopher, a mathematician, a professor, and the writer of over 80 books and papers. This was the product of a "man of vision" who possessed the foresight, courage, and imagination to work on and develop what he believed was possible and would be helpful to mankind.

Modern development of the Babbage idea

Over 100 years passed before another machine similar to the one visualized by Babbage was developed. In 1937, Professor Howard G. Aiken, a physicist at Harvard University, developed some ideas involving mechanical calculations. Through Dr. Brown, who then was a consultant to I.B.M. and a professor at Harvard, Aiken sold I.B.M. his ideas, which resulted in a research grant to Harvard for developing a sequential computer. Seven years later (May 1944), through the efforts of Aiken, an automatic sequence-controlled calculator (named the Harvard Mark I) was put into service. Its calculating elements consisted of mechanical counters driven through electromagnetic clutches controlled by electromechanical relay circuits. The Mark I has often been referred to as a "mechanical brain." It adds, subtracts, multiplies, divides, and compares quantities. Also, it has the ability to refer to any tables stored in it for the solution of specific problems. In addition, it can be adapted to solve various kinds of problems for engineers, physicists, and mathematicians. It was the first machine to do long series of arithmetic and logical functions. After the Mark I, the Mark II, Mark III, and Mark IV were constructed by Professor Aiken.

Shortly after the Mark I, between 1942 and 1946, at the University of Pennsylvania a large general-purpose computer was designed by Drs. J. Presper Eckert and John W. Mauchly, supervised by Dr. J. M. Brainerd, Head of Research and Development at the Moore School of Electrical Engineering. It was called the ENIAC (Electronic Numerical Integrator and Calculator). It is this machine (the first all-electronic computer) which the press at that time referred to as the "mechanical brain." The ENIAC was considered very fast in working out long calculations. Initially, it was used primarily for solving mathematical problems in the areas of ballistics and aeronautics. Its main drawback was the fact that it was designed for a special set of problems, thus making the change of programming relatively slow. The ENIAC was moved to Aberdeen Proving Grounds in Maryland in 1947 and continued in operation until late 1955.

Later, Dr. Irven Travis succeeded Dr. Brainerd, and the Moore School of Electrical Engineering took over the project of developing the EDVAC (Electronic Discrete Variable Automatic Computer) for the Aberdeen Proving Grounds. The EDVAC used punched paper tape for input, and a program, which controlled the sequential operations, was placed in the memory of the machine. It was the world's first commercial electronic data-processing machine.

Since then, many machines have been developed. The EDSAC (Electronic Delayed Storage Automatic Computer) was built in Cambridge, England, and the ACE (Automatic Computer Engine) in London by the National Physical Laboratory. In 1946, Eckert and Mauchly left the University of Pennsylvania and negotiated a contract with the National Bureau of Standards, forming the Eckert-Mauchly Corporation. They started to develop the UNIVAC. The UNIVAC (Universal Automatic Computer) is well known for having predicted the victory of President Dwight D. Eisenhower in the election of 1952. The Eckert-Mauchly Corporation later became a division of Sperry Rand Corporation.

In England, the "MADAM" (Manchester Automatic Digital Machine) at the University of Manchester was constructed by Ferranti, Ltd. At the University of London, the SEC (Simple Electronic Computer) and the APEC (All Purpose Electronic Computer) were developed.

Since 1958, hundreds of large and small computers have been made available for commercial purposes. Among the computer manufacturers are The International Business Machines Corporation, General Electric Corporation, Radio Corporation of America, Sperry Rand Corporation, Honeywell, Inc., Burroughs Corporation, National Cash Register, and Control Data Corporation.

The Development of the Punched Card and the Punched-Card Machine

Developments in the United States

The history of punched cards and the machines using them dates from the late 1800's. It all started because the pressing demands on the United States Bureau of the Census created a need for developing better and faster methods of processing census data. As required by the Constitution, the United States government must take a national census once every ten years. In the beginning, computation and compilation of data were performed manually.

During the nineteenth century, population increased greatly in the United States. Information of more complex nature which was demanded at every census made the manual method impractical. By the time the desired information was ready for publication, it was already obsolete and useless. To combat this situation, the Census Bureau sought the aid of a noted statistician as a special agent for the 1890 census. His name was Herman Hollerith. At that time, Dr. Hollerith was experimenting with punched-card components in the hope of coming up with a machine that would process census data faster and more efficiently than the manual system. The 1880 census took seven and a half years to finish, a total time considered by Hollerith as a tremendous waste.

By 1890, Dr. Hollerith completed a set of machines ready to process the 1890 census. It was the first large-scale punched-card data-processing machine installation. It included a card punch (a keyboard invented by Hollerith) which punched holes in 3″ × 5″ cards to record data, manually fed electromagnetic counters, and a sorting box. The census job was completed in two and one-half years, despite an increase in population from 50 million in 1880 to 63 million in 1890, a saving of over five years' time.

In 1903 Hollerith resigned his job with the Census Bureau and formed the Tabulating Machine Company, from which the International Business Machines Corporation emerged in 1912. His first customers were the railroads, which used his machines for computation of freight statistics. I.B.M.'s real name at that time was the Computing-Tabulating-Recording Company. It was changed officially to I.B.M. in 1924.

After Hollerith resigned, the Census Bureau hired James Powers, a comparatively little-known statistician from New Jersey, in 1905, to develop more equipment in a new mechanical laboratory subsidized by Congress. Powers developed several tabulating and other punched-card machines which were used successfully in the 1910 census. He developed the simultaneous-punching principle which involves the keying in of all the information to be punched in a card. Then, by depression of a certain key, the information can be punched simultaneously. This technique has the advantage of allowing the key-punch operator enough time to check and ascertain that the data to be punched are correctly keyed in. This is in contrast with the serial technique of punching, which causes a character to be punched in a column each time a key is depressed. The simultaneous principle is at present used in the Remington Rand machines.

Powers resigned his job with the Census Bureau in 1911 to head the Powers Accounting Machines Company in order to capitalize on his sorter and punching machines. His company was acquired later by the Remington Rand Corporation.

Developments in England

In 1926, work of mechanizing calculations on navigational tables was initiated by Dr. L. J. Combie, another pioneer in the field of computation, who was the Deputy Superintendent of the Nautical Almanac Office in England. Astronomical data were often faulty and unreliable because of the many mistakes resulting from the use of manual computation. Combie applied Hollerith's system in preparing the tables for the Nautical Almanac. Pertinent data were punched on cards in order to compute the position of the moon daily at noon and midnight from the year 1935 to 2000 A.D. From the results of the computations, the tables of the Nautical Almanac were prepared by the National Cash Register Company's accounting machines—hooked up in pairs and operated from a single shaft—a modern version of the Babbage Difference Engine.

REVIEW QUESTIONS

1. Why were business calculations once considered complex? Explain.
2. Explain finger counting. Demonstrate the addition of $4 + 3 = 7$.
3. Show how the product of multiplying 8×7 is obtained by the use of the fingers.
4. What is an abacus? In what arithmetic functions is it used mostly? Explain its basic operation.
5. Discuss the origin of the abacus.
6. What is the "grating" method? Who originated it? Explain its operation.
7. Who invented "Napier's Bones"? Why?
8. Explain briefly the way Napier's Bones perform the multiplication function.
9. Show how multiplying 7×9 is done by the use of the "sluggard" method.
10. Who built the world's first adding machine? What was it called? Why did he build it?
11. State briefly the main ideas of Leibnitz. What were the results of these ideas?
12. Describe the life of Henry Babbage.
13. What is the main idea around which Babbage's "Difference Engine" was centered? Explain and give an example.
14. For what reason(s) was the construction of the Difference Engine abandoned? Explain.
15. Describe generally the analytical engine. Was it completed during the lifetime of Babbage? If not, why?
16. What is the main contribution of Professor Howard G. Aiken to the computer world? Describe it.
17. Describe the ENIAC. Who built it? What was its main drawback?
18. What factors were responsible for the initiation and, later, the development of punched-card data-processing machines? Explain fully.
19. Describe the main contributions of Dr. Hollerith to punched-card data processing. What is the name of the company resulting from his works?
20. Explain the main contributions of Dr. Powers to punched-card data processing. What company was eventually formed which to date practices and develops machines based on his ideas?

Chapter 3

The Punched Card

What Is a "Punched" Card?

People who have not come into contact with punched cards are "few and far between." Such cards are used extensively as pay checks, time cards, soap coupons, gasoline credit cards, utility bills, *Reader's Digest* or *Time Magazine* bills, and even as tickets for use on turnpikes.

Basically, a punched card is a pasteboard of high-quality paper able to resist contraction or expansion due to temperature or humidity. Figure 3-1 is a replica of an IBM card with the upper right corner cut. This cut is used primarily to assure the machine operator that all cards in the deck are facing the same direction.

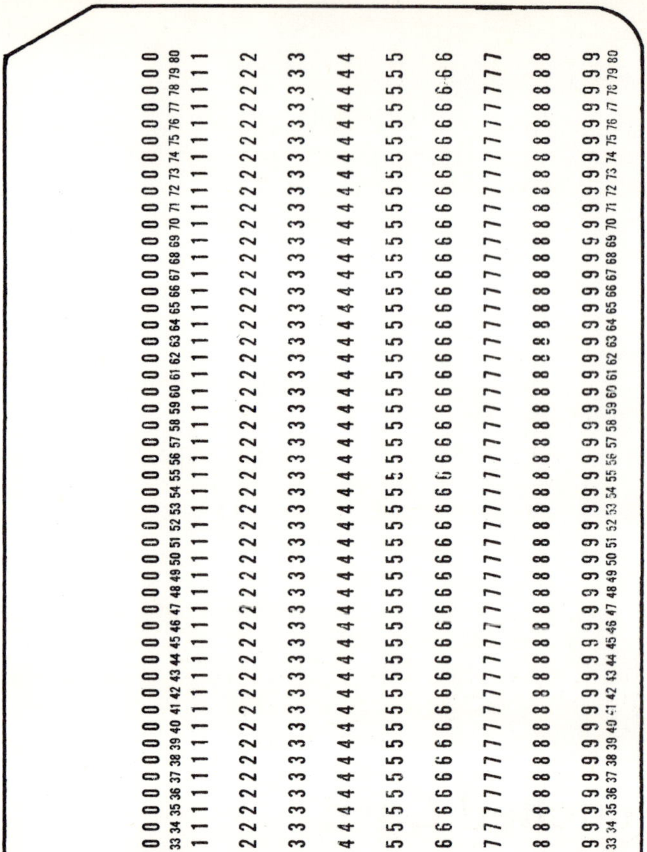

Figure 3-1. IBM card—actual size

As was mentioned in Chapter 1, the main difficulties faced in the processing of data arise from lack of standardization of information in source documents. This is due to (1) recording several different transactions on a given report, (2) the various methods used to record information, and (3) the use of different sizes of paper forms for recording information. For specific datum to be processed and reported quickly and accurately, the recording of it is standardized by punching holes on a standard-size card with only one transaction on each card.

The standard punched card is a rectangular paperboard that measures 7⅜″ long by 3¼″ wide by .007″ thick. It is a *unit record* because *only the data related to one transaction* are recorded on a given card. In the illustration given in Chapter 1, involving the customer who bought a $100 suit, three transactions ensued, thus requiring the use of three cards. The first card was prepared at the time of sale. It was merged with a second card—the customer's payment card—on January 15, to determine the unpaid balance. A third card was used on January 31 when the customer paid the balance on the suit. The updated cards replaced the other two cards, which were discarded or left in a separate file for future reference. The information on the updated cards in the customers' files is available for several purposes; that is, to determine total sales (1) for each salesman, (2) for each district, or (3) for all salesmen regardless of district.

Method of recording data on cards

The recording of data is accomplished by a key-punch machine in a coded arrangement of punched holes in data-processing cards. Once data are punched, the card becomes a permanently stored reference and can then be taken out of "storage" and duplicated when desired. Such a punched card acts as a medium of communication between the operators and the accounting or other specialized machines. In other words, the punched cards enable men to feed information about certain subjects directly to the proper special-purpose machines for processing so that these machines can "feed back" accurate answers to the problem involved. The former procedure is called "input"; the latter, "output."

Data must be recorded on a card by using a key-punch machine to punch holes in certain areas in it, and not by writing them on the card manually, because a machine cannot "read" handwriting. The holes, representing information, are "read" easily and accurately by the machine, because a predetermined machine code enables the key-punch operator to place every alphabetic, numeric, or special character in its proper location so that a special-purpose machine may treat the information mechanically in the way desired.

Sources of punched cards

There are two major manufacturers of punched cards and punched-card equipment in the United States: the International Business Machines Corporation and the Remington Rand Corporation—Division of Sperry Rand Corporation. The cards differ in that the holes in the IBM cards are rectangular and the ones in the Sperry Rand cards are round. Further, the IBM card is divided into 80 vertical columns, and the Sperry Rand card is divided into an upper row of 45 columns and a lower row of 45 columns–a total of 90 columns.

The Hollerith code

The machine code used to store information on an IBM card is referred to as the *Hollerith code.* Dr. Hollerith devised the technique of storing certain data in a standard-size card by following a predetermined code to punch holes in specific locations on it.

Columns

The IBM card is divided into 80 vertical spaces called *columns.* They are numbered horizontally from left to right: 1 to 80. In each column one letter, one digit, or a special character can be stored, or a total of 80 characters. For example, suppose we wish to punch in a card employee number *40875.* Because each column can store only one character, 5 columns would be required to store 40875. In fact, any 5 consecutive columns in the card would qualify. If it were decided to use the first five columns for that purpose, then digit *4* would be punched in column 1, digit *0* in column 2, digit *8* in column 3, digit *7* in column 4, and digit *5* in column 5.

Punching positions

In addition to the card's 80 vertical columns, the IBM card is also divided into *two punching positions:* (1) the zone punching position and (2) the digit punching position. See Figure 3-2.

The zone punching position consists of three horizontal rows, two of which are used for zone punching only. They represent the gap on the top of the card. The first row from the top is called *row 12.* The next one, row 11, is commonly called the *"X* row." One punch in row *X* (referred to as *"X* punch") in a selected column (1-80) is often used to distinguish a given card (s) from the remaining cards of the deck. The third row is known as the "0 row" and can be used *either* as a zone punching position or a digit punching position.

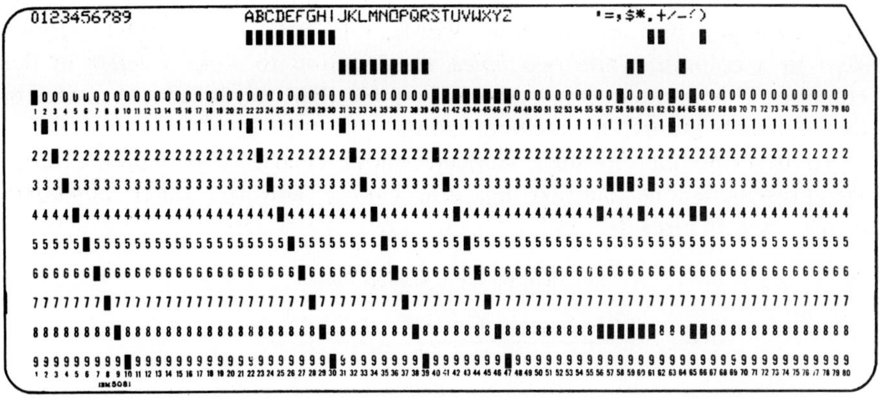

Figure 3-2. IBM card—coded punches of numeric, alphabetic, and special characters

The digit punching position consists of 10 horizontal rows, numbered vertically, to accommodate the digits *0-9* which correspond to the printed numbers on the card. Row 0 accommodates digit *0;* row 1, digit *1;* row 2, digit *2;* and so forth.

Edges and "faces"

The top edge of a punched card is called the "12-edge"; the bottom edge is called the "9-edge," to identify it with row 9. This is used to determine the side of the card which should be fed into the machine. Some machines process data on a card by feeding it in 12-edge first and others by feeding it in 9-edge first. "Face-up" means that the printed side of the card faces up as it is placed in the feed hopper. "Face-down" means that the printed side of the card faces down as it is placed in the feed hopper. Thus, if a machine processes data on a card "12-edge first, face up," the printed side of the card is up and the edge that is closest to row 12 is fed in first.

Numeric recording of information

Numbers are recorded in a card by punching only *one hole* in a column for each digit. If we need to store, for example, a nine-digit serial number in a card, it would require nine holes in any nine consecutive columns.

Alphabetic recording of information

If *alphabetic data* are to be recorded, it requires *two holes* in any column for *each letter* of the alphabet. For example, the word *HORSE* punched in a card requires five consecutive columns with *two holes* in each. One must be in the *zone* punching position and the other in the *digit* punching position. In other words, *one hole* is required to *store a digit* in a column, while *two holes* are required to *store a letter* in that column. This technique is standard on all IBM cards and is based on the Hollerith theory of machine coding.

To describe the machine language more clearly, two separate tables are presented, one entitled *numeric coding* and the other *alphabetic coding*. See Figures 3-3 and 3-5.

IBM Numeric Coding Table

Digit	Digit Punching Position	Zone Pch. Pos.	Row
0	yes	no	0
1	yes	no	1
2	yes	no	2
3	yes	no	3
4	yes	no	4
5	yes	no	5
6	yes	no	6
7	yes	no	7
8	yes	no	8
9	yes	no	9

Figure 3-3. IBM numeric coding

If we are to punch the number *14036* in columns 13-17, for example, we would proceed as follows:

Figure 3-4

Column 13 would have a hole punched in row 1 for digit *1*.
Column 14 would have a hole punched in row 4 for digit *4*.
Column 15 would have a hole punched in row 0 for digit *0*.
Column 16 would have a hole punched in row 3 for digit *3*.
Column 17 would have a hole punched in row 6 for digit *6*.

Figure 3-4 is a partial IBM card, showing the results of following the instructions in the above table.

IBM Alphabetic Coding. Because there are three zone rows for punching alphabetic characters in the card, that is, row 12, row 11, and row 0, the alphabet is divided into three parts, each part containing the number of letters equal to the number of rows in the digit punching position. This is done because *it takes two holes in a given column to represent a letter*. Depending upon the letter in mind, one of the two holes must be in row 12, 11, or 0, and the other hole must be in row 1, 2, 3, 4, 5, 6, 7, 8, or 9. Any set of columns may be used for any one of the three alphabetic groupings.

The three parts of the alphabet are:

A-I (first 9 letters)
J-R (second 9 letters)
S-Z (remaining 8 letters)

The letters *A* through *I* are each coded by punching a hole in row 12 and another hole directly below in rows 1 through 9, respectively. For example, letter *A* would be coded by a hole in row 12 and a hole in row 1 directly below. Letter *B* would be coded by a hole in row 12 and a hole in row 2 directly below, and so on for the remaining letters of the alphabet.

In Figure 3-5 the first part of the alphabet, *A* through *I*, is coded by using row 12 for the first, or zone punch, and rows 1 through 9 for the digit punch.

Letter	Zone Pch. Pos. in Row	Digit Pch. Pos. in Row
A	12	1
B	12	2
C	12	3
D	12	4
E	12	5
F	12	6
G	12	7
H	12	8
I	12	9

Figure 3-5. IBM alphabetic coding

At this point, it is apparent that letter *I* occupies the last usable row on the card. In order to code the second group of letters, *J* through *R*, it is necessary to start with row 1 again, using row 11 for the zone punch instead of row 12, and rows 1 through 9 for the digit punch. See Figure 3-6, page 36.

Letter *R* now occupies the last row on the card. In order to code the remaining letters, *S* through *Z*, it is therefore necessary to start over again, using row 0 for the zone punch and rows 2 through 9 for the digit punch. Because there are only eight letters left in the third alphabetic group, the IBM Corporation decided to use rows 2 through 9 instead of rows 1 through 8 for the digit punch. This was done, possibly, to avoid punching holes too close to each other, as would be the case if rows 0 and 1 were used, because in the early machines it was found that accuracy might be sacrificed if holes were punched too closely together. For this

Letter	Zone Pch. Pos. in Row	Digit Pch. Pos. in Row
J	11	1
K	11	2
L	11	3
M	11	4
N	11	5
O	11	6
P	11	7
Q	11	8
R	11	9

Figure 3-6

Letter	Zone Pch. Pos. in Row	Digit Pch. Pos. in Row
S	0	2
T	0	3
U	0	4
V	0	5
W	0	6
X	0	7
Y	0	8
Z	0	9

Figure 3-7

reason, a gap was decided upon and has become a part of the standard procedure, even though modern key-punch machines have been improved to such an extent that the proximity of the holes no longer makes any difference. See Figure 3-7, above.

It should be pointed out that any set of columns can be used for recording any one word, as the following discussion shows. To illustrate, see how the word *ACID* is stored in columns 17 through 20 (Figure 3-5); the word *MONK,* in columns 3 through 6 (Figure 3-6); and the word *STY* (Figure 3-7), in columns 70 through 72. In *ACID,* *A* is stored by punching a hole in row 12 (the zone) and one directly below it in column 17 (the digit). Any other columns could have been used. The above predetermined code is built into present-day key-punch machines so that all an operator must do is press the proper letter of the alphabet on the keyboard and the holes appear in the card as described. Try using the tables to code the word *INVOICE* to see if you get the idea.

Unit record principle

As mentioned earlier in this chapter, a punched card is a unit record, because it represents only one transaction. Also, because it is mobile, it can be merged with cards containing different information for the purpose of calculating or summarizing data. The accompanying Figure 3-8 illustrates an invoice containing six transactions between Do-It-Yourself, Inc., and Mr. Robert Lee Honeywell. The 50-watt amplifier transaction is used to demonstrate how each transaction is entered in a separate card. For this invoice, six cards would be required to record all the information it contains. For future processing, each of these transactions must first be punched on a card in the same manner as is the one involving the 50-watt amplifier.

Card layout requirements

The cards themselves must be of a predetermined format so that each *unit of information* occupies the same position on all cards representing any given transaction. If the customer's number occupies columns 1-5, it must always be punched in that location and this area should not be used for any other data. Standardizing the location of certain data in a specific location on a card is as important as standardizing the signature location of the bottom right side of a check or placing a postage stamp on the top right corner of a regular mail envelope. This leads us to the important concept of "field."

Field. Any one transaction contains a certain number of details called *units of information.* A *field* is a group of consecutive card columns reserved for *a specific unit of information.* Because the punched card in Figure 3-8 contains 11 *units of information* related to the last transaction in the invoice, 11 fields are used, occupying, in this instance, 77 of the 80 columns available. The length of the field depends on the maximum length of the unit of information. The minimum length of a field is one column and the maximum is the size of the card, or 80 columns. All information is of two types: fixed and variable. Fixed information never changes in regard to any one customer. It includes, for example, such items as (1) customer's name and address, (2) mode of transporting merchandise, (3) source of merchandise, (4) catalog number, and (5) description of merchandise ordered. Variable information, on the other hand, is that type of information which is subject to change. For instance, it includes (1) date of the invoice, (2) quantity of each item ordered, (3) quantity sold, (4) transportation charges, (5) terms of payment, and other items of this nature. Fixed information is usually put in the card beginning at the left side, whereas the right side of the card is reserved for variable information.

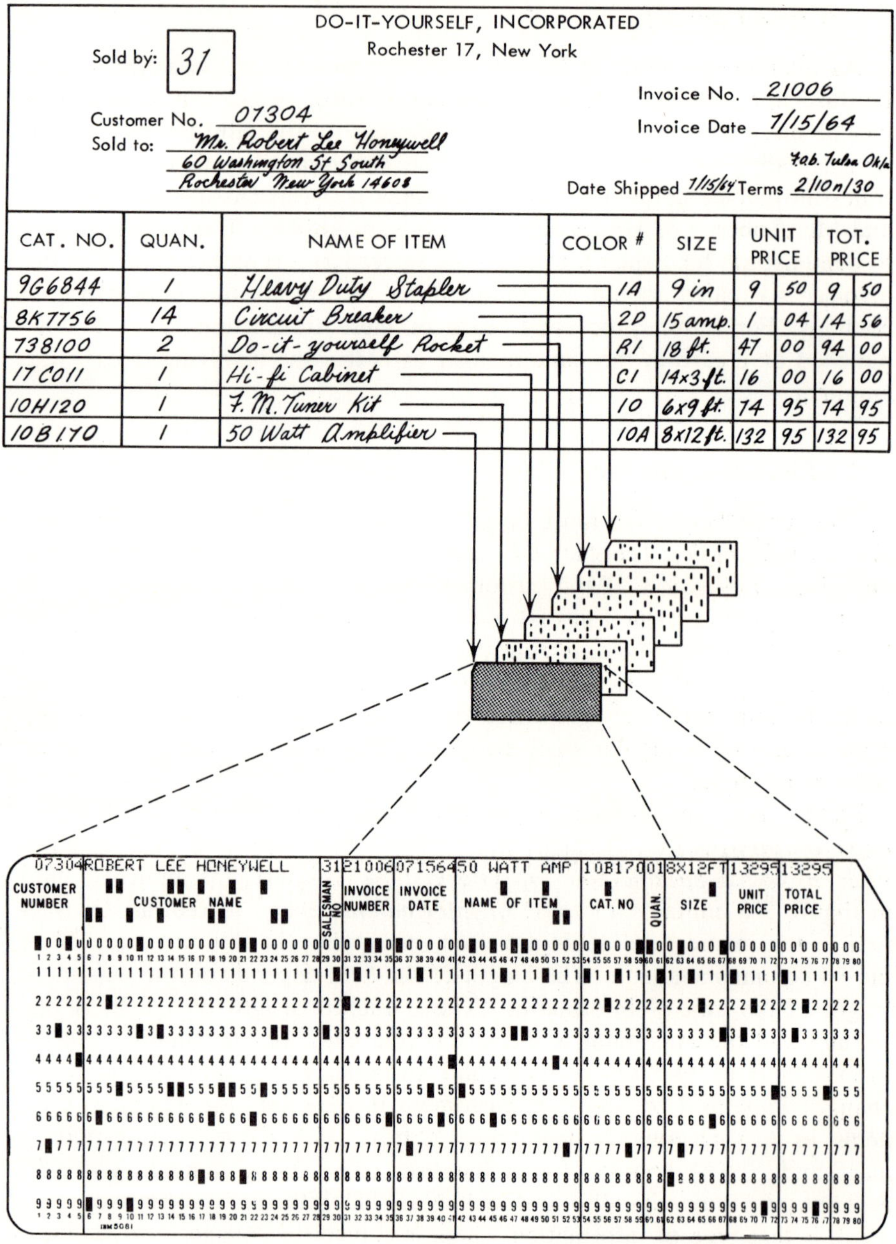

Figure 3-8. A partial invoice—the unit record principle

The first field in Figure 3-8 is the customer's-number field. It was decided to make it a five-column field because, in this case, it was assumed that, within the foreseeable future, the number of potential customers of Do-It-Yourself, Inc., would reach the 10,000 mark, but would not be likely to exceed 99,999. Recording a four-digit customer number (for example, 4461) in columns 1-5 requires the use of columns 2, 3, 4, and 5. Column 1, which is currently unused, is punched with a zero.* In designing fields for the storage of units of information, enough columns must be allotted to each field so that the longest group of digits, or alphabetic characters, can be accommodated. If the current or future need for recording several units exceeds the length of the card, abbreviations of names and other information, where possible, is the normal procedure.

Card design

Because a machine cannot think, it does not make any real difference where a certain fact is punched or in what sequence certain fields are presented. The normal procedure, however, is to lay out the fields in the same sequence as they appear in the source document. This makes it much easier, faster, and more convenient for the key-punch operator to punch the data into the card from the source document. Hence, the expense of key punching is lowered. The process of recording data from source documents is the initial step in the conversion routine and can be very annoying and frustrating to the key-punch operator if the various units of information in the document have to be punched in locations on the card that are out of sequence with the information as presented in the source document.

Identifying Marks. A card may be identified by its format, by different colors, by different corner cuts, by horizontal color stripes, or by a control field. The format shows the way the various fields are arranged on a card and distinguishes it from the other cards which enter the processing routine. For example, in a banking application, a name-and-address card may have basically a customer-number field, name field, a home-address field, and a business-address field; whereas a loan card may have a customer-number field, name field, amount-of-the-loan field, number-of-payments field, and amount-of-each-payment field. In addition to having a different format, the name-and-address card may be visually distinguished by a blue stripe while the loan card may have a yellow stripe. On the other hand, different-colored cards may be used to designate the different kinds of cards.

---

* Others use a skip of column 1 and punch the *4461* in columns 2, 3, 4, and 5, the importance being that of an established policy in reference to the above.

Control fields

A control field aids in the location and *reassembling* of a group of cards which has been merged previously with other groups of cards containing all kinds of information for processing. You frequently hear of an *X* punch in column 80 or an *X* punch in column 27. This denotes that only certain cards in a group have an *X* punched in column 80 or in column 27. Assume a group of cards containing information on each employee of a firm, including managers, foremen, and the rank-and-file employees. Assume further that, at the end of the year, the board of directors decides to grant a $500 bonus to managers only. In order to make it possible for the machine to select the managers' cards out of all the cards, some distinctive code must be placed on the managers' cards which would not appear in any other group of cards. Usually, this coding is done by punching an *X* in a column reserved for that purpose. In this example, let us assume the use of column 80 as the *X* column. Once an *X* is punched in column 80 of each manager's card in the group, the matter of picking these cards out by the machine becomes a simple matter. Every time the machine reads an *X* in column 80, it ejects the card containing it into a separate pocket, leaving the other cards to drop undisturbed into another pocket.

Remington Rand card design

Another kind of punched card in common use in the United States is the Remington Rand card. It is the same size as the IBM card, that is, 7⅜″ long by 3¼″ wide by .007″ thick. It differs in that it is divided into 90 vertical columns which are organized into two sections. The upper half represents columns 1-45 and the lower half represents columns

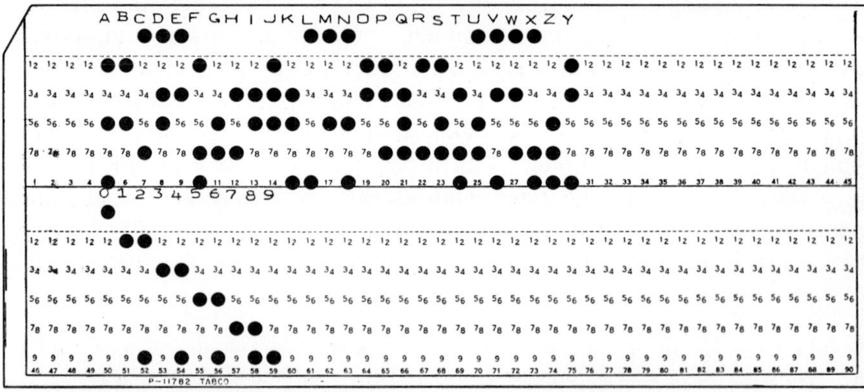

Figure 3-9. Remington Rand card—coded punches of numeric, alphabetic, and special characters

46-90. Each of the two sections consists of six horizontal rows. One group of 45 columns is for punching numeric information. The other is used for punching alphabetic information. Figure 3-9 shows a Remington Rand card. Notice the round holes, which are one of its distinguishing characteristics.

Unlike IBM, Remington Rand's coding does not follow a specific pattern. Each column has six positions. From the bottom, they are 9, 7, 5, 3, 1, and 0. A digit is represented by *one hole* in a given column *if it is odd,* or *two holes if it is even* (Figure 3-9). That is, digits *2, 4, 6,* and *8* are represented by two holes each because they are even. Digits *1, 3, 5, 7,* and *9* are represented by one hole each, because they are odd. Digit *0* is represented by one hole. Alphabetic characters are represented by a combination of two or three holes per character in any given column. Although details of each manufacturer's coding differ, the basic idea underlying the punching of the cards is the same.

The need for the punched card and punched-card equipment in data processing

Key-punch equipment which is used to punch information in cards is needed in both punched-card processing and electronic processing. Recording of data must be standardized in this manner before either punched-card machines or electronic machines can handle it. The key-punch machines are designed in such a way that either numeric or alphabetic coding can be punched by them. Some are designed to punch only. However, the latest models are designed either to punch only or to print and punch simultaneously. If it is desired to print at the same time as the card is punched, the operator need only depress the "A" key in order that the machine punch the proper holes for *A* in the column selected and print the letter *A* simultaneously. Referring to the previous examples, the words *acid, monk,* and *sty* can be printed on the card at the same time as the holes are being punched if this is so desired. If not, the operator need only suppress a switch and the machine will punch but not print. In the event that the information is printed and punched at the same time, no intermediate machine is needed to read the holes in order to print the proper information, as is the case if the card is punched only. After being key-punched, the cards can be immediately processed in the proper special-purpose punched-card or electronic machines which read the holes and proceed according to predetermined instructions.

REVIEW QUESTIONS

1. Describe the punched card. Give two examples of its use.
2. Why is it necessary to have a standard punched card? Explain briefly.

3. Explain the role of the punched card in the recording stage.
4. What is the Hollerith code? Why was it called so?
5. How many columns does an IBM card contain? How much data can be punched in each column?
6. Describe the two punching positions of an IBM card. Why are they used? Explain.
7. What is meant by "9-edge first, face down"? What is meant by "12-edge first, face up"?
8. How is alphabetic recording of data different from the numeric recording in a card? Explain briefly.
9. What is the zone punching position of each of the following letters:

   C, S, U, K, F, X, Q, Y?
10. What is the digit punching position of each of the following data:

    4, S, 7, P, I, 8?
11. What is the unit record principle?
12. An order form contains seven different types of merchandise ordered by a given customer. How many cards would be required to record them for further processing?
13. What is a field? Explain. Give an example.
14. What are the two main types of information that make up a transaction? Explain, and give an example of each type.
15. Explain the normal procedure used in converting data from source documents into punched cards.
16. By how many different ways may a card be identified? Explain each briefly.
17. What is a control field used for? Give an example.
18. What is the main difference between an IBM card and a Remington Rand card? Be specific.

PART 2

PUNCHED-CARD DATA PROCESSING

Chapter 4

The Recording of Source Information

The Processing Cycle

Processable business data have to go, in one form or another, through some or all of the stages of the punched-card data-processing cycle before any kind of result can be attained. This cycle is carried out by utilizing the various machines that perform the operations of *recording, classifying, calculating, summarizing,* and *reporting* (or printing). These are the five principal processing steps performed on data when a punched-card installation is used. By contrast, in an electronic installation, these operations are condensed into three major steps: that is, (1) *input,* which means the recording of data on punched cards, paper tape, or magnetic tape, and the feeding of these data into a computer, which is the main processing unit; (2) *processing,* which means the primary storage in the computer of the data received from step 1 and the performance of calculations and manipulation on them; and (3) *output,* which is the result of the computations performed on data in the computer, in the form of a printed page, a punched card, a punched tape, or a magnetic tape.

As was mentioned in Chapter 1, a machine has yet to be commercially developed which would be capable of reading and processing handwritten transactions recorded on various-size reports. Consequently, the need for a standard-size report led to the development of the punched card. This necessitated converting the English language into a language which could be handled by punched-card machines. Thus, a "machine language" was developed, examples of which are the Numeric and Alphabetic coding tables discussed in Chapter 3.

Recording

Before any data can be read and properly processed by machine, they must be recorded in a proper form. This, therefore, constitutes the first step in the punched-card processing cycle. The recording function is performed by utilizing a machine called the *card punch,* commonly called the *key punch,* and another machine, the *verifier,* which checks on the accuracy of the punched data made by the key punch.

The key punch

Key punching is the most widely used method of recording data in a card. The key-punch machine bears a striking resemblance to an electric typewriter. The keyboards of the two are similar, as each contains alphabetic, numeric, and special characters.* Also, recording is accomplished by stroking the keys. The depression of a key on a typewriter results in printing that particular character on a sheet of paper, whereas the same key depressed on the key punch results in punching a hole or holes in a particular column of a card. However, the idea is the same, that is, to present information on a report for further analysis, evaluation, or control. In the case of the typewriter, information is *printed* on a standard-size sheet of paper. In the case of a key punch, the same information is presented in *punched* form on a standard-size punched card. The key punch punches one column at a time, as the card moves from right to left; the typewriter prints one character at a time as the roller that controls the paper moves from right to left one space at a time. Figure 4-1 shows the IBM 26 key punch, which prints or interprets directly over the col-

* Some earlier key-punch machines have numerical keyboards only. They are still available and are currently used where the alphabetic requirement does not exist.

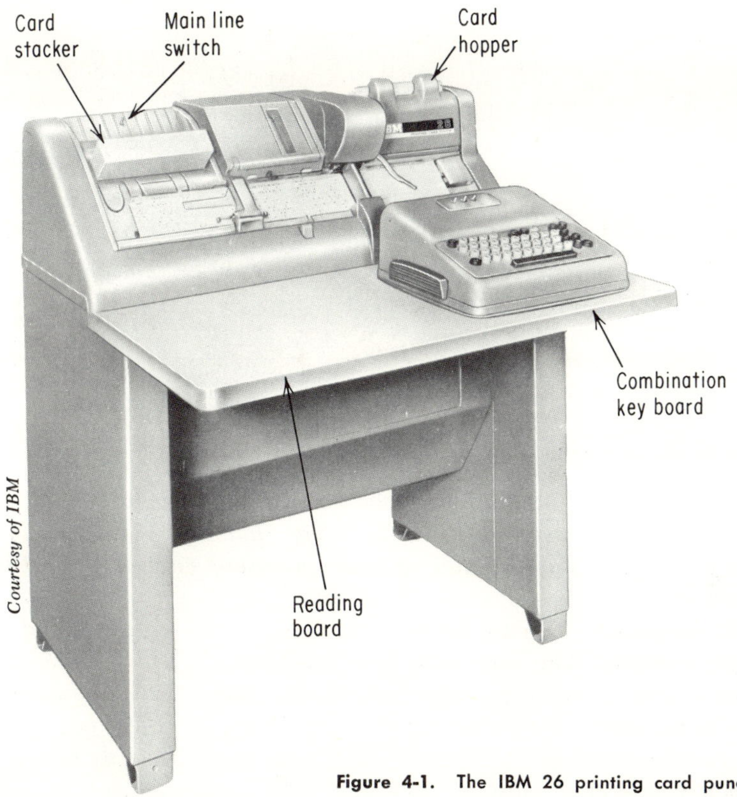

Figure 4-1. The IBM 26 printing card punch

umn(s) as it punches holes in the card. Earlier models punch only and do not print.

The primary difference between a typewriter and a key punch is in the arrangement and location of the numerical keys. The numerical keys on the typewriter are located in the top row. On the key punch, however, numerical keys are grouped together in such a manner that one hand is capable of manipulating them. This is done for the convenience of the key-punch operator. Because numeric data are punched more frequently than alphabetic data, it is more efficient for the numeric keys to be controlled by one hand rather than two, because this eliminates unnecessary movements. Figure 4-2 shows the arrangement of the keyboard on a key-punch machine.

The keyboard is normally in alphabetic mode. If numeric data are to be punched, depressing the numeric shift key manually makes the use of the numeric keys possible. If the majority of the operator's work is numeric data, it is better to shift the keyboard into numeric shift automatically by coding a program card for this purpose, as will be explained later.

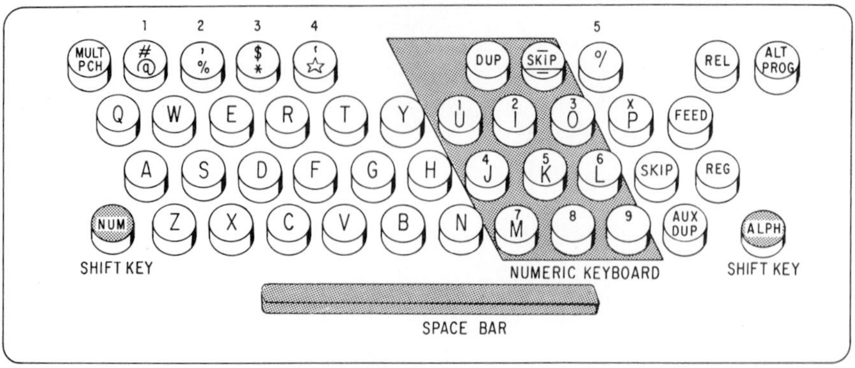

Courtesy of IBM

Figure 4-2. An IBM 26 keyboard chart

Components of the key punch

In addition to the keyboard, the other components of the key punch are: (1) the *card hopper,* (2) the *punching station,* (3) the *reading station,* (4) the *card stacker,* and (5) the *program control unit.* (See Figure 4-3.)

The Card Hopper. A great number of blank cards and a method of "feeding" or dropping them one at a time for punching are essential for the efficient recording of transactions. A device called the *card hopper* takes care of the latter requirement, while the provision of ample numbers of cards takes care of the former. Numerous cards have to be used, because each transaction must be recorded on a separate card. A card hopper holds approximately 500 cards and the cards are placed in it 9-edge first.

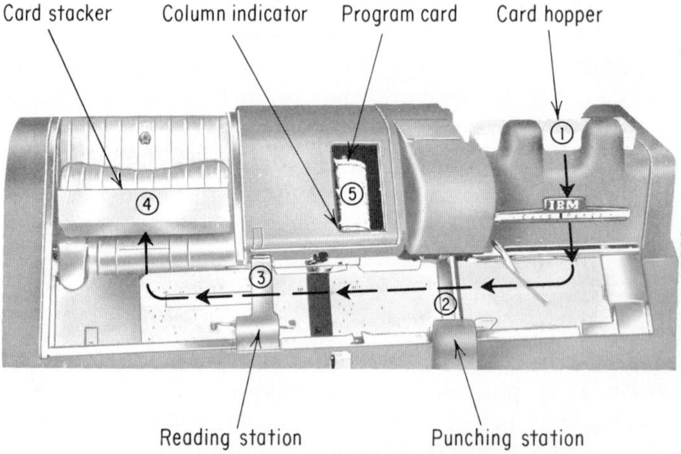

Courtesy of IBM

Figure 4-3. **The path of the card through the punch—components of the key punch are shown**

The Card Path. The cards move through the key punch from right to left as columns 1 through 80 are being punched. Upon the depression of a "feed" key, the first card drops to the card bed. The feed key is depressed a second time to cause the second card to drop to the card bed as the first card then moves to the punching station while the second card waits at the card bed. As soon as column 80 of card 1 passes the *punching station* and begins to move under the *reading station,* card 2 moves to the *punching station.* This causes another card to drop automatically from the *card hopper* to the card bed. Thus, the blank cards in the *card hopper* move continuously on their journey from the hopper through the *punching* and *reading stations* for the recording of information and, finally, to their destination in the *card stacker.*

The card hopper is used most advantageously when feeding in numerous cards involving a specific problem or project. When duplicating or punching only one or a few cards, it is faster to do the feeding job manually.

The Punching Station. The punching station is the first of the two stations along the card path, as shown in Figure 4-3. It contains 12 punch dies aligned or positioned vertically in the same sequence as the vertical layout of the card. The top three punch dies are for the zone punching positions 12, 11, and 0. The remaining nine are for the digit punching positions 1 through 9. Figure 4-4 shows the alignment of the

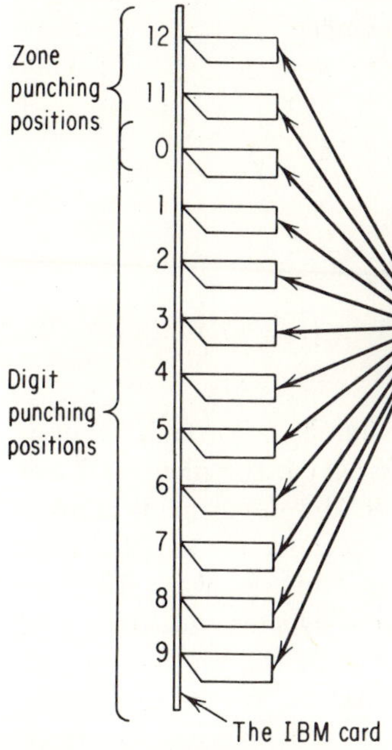

Figure 4-4

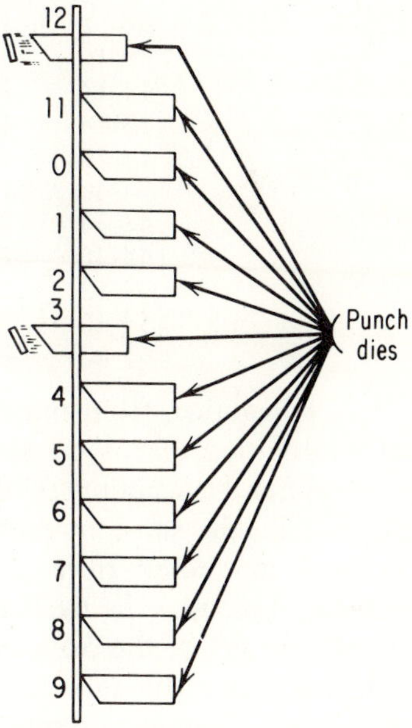

Figure 4-5. Letter "C" punched in column 1

punch dies against an IBM card which is underneath the punching station housing them. Assume that the dies are on column 1, and letter *C* is to be punched. The depression of key *C* on the keyboard causes punch dies 12 and 3 to penetrate the card, causing two rectangular holes in those locations (Figure 4-5).

The Reading Station. The key-punch operator is often faced with the need for punching certain repetitive information in a group of cards. The cards can be punched one at a time, but, because some of the information on a card is the same as that on any other card in the deck, a duplicating technique is desirable so that the job can be done more efficiently.

The reading station aids in the duplication of the data read in the card that moves underneath it and, when the duplicate ("Dup") key is depressed, causes the punching station to duplicate the holes in the card under it in the same location in the card that is under the reading station. The fact that the cards under the reading and punching stations move together one column at a time from right to left makes the duplicating function possible. In a store, for example, assume that on January 1 a television salesman from the Hi-Fi department sells 50 television sets to customers on account. Terms are net payment within 30 days. The data format on each of the fifty transaction cards is as follows:

Column	*Description of the field*
1- 5	Customer-account number
6- 8	Department number
9-10	Salesman number
11-14	Due date
15-18	Date of item
19-23	Item number
24-40	Description of item
41-44	Size
45-48	Color
49-53	Unit Price
54-60	Total Price
61-80	Blank

You will notice, from the data above, that columns 6 through 18 contain information that is the same on each of the 50 cards which represent the 50 different accounts. Columns 6 through 8, the department-number field, will be the same in each of the 50 cards, because all the television sets were purchased from the same department, that is, the Hi-Fi department. Likewise, in the case of the salesman's-number, due-date, and date-of-item fields, the 50 television sets were sold by the same salesman, on the same day, January 1, and the money will be due on the same date, January 31. Therefore, duplication of these fields through using the reading station as described is much faster than having the key-punch operator punch the information in each card separately.

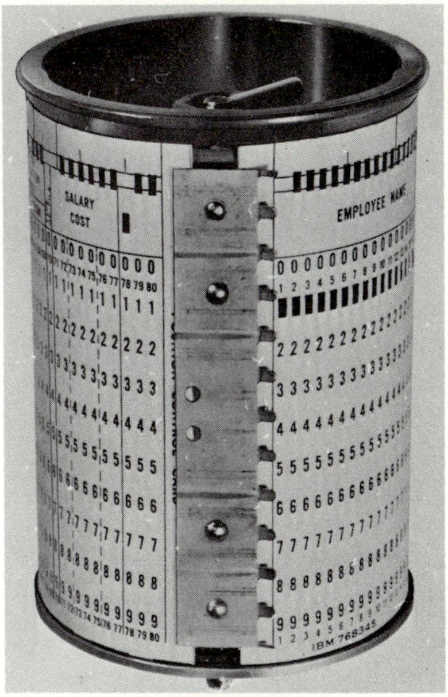

Courtesy of IBM

Figure 4-6

The Program Control Unit. The program control unit contains an IBM program card which causes duplicating, skipping, or shifting to take place automatically because of a predetermined series of coded holes, or program, punched in it. It is wrapped around a drum and placed in position before any keypunching begins, as is illustrated in Figure 4-6. In this way, repetitive information in a deck of cards is duplicated in approximately one-sixth of the time taken by the keypunch operator to do the job manually. The degree of accuracy is also increased because of the decrease in the possibility of error due to the substitution of machine operation for human operation.

Automatic *skipping* through the program card is initiated by an *11* punch (the *1* hole in row 11) in the far left column of the skip field in the program card. From then on, the number of columns to be skipped is indicated by the sensing of consecutive holes in row 12 of the columns immediately following the *11* punch (Figure 4-7). Again, using the television salesman example for clarification of this function, we find that columns 61 through 80 are blank columns. It would be a waste of time for the operator to use the space bar once for each blank column. It is more convenient if skipping can be done

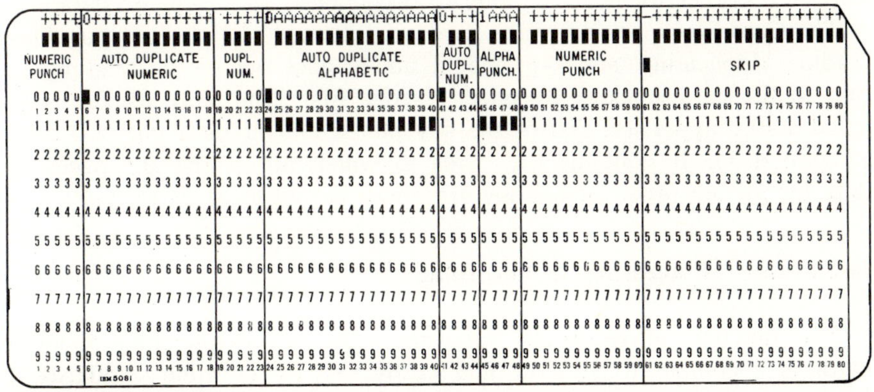

Figure 4-7. A program card

automatically. To do this, column 61 of the program card is punched with a hole in row 11 to indicate the beginning of the skip operation. When sensed, it will tell the key punch to begin skipping. In order for the machine to skip columns 62 through 80, consecutive holes in row 12 of these columns, referred to as "12 punches," are made in the program card immediately following the *11* punch in column 61, as shown in Figure 4-7. Skipping is done at the rate of one card, 80 columns, per second.

Shifting to alphabetic mode from numeric automatically can be controlled through the program card. The keyboard is always in alphabetic mode when the program unit is not activated. The keys are then used like the keys in any typewriter. When numeric punching is desired, the numeric shift key is depressed. However, when the program control unit is activated, the keyboard is *shifted* into *alphabetic* mode automatically when a *1*-punch is detected in any column of the program card. In Figure 4-7 a *1* punch is made in column 24. The zero punch in that column initiates automatic duplication of the field. The size of the shift field is determined by consecutive holes in rows 12 and 1 in each column. For example, column 24 will have a punch in row 0 and row 1, and columns 25 through 40 will each have a hole in row 12 and a hole in row 1, as shown in Figure 4-7.

The program card can also be used to shift from alphabetic into numeric mode. The absence of a *1* punch in the far left column of the numeric field of the program card accomplishes this. For example, columns 49 through 53 in the television salesman illustration can be punched manually with the unit price if column 49 in the program card is left blank. Therefore, columns 50, 51, 52, and 53 should have consecutive 12 punches immediately following the blank 49 column. When the operator is ready to punch the unit price into column 49, the keyboard is already in numeric mode. If it were not, the operator would have to shift manually by depressing and holding the "numeric shift" key at the lower left corner for every column to be punched with numeric data.

The Card Stacker. After the card goes through the steps of punching, reading, duplicating, and skipping, it finally goes out of the reading station to the card stacker. It is fed 12-edge first. The card stacker is located at the upper left end of the key punch and holds about 500 cards (Figure 4-3). It contains the cards in which are stored the necessary data for further processing. They are now referred to as *data cards.*

Importance of Accuracy in Recording

The function of recording data manually by key-punching them in cards is a comparatively slow and costly one by machine standards. It is slow because, at the initial point of converting source documents into a group of cards for further processing, humans do the reading of the source document and the punching of its contents, one column at a time, one card at a time, until the job is completed. Assuming that the key-punch operator is of average quality, she can punch so many cards per hour and no more. The degree of accuracy is dependent upon the time allowed for the job as well as upon the legibility and accuracy of the source document itself. Because the punched facts can be no more accurate than the source documents from which they were punched, source documents should be clearly written or printed. A key-punch operator can punch in the neighborhood of 160 key strokes per minute. Naturally, her speed fluctuates, based on the type of information she is punching. When either the time allotted for the job is limited, creating pressure on her to punch faster than her normal rate of speed, or the source document is not clear, errors are bound to creep into her work. They must be corrected immediately, because it is less costly to locate and correct a mistake at this point than at a later time when processing is being done. Once data have been stored in cards for processing, the cards become a part of other decks of cards, and the values which they contain become a part of the over-all results. Errors discovered when processing is under way cause frustrating interruptions, and the time it takes to locate them multiplies with the type of error made and the complexity of the system itself. Efficiency is drastically reduced and costs can easily mount beyond a reasonable limit. Therefore, it is of utmost importance that the facts punched in cards be correct. In order to verify and check the accuracy of the key-punched data, a machine called the *verifier* is used.

The verifier

A verifier looks like and works almost exactly the same as a key punch. However, the objective is different: The verifier checks or verifies the accuracy of the contents of the data cards. In place of the punching station containing the punch dies, the verifier has a verifying station containing sense pins to feel the holes in the column(s) and compare them with the keys depressed by the operator. The verifier operator uses the information from the source document and keys it in on the keyboard. If there is agreement between the punched card and the keyed-in data, a notch is made on the right edge of the card opposite row 1 (Figure 4-8). If there is disagreement, the verifier produces a red signal to indicate that the stored information in the data card may be wrong. This can be the result of error on the part of either the key-punch operator or the verifier operator. To eliminate the possibility of error on her part, the verifier operator rekeys the information and, if it is still in disagreement with the data card, she tries a third time. If disagreement continues to result, the error is assumed by the verifier to be in the data card and to have

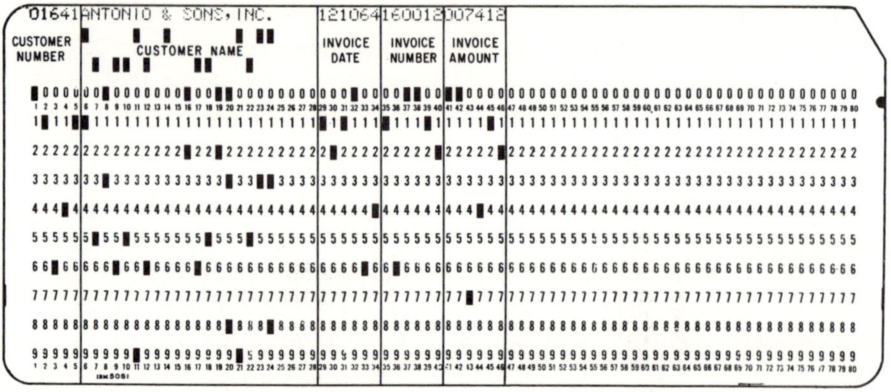

Figure 4-8. A verification notch indicating the accuracy of the punched facts

been made by the key-punch operator. Consequently, a notch is made on the top of the column(s) where the error(s) occur (Figure 4-9).

The error(s) are corrected by punching the correct information in a new card and replacing the incorrect data card with the new card. Figure 4-9 shows the same card and contents as that shown in Figure 4-8 except that a punching error was purposely made in columns 33 and 34 by the key-punch operator to illustrate the role of the verifier in detecting errors. Instead of punching *64* for "year" in columns 33 and 34, respectively, as shown in Figure 4-8, the reverse of the data, *46,* was punched in these two columns (Figure 4-9). The card was then placed in the verifier and the correct information was keyed-in from the original source document. The verifier compared the two sets of data, and after three tries by the verifier operator, disagreement in the data card was confirmed. Consequently, two notches were made on top of the two incorrect columns 33 and 34.

Figure 4-9. Error notches—see columns 33 and 34

Significance of verification

Verification of punched cards takes almost as much time as the actual punching of the cards themselves. Despite this fact, it should be patiently done because it costs less to locate errors now than later. It also assures that the stored data is 100 per cent reliable and can be used with confidence for future processing. At times, information that has little future processable value is not verified; alphabetic data are also frequently bypassed.

QUESTIONS AND PROBLEMS

1. List in the correct sequence and describe the five punched-card data-processing machine functions. Contrast them with the major steps in an electronic installation.
2. Discuss the similarities and differences between a typewriter and a key punch.
3. What is a program card? How is it different from a regular punched card? Why is a program card used?
4. What is the function of the card hopper? The card stacker? Which of the two holds the blank deck of cards?
5. What is the difference (in functions) between the reading station and the punching station? When is the reading station used along with that of the punching station?
6. You are a part-time employee in a small data-processing department of a local retail store. Your supervisor asked you to design a card to include the following information:

Quantity—	2 digits
Account number—	3 digits
Total price—	7 digits
Customer's address—	25 digits
Unit price—	5 digits
Customer's name—	20 digits

   (a) How many columns are used?
   (b) How many data fields are included?
   (c) Show on an IBM card the sequence in which these fields should be punched by giving an example pertinent to the above information.
7. In what ways are data cards duplicated on a key punch?
8. Suppose you have 200 blank cards in which student number *0561* is to be punched in columns 1, 2, 3, and 4 of each card. You have only a key-punch machine at your disposal. What is the most efficient method of punching the number in the cards?
9. What is the difference between the verifier and the key punch? Explain.
10. Assume that the amount *81945* was punched in a given card in columns 45–49 as *89944*. Explain what happens when the card is fed through the verifier. Identify the location and number of notches that are made (if any).
11. Explain why it is important to ascertain the accuracy of data at the key-punching stage.

Chapter 5

The Reproduction of Recorded Information

Duplicating Stored Data

Stored data are duplicated by reproducing, gang punching, or mark sensing. Duplicating is done by a machine called the *reproducer*. It has three purposes: (1) reproducing of data from one card into another card; (2) comparing data punched into a card from another card for accurate results; and, (3) gang punching data from a master card into a number of blank cards.

The Reproducer

Components of the reproducer

The reproducer (IBM 514)* is divided into two major parts: (1) the reading unit and (2) the punching unit.

* The 519 IBM reproducer is also available. Its function is similar to that of the 514 reproducer. The major difference is that the 519 has the end printing device, three entries to the punch unit, greater selection capacity, and wired switches.

The reading unit contains a hopper, called the "Read" hopper, to hold the cards to be reproduced, and two sets of reading brushes, each set containing 80 brushes to read 80 columns in a card. The first set, called the *reproducing* brushes, read the holes punched in that row, one row at a time. The second set, called the *comparing* brushes, aid in comparing the holes read by the reproducing brushes with those punched in another card by the punching unit to insure accuracy (Figure 5-1).

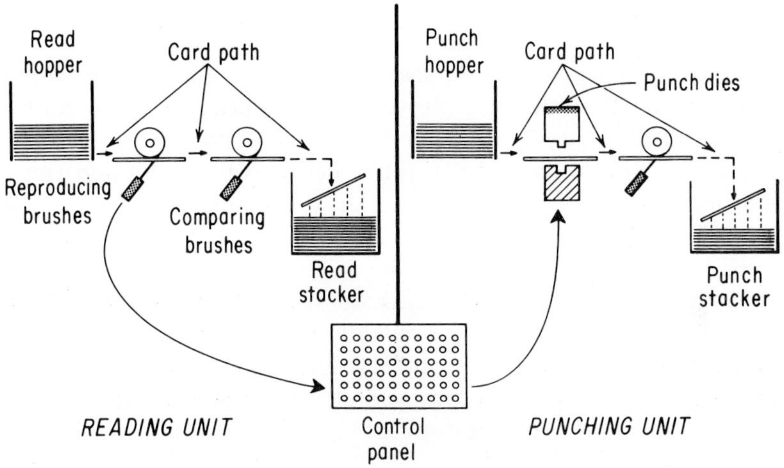

Figure 5-1

The other part of the reproducer is the punching unit. It contains a set of 80 punch dies to punch up to 80 holes, if necessary, in any row of a card, as well as a set of 80 punch brushes to read what is punched and to work with the comparing brushes, through a control device, to insure accuracy of the results.

For example, suppose that we have a card containing number *3333* in columns 4, 5, 6, and 7, and that it is desired to put this number into a blank card. The following procedure takes place: The data card with the number *3333* in columns 4, 5, 6, and 7 is placed in the "Read" hopper 12-edge first, face down. A blank card is also placed in the "Punch" hopper 12-edge first, face down. If the control panel is properly wired, the depression of the "START" button will cause both cards to move together. Row 12 of the data card moves over the reproducing brushes while row 12 of the blank card moves under the punch dies. No impulse is created, because no holes are present. Only the presence of a hole can cause the brush to make contact with the cylinder above the card to create an electric impulse for action. The cards keep moving in unison, and rows 11, 0, 1, and 2 pass by with no results. However, when row 3 with holes in it reaches the reproducing brushes, dies 4, 5, 6, and 7 punch holes in the blank card instantly. The cards keep moving through, and rows 4, 5, 6, 7, 8, and 9 pass by the brushes with no impulse.

After the data card is read by the reading brushes, it is also read by the comparing brushes and then drops into the "Read" stacker. At the same time, the blank card which was just punched by the punch dies is read by the punch brushes and drops into the "Punch" stacker. The job is completed.

Uses of reproducing

Reproducing is common and has many uses, a number of which can be inferred from the following illustrations. A master deck of cards containing basic information, such as the hourly rate of employees, their overtime, their rate of pay, and so forth, becomes worn out and can cause jamming as a result of excessive use. Such jamming may not only result in loss of machine time, but in some cases the master card is twisted and mutilated to the extent that part of the information in it is destroyed. The data-processing employee would have to resort to the source document from which the master card was originally prepared if an alternative were not available to him. This could take a lot of time and run up the cost of processing. In order to avoid any such undesirable incident, it is wise for the department to make a duplicate of the master cards. The master

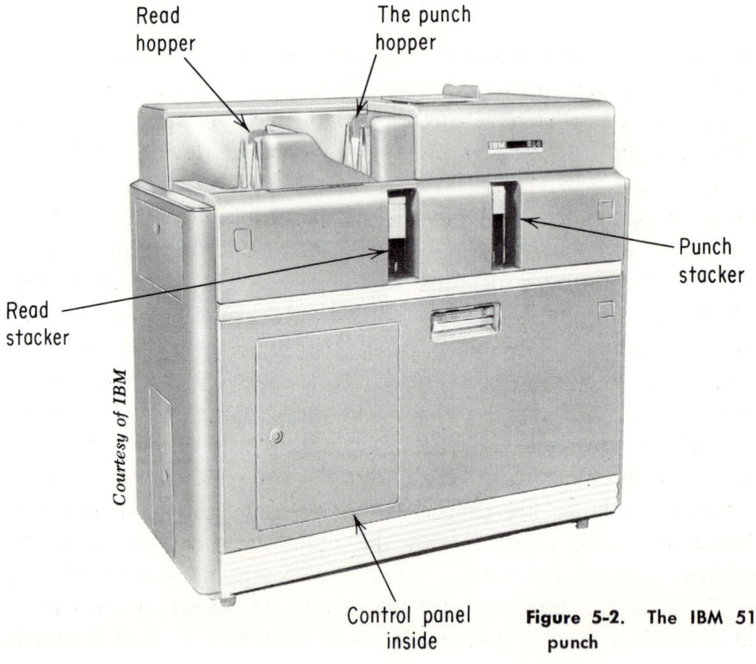

Figure 5-2. The IBM 514 reproducing punch

deck can be duplicated simply by placing it in the read hopper and an equal number of blank cards in the punch hopper. (See Figure 5-2.) The control panel can be wired to read and reproduce columns 1 through 80 of the master card into columns 1 through 80 in a blank card in the punch hopper. The reproduced deck drops, one card at a time, into the punch stacker and the original master deck also drops, one card at a time, into the read stacker. This type of reproduction is commonly referred to as the "80-80" method, and 100 cards per minute can be reproduced.

Another use of the reproducing punch is in copying certain data, or fields, from a card(s) in the read hopper into any location in another card in the punch hopper. This process is referred to as "offset punching." For example, assume that Pocket-the-Profit, Inc., a small discount store in Rochester, New York, employs a total of five employees (Nos. 01, 02, 03, 04, and 05). Their hourly rates of pay are set at \$1.25, \$1.50, \$1.75, \$2.00, and \$2.25, respectively, and they are paid on Friday of each week.

At the time he is employed, a new employee is assigned a number, and a master card is immediately prepared to include the following information:

Column	1- 2	Employee number
	3-30	Employee name
	31-49	Employee's home address
	50-57	Telephone number
	58-64	Employee title
	65-67	Hourly rate
	68-80	Blank

The payroll is prepared on Friday morning. It is computed as follows: The manager of Pocket-the-Profit, Inc. inspects the time cards to get the number of days and the amount of time each of his five employees worked. He reports it to the key-punch operator, who punches the data in five separate cards as follows:

1- 2	Employee number
3-30	Employee name
31-45	Employee title
46-47	Total number of hours for the week

(See Figure 5-3.) It is assumed in this example that Pocket-the-Profit, Inc. does not work overtime.

The five cards are referred to, from this point on, as the *detail* cards,

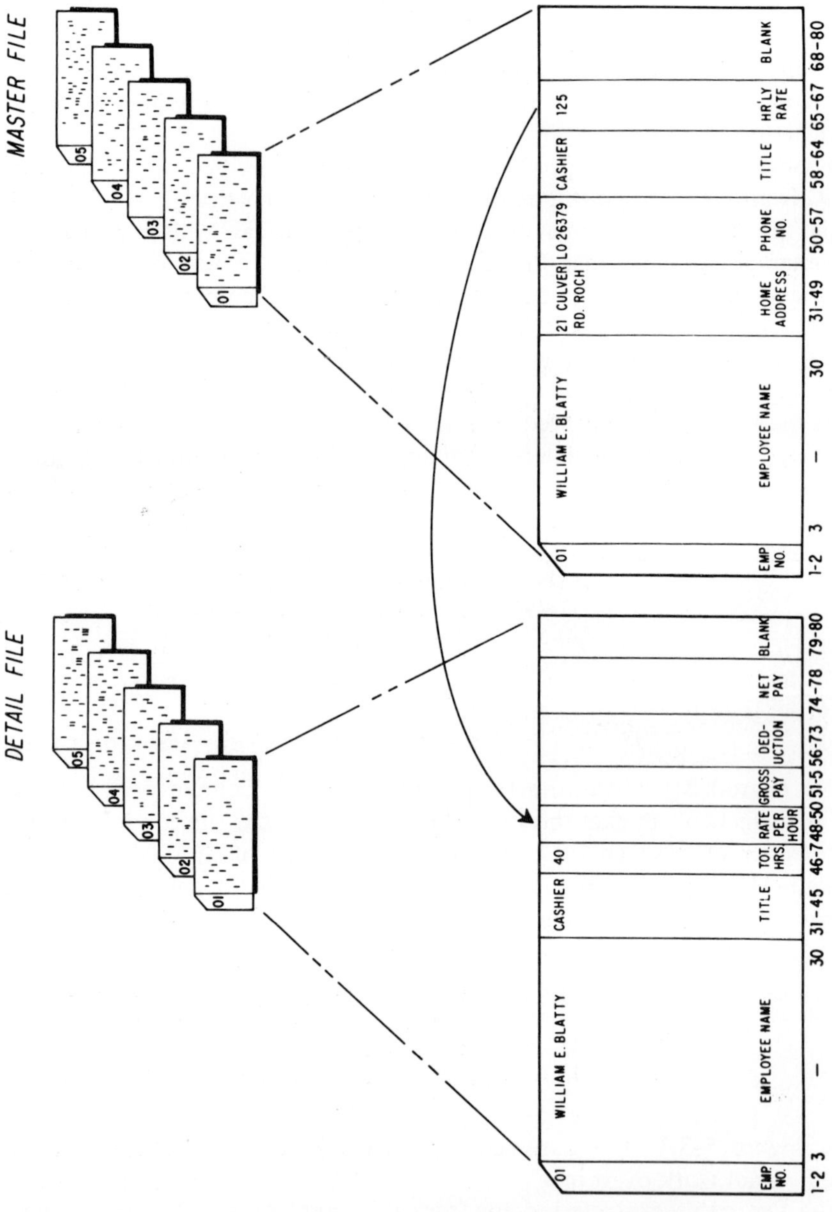
MASTER FILE
05
04
03
02
01
01
WILLIAM E. BLATTY
21 CULVER RD. ROCH
LO 26379
CASHIER
125
EMP NO.
EMPLOYEE NAME
HOME ADDRESS
PHONE NO.
TITLE
HR'LY RATE
BLANK
1-2 3 — 30 31-49 50-57 58-64 65-67 68-80
DETAIL FILE
05
04
03
02
01
01
WILLIAM E. BLATTY
CASHIER
40
EMP NO.
EMPLOYEE NAME
TITLE
TOT. HRS.
RATE PER HOUR
GROSS PAY
DED-UCTION
NET PAY
BLANK
1-2 3 — 30 31-45 46-47 48-50 51-55 56-73 74-78 79-80

Figure 5-3

or *detail file*. After all computations are made and punched in them, the cards will contain details pertinent to the employees and indirectly to their company. From these cards, pay checks can be written and prepared. The management, too, can obtain information from them on the amount of tax withheld for the preparation of periodical tax reports and other related statements in the future.

Based on the data in the detail cards in Figure 5-3, it appears clear that before any computations for net pay are made, the hourly rate of each employee must be punched in the card, that is, in columns 48, 49, and 50. The hourly rate is available only in the master card (in columns 65, 66, and 67). The data-processing department first checks to make sure that the master file and the detail file are arranged in the proper sequence. The first card in the master file, employee number 01, should correspond to the first card in the detail file, employee number 01. (See Figure 5-3.) Next, the master deck is placed in the read hopper while the detail deck is placed in the punch hopper. The control panel is wired to read the contents of columns 65 through 67 of the master card and to cause the punch dies to punch these data in columns 48 through 50 in the detail card. Once this job is done, the detail card contains the employee number, his name, his title, his total hours for the week, and his hourly rate. This card is then placed in the calculator, which multiplies the number of hours times the hourly rate in order to arrive at the gross pay. The gross pay is punched by the calculator in the same card in columns 51 through 55. Deductions are later determined and subtracted from the gross pay, leaving the net pay for the week. The master deck from which the hourly rate was reproduced should then be taken to the master file until it is needed again.

From the foregoing example, it should be noted that, through the control panel, any column(s) from the card(s) placed in the read hopper can be reproduced into any column(s) in the card(s) placed in the punch hopper. The system is flexible and allows the reproduction of one column, or of one or several fields, in entirely different locations in blank cards.

The comparing function of the reproducer

To check on the performance of the reproducer, a unit is built into it which can compare what is reproduced with the original data to insure accuracy. This is similar to the work of the verifier. As is true of the verifier, the comparison made by the reproducer proves agreement between the reproduced cards and the master cards. (Figure 5-4.)

In the diagram, let us assume that another deck of five cards is desired, which will contain only the employee number in columns 1 and 2. Assume, further, that the control panel is wired so that brushes 1 and 2 would actuate punch dies 1 and 2 upon detecting a hole in columns 1

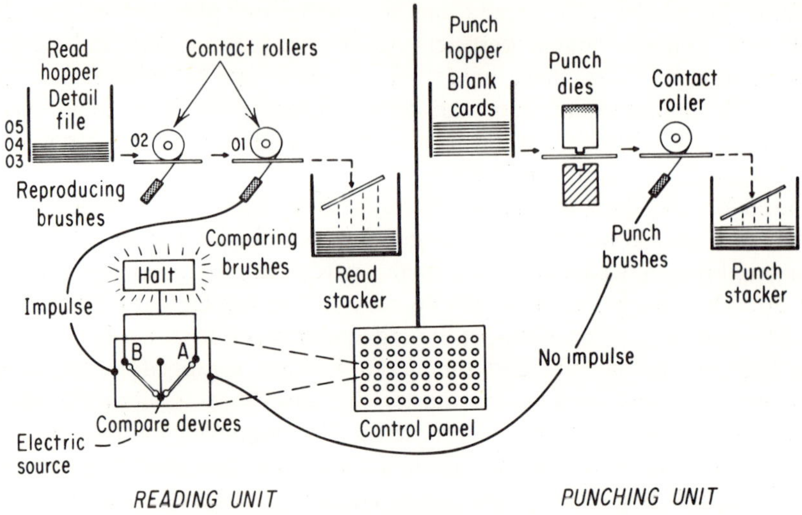

Figure 5-4. A schematic of the reproducer showing the comparing function

and 2. The machine is started and the first data card bearing employee number *01* is read by reproducing brushes 1 and 2. Brush 1 detects hole *0* in row 0 of column 1—the first available hole, because the card is fed 12-edge first, causing punch die 1 to punch in the same location in the blank card. (Refer to Figure 5-5.) The data card moves further and brush 2 detects a hole in row 1 in column 2, also causing punch die 2 to punch a *1* in the same location in the blank card.

Suppose that the punch dies do not respond properly to the impulses received from the reproducing brushes and that employee card number 01 was not punched. In this case, when the detail card moves over the comparing brushes in unison with the blank card which moves over the punch brushes, the comparing brushes send an impulse to a compare box, but

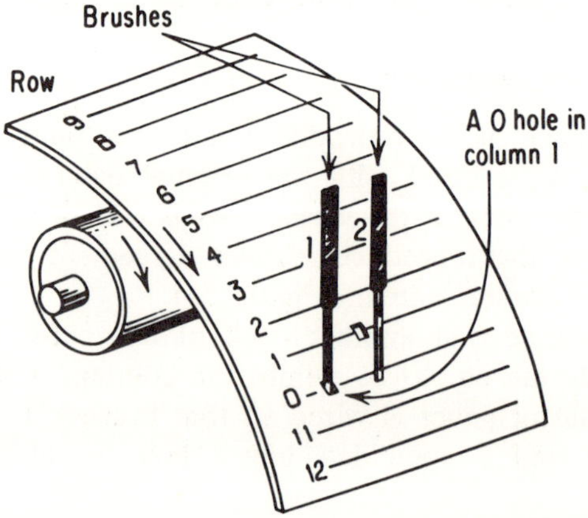

Figure 5-5. Reproducing brushes 1 and 2 sensing holes 0 and 1 in sequence.

the punch brushes do not send any impulse, because no holes were punched. This causes an imbalance in the compare device and a contact is made internally, halting the reproducer immediately. An arrow in a box on the outside indicates to the operator the location of the error.

Gang Punching

Gang punching is the automatic copying of punched data from the master card into one or more blank cards. Although the reproducer is used to do it, gang punching differs from reproducing in that the reproducing operation requires use of both the reading unit and the punch unit, whereas gang punching requires use of the punching unit only. A connection is made between the punch brushes and the punch dies through the control panel.

Figure 5-6 is a diagram of the punch unit of the reproducer and the path of cards in a gang-punching operation. The master card moves to the punch brushes and the first blank card following it moves to the punch

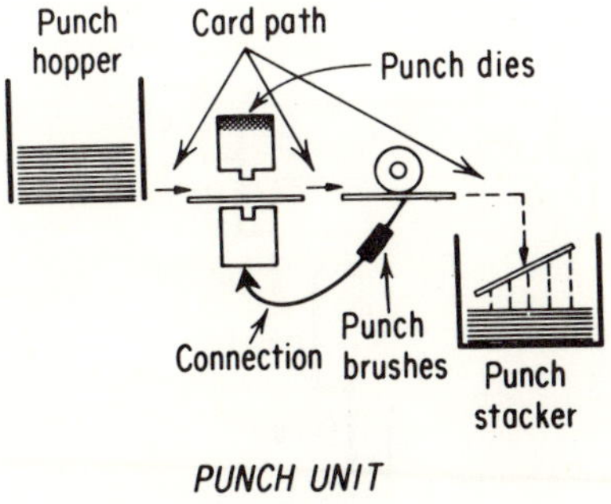

Figure 5-6. Punch unit of the reproducer used for gang punching

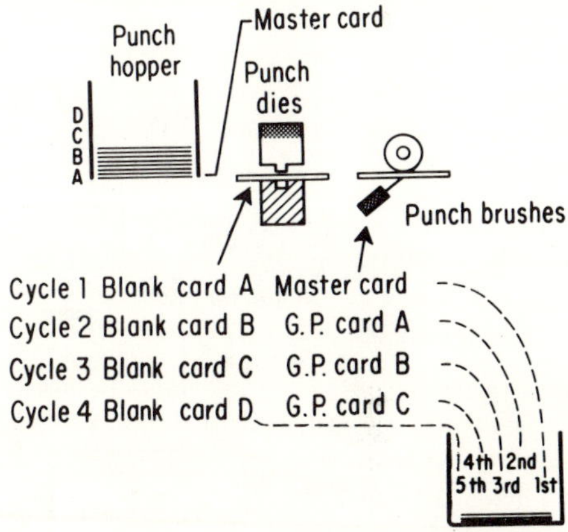

Figure 5-7. Single master-card gang punching

dies. The punch brushes sense the holes in the master card and, because of direct wiring through the control panel, actuate the punch dies to duplicate the same holes in the same location. Next, the master card drops into the stacker, the reproduced card moves to the punch brushes, and the second blank card moves under the punch dies. At this stage, the reproduced card is considered the same as the master card, because now it has the same information and is positioned at the punching brushes. Its contents are punched in the blank card following it in the same manner as the previous cycle. This cycle is repeated until all cards are completed.

To clarify, assume that a master card is to be gang-punched in four blank cards (*A, B, C,* and *D*) following it. Figure 5-7 presents the cycles necessary to complete the operation.

In cycle 1, the master card is copied into blank card *A*. The master card drops into the stacker. In cycle 2, gang-punched card *A* moves to the punching brushes and is copied (by punching) into blank card *B*. Gang-punched card *A* drops in the stacker while *B* moves to the punching brushes and card *C* to the punching dies. The same procedure applies for cycle 3 and cycle 4. At the end of cycle 4, gang-punched cards *C* and *D* drop in the stacker, respectively.

The illustration in Figure 5-7 works well in *single master-card gang punching,* that is, when only one master card is involved and a number of cards are to be duplicated from it. However, when information varies from one group of cards to another, the *interspersed gang-punching method* is used. In this method, a master card heads a group of cards to be gang-punched. On the first master card, the procedure is the same as in the single master-card gang-punching method. When the second master

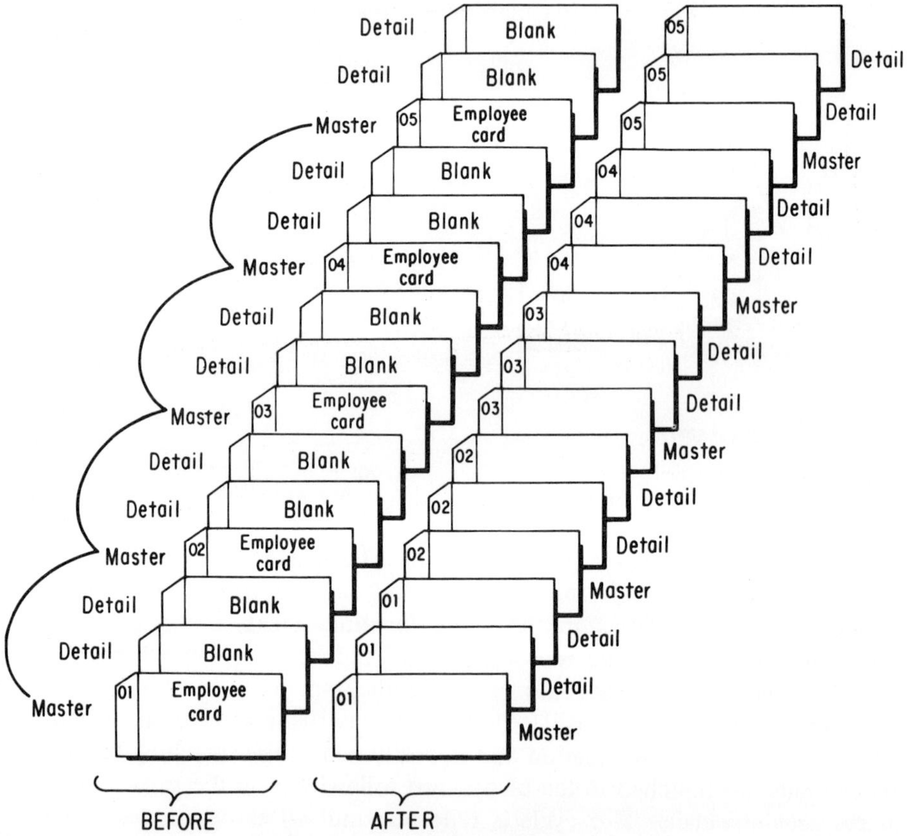

Figure 5-8. Interspersed gang punching

card is detected by the machine, the punching pattern then changes to conform to the details in it. (See Figure 5-8.)

Gang punching can be performed on a key punch. However, it is more convenient and efficient to use the reproducer because the job can be done faster on it than on the key punch.

Mark Sensing

Have you ever observed a representative of the gas and electric company taking a utility meter reading? The meter reader is provided with an IBM card in which are punched basic data, such as the customer's name, his meter number, and other related data. Also, on the right-hand section of the card, short lines are provided to be blackened with a special electrographic pencil to represent numeric data. The reader blackens the proper numbers with the pencil after he reads the meter. This is called *Mark Sensing*. The cards are later fed into the reproducer, which senses the strokes, or marks, and, through the control-board wiring, translates them into punched holes. This conversion step is necessary before the data from the mark-sensed cards can be integrated and properly processed for the eventual preparation of customer bills or financial statements.

Mark sensing is usually used for reproducing small quantities of numeric information. Alphabetic information requires double the space (2 holes to each letter) compared with that of numeric information (1 hole to each number). Further, alphabetic mark sensing is not so convenient for use by the layman.

Mark sensing is also common in scoring examination sheets where the student answers a specific question by blackening a short line or a column for an answer. Care must be taken when using this method, because the machine does not know when the student changes his mind, even if he blackens a different column for an answer, if he neglects to erase the previous answer well. Also, the machine will ignore the second answer if the spot is not marked heavily. Many times students pay heavily in unnecessary loss of points because of their neglect to read carefully the instructions prepared by the manufacturer.

Interpreting

Interpreting is converting machine language into human language. Figure 5-9 is a photograph of the IBM 548 Interpreter, the most commonly used one in data-processing departments. A distinction can be made easily between printing by the interpreter and that done by the key punch.

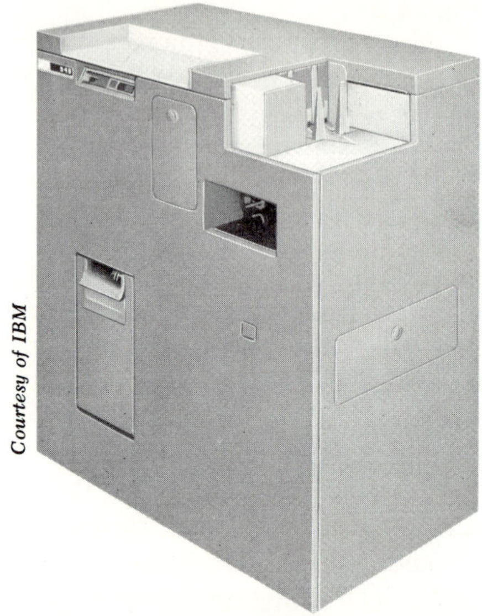

Figure 5-9. The IBM 548 interpreter

The latter machine prints on the top of the same column that contains the hole(s), whereas the interpreter merely prints across the face of the card.

Interpreting is a helpful supplementary aid in the reproducing function. Because many cards are reproduced or gang punched, a person can read them more easily if the cards are interpreted first than if he has to read the punched holes, a job which is both time-consuming and extremely boring.

QUESTIONS AND PROBLEMS

1. For what purpose(s) is a reproducer used?
2. Describe the reading unit and the punching units of a reproducer. Draw a schematic of a reproducer.
3. Identify the two sets of reading brushes of the reading unit. What is the function of each set?
4. Describe the procedure in reproducing a data card into a blank card.
5. What is meant by reproducing "80-80"? Explain.
6. Explain how the comparing function of a reproducer is similar to that of a verifier.
7. What is gang punching? How does it differ from reproducing?
8. Assume that a master card is to be punched in seven blank cards. Present and explain the cycles necessary to complete the operation.

9. What is the difference between single master-card gang punching and interspersed gang-punching methods?
10. You are a tab operator in a data-processing department of a local furniture store. Your supervisor asked you to duplicate three master cards bearing employee numbers *102, 106,* and *702,* respectively, into five blank cards each.
    (a) What machine is best suited for the job?
    (b) What is the name of this operation?
    (c) Show (by drawing) the sequence of cards as they appear *before* and *after* the operation is completed.
11. What is *mark sensing?* When and how is it used?
12. How can you distinguish between the printing of an interpreter and that of a key punch?

Chapter 6

Classifying Information by Sorting

As stressed in Chapter 1, the primary purpose of processing data is to prepare and report business facts vital to management in making informed decisions. After the conversion of source documents into unit records by key punching, the cards are checked and errors corrected by use of the verifier. Once they have been verified and any errors corrected, they are ready to be classified.

Reports to management must be presented in proper and useful form. What is "proper and useful" varies with the type of report required, because reports are needed for various reasons. The sales volume of a company for the fiscal year, for example, can produce many useful and informative facts. The many products sold during the year can be analyzed in order to determine whether or not they contributed enough to the over-all profit margin. Such information helps executives make decisions and future plans about maintaining the present products in stock and about the possible profitability of adding new products. Company sales can be analyzed also in order to see whether or not the salesmen have met the sales quotas set for them in the product lines which they were responsible for selling. The performance of a particular salesman can be compared with that of other salesmen employed in the same department, based on his sales quota and other pertinent factors, in order to determine whether he qualifies for a raise in salary or in rank within his department or, in some cases, for a transfer to a different branch with a promotion in both rank and salary.

The above example is but one of many situations which can be dealt with intelligently if facts concerning it are *classified* correctly before they are printed and reported. The purpose of classifying, thus, is to facilitate the arrangement of data in proper form for their use in various business reports. If a sales report by salesman is required, for example, it would be useless for the data-processing department to present a sales report by product or by customer number instead. In other words, the preparation of business transactions in a definite form contributes greatly to their effective use when they are finally printed and reported to management.

What Is Classifying?

Classifying, or sorting, is a process in which like transactions are grouped, or arranged together, in either alphabetic or numeric sequence based on the data punched in them. This is referred to as *sorting in sequence*. It is one of the three primary types of classifications performed on a machine called the *sorter*. The other two types are: *selecting,* or classifying by extraction; and *grouping,* or classifying according to common characteristics.

Sorting in sequence

Sorting in sequence is a process of preparing like data in either alphabetic or numeric order. Figure 6-1, (a) and (b), shows five cards being sequenced in numeric and alphabetic order, respectively.

Selecting

Selecting, or classifying by extraction, is the operation which involves pulling a number of cards from a certain file that require special attention without disturbing the sequence of the remainder of the file. In a

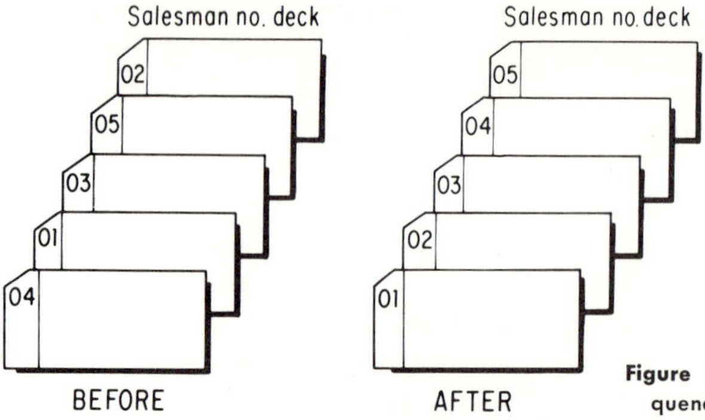

Figure 6-1 (a). Sorting in sequence—numerically

Figure 6-1 (b). Sorting in sequence—alphabetically

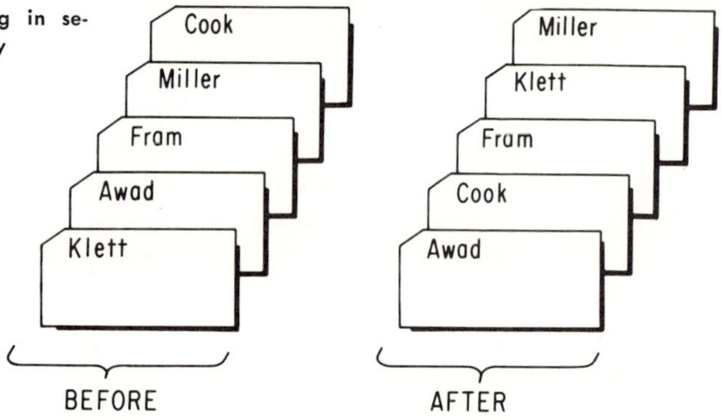

public relations department of a business firm, for instance, all employees who have been with the company for 20 years or more would have an *X* punched in a specific column (assume column 75) of their cards in a master file. Suppose that the public relations department is responsible for honoring these employees at an annual banquet. The data-processing manager is instructed to prepare a list of employees eligible for this honor. His department sorts the complete master file and, through the use of the sorter, extracts all cards having an *X* punched in column 75 without disturbing the sequence of the remainder of the file. Once the eligible employees' cards are extracted from the master file, they are listed and a copy is mailed to the public relations office. Figure 6-2 presents a condensed picture of the above example.

The selecting technique is used in many other connections in business data processing. In a banking application, for example, certain delinquent-customer loan cards can be extracted from the master loan file so that listing of these customer accounts can be made and notices mailed to them reminding them of the overdue payment. In an insurance application, there can be extracted from a master policyholders' file all cards pertaining to those policyholders whose insurance policies expire within

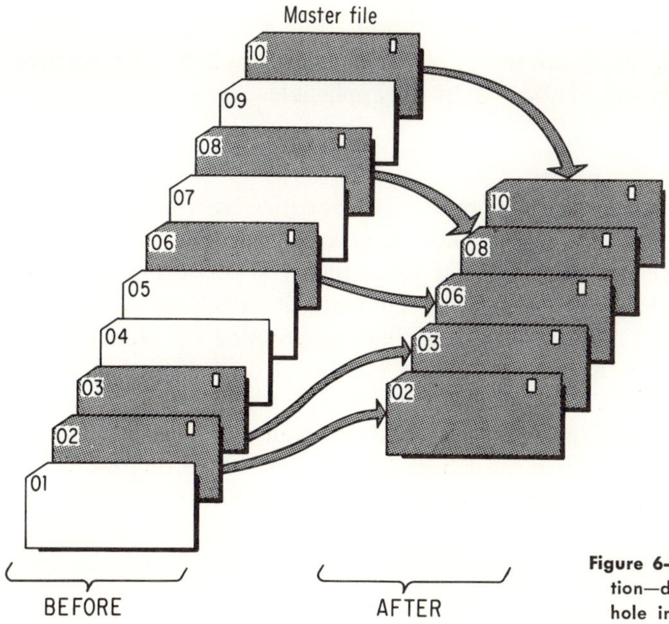

Figure 6-2. Selecting by extraction—denotes an X punch (a hole in row 11) in column 75

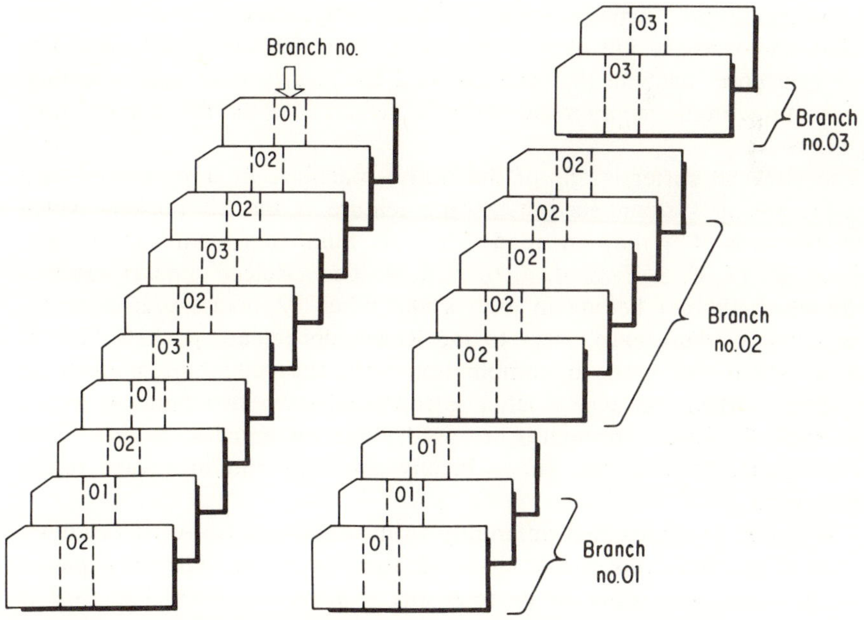

Figure 6-3. Grouping—classifying by common characteristics

the current month, for the purpose of preparing a statement of policy renewal. Numerous other examples can be thought of by the student where classifying by extraction would be applicable.

Grouping

Grouping, or classifying by common characteristics, is a process where a mass of data is arranged into related groups, each group having common characteristics. For example, if a sales report is to be presented by branch number instead of by product number, the deck of cards containing the data for a sales report must first be grouped by branches. In this way, all sales cards having branch number 1 will be listed under branch number 1, all cards in branch 2 will be listed under branch 2, and so forth, until the total number of sales cards in the deck would be grouped under their respective branches. This is done by sorting the cards according to the branch-number field, as shown in Figure 6-3.

The Sorter

Sorting is similar to filing and can be done manually on an economical basis in some small applications. A simple illustration of it is distributing the mail in the proper mail racks or in the "In" and "Out" mail baskets. In large volumes of data, however, manual attempts to rearrange them for specific report purposes would be too costly; thus, if a machine can be devised to do the job, it will be used if it cuts down on the cost. The special-purpose machine that can be used for sequence sorting, selecting, or grouping on an economical basis is referred to as the *Sorter*. (See Figure 6-4.)

The IBM 83 sorter is one of the fastest machines in the punched-card data-processing system. Its outstanding feature is the 13 pockets which hold the cards after they are read. They are numbered from right to left: *Reject, 12, 11, 0, 1, 2, 3, 4, 5, 6, 7, 8, 9*. The "Reject" pocket receives cards which do not belong in any of the other 12 pockets, an example of which is a blank card. Next to the Reject pocket are pockets 12, 11, and 0, which are used in combination with the remaining pockets in alphabetic sorting, because a letter is represented by two punches in the IBM card. Pockets 0 through 9 are used alone for numeric sorting. They are adequate, because one punch in any given column in a card represents a digit.

The sorter is constructed differently from other punched-card machines in that it has only *one brush* mounted above a roller. The card passes between brush and roller to be read *one column per pass*. The card is fed into the sorter 9-edge first, face down. This means that row 9 of a specific column passes under the reading brush. If a hole is detected, the

Figure 6-4. The IBM 83 sorter

brush makes contact with the roller underneath the card, causing the card to be ejected into pocket 9. If a hole is detected in row 8, however, the Sorter will eject that card into pocket 8 instead. This goes on until all the twelve rows of card 1 are read. When the brush passes row 12 of card 1, row 9 of card 2 follows immediately. This process continues until all the rows in a specific column of all the cards in the hopper are read and, consequently, the cards are ejected into their respective pockets.

Sorting in sequence on the IBM 83 sorter

For purposes of illustration, let us take the first primary type of classification performed on the sorter, that is, "sorting in sequence." It is divided into Numeric Sorting and Alphabetic Sorting.

Numeric sorting

Numeric sorting involves the rearrangement of cards in numeric order by sorting a specific digit field in the cards. The size of the field can be one or more columns, the location of which is immaterial to the sorter, because the reading brush can be moved manually to read any given column regardless of its location in the card. Sorting a deck of cards on a one-column digit field is done by moving the "read" brush to the desired column. All cards having a zero in them will eject into pocket zero, those containing "1" will eject into pocket 1, and so forth, until the deck is completely sorted. For instance, Figure 6-5 shows a deck containing 10 cards in random order face down.

Assume that the cards are to be rearranged sequentially on column 1 containing the digits shown at the right in the illustration. The reading brush is moved to the location of column 1 and the bottom card moves

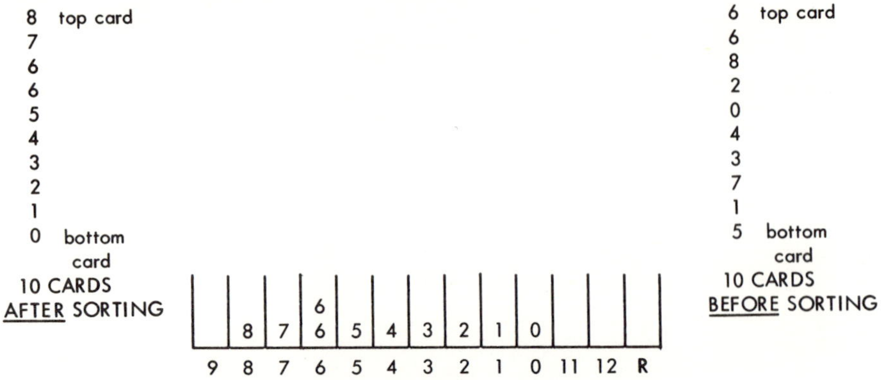

Figure 6-5. Numeric sorting—1 digit field

under the brush 9-edge first. The brush detects a hole in row 5, which would cause it to drop into pocket 5. The next card moves along, and a hole in row 1 is detected. It drops into pocket 1. This process continues until the top card is sensed and consequently dropped into pocket 6. The middle of Figure 6-5 shows the location of the cards in the sorter pockets. The operator reassembles them as follows: The cards in pocket 1 are placed on top of those in pocket zero. They are followed by pocket 2 cards, which are placed on top of the combined deck of cards 1 and 0; those from pocket 3 are placed on top of those from 2; those from 4, on top of those from 3; those from 5 on top of those from 4; and so forth. After reassembly is completed, card 8 should be on the top of the deck and card zero on the bottom, face down. When turned over as a complete deck, zero appears first and behind it, in ascending order, cards 1 through 8.

Another method of reassembling the cards from the pockets of the sorter is to start with the 9's (cards in pocket 9) and place cards from each succeeding pocket to the right underneath those already removed until cards from pocket 0 are placed last.

The Reverse-Digit Method of Sorting. For fields larger than one column, the reverse-digit sorting method is used. That is, the numeric field is sorted from right to left across the field, one column per pass. All cards have to be sorted on the right-hand column first. When this step is completed, *it is referred to as "pass 1."* The cards are reassembled and the stack is placed in the hopper to be sorted on the second column from the right. This is referred to as "pass 2." The process continues until the whole field is sorted. Therefore, the number of passes necessary to sort a numeric field is equal to the number of columns in it. Figure 6-6 illustrates, step by step, numeric sorting by the reverse-digit method, the

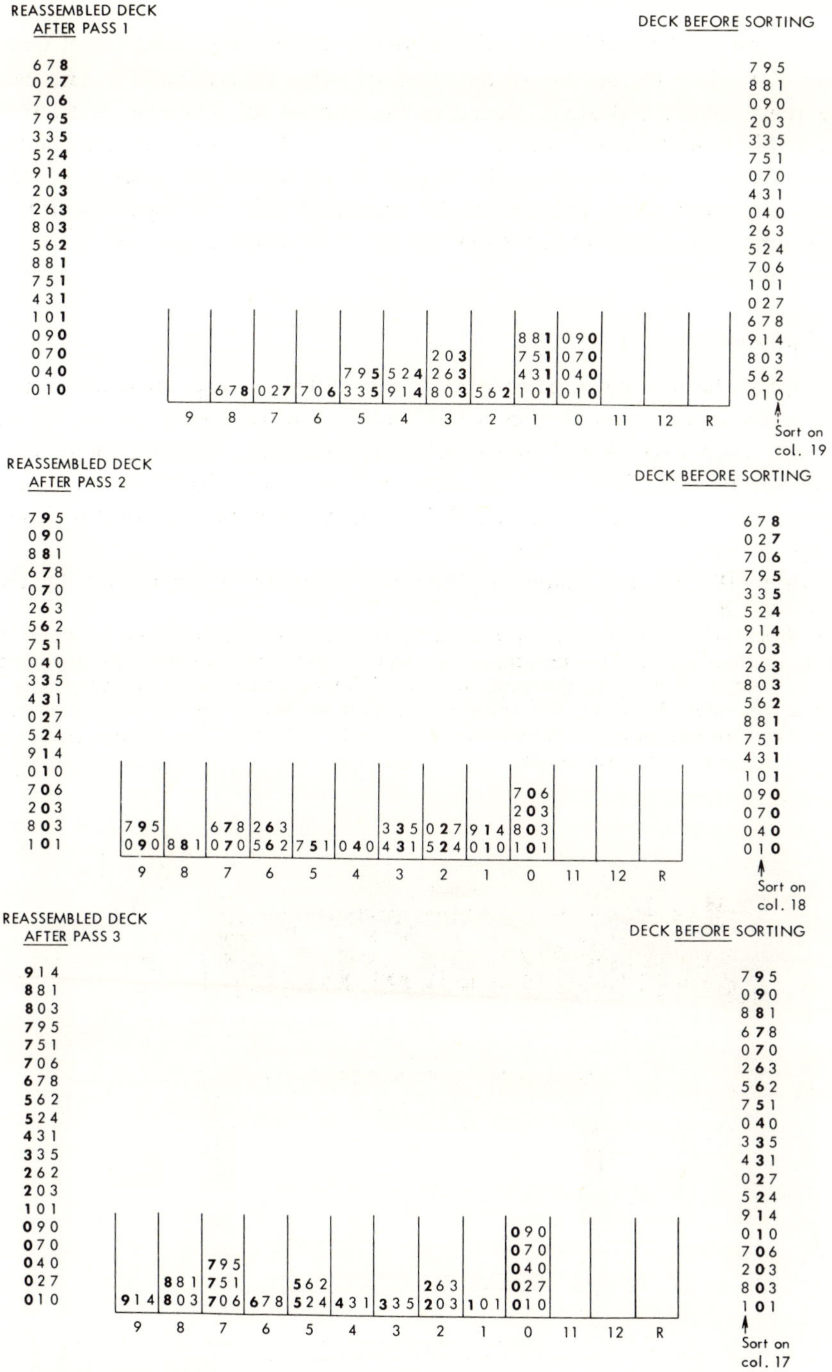

Figure 6-6. Numeric sorting—(a) more than one column; and (b) steps of the reverse digit method

fastest and most commonly used method of sorting large volumes of data.* Pass 1 involves the sorting of the stack of cards on column 19. The cards are reassembled and again placed in the hopper for a second pass. However, this time they are sorted on column 18. The cards are reassembled a second time and placed in the hopper to be sorted on column 17 for a third and final pass. The cards are reassembled by the operator for the final time. The result should show the stack of cards in the proper ascending numeric order.

Alphabetic sorting

Alphabetic sorting is performed in two different ways, depending upon the sorter model used. The two IBM models in use today are the 82 and the 83. (See Figures 6-7 and 6-4.) One difference between them lies in their speed. The IBM 82 sorter sorts at the rate of 650 cards per minute, whereas the 83 model sorts at 1,000 cards per minute. Another difference is the methods in which they sort.

Alphabetic Sorting Using the IBM 82. Alphabetic sorting on the IBM

* When several sorters are available, it is often more convenient to divide the work among them. In this technique, the deck is first sorted on the leftmost column of the field, thus dividing the cards into 10 different groups, each of which can be sorted separately by using the reverse-digit method. When the 10 groups of cards have been sorted, they are recombined in a proper sequence. This process is referred to as the *block sorting* technique.

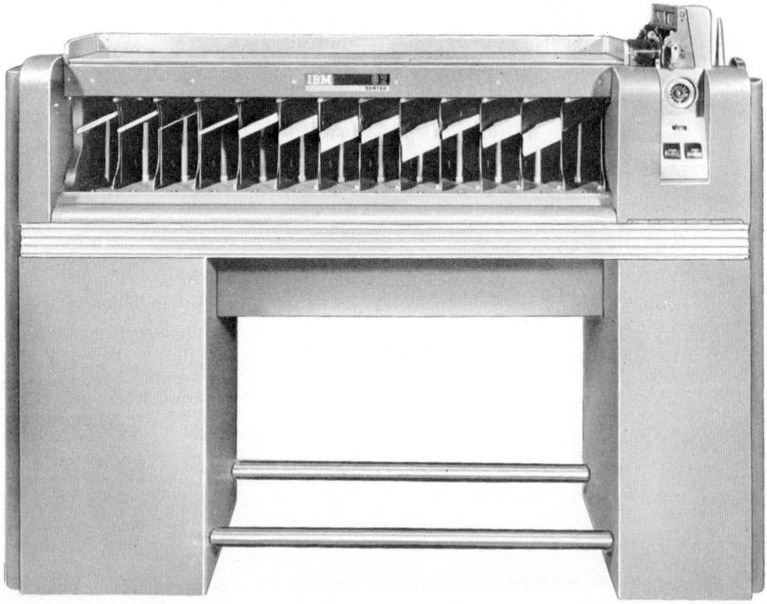

Courtesy of IBM

Figure 6-7. The IBM 82 sorter

82 takes twice as much time as numeric sorting. Because a letter is represented by two holes in a given column in a card, it would take two passes to sort on that column. The first pass sorts the digit part of a given column of each card, so that the whole deck is grouped by digits *1* through *9*. Only holes 1 through 9 are sensed in this pass. The second pass sorts the *zone* portion of the same column. In the second pass, the brush will sense holes in the zone punching positions only. The cards fall in one of the zone pockets 12, 11, and 0, in the proper alphabetic sequence. Pocket 12 holds all cards with letters represented by zone 12, that is, *A-I*. Pocket 11 holds all cards with letters represented by zone 11, *J-R*. Pocket zero holds all cards with letters repersented by zone 0, *S-Z*. As in numeric sorting, cards are fed into the sorter 9-edge first, face down.

Figure 6-8 shows, step by step, the alphabetic sorting of a deck of 26 alphabetically punched cards. For purposes of illustration, only a one-column alphabetic field is applied. However, in the case of a two-letter field, for instance, four passes are required: two passes per column. The right-hand column is sorted first, and the left-hand column is sorted next, as is true in numeric sorting.

Alphabetic Sorting Using the IBM 83. The IBM 83 sorter is similar to the 82 model in that each has 13 pockets and one brush to read one column at a time, from right to left across the field on which sorting is to be performed. Also, cards are placed in either machine 9-edge first, face down. However, the alphabetic procedure differs in the 83 model.

In the first pass, the IBM 83 sorter ejects cards bearing letters *A-I* to pockets 1-9, that is, sorting on the digit portion of these letters. The remaining cards are treated as follows: cards containing letters *J-R* are ejected into pocket 11. Cards containing letters *S-Z* are ejected into pocket 0.

In the second pass, cards *A-I* are excluded because they are already in sequence when reassembled. Cards in pocket 11 are sorted on their digit punching positions and ejected into pockets 1-9, that is, pocket 1 contains *J*'s; pocket 2, *K*'s; pocket 3, *L*'s; and so forth. They are reassembled and placed behind cards (*A-I*) sequenced in the first pass.

In the third pass, the cards containing *S-Z* are sorted on their digit punching position and ejected into pockets 2-9. That is, pocket 2 would contain cards with *S*'s; pocket 3, *T*'s; pocket 4, *U*'s; and so forth. When reassembled, they are placed behind the partial deck containing cards *A-R* (*A-I* plus *J-R*) from the previous two passes (Figure 6-9).

Alphabetic sorting on the IBM 83 sorter is, thus, faster than on the earlier model 82, because, after the first pass, the deck of cards to be sorted is progressively decreasing. With fewer remaining cards to be sorted in each of the second and third passes, plus the greater rate of

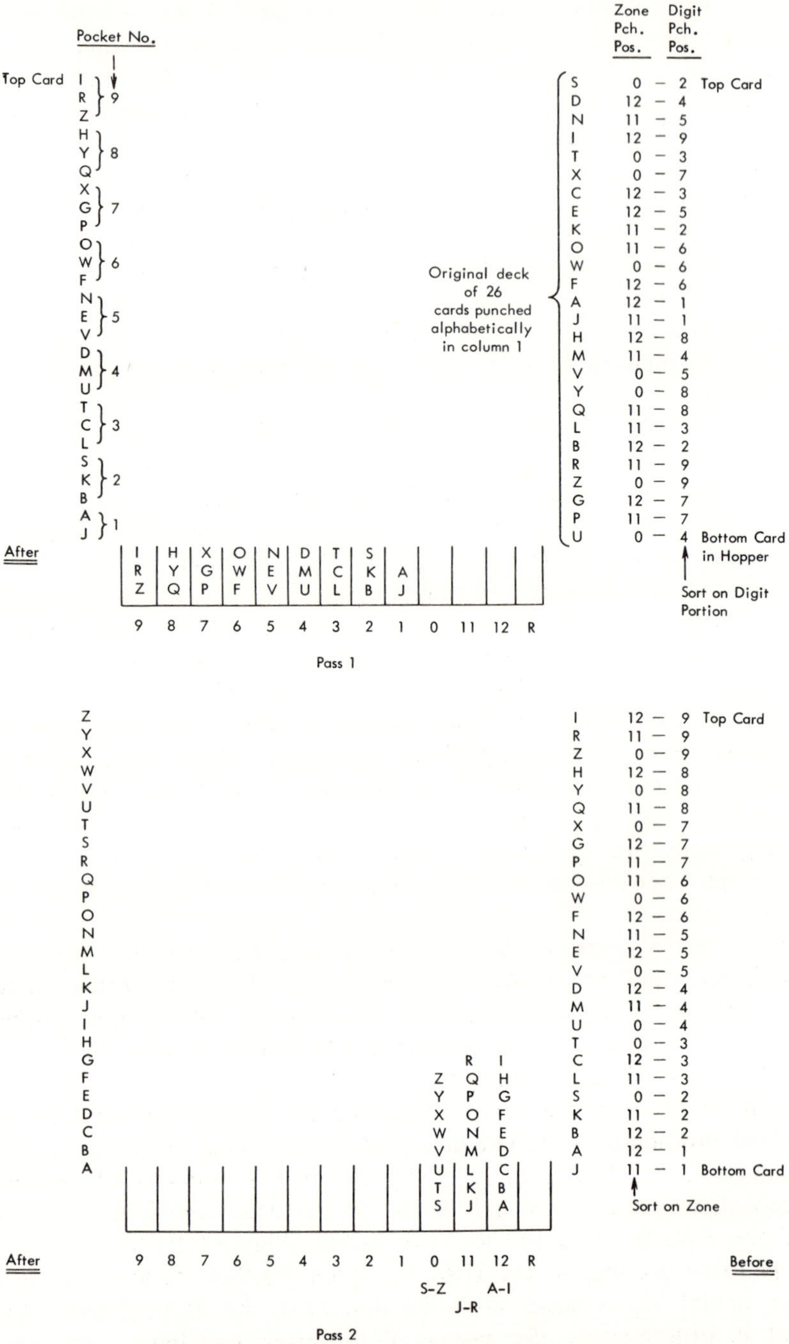

Figure 6-8. Alphabetic sorting—the IBM 82 sorter

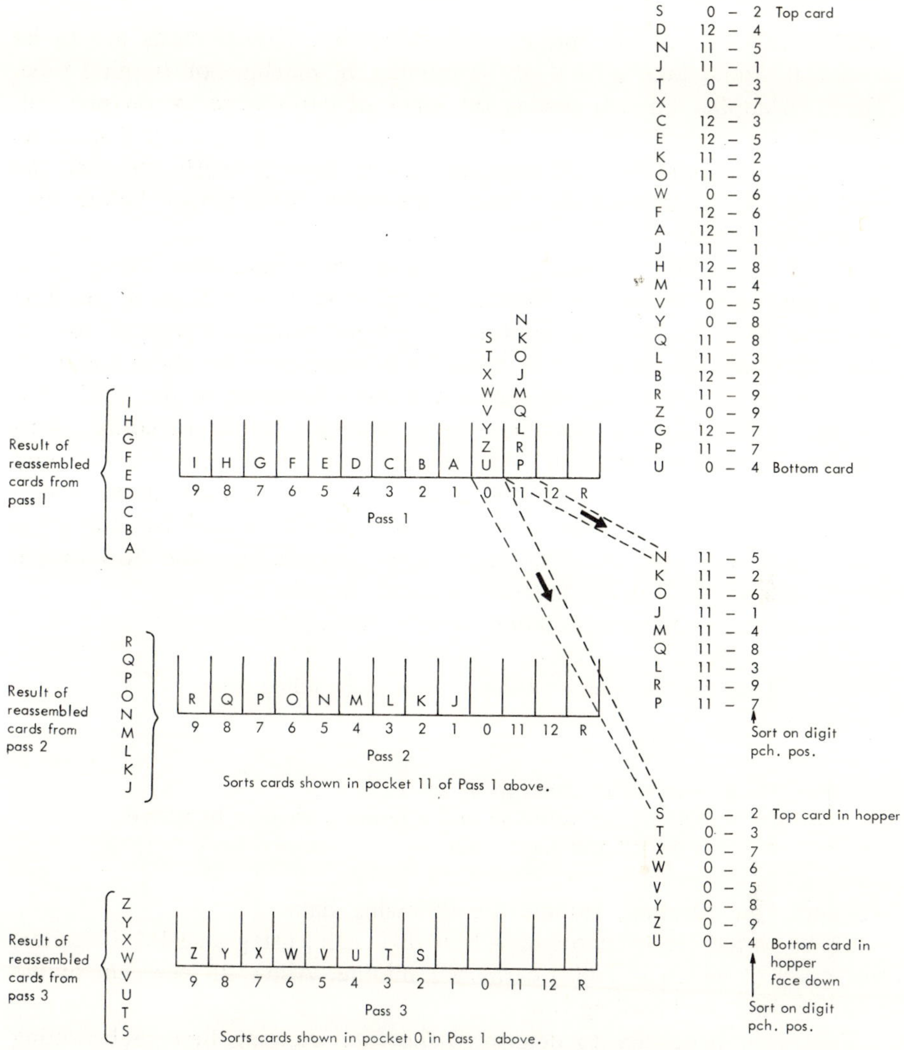

Figure 6-9. Alphabetic sorting—the IBM 83 sorter

speed of the model itself, the job can be done in a shorter period of time on the 83 than on the 82.

Computation of Sorting Time

The time it takes to sort a given deck of cards depends largely upon factors such as the number of cards in the deck, the size of the numeric field to be sorted, the speed of the sorter to be used, and the degree of experience of the operator. The IBM 83 sorter (Figure 5-4) reads at the rate of 1,000 cards per minute. Assuming that 10,000 cards are to be sorted, it would take a total of 10 minutes of machine or running time. The time applies only to sorting the stack of cards once, or on one column. If, for example, the 10,000 cards are to be sorted on a 3 numeric field, then it would take 30 minutes to sort them properly, because the cards have to go through the sorter three times, three passes, before they are finally sorted.

The human effort in sorting is time-consuming and, thus, costly. It is time-consuming because a human operator is slower than a machine and less adept in handling continuous routine processes without loss in time, accuracy, or speed. It is considered reasonable to allow about 25 per cent of the total running time for human handling of the cards and the manipulation of the machine. The actual time would, of course, vary with the individual operator. An operator with little experience would very likely increase the percentage allowance by causing more delays and *avoidable* interruptions, whereas the opposite would be true of a well-experienced operator who knew what steps to take and how to use proper "short cuts" to do the job fast and accurately.

A formula for the computation of total sorting time is:

$$\text{Total sorting time} = \text{Running time} + \text{handling time.}$$

$$\text{Running time} = \frac{V \times Nc}{S}$$

V = Number of cards to be sorted
Nc = Number of columns in the numeric field to be sorted
S = Speed of the sorter used

To apply the formula, assume the following data:

To be sorted: 2,500 cards on a four-digit field, using an IBM 83 sorter, the speed of which is 1,000 cards per minute. Allow 25 per cent of the running time for handling time.

First, it is necessary to determine the total running time. Substituting values in the formula, we would get:

$$\frac{2{,}500 \times 4}{1{,}000} = 10 \text{ minutes — running time}$$

$$\text{Total sorting time} = 10 \text{ minutes} + 2.5 \text{ minutes handling time} = 12.5 \text{ minutes.}$$

If an operator were being paid $1.50 per hour to run the machine, the total labor cost would be: 12.5 × .025 = $0.3125, or 31¼ cents. Compare this with the labor cost involved if sorting this deck were done manually by the same operator.

QUESTIONS AND PROBLEMS

1. Define the following terms and give an example of each:
   (a) Classifying
   (b) Selecting
   (c) Grouping
2. Sort the following cards in ascending sequence:
   (a) By student number
   (b) By student name
   (c) By course number

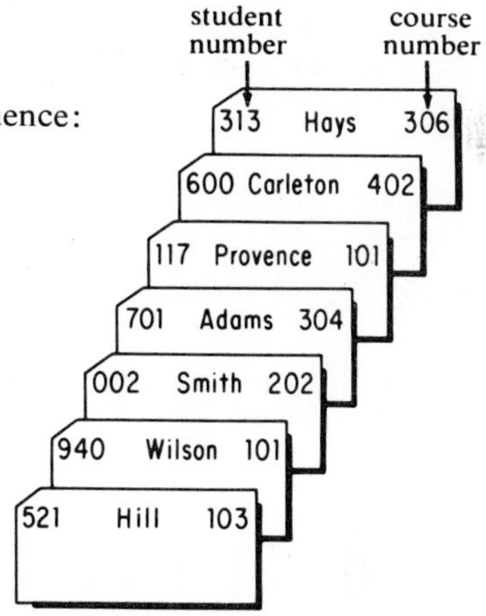

3. Assume that *100-103* denote a freshman-course level; *200-203,* sophomore-course level; *300-304,* junior-course level; and *400-403,* senior-course level. Using the data in the seven student cards in Problem 2 above,
   (a) Group the cards under the four categories (that is, by class level).
   (b) Sort the cards in each category by student number.
4. Show how the following numbers (each represented by a card) are placed in the sorter pockets:

   3, 5, 9, 2, 0, 1, 4, 7, 8, 9, 0.
5. Assume the following deck of 20 numbers, each of which represents a card:

20 (top card)	67	10	80	18
08	75	72	95	26
20	11	52	33	51
33	46	07	64	93 (bottom card)

   (a) How many passes are required to sort the deck?
   (b) Using the reverse-digit method of sorting, present in ascending order a reassembled deck after each pass.
6. Sort the following letters, each representing a card, using the IBM 82 sorter, by showing their location in the proper sorter pockets (refer to Figure 6-8).

Q (top card)	T	L	E	F
S	K	G	V	P
N	L	C	U	R
B	J	W	M	Y (bottom card)

Explain also how these letters are sorted, using the same sorter.

7. Suppose we wish to sort 9,000 cards on a four-digit numeric field using the IBM 83 sorter.
   (a) How many passes would be required to sort the deck?
   (b) Assuming a speed of 1,000 cards per minute, what is the running time of this sort?
   (c) What is the total sorting time if 25 per cent of the running time is allowed for handling?

Chapter 7

The Collation of Sorted Data

After data cards have been carefully prepared from source documents and sequenced, they are placed in a master file for future use. Management may want to use these stored data for a variety of purposes, some examples of which would be the preparation of sales reports, reports on items purchased for resale, classified information on parts ordered for the manufacturing process, information as to the number of employees hired in different departments during the year, and knowledge of the profit made on various lines carried, of the costs involved in certain departments, or of the location of customers. All of this information is stored in cards in the master file in proper sequence. In order to obtain all of the pertinent information for a specific report, the cards containing it must be gathered together from the total number in the master file, or files, involved. The process of picking out cards containing the desired stored data from the mass, or combining information in two different files, is called *collating,* and the machine that has been developed to do this routine job is called the *collator*.

The Collator

The *collator* is actually an auxiliary high-speed filing machine used after classification has been completed. (See Figure 7-1.) Although a few of its functions are somewhat similar to those of the sorter, it is a flexible, multipurpose, more complicated machine than the sorter. Because it has hoppers to handle two different groups of cards, it can read several columns of two cards at once, whereas the sorter can read only one column of one card at a time—which limits its application in the collating process.

Purpose of the collator

In an operation where funds are limited for data-processing equipment, functions such as selecting and merging can be done on the sorter instead of the collator. However, the sorter's limitations must be strictly

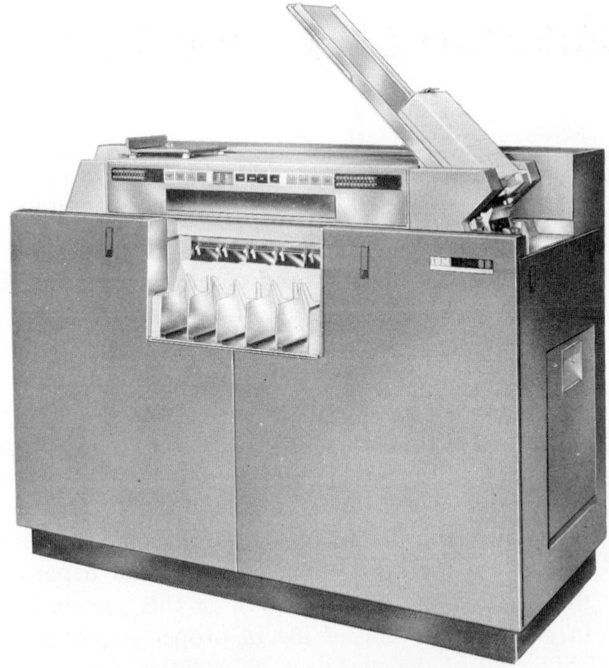
Courtesy of IBM

Figure 7-1. The IBM 88 collator

observed if it is to be used in this way. In a merging operation, for example, the sorter can be used *if the merging field is in the same location in each card.* The collator, on the other hand, is designed for merging two different decks of cards much faster than the sorter, and it does *not* require that the merge field in the two decks of cards be located in the same location. The purpose of the collator is to arrange a deck or two of sorted cards into a predetermined sequence for filing or for further processing.

Description of the IBM 88 collator

The IBM 88 collator is designed to collate information by merging, matching, merge-matching, sequence checking, selecting, or editing. (Figure 7-1.*) In order for it to perform these functions, it has two separate feed units, each of which has two sets of 80 reading brushes. The right side of the machine is called the *primary feed unit.* The left side is called the *secondary feed unit* (Figure 7-2).

---

* The IBM 77 and 89 collators are still available. They perform the same basic functions as the 88 collator above, except that the latter machine includes features such as editing, separate indicators for primary and secondary errors, and an extra stacker for more versatile use. These factors, along with the greater speed, make the 88 collator a superior and a costlier machine.

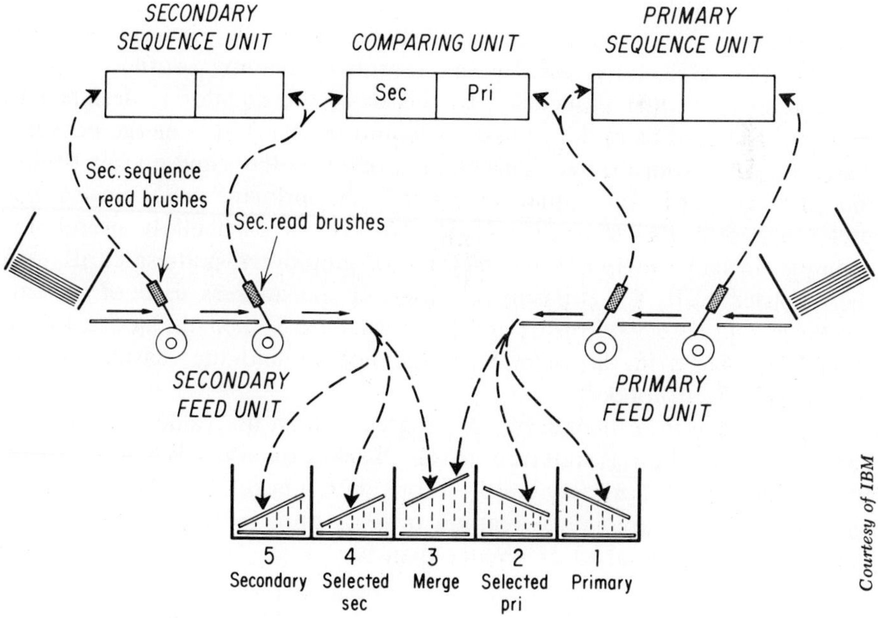

Courtesy of IBM

Figure 7-2. A schematic of the main components of the IBM 88 collator

Cards moving through from either side eject into one of the five pockets, based on the type of operation in action. Because the cards move from two opposite directions, they are placed into the hoppers differently. The primary cards are fed 9-edge first, face down, whereas the secondary cards are fed 12-edge first, face down.

The Merging Function

One of the main capabilities of the collator is the ability to compare two values. Comparing two values manually involves the use of the eyes and the mind. A person looks at one value and then looks at another. Next, he compares and sequences the cards bearing the two values in a predetermined manner. The same basic steps take place in a collator. The brushes are the eyes of the machine, and the control unit (panel) is its mind. The brushes read the values in two cards from separate hoppers. The comparing unit can determine whether they are equal, whether one value is greater than another, or whether one value is less than another.

Merging is taking two separate decks and arranging them into one deck in a given sequence. Before merging, each of the two decks must be in sequence. The card read at the primary reading brushes is compared with that read at the secondary reading brushes. One of three possibilities can exist:

1. The value in a card read by the primary reading brushes is equal to the value of a card read by the secondary reading brushes. This is referred to as "equal sequence." In this case, the collator is designed to eject first the card from the primary side into pocket 3 (the merge pocket). Then the card from the secondary side drops into the same pocket behind the primary card. In "equal sequence," the primary feed always has preference over the secondary feed. This fact is particularly useful, for example, in cases involving the merging of employees'-address cards with their master cards for printing purposes. If the address card of an employee is supposed to drop behind his master card, then the address deck should be placed in the secondary feed hopper and the master card in the primary feed hopper.

2. The value in a secondary card is greater than the value in a primary card. This situation is referred to as "Low Primary." When it arises, the smaller-value (primary card) drops into pocket 3. The secondary card waits at the secondary reading brushes until another primary card contains a value equal to or greater than it.

3. The value in a secondary card is less than the value in a primary card. This is referred to as "Low Secondary." In this case, the secondary card (being a smaller value) drops into pocket 3 and the primary card waits at the primary reading brushes until another secondary card contains a value equal to or greater than it.

For purposes of illustration, assume that three customer cards were selected out of the master file for temporary use with other information, and merging these cards into the master deck is now desired. In Figure 7-3, the three customer cards are placed in the secondary hopper and the incomplete master file is placed in the primary hopper. The result is a merged deck in pocket 3 of the collator, because pocket 3 is the only pocket that accepts cards from both the primary and the secondary feed units.

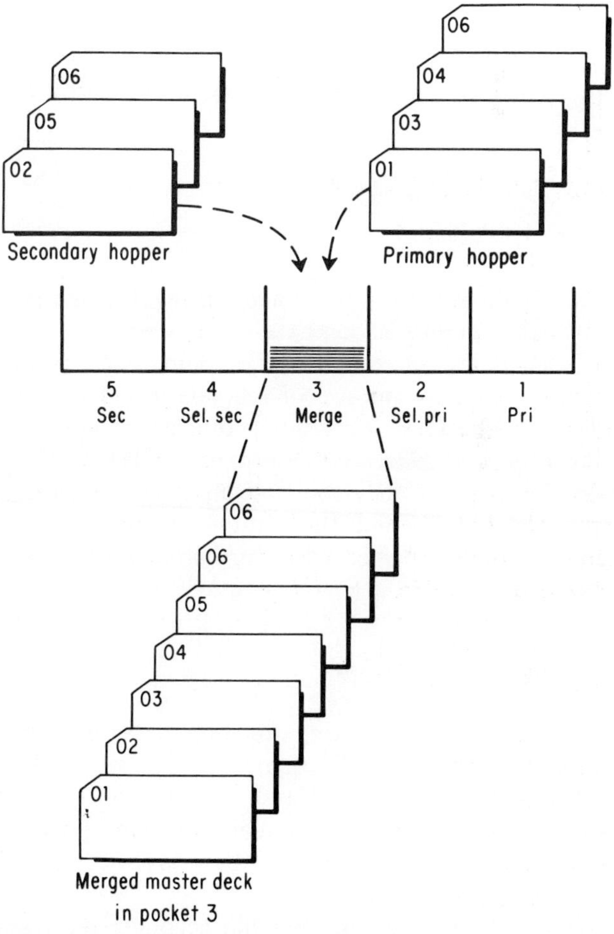

Figure 7-3. Merging—an example

During the course of the merge operation in Figure 7-3, the collator made the following comparisons:

Comparison number	*Secondary card*		*Primary card*	*Result of comparison*	*Action taken*
1	02	—	01	Low Primary	Primary card 01 drops into pocket 3, while sec. card 02 waits at sec. read. brushes.
2	02	—	03	Low Secondary	Sec. card 02 drops into pocket 3, while pri. card 03 waits at the pri. read. station.
3	05	—	03	Low Primary	Pri. card 03 drops into pocket 3, while sec. card 05 waits at the sec. read. brushes.
4	05	—	04	Low Primary	Pri. card 04 drops into pocket 3, while sec. card 05 waits again at the sec. read. brushes.
5	05	—	06	Low Secondary	Sec. card 05 drops into pocket 3, while pri. card 06 waits at the pri. read. brushes.
6	06	—	06	Equal	The primary feed has preference over the sec. Primary card 06 drops into pocket 3 first, followed by sec. card 06.

Six comparisons were made during the merge operation. The speed at which merging is done varies between 650 and 1,300 cards per minute, depending on results of the comparisons made. The merge operation requires basically the use of secondary and the primary reading brushes. However, the sequence reading brushes of both sides can be used simultaneously to check on the proper sequence of the cards coming from both hoppers. If they are activated, and a card is found to be out of sequence, the machine stops automatically and an error light turns on to tell the operator which card (primary or secondary) is out of sequence.

The Matching Function

Matching is a checking function performed by the collator to determine the equality of a specific field in two decks of cards. One deck is fed into the primary feed and the other deck into the secondary feed. In an equal comparison, the equal cards are ejected into pockets 2 and 4. If the comparison is unequal, they are ejected into the extreme pockets (that is, pockets 1 and 5).

To illustrate, suppose that the accounts receivable file of a small business firm contains 09 active accounts. At the end of a specific day, four

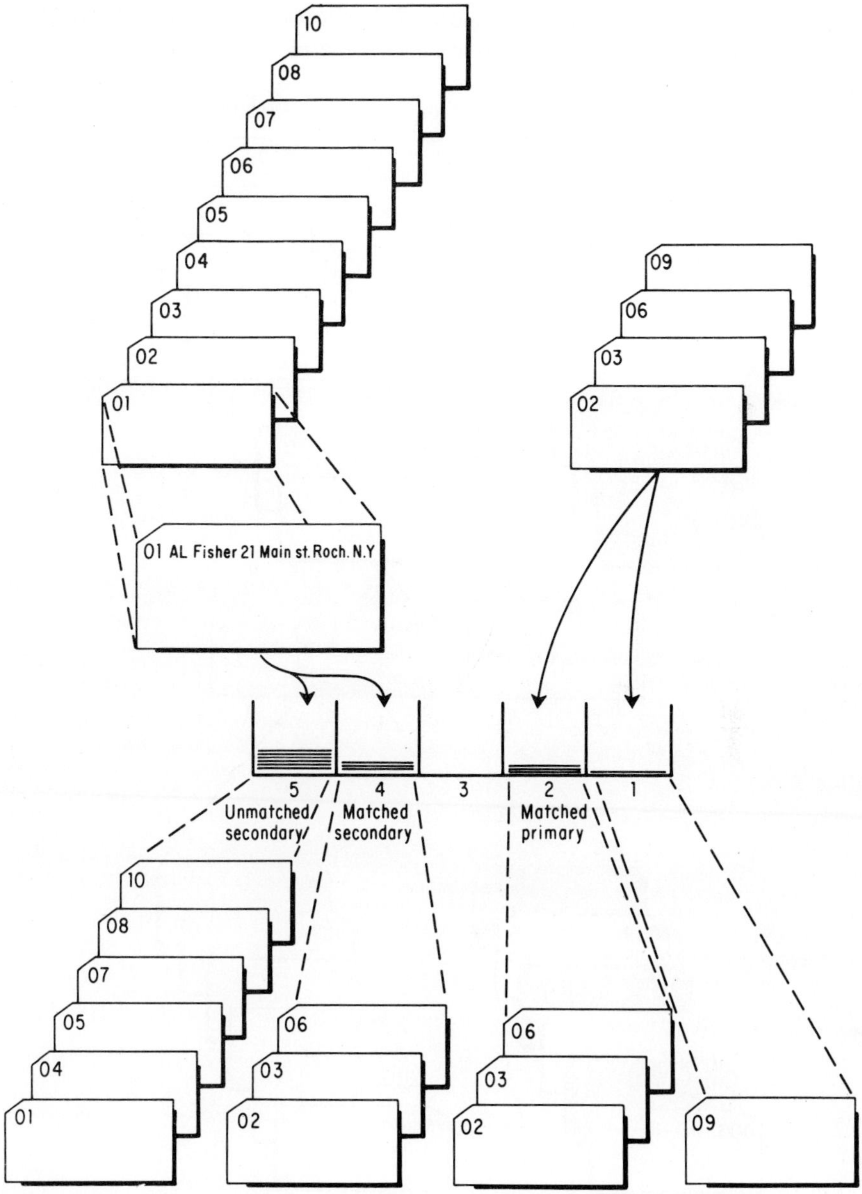

Figure 7-4. Matching—an example

of the accounts are paid up. Assume, further, that the business keeps a separate name-and-address card for each accounts receivable card. In order for the name-and-address file to be updated—that is, to contain only the names and addresses of the unpaid accounts—it is necessary to match the paid-up accounts receivable (four cards) against the name-and-address file (09 cards). Figure 7-4 shows the matched cards in pockets 2 and 4. The cards in pocket 5 are the name-and-address cards

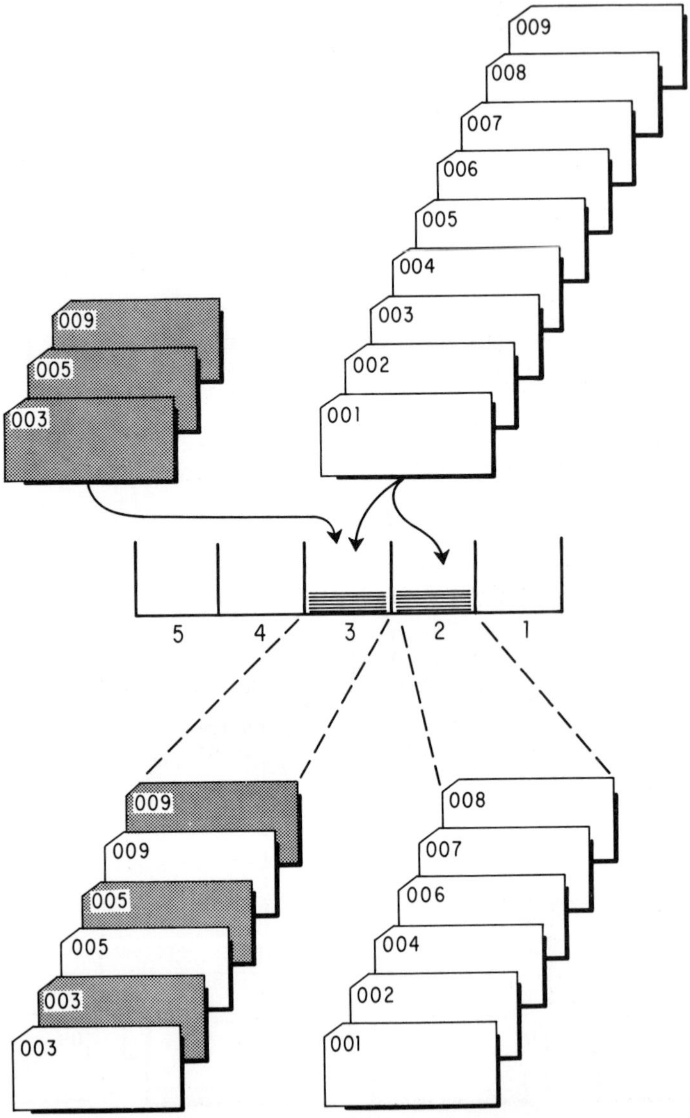

Figure 7-5. Match-merge—a further exampl‹

pertaining to the remainder of the accounts receivable file. The card bearing customer number 09 is dropped into pocket 1, because it is unmatched, since there is no name-and-address card bearing the same number.

The Match-Merging Function

The match-merging function combines the machine's matching and merging capabilities into one operation. *Match-merging* is a routine in which cards in both decks are compared. The cards that match are merged and dropped into one pocket (pocket 3) instead of being placed separately into two different pockets. It is one of the most common operations performed on the collator. In a banking application, for example, the consumer credit department keeps a file containing a to-date balance card for each loan made by the bank to a given customer. It is referred to as the *balance file*. Periodically, the bank receives payment of installments made by some customers toward the payment of their loans. After these payments are punched into payment cards, they are compared with the balance file so that each payment card will merge with the balance card bearing the same customer number. This is done for the purpose of calculating the unpaid balance, if any. Figure 7-5 shows three payment cards placed in the secondary hopper and the balance file placed in the primary hopper. The two decks are compared. Cards 003, 005, and 009 in both decks agree. Under the match-merge operation, they merge together and drop into pocket 3. The remaining cards in the balance file drop into pocket 2 because they find no match in the secondary file.

If, for example, balance card 009 in the primary hopper were missing, the payment card 009 in the secondary hopper will not find a match and will drop into pocket 4 instead of pocket 3. When such a situation occurs, it is investigated and proper corrections made.

The Sequence-Checking Function

Sequence checking is the process of determining whether the IBM cards in a given file are in the proper order by comparing each card with the one ahead of it. Depending upon the wiring of the control panel, the primary and secondary files can be sequence-checked either separately or simultaneously. Usually sequence checking is done along with merging, with matching, or with match-merging operations, but it can also be performed as a separate function on the collator if the occasion demands this.

In sequence checking, three possibilities can occur: (1) The value in

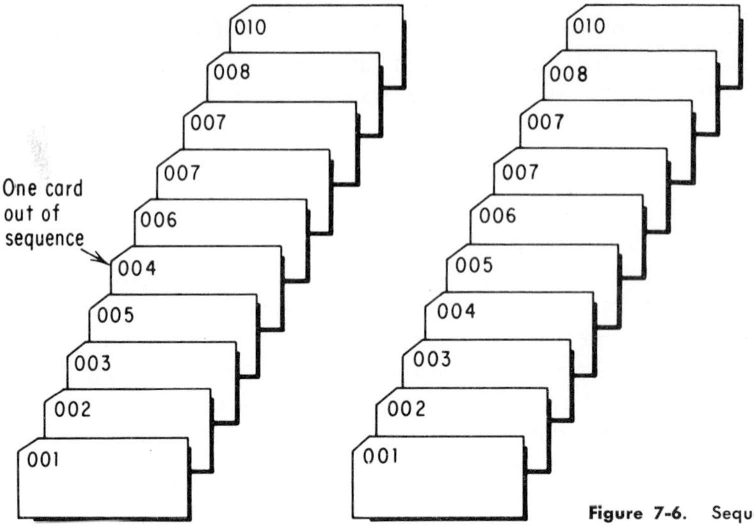

Figure 7-6. Sequence checking

one card may be greater than the value in another card preceding it. This is referred to as *high sequence.* (2) The value in one card may be equal to the value in another card preceding it. This is referred to as *equal sequence.* (3) The value in one card may be less than the value in another card preceding. This is called *low sequence.*

In ascending sequence checking, for instance, the file is considered in order if the value of any given card is either equal to or greater than the value of the one preceding it; and vice versa, in a descending sequence-checking operation. Figure 7-6 shows a deck of 10 cards, Numbers 001-010. When a sequence check is desired, the following pairs of comparisons are made:

	Cards compared	*Result*	*Action taken*
1.	001-002	High sequence	Continue to next comparison.
2.	002-003	High sequence	Continue to next comparison.
3.	003-005	High sequence	Continue to next comparison.
4.	005-004	*Low sequence*	Card 004 is out of order. The machine stops immediately. Sequence of the two cards is corrected by the operator, and then the operation resumes.
5.	004-005	High sequence	Continue to next comparison.
6.	005-006	High sequence	Continue to next comparison.
7.	006-007	High sequence	Continue to next comparison.
8.	007-007	Equal sequence	Continue to next comparison.
9.	007-008	High sequence	Continue to next comparison.
10.	008-010	High sequence	Sequence is in order. But because no more cards are left in the hopper, the collator halts automatically. The operator would have to "run-out" cards 008 and 010 from the machine to complete the deck and also to clear the machine for a new operation.

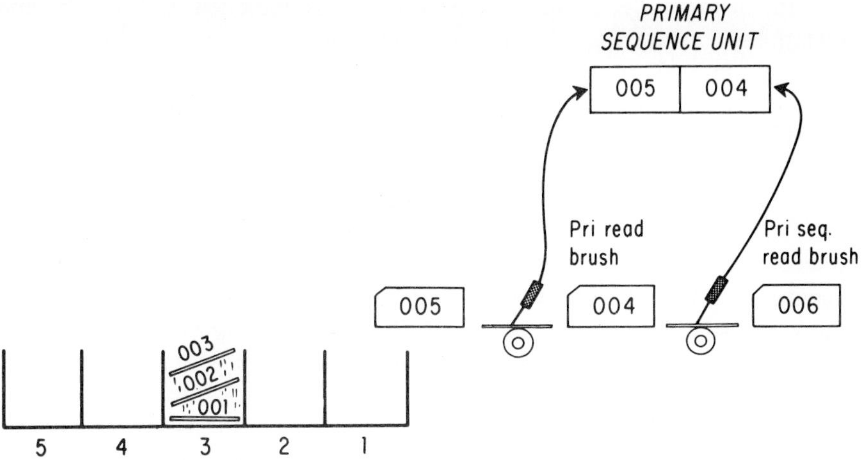

Figure 7-7. Sequence checking—connections of the two sets of primary brushes to the primary sequence unit

The collator compared 10 different pairs of cards, detecting only one card out of order. At that moment, the machine would stop automatically if another operation were being performed. This response is normal when sequence checking is done along with merging.

In sequence checking, two sets of brushes are wired to a sequence unit. They are reading brushes and sequence-checking brushes. Assuming that the procedure in Figure 7-6 is done through the primary hopper; then the primary reading brushes and the primary-sequence reading brushes would be activated (wired) to the primary-sequence unit (Figure 7-7).

The Selecting Function

The selecting function is another basic collating function performed on a collator. It is the pulling out of a file of a card, or a number of cards, having a specific code or value punched in it. A common application involves the selection of cards with an *X* punched in a specific column out of a file for special processing. Likewise, other types of cards can be selected. Some of these types are:

1. Cards in a file with no code or *X* in them (*NX* cards)—for instance, suppose that a master deck of cards contains both male and female employee cards. Assume, further, that all male-employee cards have an *X* punched in column 80. Female-employee cards can be selected out of the master deck and dropped into a separate pocket every time the collator fails to detect an *X* punch in column 80.

2. A zero-balance card—in an accounts receivable application, all paid-up customer accounts would have zeros punched in the "balance outstanding" field. For the purpose of notifying those customers that they have paid their accounts, the "zero-balance" cards are selected out of the accounts receivable file and dropped into a separate pocket.

3. Cards between minimum and maximum limits—the collator can be wired to select cards that have a value in a specific field which is between two values. For instance, assume that a manufacturing enterprise has 12 branches primarily involved in the sale of given merchandise. Assume, further, that the company desires a sales report involving branches 03, 04, and 05 only. A blank card is punched with a minimum and a maximum of branch numbers 02 and 06, respectively. Then it is placed in front of the master deck containing the sales cards from the 12 branches. The collator would read the first card containing the minimum and maximum values and would select and eject into a separate pocket all cards between these limits. Once they are selected, these cards can be used later in another machine (the accounting machine) for the printing of a report. Figure 7-8 presents a condensed application of the above example. The coded card is placed in the front of the file. All sales cards from branches 03, 04, and 05 were selected and dropped into pocket 2. The remainder of the file was ejected, undisturbed, into pocket 1.

Unlike merging, matching, or sequence-checking, the selecting function does not require that the deck of cards be in any given sequence or order. The collator selects the cards out of the file independently of their sequential order when compared with the other cards in the deck.

QUESTIONS AND PROBLEMS

1. What advantages does a collator have over a sorter?
2. Describe the IBM 88 collator. What are its main functions?
3. Define the following terms:
   (a) matching
   (b) merging
   (c) sequence checking
   (d) match-merging
   (e) selecting
   (f) editing
   (g) low primary
   (h) low secondary
   (i) high sequence
   (j) equal sequence
   (k) low sequence

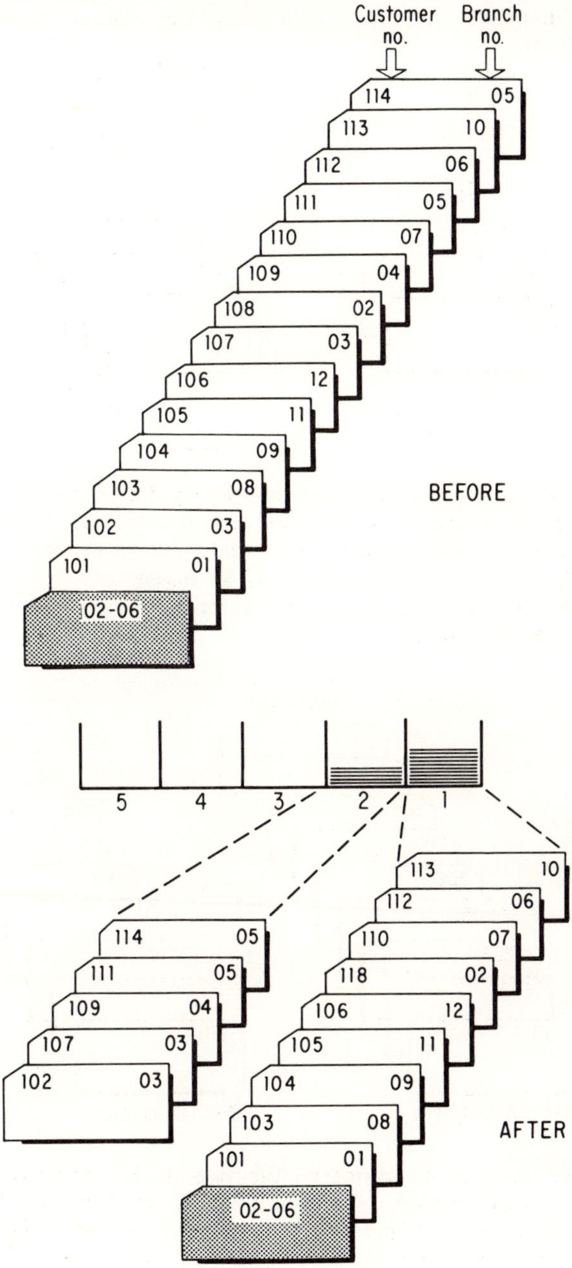

Figure 7-8. Selecting—an example

4. Suppose we wish to merge the following two decks of cards:
   (a) What step(s) must be taken before any merging can take place?
   (b) How many comparisons are made by the collator during the merging operation?
   (c) What pair(s) of cards result in low secondary? In low primary?

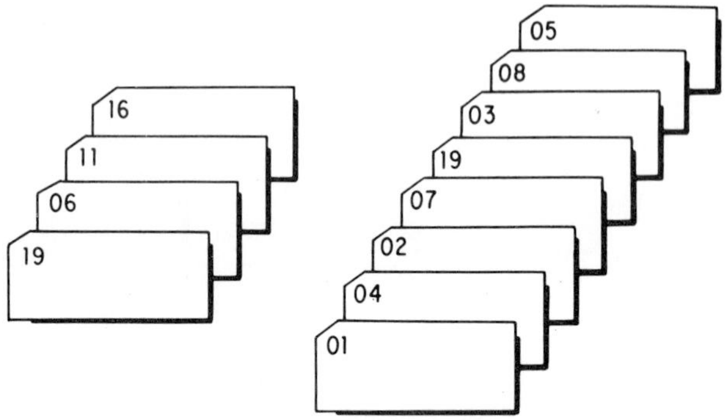

5. Given are two decks of data cards, the primary deck consisting of employees' withholding-tax information, and the secondary deck including the employees' name-and-address cards. In a matching operation:
   (a) Which cards (or card) in both decks match?
   (b) Which cards (or card) in both decks do not match? In which pocket(s) do they drop?

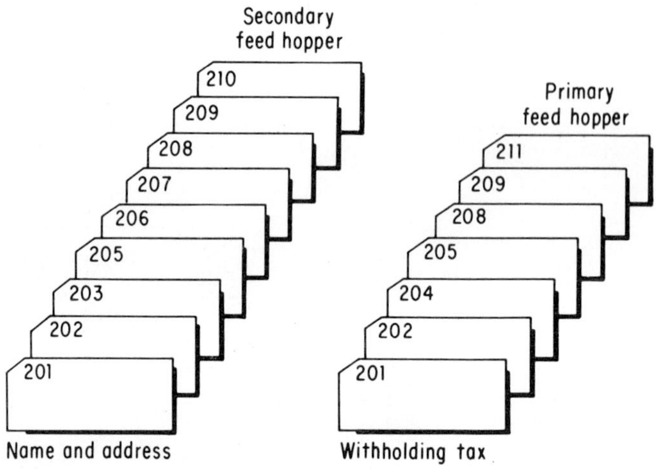

6. Suppose we wish to match-merge the two decks of cards in Problem 5 above with each employee's withholding-tax card behind his name-and-address card. Assuming that the control panel of the collator is wired to perform a match-merge operation,
   (a) In which hopper (that is, primary or secondary) is the name-and-address deck placed? Why?

(b) In which pocket do the merged cards drop?
(c) In which pocket do the rest of the cards from both decks drop? Specify.

7. What types of cards can be selected out of a deck of punched cards? Explain each type briefly.

Chapter 8

The Calculating Function

Modern business firms would be greatly handicapped without the use of calculations in solving the many problems and applications generated by daily business events. These calculations are the basic arithmetical ones of addition, subtraction, multiplication, and division. Because most business problems usually involve some mathematical considerations demanding facility in simple calculation in arriving at intelligent solutions, a machine called the *calculator* has been developed to handle the routine, repetitive work necessary in this connection. The most commonly used calculator in a punched-card data-processing system is the IBM 604 electronic calculating punch, referred to as the *electronic calculator* (Figure 8-1).

The title "Electronic Calculator" might lead the reader

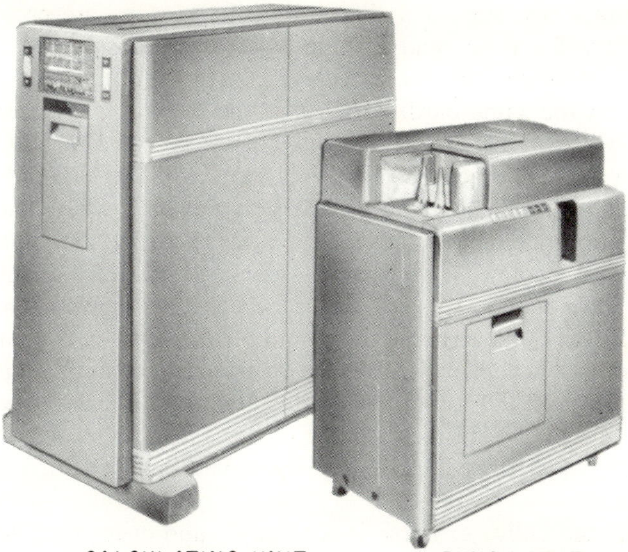

Figure 8-1. IBM 604 electronic calculating punch

to believe that the machine should be classified under the category of electronic data processing. Although it is similar to an electronic computer, in that it calculates at electronic speed and uses electronic tubes in its arithmetic and storage units, it is used primarily in punched-card data-processing systems rather than in electronic ones. An electronic tube has two states: a 0 (zero) state, when the tube is turned off, and a 1 state (or value) when it is turned on. A number of electronic tubes are combined for the storage and representation of digits *0-9*. However, the calculator is distinctly different from an electronic computer in the way it is controlled and also in the manner in which it is fed input and presents output. The calculator receives data through a punched card as input and punches the results in a punched card. The electronic computer, on the other hand, receives input from paper tape, magnetic tape, and so forth, as well as from the punched card. Likewise, output in the electronic computer is made on magnetic tape, paper tape, or other related means.

Essentially, calculating is reconstructing data or creating new data. It is done by the application of simple arithmetic formulas. For instance, the value of four bars of chocolate at a price of five cents each is obtained by multiplying quantity times unit price, or $4 \times 5 = 20$ cents. The product, *20,* is new data, a value obtained as a result of applying the formula "Quantity $\times$ Unit Price = Total Value."

The IBM punched-card calculator performs any, or all, of the four basic arithmetic operations based on program steps or wiring a control panel. It takes one step at a time until all the steps are completed. The first step, usually, is to read a field or several fields from a card. Then the machine performs the necessary calculating operations and punches the answer(s) in the same card. Physically, the electronic calculator is composed of two separate units connected by a cable. The first unit has a card hopper and a stacker. This is called the "Punch Unit." The other unit is called the "Calculating Unit." It is the area where factor storage and calculations are made. (See Figure 8-1.) Using the example of the four bars of chocolate, a card is first punched with the quantity and the unit price (five cents). It is fed (12 edge-first, face down) into the punch unit, which reads one row at a time until all the rows in the card are read. The necessary data in the card are transferred from the punch unit to the calculating unit. In the calculating unit, multiplication is performed and, instantly, the product, 20, is fed to the punching station of the punch unit, which punches the 20 cents in a predetermined field in the original card.

Although the above example is too simple and elementary to justify the purchase or the rental of an electronic calculator, it does illustrate simply the basic components and operation of the units themselves. A routine problem performed on the calculator is a payroll application. It involves calculation of the net pay of each employee after certain required deductions, such as federal income tax withholding and Social Security tax, are made. Although the application may seem too complex to comprehend, it is, in reality, only the result of a series of basic arithmetic operations presented in a definite sequence. Planning the operations in advance is very important, because the machine can perform only those steps which are wired into the control panel. The steps themselves are basic and must be in proper sequence.

For the purpose of illustration, we shall introduce the payroll steps involved in: (1) Calculating an employee's gross pay. (2) Calculating his federal income tax withholding. (3) Determining his Social Security tax. These deductions are mandatory. Calculation of them is, therefore, necessary before net pay can be obtained.

1. *Calculations for Gross Pay.* Most business firms, whether manufacturing or service, must have various men and women capable of performing various duties and functions. At the rank-and-file level, most employees earn their wages on an hourly basis. Assuming that the hourly rate is a standard $1.50 per hour, and no overtime is involved, the formula for gross pay would be:

$$\text{Total Hours for the Week} \times \text{Rate per Hour} = \textit{Gross pay}.$$

If an employee works 32 hours during a given week, at the rate of \$1.50 per hour, then his gross pay for that week would be 32 × \$1.50 = \$48.00.

The product, \$48.00, is new data created by the calculator as a result of multiplying two factors: (1) the multiplicand, or the total hours (32), and (2) the multiplier, or the rate per hour (\$1.50). These factors can be fed to the calculator either on two separate cards or on one card.

2. *Calculations for Federal Income Tax.* An employee's net pay is always less than his gross pay, owing to the required deductions, one of which is the federal income tax withholding. According to the federal income tax schedule, a single employee pays proportionately more tax than a married employee does, because of the factor of dependents. The more dependents an employee claims, the less the amount of tax he is likely to pay. In fact, some employees are in a bracket where they pay no federal income tax, because the amount allowed as deduction for their dependents equals and sometimes exceeds their gross pay.

An employee's gross pay per week is reduced by the amount of \$13.00 for himself and for each dependent, called an *exemption.* An employee is allowed an exemption in the amount of \$13.00 for himself and for each dependent. The amount of the total exemption is nontaxable. For example, if William Blatty's gross pay for the week is \$100.00 and he claims his wife and son as dependents, then the nontaxable amount is \$13.00 × 3 = \$39.00. This means that no tax is computed on the first \$39.00 of his pay. The taxable amount is computed by subtracting the nontaxable amount (\$39.00) from his gross pay. That is, \$100.00 − \$39.00 = \$61.00. The amount of tax to be deducted from his gross pay for federal income tax withholding is calculated by multiplying the taxable amount (\$61.00) by 18 per cent. That is, \$61.00 × 0.18 = \$10.98, Federal Withholding Tax. If Mr. Blatty's gross pay was \$39.00 for the week, however, no tax would be deducted, because the nontaxable amount (from 3 exemptions @ \$13.00 per exemption) would be equal to his gross pay.

From the foregoing description, three main factors are required before a calculation for federal income tax withholding is feasible. They are:

1. Total hours for the week.
2. The rate per hour.
3. Number of exemptions.

As far as the arithmetic operations are concerned, the calculator would perform three multiplication steps and one subtraction step before it arrives at the amount of federal income tax to be withheld. Assume the following data:

John Huntley, an employee with Acadia Oil Company, worked 39 hours for the week ending January 10, 1965. The hourly rate is \$4.00. He claims four dependents (himself, his wife, and two children). Calculate the federal income tax withholding for the week:

Step 1. Multiply: Total Hours for the Week × Rate/Hr. = *Gross Pay,* or 39 × \$4 = \$156.00.

Step 2. Multiply: Number of Exemptions × \$13.00 = *Nontaxable Amount,* or 4 × \$13.00 = \$52.00.

Step 3. Subtract: Gross Pay less Nontaxable Amount = *Taxable Amount,* or \$156.00 − \$52.00 = \$104.00.

Step 4. Multiply: Taxable Amount × 18 per cent = Federal Income Tax Withholding, or \$104 × 0.18 = \$18.72.

The federal withholding tax is \$18.72, and it can be punched in a reserved field in the card if it is the only result desired. However, because it is, most likely, a part of the over-all payroll deductions, the amount is stored temporarily in a storage unit of the calculator until other related calculations are completed.

3. *Calculations for FICA Tax.* Under the Federal Insurance Contributions Act (FICA), a deduction from gross pay is required by law for Social Security purposes. A percentage of the first \$4,800 of an employee's earnings in a calendar year is withheld every time a calculation for net pay is made. For the sake of illustration, assume that 3½ per cent of the gross pay is withheld for FICA tax. FICA deductions terminate as soon as the accumulated employee's earnings reach \$4,800 in the calendar year, or as soon as his accumulated FICA deductions reach \$168.00 (3½% of \$4,800). Therefore, two main points are involved in the calculation: (1) To calculate the FICA tax. (2) To check on the accumulated FICA tax to date.

To apply the example of John Huntley, the amount of FICA tax is calculated by multiplying his gross pay by 3½%, or

$$\frac{\$156.00 \times 3.5}{100} = \$5.46.$$

The FICA calculation is deducted in full, if the year-to-date FICA including this week's FICA has not reached the limit of \$168.00. When this limit is reached, no further Social Security deduction is made in that year.

Once the federal withholding tax and the FICA tax are determined, the calculation of net pay is comparatively simple. Assuming that no other deductions are mandatory, net pay is attained by the following formula:

Net pay = Gross pay *less* (federal withholding tax + FICA tax).

To calculate the net pay of John Huntley, we substitute:

Net pay: \$156.00 − (\$18.72 + \$5.46) = \$131.82.

The electronic calculator is capable of performing all of the arithmetic in connection with gross pay, federal withholding tax, and FICA tax. It stores the amounts individually and punches them in their related fields in the card at the rate of approximately 100 cards per minute. The value of using an electronic calculator can be realized readily if one visualizes a concern employing anywhere from 100 employees to 10,000 and upward.

QUESTIONS AND PROBLEMS

1. What is meant by the term *calculate?* Give an example.
2. What are the main arithmetic functions of the IBM punched-card calculator? Explain.
3. Explain how the punch and the calculating units are used to calculate a given problem.
4. Show (by giving an example) how new data are created in a "gross pay" calculation.
5. What factors are needed in calculating for federal income tax withholding? Explain by giving an example.
6. What is meant by *FICA?* For what purpose is FICA tax withheld?
7. Steve Abromowitz, a college student, accepted a summer job with a local contractor to pave driveways. He worked 32 hours a week and was paid at the rate of $4.35 per hour. His year-to-date gross earnings are $4,680. He is single and has no dependents.

   Assuming that Steve's employer deducted federal income tax withholding, FICA, and $1.50 for health insurance premium, calculate:

   (a) Gross pay.
   (b) Federal income tax withheld.
   (c) FICA.
   (d) Net pay.

Chapter 9

The Preparation of Reports

The end result of any punched-card data-processing application is the production of final reports containing essential facts without which management cannot function well. Printing aids us in the formulation or reconstruction of data to produce those reports by listing or compressing the pertinent facts into a concise and presentable form. Report preparation is, therefore, considered one of the most important functions to be performed.

The machines involved in report preparation are called *tabulators*. The two IBM tabulators most commonly in use are the IBM 402 and 407 accounting machines (Figure 9-1, (a) and (b)). Although their basic functions are the same, the latter is a more versatile machine than the former.

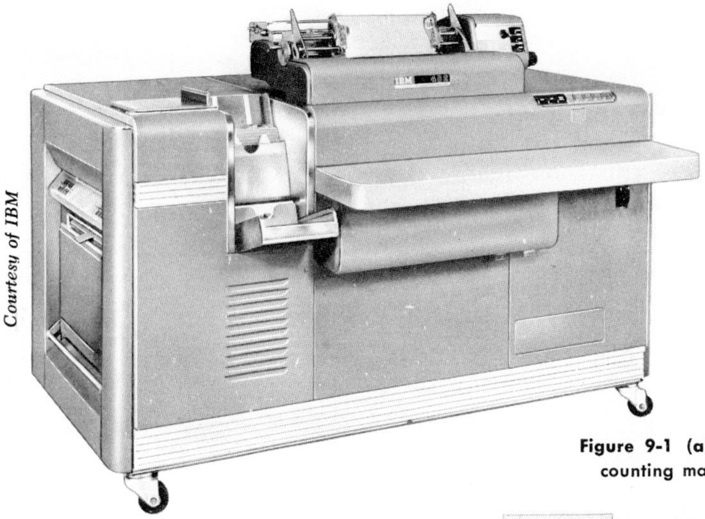

Figure 9-1 (a). IBM 402 accounting machine

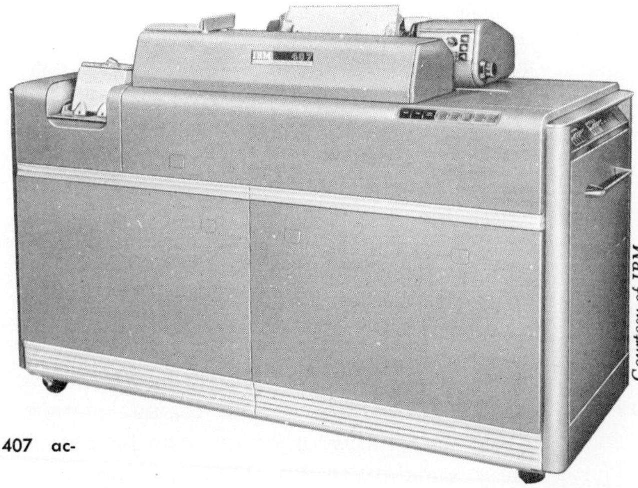

Figure 9-1 (b). IBM 407 accounting machine

The accounting machine processes data through instructions given to it by a control panel. The control panel gives the machine its versatility, in that it tells it what part(s) of the data punched in a card to print, where to print it on the form, what to accumulate, and when as well as where to print the accumulated total or to clear the counters for another operation. Each control panel contains a set of instructions for a specific operation. With the exception of minor adjustments through switches and paper alignment, the accounting machine is made ready to process a new application when the operator simply inserts the proper control panel containing the instructions related to it

Card Reading

Cards are placed in the hopper 9-edge first, face down. When the machine is started, the first card moves to the first reading station. It is held there until the machine reads all the necessary data punched in it. The reading station contains 960 reading brushes to scan any one of 960 possible holes in a given card; that is, 80 columns × 12 rows of holes = 960 holes. Once a hole is detected, a contact is made, the impulse of which is transmitted to the control panel, which controls the specific functions to be performed by the machine. (See Figure 9-2.)

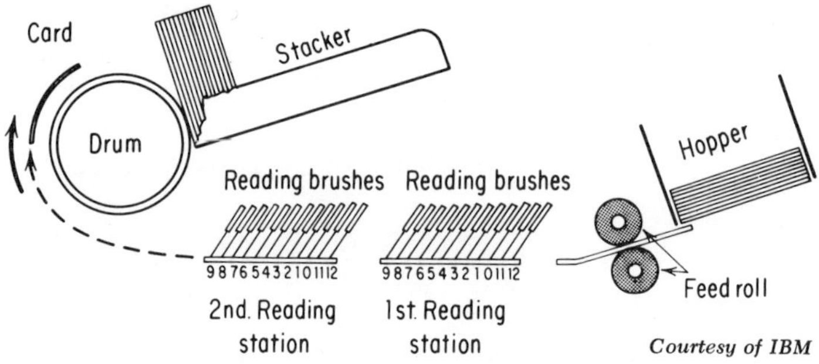

Figure 9-2. Card path schematic, IBM 407 accounting machine

After the card is read, it moves over the second reading station and around a drum (clockwise) on its way to the stacker. The speed at which cards are read on the IBM 407 model is 150 cards per minute. The first reading station is used for comparing certain values in a card with those in another card at the second reading station. Addition and subtraction, as well as printing, normally use the second reading station.

The primary capabilities of an accounting machine are: (1) *summarizing,* (2) *printing,* (3) *controlling, spacing,* and *positioning* of the form on which data are being printed to the exact location on it, and (4) *summary punching.*

The Summarizing Function

Summarizing aids in the reconstruction of data by compressing them into a more concise and presentable form. It is the end result of calculating and creates data in a new form. The income statement, for instance, is a summary of the operations of a particular business firm through a specific period of time.

In an accounting machine, summarizing takes place in counters capable of accumulating totals after addition or subtraction of numeric values punched in the cards is completed. Counters can total digits, the number of which depends upon their size. A two-position counter, for instance, is capable of totaling up to 99. A three-position counter totals up to 999, and so forth. In the 407 accounting machine, counters range in size from three to eight positions. One hundred sixty-eight (168) is the maximum number of possible accumulating positions. This number of positions is achieved by coupling counters together to formulate or total an amount of a size that large. It is accomplished through control-panel wiring. Figure 9-3 shows a control panel inserted in a 407 accounting machine.

Counters can be used to accumulate three main types of totals. They are: (1) Major, (2) Intermediate, and (3) Minor. A *major* total is the total of each of the major sections or divisions making up a business firm, thus representing the largest grouping. An *intermediate* total represents the total of the subdivisions of a business firm. A *minor* total represents the smallest part of a section or a division. It is, in fact, a part of a subdivision or a subsection of a business firm. Assume, for instance, that Company *A* has three districts, each of which supervises two offices

Courtesy of IBM

Figure 9-3. A control panel inserted in the IBM 407 accounting machine

A B C Company Sales Report For the month ending Dec. 31, 1964					
District	Office	Salesman No.	Total by salesman	Total by office	Total by district
	A	11	5.00		
		12	8.00		
		13	7.20		
Eastern		14	6.80	27.00 *	
	B	21	10.00		
		22	8.00		
		23	16.00		
		24	2.10	36.10 *	63.10 **
	A	31	4.40		
		32	3.65		
		33	5.00		
Southern		34	4.20	17.25 *	
	B	41	10.00		
		42	8.00		
		43	8.05		
		44	6.00	32.05 *	49.30 **
	A	51	81.00		
		52	62.00		
		53	1.29		
Western		54	15.04	159.33 *	
	B	61	7.14		
		62	16.02		
		63	4.06		
		64	9.00	36.22 *	195.55 **
					307.95 ***

Figure 9-4. Sales report, showing the three different types of totals

of four salesmen in each office. In a formal printed statement of the sales operations of the firm during a specific period of time, the total sales of each salesman is considered a minor total occupying usually the far left-hand column. The sum of *each* of the two offices consisting of four salesmen is called an *intermediate* total. It is usually printed in the middle column. The total of the two offices combined represents the *major* total and is printed in the right column. A final or a grand total of the firm can be obtained simply by the addition of the individual major totals of each of the three districts in the right column. The grand total is usually printed with three asterisks to its right (Figure 9-4).

Figure 9-4 shows the total sales made by each of the 24 salesmen hired by Company *A*. The total for each is called a *minor* total, because it is considered as the smallest grouping as shown in the left-most total column. The middle total column contains six amounts, each of which is the total of the four salesmen reporting to their respective offices. These are called the *intermediate* totals. The right column contains three district amounts, each of which is the total of the two offices. These are called major totals, because they are considered the largest grouping. The grand sales total of $307.95 is obtained by the addition of the three major totals in the right column.

The Printing Function

Another function of the tabulator is to print the data accumulated in the counters, in addition to other information which is read from the IBM card. Figure 9-4 is a printed sales report of the Company *A* by salesman, office, and district. It is presented under the summarizing function in order to clarify the three different types of totals which the counters are capable of accumulating.

There are two methods of printing: the serial, and the parallel. A typewriter types one character at a time as the carriage holding the paper in place moves from right to left, until the line is fully printed. This is referred to as *serial* printing. The IBM accounting machine, on the other hand, utilizes the *parallel* method of printing, because it prints one complete line at a time. All the required data are printed simultaneously on it. Speed is the main advantage of the parallel printing over the serial printing method.

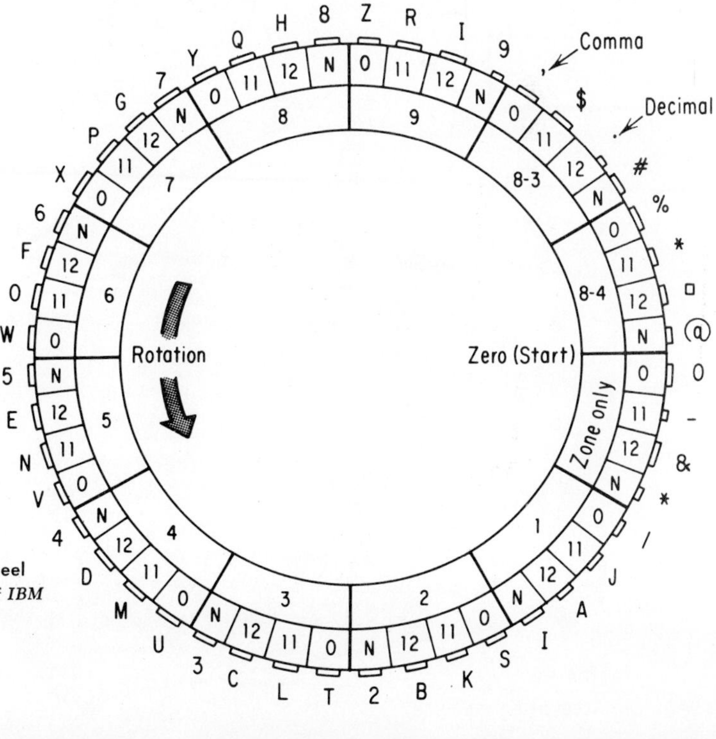

Figure 9-5. A printwheel schematic *Courtesy of IBM*

Printing on the IBM 407 accounting machine is performed by means of print wheels which rotate to the specific digit, letter, or special character. When all of the print wheels are positioned correctly, they are actuated simultaneously, resulting in the printing of a complete line. There are 120 print wheels, each of which can print the 10 digits, 26 letters, and 11 special characters (Figure 9-5). They can print within a width of 12 inches, 10 characters per inch.

Printing methods

The two printing methods used by the IBM accounting machines are: (1) *detail printing,* and (2) *group printing.*

Detail Printing. Detail Printing, or Listing, is the printing of part or all of the information punched in a card onto a report form with the added function of addition or subtraction performed by the counters on the amounts in the cards for various types of totals. Detail printing is performed when a detailed report including each transaction is required. There is a line for each card read by the machine (Figure 9-6).

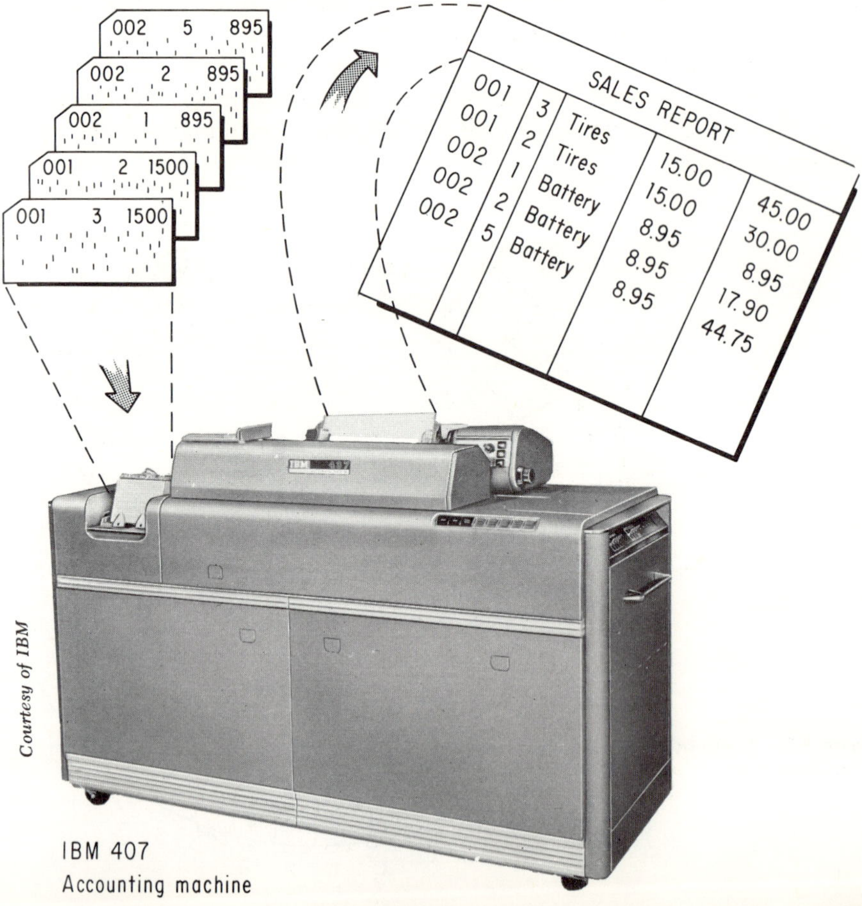

Courtesy of IBM

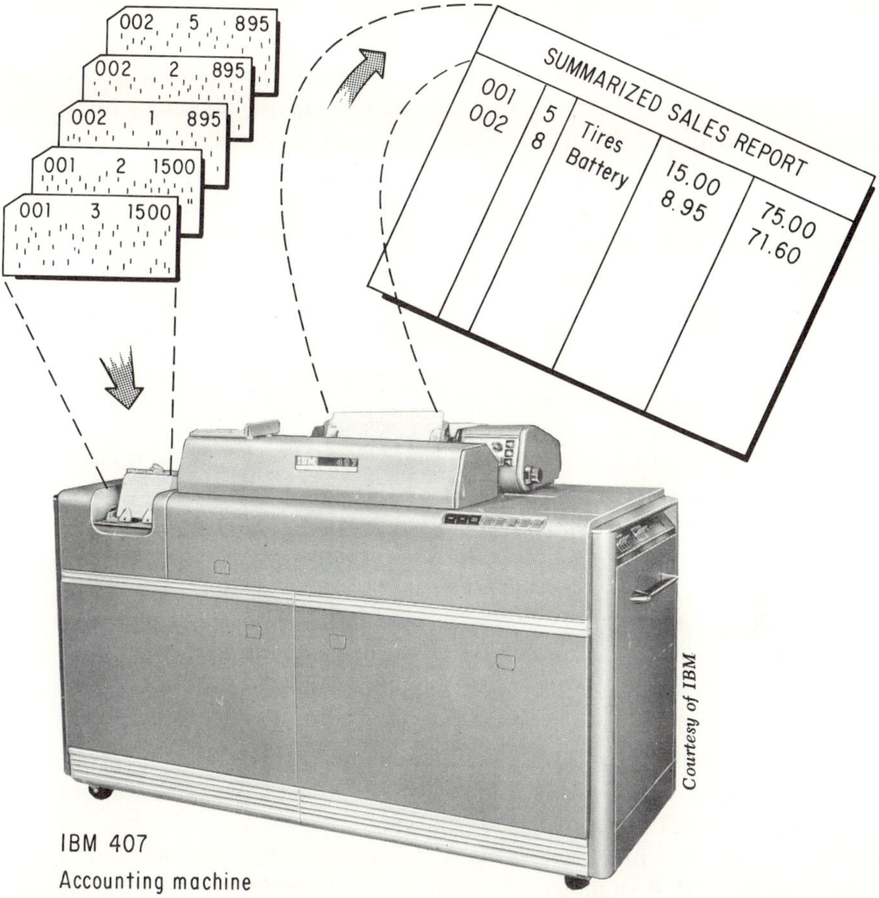

Figure 9-7. An example of group printing

Group Printing. Group printing is summarizing a group of cards and printing their totals on a report. Values from the punched cards are entered in specific counters. The counters are "read out" at the end of the group of cards, and their contents are printed on a line. Figure 9-7 is an example of group printing based on the data shown in Figure 9-6 above. Initially, certain data are read from the first card of a group for identification purposes. This data is printed first on the report. The remaining data in the group of cards are read and their values accumulated in counters. When the last card in the group is sensed, the contents of the counters are printed on the same line with the identifying information.

Group Printing Comparing. Group printing can be done because of the ability of the accounting machine to distinguish a card of one group from a card belonging to another group. A specific field in one card is compared with the same field in another card. If they are equal, the machine considers the two cards as a part of the same group. Addition or subtraction is made and certain values from the second card are accumulated in a counter (or counters) containing values from a previous card (or cards). If, however, the specific field in the second card is not the same or equal to the same field in the card previous to it, an unequal compare exists. The second card is considered as a part of a different group. At this time, before reading and starting a new group, the machine goes through a number of steps called "Total Cycle." The last card belonging to the present group is added to or subtracted from its respective counter (or counters). The group total is then printed on one line. A space is made, and the machine is ready to handle a new group.

Figure 9-7 is an example of group printing. Card 1 bearing part number 001 is compared with card 2 bearing part number 001. The result is *equal compare.* The machine adds the number of units sold in card 1 (3) in one counter and its value (45) in another counter. Next, card 2 bearing part number 001 is compared with card 3 bearing salesman-number 002. The result is *unequal compare.* Before card 3 is read and processed, the accounting machine goes through a total cycle. The units sold in card 2 are added to the same counter which stores the units sold in card 1. Now the amount accumulated in it totals 5 (3 + 2). The value of the units sold in card 2 also is added to the same counter which stores the value of the units sold in card 1. Now the amount accumulated in that counter is 75 (45 + 30).

When this addition is completed, the machine prints on one complete line the contents of the two counters, in addition to the part number and a description of the item which the amounts represent. When this is completed, the machine reverts to the comparing function and compares card 3 with card 4, and so on, until the last card is compared and its group total is printed.

Form spacing

An accounting machine, like a typewriter, has a carriage into which a sheet of paper is placed and positioned for the preparation of a statement or a report. The carriage of an accounting machine differs from that of a typewriter, however, in that its vertical movement is made automatically through a control tape. Further, because the accounting machine uses the parallel method of printing, the automatic carriage does not move horizontally from right to left as a typewriter normally moves. (Figure 9-8.)

It is impractical to insert and position one form at a time into the carriage. Because such an effort is time-consuming, continuous forms are used which are perforated in such a way that each form can be detached (burst) easily from the other forms. To aid in the automatic vertical spacing of the form itself, its extreme ends are mounted on tractor pins, the movement of which is determined by the location of a punched hole in a control device called the *control tape.*

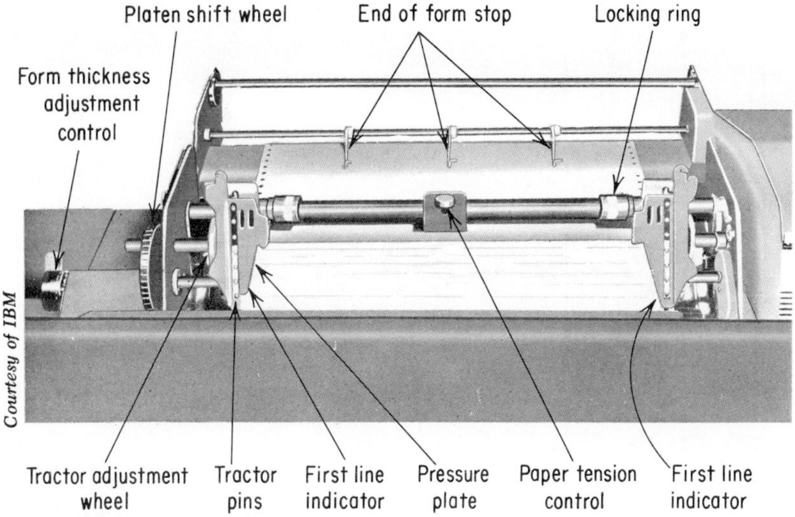

Figure 9-8. Paper form positioned around the automatic carriage of the IBM 407 accounting machine

The Control Tape

The control tape is a piece of standard-size paper designed to control the movement of the form by punching holes in specific locations in it. It is divided into 12 vertical spaces, called *channels* (Figure 9-9). Horizontally, it contains a maximum of 132 lines for the control of the form. In the middle, prepunched round holes are mounted on a sprocket wheel to advance the tape so that its movement is synchronized with that of the form. For instance, if the form is on line 10, the control tape is positioned and is synchronized on line 10. Therefore, the length of the control tape is determined by the number of lines the form contains. If a form contains 37 lines, the control tape should be cut to conform to the length of the form (37 lines) (Figure 9-9).

A form is divided into two parts: (1) the head, and (2) the body. The *head* of a form includes usually the name and address of the customer, his number (if any), and the date of the statement. The *body* of the statement consists of all the details necessary for the statement being printed. In an invoice, these include the date of the order of the item, the item catalog number, the description of the item, the quantity ordered, the price of each unit, and the total price. Upon determination of the location of all the information to be printed on the form, the top of the control tape is aligned with that of the form and the required holes are punched in it in order: (1) to direct the machine to start at the first printing line and to print the address and other related information, (2) to skip to the first body line for printing all the body details, (3) to

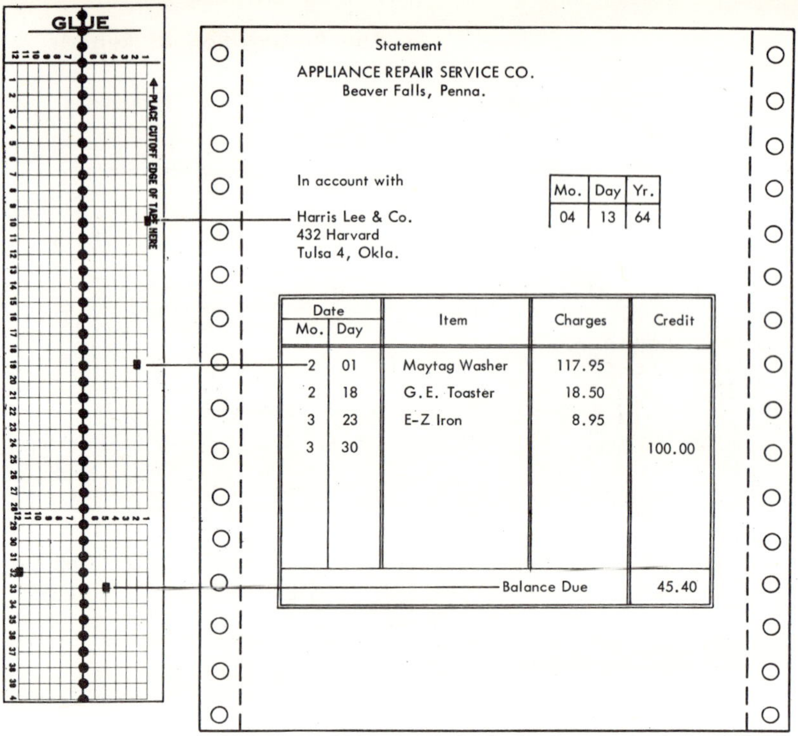

Figure 9-9. A punched control tape (left) based on predetermined printing locations (right)

indicate the first overflow line, and (4) to skip to a predetermined "total" line after the last body line is printed.

The rectangular holes in a control tape indicate to the machine the location of the significant lines. They are punched by an IBM tape punch (Figure 9-10). A hole punched in *channel 1* always indicates the first printing line of a form. *Channel 2* usually indicates the first body line of the form to be printed. *Channel 12* indicates the last printing line or overflow, and *channel 4* indicates the location of the predetermined total line.

In Figure 9-9, a hole is punched in channel 1 and line 10 to indicate the location of the first printing line. A hole is also punched in channel 2 and line 19 to indicate the first body line. The intersection of channel 12 and line 32 is punched to indicate the last printing line. Another hole is punched in channel 4 and line 33 to indicate the location of the predetermined total line. Once the tape is punched, its ends are glued and then inserted into position (Figure 9-11). A "Restore" button is depressed to synchronize the control tape with that of the form. From this point on, after the machine is started and the cards have been placed in the hopper, the spacing of the form, the printing of data, and the skipping to the desired location and to the next form are done entirely automatically. In fact, the complete operation can be done without any need for human attendance. The last card stops the machine automatically.

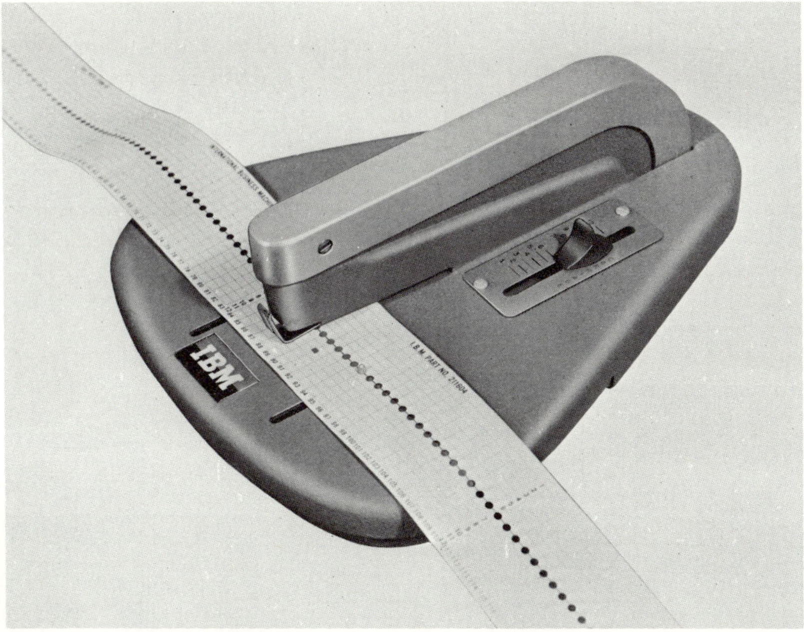

Courtesy of IBM

Figure 9-10. An IBM tape punch

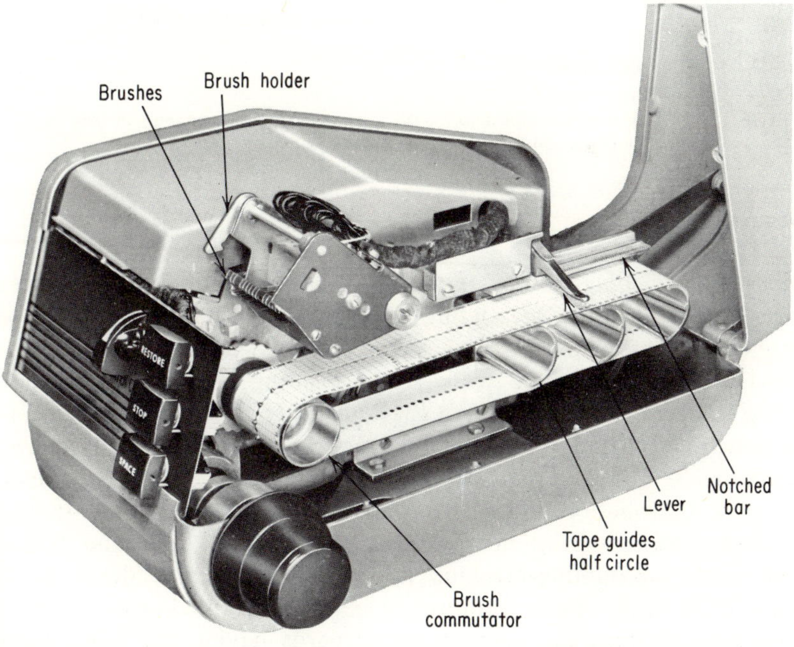

Courtesy of IBM

Figure 9-11. Inserting a punched control tape in the accounting machine

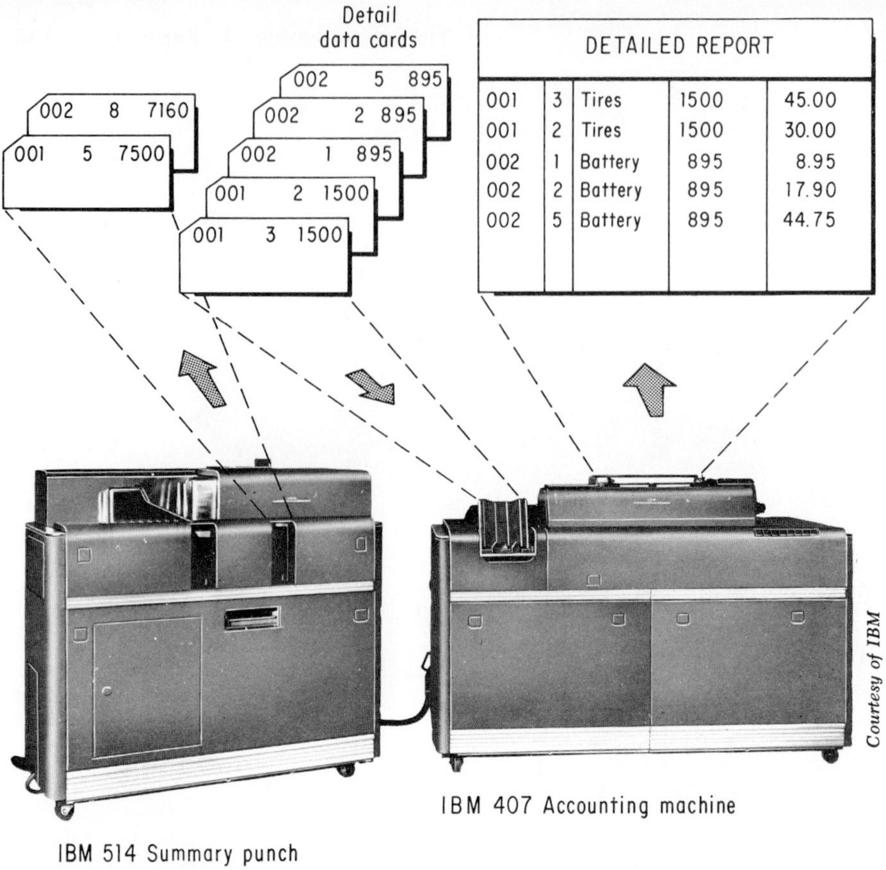

Figure 9-12. A summary punch connection between the accounting machine and a summary punch machine

Summary Punching

Summary punching is the automatic conversion into punched holes of data accumulated in the accounting machine from detail cards. These data represent the total of a particular group of cards. Summary punching can be, and is, frequently done while detail printing is going on, if the accounting machine is attached by a cable to an IBM 514 reproducing summary punch and if the proper control panels are inserted in both machines. (See Figure 9-12.) The main value of summary punching is to punch in a new card information which is not shown on any other card. In Figure 9-12, five cards, bearing numbers *001, 001, 002, 002,* and *002*, are placed in the accounting-machine hopper. The machine detail prints a line for each card. While printing is being performed, the counters in the machine perform the addition of all cards having the same number. After the second card (001) is printed and before card 002 is read, the accounting machine actuates the summary punch to punch in a blank card the total of the first two cards stored in a specific counter or counters. Once punched, the accounting machine prints the contents of the first card 002 and the remaining two cards, the total of which is also punched in another blank card in the summary punch machine.

QUESTIONS FOR REVIEW

1. List and explain briefly the main functions of the control panel of an accounting machine.
2. How are data cards read in an IBM accounting machine?
3. List the four primary functions of an accounting machine. Explain each function briefly.
4. How is summarizing performed in an accounting machine? Illustrate.
5. What is the function of a counter? What is the maximum value which can be stored in a four-position counter?
6. What types of totals can be represented or stored in a counter? Define each type and present an illustration of your own, showing their significance and their location on a paper form.
7. How is a final or grand total derived?
8. What are the two methods of printing? Explain and give an example of each method.
9. What is detail printing? What is group printing?
10. A deck containing eight cards (account numbers 201, 202, 203, 203, 204, 205, 205, and 206) are placed in the card hopper of an accounting machine. Assuming that detail printing is desired, how many lines would the machine print? How many lines would be group-printed? Why?
11. What is meant by "total cycle"?
12. How does an accounting machine differ from a typewriter with respect to form spacing?
13. What is a control tape? What four main functions does it perform? For what purpose are round holes prepunched in the middle of the tape?
14. Explain the two parts of a form. How are they controlled by a control tape?
15. What is summary punching? On what machine(s) is it used? Why?

Chapter 10

Case Illustration

This chapter introduces an actual banking application involving the use of the punched-card data-processing machines in the "DAILY PAYMENTS" section at the Consumer Credit Department, Lincoln Rochester Trust Company, Rochester, New York. For classified reasons, the customer's and dealer's names have been changed. The remainder is a step-by-step description of the data as they flow through the various stages and are processed by most of the machines involved in the punched-card data-processing cycle.

Background Information

Dr. Wilhelm Z. Blatty, an associate professor of Business Administration at a local university, purchased an unfurnished cottage on Lake Ontario, where he intends to spend his future summer vacations. On January 1, 1964,

Harry L. Gordon, a furniture dealer in Rochester, New York, advertised in the local newspaper an attractive sale of home furniture, including sofas, tables, lamps, and other similar items.

Even though it was too early in the year for the use of the cottage, Dr. Blatty decided to respond to the advertisement, and he negotiated a sale with Mr. Gordon, the store manager and owner, to furnish the cottage for a total cost of one thousand dollars ($1,000.00). Terms: no service charge if the amount is paid in full within 90 days from the date of purchase, that is, before April 1. The amount of any unpaid balance, however, can be financed after the 90-day privilege elapses. On January 1, Dr. Blatty agreed to the terms and signed a conditional sales contract for the amount of the purchase ($1,000.00). The furniture was delivered to the cottage the same day.

It is not uncommon for a business firm like Harry L. Gordon, Inc., to make arrangements with a local commercial bank to which he sells the conditional sales contract(s) for immediate cash. At times, a firm is willing to pay a fee or an amount based on a predetermined percentage for the purpose of converting some or all of its notes or, in this case, its sales contracts into cash when cash is needed. However, regardless of the exact reason(s), Harry L. Gordon transferred the contract signed by Dr. Blatty to the bank and received $1,000.00 less a fee which the bank charged for holding it for 90 days. The customer at any point in this process is held liable for $1,000.00 only, regardless of the fee which the bank charged Mr. Gordon, the furniture dealer, himself. The bank fee is merely a cost to the dealer for receiving the amount today rather than waiting 90 days for payment.

In the foregoing discussion, it is assumed that the bank accepts the sales contract only after investigating and ascertaining the satisfactory credit standing of the customer (in this example, Dr. Blatty's). After Mr. Gordon transferred the contract to the bank, the latter party notified Dr. Blatty that in the future he must deal directly with the bank's main office or any of its branches. Included in the letter, a statement is made to the effect that, if Dr. Blatty did not find it convenient to pay the amount within 90 days, the enclosed coupon book acknowledges the payment by installments. It contains coupons each of which represents one monthly payment including interest, to be made by Dr. Blatty. (Figure 10-4). That is, if the loan were extended into 12 monthly payments, the coupon book would contain 12 coupons.

Data Preparation

Upon the receipt of the sales contract, the bank sends it to the consumer loan division for processing. The consumer loan division has a primary function of processing accounts and forwarding them to data processing. Because it is necessary to distinguish one form of loan from another form, the loans are recognized by "type." The 10 different types of loans are:

0 Home Modernization Loan—for the purpose of remodeling or improving the interior or exterior of a house that is not eligible under FHA. See type 6 below.

1 American Installment Credit Corporation (AICC) Loan—a conditional sale contract made through automobile dealers for a customer automobile loan.

2 Commercial Contracts Loan—primarily extended to business firms, usually referred to as *business loans*.

3 Cash Payment Auto Loan—distinguished from type 1 above in that the customer negotiates with the bank directly and receives a sum of money for the purpose of buying an automobile.

4 Residential Loan—results from conditional sales contracts for the purchase of electric appliances such as refrigerators, toasters, irons, vacuum cleaners, and other similar items.

5 Home Furnishing Loan—all loans resulting from the purchase of home furniture on credit. Dr. Blatty's purchase of furniture from Mr. Gordon is considered a type 5 loan.

6 Federal Housing Authority (FHA) Loan—primarily used for home improvement, with conditions set by the authority.

7 Insurance Dealer Auto Loan—extended to a customer for the purchase of an automobile directly through the insurance company which writes the insurance policy.

8 Cash Personal Loan—approved for any reason not properly labeled under any of the other types of loans. For instance, a customer in need of $200.00 for travel expenses.

9 Education Loan—extended to those customers who need financial aid for educational expenses. Students as well as teachers are included.

A clerk types from the original sales contract the required data on a *loan detail* card (Figure 10-1). Hereafter, all data pertaining to the processing of Dr. Blatty's account will be obtained from this detail card. The loan detail card is not used in the processing of data, but is considered a master card for reference in the future. It is placed in a loan detail file.

On the top of the card, the name and address of the customer are typed. In the middle of the card, the clerk also types an account number and the branch number (*19*) of the bank to which the furniture dealer transferred the sales contract. Next, the dealer number, *502,* is typed, a code assigned solely to Harry L. Gordon, Inc. Each dealer has a different number, a fact which will be useful in later applications in the preparation of sales reports by *dealer* rather than by customer number or by branch.

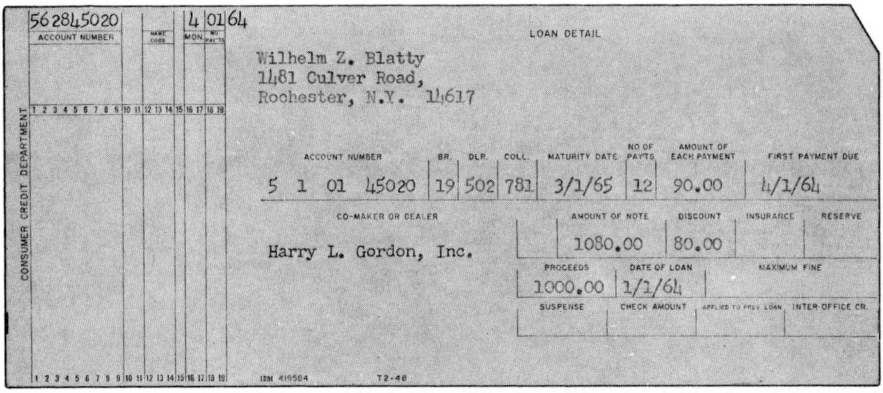
56 28 45020 | 4 01 64
ACCOUNT NUMBER | MAKE CODE | MON. | NO. PAY'TS
CONSUMER CREDIT DEPARTMENT
LOAN DETAIL
Wilhelm Z. Blatty
1481 Culver Road,
Rochester, N.Y. 14617
ACCOUNT NUMBER | BR. | DLR. | COLL. | MATURITY DATE | NO OF PAY'TS | AMOUNT OF EACH PAYMENT | FIRST PAYMENT DUE
5 1 01 45020 | 19 | 502 | 781 | 3/1/65 | 12 | 90.00 | 4/1/64
CO-MAKER OR DEALER | AMOUNT OF NOTE | DISCOUNT | INSURANCE | RESERVE
Harry L. Gordon, Inc. | 1080.00 | 80.00
PROCEEDS | DATE OF LOAN | MAXIMUM FINE
1000.00 | 1/1/64
SUSPENSE | CHECK AMOUNT | APPLIED TO PREV. LOAN | INTER-OFFICE CR.
IBM 419584 T2-48

Figure 10-1. A loan detail card (Courtesy of Lincoln Rochester Trust Company)

Next to the "dealer" column is the "collateral" column, bearing number *781*. In the case of Dr. Blatty, his furniture acts as a collateral and can be repossessed in the event that he defaults in his payments. The collateral code for merchandise of this type is 781. The maturity date of the loan is one year from the payment of the first of 12 monthly installments due April 1, 1964. The amount of each payment ($90.00) is computed as follows:

$$\text{Amount of each payment} = \frac{\text{Principal} + \text{interest for year } (8\%)}{\text{Number of payments}}$$

$$\text{To substitute: } \frac{\$1{,}000.00 + 8\% \text{ of } \$1{,}000/\text{yr.}}{12} = \frac{\$1{,}080}{12} = \$90.00$$

The interest rate in this case is eight per cent per annum.

In the top left corner of the card (Figure 10-1) is the account number *5 6 28 45020* and the due date of the first payment, April 1, 1964.

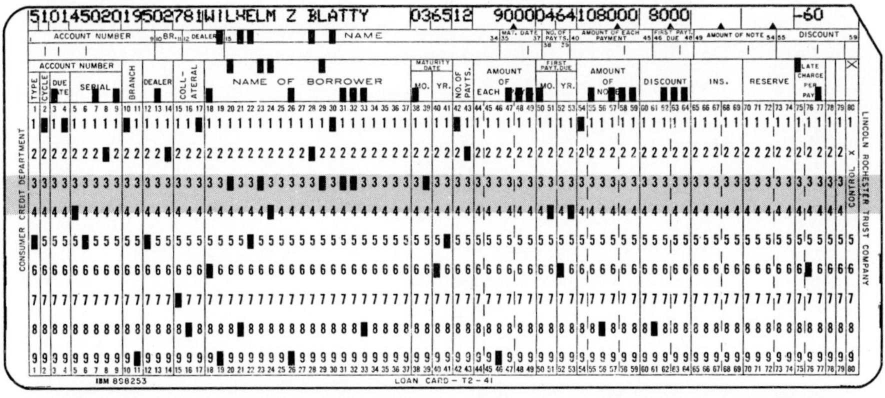
5101450201950278IWILHELM Z BLATTY 036512 90000464108000 8000 -60
ACCOUNT NUMBER | BR. | DEALER | NAME | MAT. DATE | NO. OF PAYTS. | AMOUNT OF EACH PAYMENT | FIRST PAYT. DUE | AMOUNT OF NOTE | DISCOUNT
ACCOUNT NUMBER | TYPE | CYCLE | DUE DATE | SERIAL | BRANCH | DEALER | COLL-ATERAL | NAME OF BORROWER | MATURITY DATE MO. YR. | NO. OF PAYTS. | AMOUNT OF EACH | FIRST PAYT. DUE MO. YR. | AMOUNT OF NOTE | DISCOUNT | INS. | RESERVE | LATE CHARGE PER PAY | X | CONTROL
CONSUMER CREDIT DEPARTMENT
LINCOLN ROCHESTER TRUST COMPANY
IBM 898253 LOAN CARD - T2 - 41

Figure 10-2. A new-loan card (Courtesy of Lincoln Rochester Trust Company)

Recording Data on a New-Loan Card

Once a nonprocessable *loan detail* card is prepared (Figure 10-1), the same basic data are punched by a key-punch operator on an IBM card, referred to as a *new-loan card* (Figure 10-2). The new-loan card will be used later in the preparation of a balance card to represent Dr. Blatty's loan in the balance file and also in producing a coupon book to be mailed to him for monthly payments.

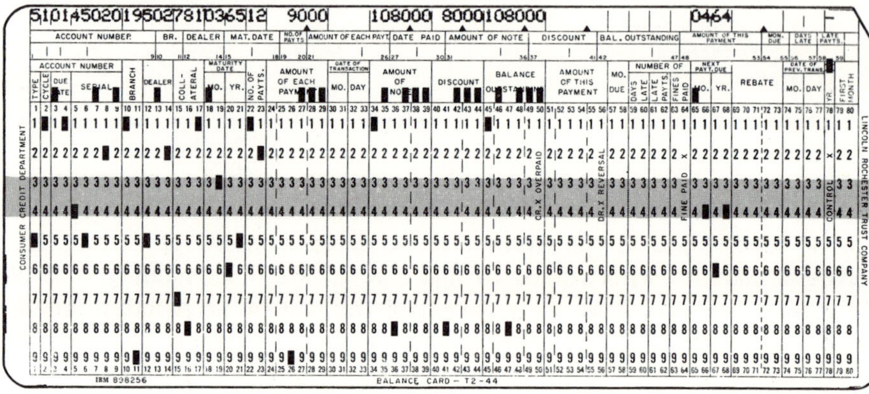

Figure 10-3. A balance card (Courtesy of Lincoln Rochester Trust Company)

Preparation of a Balance Card

The next formal step in the data preparation routine is the preparation of a balance card (Figure 10-3). The balance card is punched with the basic data copied from the new-loan card (Figure 10-2).

From left to right, the data fields are:

Columns

- 1-09 Dr. Blatty's account number.
- 10-11 The branch number of the bank to which the note was originally transferred.
- 12-14 Harry L. Gordon's number.
- 15-17 The collateral number of the furniture purchased by Dr. Blatty.
- 18-21 The maturity date of the note.
- 22-23 The number of payments to be received by the bank.
- 24-29 The exact amount of each installment.
- 30-33 The date of the current payment. Note that no data are punched, because at the time the balance card is prepared, no payment has been made or anticipated.
- 34-39 The amount of the note.
- 40-44 The discount or the amount which the bank charged on a

$1,000 note, which in effect is an interest expense to the customer. He has to pay the discount in addition to the principal amount ($1,000.00), or $1,080.00, which is the total amount of the note.

45-50 Balance outstanding. At this point, the balance outstanding is the same as the amount of the note (cols. 34-39), because no payment by Dr. Blatty has been made yet.

51-56 Amount of this payment field will be punched with the first installment or whatever Dr. Blatty makes on his first payment, due April 1, 1964.

57-58 Is not used in this application.

59-64 Are used to keep track of the number of days Dr. Blatty was late on his payments, the number of late payments, and the number of fines paid.

65-68 The due date of next payment. At this stage, the next payment due date is the first installment on April 1, 1964.

69-73 The rebate field. This is used to compute the amount of rebate due the customer, if and when he pays in advance of the due date or beyond the regular monthly amount. Some customers, for example, make two payments in a month instead of one payment. The second payment, which is paid one month in advance, requires the computation of a rebate to be paid to the customer. This amount is punched in the Rebate column.

74-77 The date of the previous transaction, if any.

78 A control field. Note the *X* punch in column 78. Later, it will be necessary to merge the balance cards with other cards for various applications or to pull it out of a merged deck.

79-80 Is not used in this application. Column 80, however, will be used (*X* punched in 80) to aid in separating the balance card from the file after a new balance card is made. This is done by sorting on column 80.

Why a nine-digit account-number field?

The nine-digit account number assigned to Dr. Blatty's loan reveals related and useful information. It is described as follows:

Column

1 Contains digit *5*, which stands for the type of merchandise (furniture) for which a loan was extended to Dr. Blatty.

2 The cycle or the code represents a range between which payment on certain loans is due. Some customers pay toward their loan regularly on the first of the month, others on the fourth, and the remainder at other times during the month. Date of payment on a loan comes under one of the following cycles:

Cycle 1 All regular payments to be paid between the first and the 5th of the month.

2 Regular payments expected between the 6th and the 10th of the month.

3 Payments that fall between the 11th and the 15th of the month.

4 Payments that fall between the 16th and the 20th of the month.

5 Payments due between the 21st and the 25th of the month.

6 Payments that fall due between the 26th and the end of the month.

Dr. Blatty's payments are due on the beginning of each month, beginning on April 1. Therefore, his payments fall in cycle 1, punched in column 2. After a grace period is allowed, sorting on column 2 for a specific cycle will select all the balance cards the payment on which is past due. This function is related to a punched-card data-processing application which selects the delinquent accounts out of the file for the purpose of mailing to the customer(s) "Past Due" statements.

3-4 Due-date field; a part of the account number. In Figure 10-3, 01 is punched in it, denoting the date of payment of each installment. This field can be used also for pulling out the cards with a certain date and then matching them against the payment cards received by the bank during that day. All balance cards that do not match reveal that no payment was made. This will result in the preparation of reports or statements concerning their delinquent status.

5-9 Serial number which is assigned to a customer. For the next customer, it is incremented by one for each additional loan extended.

The Coupon Book

At the same time that a balance card is punched, a coupon book is prepared, containing coupons the number of which is equal to the number of payments set by the bank and agreed upon by the customer (Figure 10-4). The data punched in each coupon are copied from the

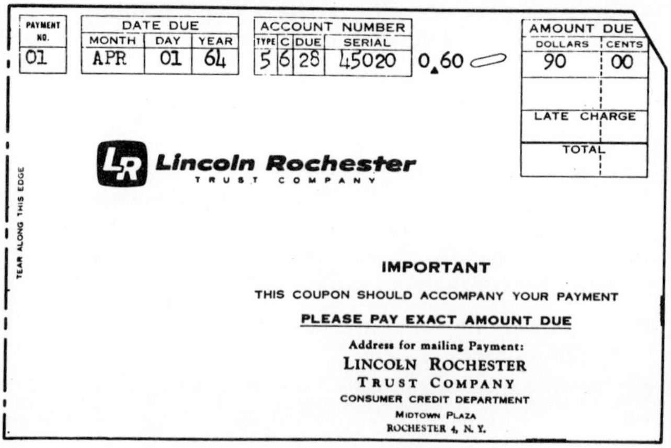

Figure 10-4. An example of a coupon (Courtesy of Lincoln Rochester Trust Company)

new-loan card (Figure 10-2). Dr. Blatty receives a coupon book containing 12 coupons representing 12 equal monthly payments toward his loans.

Each coupon contains the following information:

Payment Number The serial number of a coupon. For instance, Figure 10-4 shows the coupon which Dr. Blatty should present to the teller with his first payment of $90.00. The payment number of each of the remaining 11 coupons is incremented by 01.

Date Due Printed on each coupon is the exact date on which payment should be made. For example, coupon No. 01 is due on April 1, 1964. The next coupon (No. 02) is due on May 1, 1964, and so forth, until coupon No. 12, which is due on March 1, 1965.

Account Number Printed, remains constant on each coupon.

Late Charge In Figure 10-4, a late charge of $.60 will be required in addition to the regular payment of $90.00 if Dr. Blatty fails to pay on the due date.

Amount Due Essentially is the monthly installment. A late charge will be added if payment is made at a later date than April 1.

In addition to the 12 coupons formulating the coupon book, the bank also attaches a copy of the loan detail card (see Figure 10-1) for the customers to keep for income tax purposes. (See Figure 10-5.)

The Data-Processing Procedure

No data processing can be done in the "Daily Payments" application until the steps discussed earlier in this chapter are properly taken. From the standpoint of the punched-card data-processing routine, the "Daily

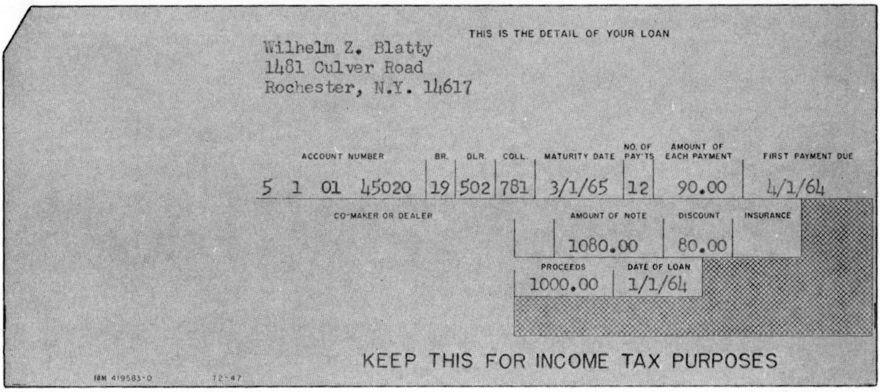
THIS IS THE DETAIL OF YOUR LOAN

Wilhelm Z. Blatty
1481 Culver Road
Rochester, N.Y. 14617

ACCOUNT NUMBER	BR.	DLR.	COLL.	MATURITY DATE	NO. OF PAY'TS	AMOUNT OF EACH PAYMENT	FIRST PAYMENT DUE
5 1 01 45020	19	502	781	3/1/65	12	90.00	4/1/64

CO-MAKER OR DEALER	AMOUNT OF NOTE	DISCOUNT	INSURANCE
	1080.00	80.00	

PROCEEDS	DATE OF LOAN
1000.00	1/1/64

KEEP THIS FOR INCOME TAX PURPOSES

IBM 419583-0 72-47

Figure 10-5. An example of Dr. Blatty's copy showing the detail of his loan (Courtesy of Lincoln Rochester Trust Company)

Payments" application begins only after a customer's loan is approved, a master card (loan detail) prepared, a "new-loan" card punched with the basic data of the loan, a balance card representing the specific loan prepared and merged in the balance file, and a coupon book mailed to the customer out of which he is able to secure the information with which he can conveniently pay his installments properly.

On April 1, 1964, Dr. Blatty walked to the teller's window of a Lincoln Rochester Trust Company branch. He detached coupon number 01 from the coupon book and handed the teller $90.00 to pay the first installment due in full. At the end of the banking day, all coupons received are sent to the data-processing department, where consumer loans are handled. All coupons go through the same procedure and are processed by the same machines as that received from Dr. Blatty. For purposes of illustration, however, Dr. Blatty's case will be emphasized in detail.

I. Recording by reproducing

The first logical and required step in the "Daily Payments" application is to record the data from the coupon received to a standard-size IBM punched card, referred to as a *payment card* (Figure 10-6). The title is self-descriptive, because the payment card represents primarily the amount paid by Dr. Blatty toward his loan. It is punched in the "amount field" or in columns 51-56. In addition to the amount of the installment payment, the date of the payment, April 1 (cols. 30-33), and the account number (cols. 1-9) are punched so as to relate the payment to the right party and the correct date, thus facilitating proper processing.

A key-punch operator could take Dr. Blatty's coupon and key punch from it his account number, date of payment, and the amount of payment on the payment card. This method offers the same result as otherwise would be the case in punching the same data by the use of the

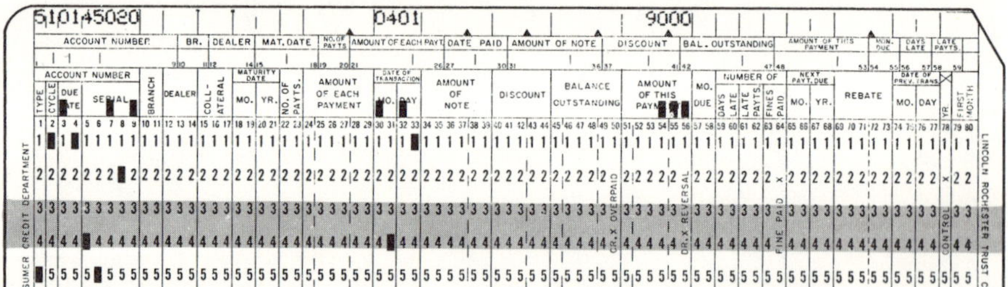

Figure 10-6. A payment card pertaining to Dr. Blatty's first installment on the loan (Courtesy of Lincoln Rochester Trust Company)

reproducer. However, because a bank such as Lincoln Rochester handles hundreds of payments related to their respective loans daily, the recording of data into a payment card from a coupon can be accomplished more effectively by the use of the reproducer; therefore, recording by reproducing is used.

The coupons are placed in the "Read" hopper and a deck of blank payment cards is placed in the "Punch" hopper. With the insertion of a wired control panel for this routine, each of the coupons will be reproduced on a payment card.

II. Tabulating payment cards

After the coupons are converted into payment cards, the latter deck is placed in an accounting machine and the amount listed for arriving at a total for that day. This move is necessarily performed in order to check on the accuracy of the conversion routine thus far. The total obtained on the accounting machine is compared with the one held at the main office. If both totals agree, it is assumed that the recording stage has been completed successfully. The data-processing department can go on with the application routine. If the total obtained on the accounting machine disagrees with that of the central office, then the error(s) must be located and corrected before any other step(s) is taken.

III. Sorting payment cards

The sorting step involves the sequencing of the payment cards by account number. In effect, they are being prepared to be match-merged with the balance file, the cards of which are already sequenced by account number. Sorting the payment cards by account number requires 9 passes: one pass for each of the 9 columns of the account-number field. Pass 1 sorts column 9 first. When the cards are reassembled, they are placed in the hopper again and the sorter brush is set to read column 8. The operation continues until the nine columns have been sorted.

IV. Match-merging payments with balance file

The payment cards can be useful only when they effect a reduction in the balance outstanding of the loans pertaining to them. For example, prior to April 1, Dr. Blatty's balance outstanding of his loan was $1,080. As a result of the payment of his first installment of $90.00 on April 1, the balance outstanding of his loan should be reduced to $990 ($1,080.00 − $90.00 = $990.00). The calculating step cannot be performed, however, until both the payment card and the balance card of each loan are merged together. This step is performed on the collator and referred to as the *match-merge* step.

The payment cards are placed in the secondary hopper and the balance cards placed in the primary hopper. A control panel is wired to match-merge the two decks. A payment card drops behind a balance card in pocket 3 of the collator *only* if the account number in both is equal. Otherwise, all *payment* cards that have no balance card to match their account numbers are dropped in pocket 5 (the secondary pocket). All *balance* cards that have no payment cards to match their account numbers are dropped in pocket 1 (the primary pocket). In the case of Dr. Blatty's balance card and payment card, both were available and, because the account number in each card is the same (equal), they were merged in pocket 3 (Figure 10-6). Note that the balance card is in front of the payment card. Each of the other payment cards in the stacker should be preceded by a balance card bearing the same account number.

V. The calculating function

The merged cards are then placed in the IBM 604 electronic calculating punch. The balance card is read first. The amount of payment ($90.00 in cols. 51-56) is read from the payment card behind the balance card. The calculator subtracts the amount from the balance outstanding ($1,080 in cols. 45-50) located in the balance card. The remainder (that is, $1,080.00 − $90.00 = $990.00) is punched in cols. 45-50 in the payment card. (See Figure 10-7.) Note that the balance outstanding (cols. 45-50) is $90.00 less as the result of subtracting Dr. Blatty's payment from the initial amount.

The payment card will be considered a new balance card for the next payment due May 1, 1964. Therefore, when the calculator punches the

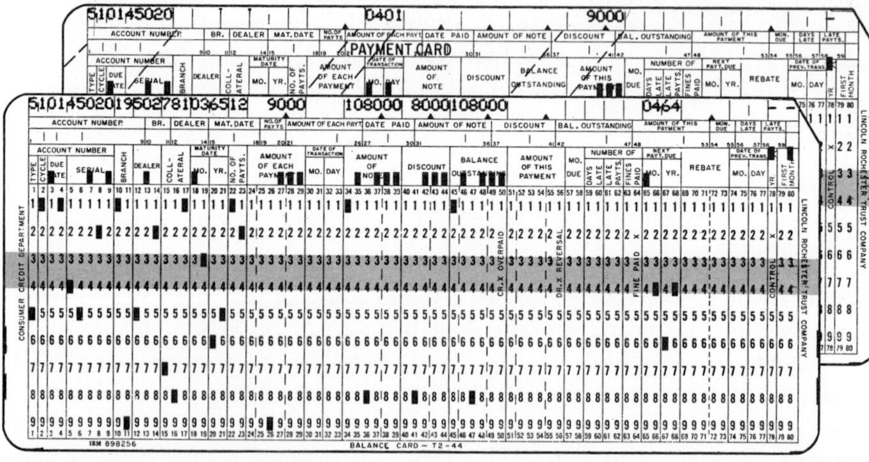

Figure 10-7. The sequence of the balance card and payment card after a match-merge operation of Dr. Blatty's loan (Courtesy of Lincoln Rochester Trust Company)

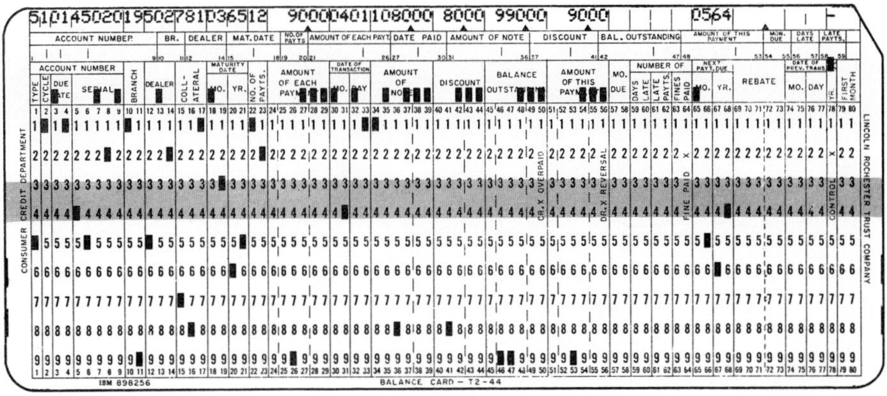

Figure 10-8. The payment card becomes an updated record of Dr. Blatty's loan after calculation was performed (Courtesy of Lincoln Rochester Trust Company)

difference after subtracting the amount of payment ($90.00) from the balance outstanding, it also copies from the balance card into the payment card all the data which were not originally punched in it. See Figure 10-8 and compare it with the payment card in Figure 10-7. This transfer of data makes the balance card in Figure 10-7 useless, because the payment card shows the up-to-date balance outstanding plus the contents of the balance card. From this point on, it is called a new balance card for next month's "Daily Payments" application. The calculator has already punched 0564 (May 1964) in columns 65-68 of the payment card.

VI. Sorting old balance cards from the file

Now that a new balance card is available, the old balance card should be pulled out or separated. The file is placed in the hopper of the sorter to eject into a separate pocket all cards with an *X* punch in column 80. Only the old balance cards have an *X* punched in that column. The collator is, usually, used to extract the desired card from the file, because of the convenience factor. A control panel is wired to cause all cards with *X* in column 80 to eject into a pocket separate from the rest of the cards in the file.

VII. Checks and balances

Once the old balance cards are extracted, the new payment cards are placed in the accounting machine for a card-for-card listing. In Figure 10-9, a payment journal is used. Dr. Blatty's account number, new outstanding balance brought forward on April 1, the amount paid, and the next due date are printed. This step is considered necessary because a final check is made by comparing the total "amount of payment" column in the journal with the original amount received by the teller of the bank. If the

CONSUMER CREDIT DEPARTMENT - PAYMENT JOURNAL - LINCOLN ROCHESTER TRUST COMPANY

ACCOUNT NUMBER T	C	DUE	SERIAL	OUTSTANDING BALANCE	DATE MO.	DAY	AMOUNT OF PAYMENT	MO. DUE	PREVIOUS PAYMENT MO.	DAY
5	1	01	45020	990 00	4	01	90 00	5		

Figure 10-9. A partial payment journal, showing Dr. Blatty's account listed (Courtesy of Lincoln Rochester Trust Company)

two amounts agree, then the new payment cards can be merged in the main file. If the two totals disagree, it would be necessary to locate and correct the error or errors before final merging.

VIII. Merging new payment cards in the balance file

Assuming that the total payments amount is correct, the final step in the application is to merge the new payment cards in the balance file. The primary hopper of the collator is fed with the balance cards. The secondary hopper is fed with the new payment cards. The merging process causes both feeds to drop into the proper sequential order in pocket 3 of the collator.

After the merge operation is completed, the balance file is ready for another cycle when other customers pay their installments the next day. In the case of Dr. Blatty, the same cycle presented in this chapter will recur on May 1, when he makes his second payment.

PART 3

ELECTRONIC DATA PROCESSING

Chapter 11

The Effect of Research on Business Data-Processing Systems

Punched-card data-processing systems and the equipment associated with them are in wide use today and most likely will be used by business firms for a long time to come. In the face of this, the question arises as to why there is any demand for automatic computers to process business data already processable by punched-card machines. The answers to this question widen our knowledge about data-processing systems by describing an advanced processing routine, still in its infancy, involving the use of electronics, which is designed to serve business firms in a much more efficient, more accurate, more economical manner than the punched-card routine. The development of computer systems for business data processing, side by side with the improvement and perfection of punched-card systems, is a perfect example of how rapid technological change can be in new industries and of what is meant by the statement that "what is new today may become obsolete tomorrow."

Although electronic systems are a decided improvement over punched-card systems, the fact remains that, until more is known about how to adapt them to all types of situations economically, punched-card systems remain the most practical for business firms where the volume of repetitive paper work is such that their installation can be justified. Although the "old" is serving to alleviate the present situation, research, experimentation, and actual use in industries which find it economical are forging ahead on the "new." Whether one will displace the other, or whether they will supplement each other, only time will tell. The "new" improves on the basic ideas behind business data processing in use by the "old" just as the "new" punched-card systems supplanted the "old" manual methods.

Thus, to give students a well-rounded picture of all developments in the business data-processing field, a description and analysis of the development of the "Babbage" ideas on a practical basis in modern computer systems is essential. A computer system is usually installed as it becomes economically feasible to do so. Thus, as research progresses, the everyday use of computer systems in business continues to widen. Today's students will be likely to find themselves involved in either an actual operation, or a consideration of the feasibility of its installation, when they enter upon their business careers. Hence their need for understanding the ideas involved in both punched-card and electronic systems stands out in clear relief.

The purpose of Part 3 is not to prepare anyone to become a systems analyst or a programmer. It is, instead, to instill understanding about electronic data processing in the student's mind by showing (1) why there is so much interest in electronic computers and (2) how an electronic computer works. A clear-cut picture of its basic elements, its language, the means by which it calculates and processes data, and how instructions are written so that it can perform its various calculations should enable students to think intelligently rather than "awesomely" about these machines and their purposes in business.

Digital computers used in business are built to aid man in doing the many required repetitive tasks that make up the course of his business. Their use boosts his productivity and improves the quality of his output regardless of whether it is a tangible product or an intangible service. These goals can be met by an electronic computer more successfully than by a punched-card system in four ways: (1) By processing a greater number of items per second, the exact amount depending upon the type and size of the computer. Because the speed of the electronic computer is measured in thousands or millions of steps per second, it is, therefore, faster than any other type of machine designed to do similar work. (2) By processing business data more accurately than alternative methods. A clerk, *at his best,* makes at least five mistakes per 100 manual calculations, whereas the computer's rate of error is a fraction of 1/10,000 of one per cent, or 99.999+ per cent accuracy. A punched-card system operates with a much higher degree of accuracy than any manual system, but it cannot operate with as great accuracy as an electronic system, because it is composed of mostly mechanical parts. Although electricity is used to operate most punched-card systems, the fact that they are mechanical makes their operation subject to slightly greater error than a computer system which operates by means of electronic circuitry. (3) By allowing more time for creative and intelligent planning than is provided by a punched-card system. A computer's greater versatility in performing millions of operations tirelessly frees even greater amounts of time for more productive use. (4) By lowering costs. The cost of each application processed by a computer, in general, is lower than when alternative machine methods are used. Although the initial cost of obtaining the computer is high, the saving resulting from its speed and accuracy in many cases justifies the decision to install it.

The development of interest in the practical use of electronic systems is due to various reasons, among which the following are significant. A hundred years ago, electronic computers were not really needed for the comparatively slow pace of events characteristic of an agricultural economy. If they had been, there would have been interest in building them, because the ideas governing their operation and behavior were already known, as was brought out in Chapter 2. However, as economies were transformed from basically agricultural ones to predominantly manufacturing or industrial ones, the need for machinery and the adoption of automated techniques to mass-produce for expanding markets became more and more apparent. Business executives have become very conscious of the fact that, if they are to compete in rapidly growing competitive markets, they must have essential business data regarding their products as quickly as possible in usable form. Therefore, the elements of time, speed, and accuracy in data preparation become more important, rather than less important, as economies grow and markets expand. The saving of time through speed can be, and is, solved by increasing clerical help to process and handle paper work. However, increasing the clerical staff results in the generation of new problems. (1) A firm finds it necessary to hire supervisors to organize and direct the many plans and procedures handled by clerks, with resulting increase in the cost of data-handling tasks. (2) Morale problems increase with the increase in human help. Many office workers become bored with the repetitive nature of their work, and its monotony causes them to brood about many things, at the expense of their accuracy and efficiency. (3) Storage becomes a problem, because all business data must be filed daily.

Even though the problems of time and speed are solved in this manner, the high costs associated with such a solution are illustrated by the fact that clerical workers receive approximately one dollar out of every eight paid for wages and salaries in the United States. The basic problem of lowering the cost of data handling and data processing, thus, remains. To solve it, some industries have moved ahead successfully in the areas of punched-card and electronic data processing. The banking industry, for instance, processes, on the average, ten billion checks every year. Each of these checks is handled several times and must go through a tedious routine before it is finally paid and returned. At present, more and more of the larger banks are using magnetic character sensing by reader-sorter machines which read the depositor's account number and other related data printed in magnetic ink on the face of the check. Checks are sorted into the desired classifications or sequence in a fraction of the time it takes to do it manually.

As economies have grown industrially, progressive business firms have expanded their operations. The emergence of the large firm with many branches is well known. This requires the intelligent use and coordination of the five *M*'s of Management, that is, *Money, Men, Methods, Materials,* and *Managerial Talent,* in order to operate profitably. Productive use of these elements demands greater amounts of data. For example, the obtaining of *money* involves contacts with financial institutions and the presentation of financial statements and plans for the purpose of establishing lines of credit for the negotiation of loans. The mounting need for labor (*men*) requires the gathering together and processing of various forms for interviewing, testing, screening, and selecting the men best suited to the various kinds of jobs. *Methods* must be constantly devised and procedures prepared so that the firm's goal can be attained. *Materials* used in the manufacture of the product must be ordered. None of the foregoing factors are of much use to a firm without *Managerial Talent.* Because management is basically defined as "getting things done through people," executives with a background in the literature of management are in great demand to coordinate and synchronize the work of many people who follow *preplanned* methods and procedures.

Maintaining relationships with workers and their supervisors, on the one hand, and being informed about the performance of the equipment, the quality of the products, the status of the raw materials, and the level of production, on the other, require that accurate facts be made available quickly. Each and every report must be prepared in such a way that it aids management in making better decisions. The speed and accuracy with which these reports are prepared and disseminated to key executives give a firm a better chance for survival in the business community, provided the information is put to intelligent use by the top-management officials who receive it. To meet competition, by utilizing their physical plants to capacity, many firms diversify their products. Ford Motor Company, for instance, introduces each year a variety of different-size and different price-level automobiles in addition to their basic model. The consumer can choose between two or more sizes, colors, and price ranges. Engines of different power ratings are available upon request. Accessories can be easily provided for, including colored white-wall tires or hubcaps to match the owner's attire. Other automobile companies do the same. Accompanying the introduction of a variety of basically similar, yet different, products on the market is the need for data for analysis and comparison so that decisions can be made as to the competitive advantage to be derived from such "differentiation." Can the company justify the mass production of a given product, considering the initial manufacturing and marketing costs? What portion of the market does it hold? How does it rate when compared with a competitor's product of similar specifications? How long is it expected to be in demand? How long would it take before a breakeven point is reached? All these and other questions must be answered. Management cannot plan wisely without access to all the basic data pertaining to its products. Unlike the Spartans who didn't question the number of the enemy but only asked where it was, a business firm must measure its own strength against that of its competitors in order to prepare the right "weapons" for the competitive "battle."

Punched-card data-processing systems and equipment became commercially available in the 1930's and are still in widespread use today. They are a big step forward in the area of business data processing in advance of manual methods. Because continuous research for better ways to save time and money has shown that electronics can be adapted successfully to business data processing, electronic systems are being built on a practical basis for industries where the volume and kind of data to be handled justify the expense of their installation.

In many operations, manual systems of handling data are used because managements cannot justify the installation costs of either punched-card or electronic systems. Although machine methods provide cheaper handling once the systems have been installed, each firm must be able to justify the initial costs on the basis of the nature of its operations and the mass of data generated by them. Thus, manual, punched-card, and electronic systems exist side by side in the modern business world. In all systems, the same basic processing steps must be followed. Because this text is concerned primarily with machine methods of data handling, attention is, therefore, focused on a description and analysis of punched-card and electronic systems so that students can develop an awareness of the significant developments in machine handling in the rapidly changing business data-processing field.

QUESTIONS FOR REVIEW

1. "What is new today may become obsolete tomorrow." Do you agree with this statement? Write a 200- to 400-word report to defend your answer.
2. In how many ways can an electronic data-processing computer help a business firm boost productivity and/or improve the quality of its products? Explain each way briefly.
3. What are some of the disadvantages of increasing clerical help in a manual system? Explain.
4. Explain briefly each of the five *M*'s of management.
5. How can speed and accuracy of reports' preparation help key executives increase the chance of their firm for survival?

Chapter 12

Business Computer Systems: Their Nature, Capabilities, Limitations, and Make-up

The Automatic Business Computer

An *automatic business computer* is defined as a machine that manipulates bits of business information within its main unit, based on a predetermined series of steps or sets of instructions, with a minimum of human intervention. To be more exact, a better name for a business computer is "Automatic High-Speed Electronic Business Data-Processing Digital Computer." *

The term *automatic* is synonymous with *self-directing,* because, once the computer receives a set of instructions,

---

* Ned Chapin, *An Introduction to Automatic Computers,* 2nd ed. (Princeton, N.J.: D. Van Nostrand Co., Inc., 1955-63). The idea for the approach used in this chapter has been adapted from Chapter 2.

which tells it what to do and how to bring about the desired results, it performs all the required work independently of human intervention. In this respect, the computer is referred to as being *automatic* or *self-directing*. Its self-direction is limited, however, by the instructions made available to it by a human programmer.

The term *high-speed* represents the ability of the computer to perform needed operations at the speed of light. The average speed of most computers ranges from a minimum of 100 operations per second up to 500,000 per second. Only a few computers are found beyond this limit.

The term *electronic* explains why a computer is referred to as a high-speed machine. "Electronics" relates to the flow of electrons behaving as signals in the circuitry of electronic equipment. These signals are manipulated to represent codes, which can be numeric, alphabetic, or special. The electron's high speed causes electronic computers to operate efficiently, as a result of which information flows thousands of times faster than through mechanical or electromechanical machines.

The term *business data processing* refers to the manipulation of known business facts for the purpose of a desired result in terms of printed financial reports or other business statements.

The term *digital* refers to the type of computer. Such a computer utilizes counting devices and numbers for expressing variable quantities as well as for calculations. In contrast, the analog computer transforms physical flows, such as temperature or pressure, into electrical quantities in solving a given problem.

The term *computer* is used to designate a machine that can be used to solve problems in their entirety, and not merely the arithmetical operations which can be performed on any calculator. Although referred to as a "human brain," a computer is no more human than an electric saw or an automobile. A computer is assembled from many different parts. However, the manner in which it processes data is seemingly "human," primarily because it is designed to follow the same routine that a human being would have to follow in solving the problem.

Essential Capabilities of a Business Computer

1. *Ability to Handle Information:* A digital computer which is designed to process business data is capable of storing (remembering) the data being worked on, and of transferring it from a given part in storage to any other desired location in the system at high speed. The speed is usually measured in one-thousandths of a second, referred to as *milliseconds* (abbreviated ms), or in one-millionths of a second, referred to as *microseconds* (abbreviated μs). With this capability, it is convenient for a business firm to update each and every record, because actual calculations take very little time.

2. *Ability to Handle Repetitive Tasks:* In general, a business computer is designed to handle any repetitive, recurring problem using different data as long as it follows the same prescribed procedures.

3. *Self-Operational:* The business computer is capable of storing temporarily, or permanently, both business data and the set of instructions, called a *program,* that tells it what to do, in a common storage so as to effect direct access to the data. This constitutes a self-operating situation with a minimum of human intervention.

4. *Ability to Communicate Effectively:* In order to be effective and useful, a business computer must be capable of accepting information and, after performing the desired routine, of giving correct results.

5. *Ability to "Make Decisions":* A computer cannot do anything a man couldn't do if he had the time. A digital computer is capable of following instructions stored in it and of modifying any of those instructions if necessary. In other words, the computer is preset so that it can choose between alternative courses of action to perform the right routine. In this respect, the act is referred to as "decision making." However, the choice between alternatives is limited to those prepared for it by the programmer. The computer can decide on the correct sequence of steps necessary to solve a given problem on the basis of conditions occurring in the interim. In computer terminology, this is referred to as "feedback."

6. *Ability to Check on the Correctness of Its Own Work:* A business computer is capable of checking on the accuracy of its own work by means of a "code check." In this, the computer counts the number of characters it has in storage and keeps track of every character as a result of an arithmetical, or other, operation.

7. *Ability to Do New and Additional Tasks:* A computer can be instructed to do additional tasks, such as the printing of an order every time the stock level of a given item falls below a desired minimum. By the same token, it can print a list of all the items currently available in stock with a specific color, size, and/or other specifications. It can tabulate or summarize quantitative information more effectively than any human clerk because it is not subject to "boredom."

Limitations of a Digital Computer

1. A computer can handle the business information it has been programmed to handle, and can communicate the information to the user. It cannot do anything beyond this limit. In other words, it cannot make a decision in situations where *qualitative* factors are involved. A computer, for instance, can show certain expense items which exceed a desired maximum, but it cannot take action to stop the expense.

2. A computer can neither make its own program nor determine its own course of action. Because it is made of metal, it has to be told in a

very detailed manner how to do any given job. All alternative courses of action are predetermined and stored as a part of the program by a human programmer. The computer can choose a desired routine only if it is provided for in the program.

3. Even though a computer processes business data close to perfection, it cannot be perfect. Anything made by man is subject to occasional breakdown. A computer occasionally develops "bugs." An amusing story is told of a digital computer that sold the wrong stocks, because of a slipped cog. Another concerns the computer operated by the army that ordered millions of dollars' worth of items which were never required, to be shipped to Europe. These stories, while anecdotal, do point out that environmental, technical, and human factors can contribute to the failure of a computer. All manufacturers prescribe the manner in which their computers are to be treated and operated. A workable series of steps is outlined that lead to the attainment of the results desired. When the instructions are followed exactly by the user, a computer's accuracy, compared with that of a human being, is almost perfect. Computers are now being built to perform over 9 billion operations without an error.

4. The best justification for the use of a computer in business lies in its application to routine, continuous, repetitive tasks. A computer should not be expected to do nonrecurring or nonrepetitive calculations on small amounts of data. As was mentioned previously, every application requires the preparation of a program to tell the computer what to do and how to go about reading a solution to the problem. It is normally anticipated that, with the expenditure of human effort and time in the preparation of the program, the application will be used over and over again. The many hours involved in writing the program become only a matter of minutes to the computer when it processes the complete application. Therefore, programming effort should be applied toward routine and recurring applications and not toward those jobs that involve *many exceptions* and which are *not to be processed frequently*.

Elements of a Business Data-Processing Computer System

A. The human thinking process

The elements comprising a business data-processing computer system are a copy of those comprising the human thought processes involved in any kind of data processing. For this reason, it is well to outline the manner in which a human being solves problems, and to review the steps involved in the attainment of the correct result. For example, assume that George Cook, a freshman student at a local community college, was asked on an accounting exam to determine the amount of the new cash balance of ABC Company, by adding the previous balance of $30.00 to today's receipts of $5.00. What elements are required for a correct solution to this problem?

1. Communicate. The student cannot give the correct answer unless he is capable of communicating. Communicating is a transportation device. The instruction implying addition of the previous balance of $30.00 to today's receipts of $5.00 must be accessible and properly visualized. (Figure 12-1.)

2. Hold Information and Make Decisions. After the instruction (*Add*) and the amounts to be added (*30* and *5*) are visualized, they are retained in the mind (memory) of the student. Memory retains the desired data as long as it is needed. In memory, logical decisions are made concerning the problems also. The student determines whether or not both amounts have positive signs, checks to ascertain that no fractions are ignored, and decides whether the amounts in memory are sufficient data for a satisfactory answer. (Figure 12-2.)

3. Do Arithmetic. The next step is to add *30* plus *5* to realize the sum, $35.00—the new cash balance. (Figure 12-3.)

4. Produce Reports. Upon arriving at the sum ($35.00), the student writes down the answer on the exam paper, along with the proper description. (Figure 12-4.)

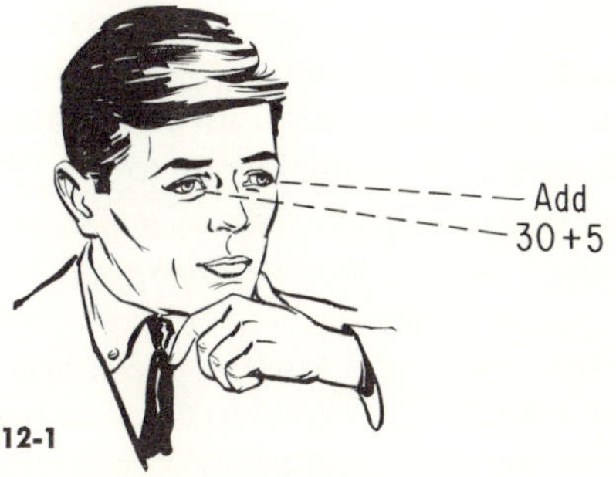

Figure 12-1

Figure 12-2

Figure 12-3

Figure 12-4

B. The elements comprising a business computer system

You will note from the foregoing illustration of the human thought process that the brain cannot work effectively without the aid of its auxiliary units or organs. The eyes, for instance, read the data written on the blackboard and communicate (transport) the instruction (*Add*) and the amounts, *30* and *5,* to be added by the brain. After addition, the hand communicates the answer to the instructor by writing it on the examination paper.

Like the human brain, the business computer cannot function effectively without the aid of its auxiliary units. That is the reason why we speak in terms of a computer system rather than of a single computer. The main elements comprising any business data-processing computer system are:

1. *Communication.* In order to work on business problems, a computer, like the human brain, must be capable of receiving business data in an orderly manner. The business information is called *INPUT* (Figure 12-5). Data are placed in a unit called the *input* unit, which is the "eye" of the computer. It reads the desired data and communicates (through cables) to the memory unit of the computer (see the square in the middle of Figure 12-5).

2. *Storage.* Once read by the input unit, data are transferred to the primary storage section of the computer, called "memory." They are held there until arithmetic is performed. It is important to remember that primary storage is the heart of the computer. It is analogous to the "human brain." (See the square in Figure 12-5.)

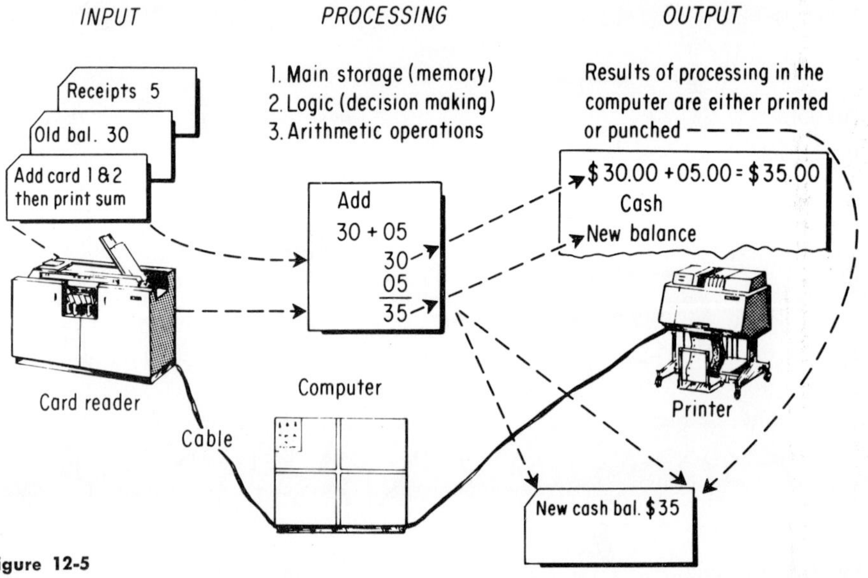

Figure 12-5

3. *Decision Making.* The computer has the ability to compare two values "logically" to determine whether they are equal or unequal, distinguishing between a positive and a negative value and determining whether a number is greater or less than 0. These important capabilities take place in the central processing unit.

4. *Arithmetic Computation.* The computer, referred to frequently as the *central processing unit,* contains an arithmetic unit where a part of the memory is used for arithmetical calculations. The computer has a very basic mathematical education. It can only add, subtract, multiply, divide, and compare. Its ability to compare makes the computer useful. It can tell whether a number is positive, negative, or *0.* Only in the central processing unit are calculations of any kind performed. The external units are merely assisting units that facilitate transmission and storage of information. Elements 2, 3, and 4 constitute the heart of the computer, referred to from now on as the *central processing unit* (C.P.U.).

5. *Report Preparation.* The final element of a computer system is the preparation of reports based on the calculations made in the central processing unit. This step is referred to as *readable output* and is usually expressed in the form of a printed report. Nonreadable output is usually expressed either in the form of a punched card or of magnetic tape. In certain systems, punched paper tape is also available as a form of output. In the example involving the human being, the examination paper is the output medium and the pencil is the output unit or device.

6. *The Stored Program.* If the computer system is to read, remember, make decisions, calculate, and write, it must do them in proper sequence. The stored program contains instructions which tell the computer what steps to take, what data to work on, and what to do with the results. A control element instructs the computer what instructions to use from the stored program which a human programmer has prepared. This causes all other units to operate in the proper manner so that correct results are obtained.

QUESTIONS FOR REVIEW

1. What is meant by the term *computer?* What is meant by the term *digital?*
2. List and explain in detail the essential capabilities of a business computer.
3. "A computer cannot do anything a man couldn't do if he had the time." Do you agree with the statement? Defend your answer.
4. In what respect is a computer referred to as "making decisions"?
5. What is meant by *code check?*
6. What are the four limitations of a digital computer? Explain each limitation briefly.
7. What are the elements which comprise a business data-processing system? Explain each element in detail.

8. What elements constitute the central processing unit?
9. What does an electronic data-processing installation normally consist of, if it is to operate as a complete system? Why? Explain. (See Figure 12-5.)
10. Is there a difference between a stored program and logic? Explain.

Chapter 13

Input and Output: Media and Devices

Introduction

One of the most important aspects of processing business data by using an electronic computer is to prepare accurately and in the proper sequence the raw data that are to be processed. It is helpful to keep in mind that all incorrect information used as input will result in inaccurate output. For example, in anticipation of the sum *3* for an answer (output), only certain digits or a combination of digits can be used (input). The alternatives can be either $3 + 0$, $2 + 1$, $2 + 1 + 0$, or $1 + 2 + 0$. Using a combination such as $3 + B$, or $A + 2$, and so forth, as input, obviously will not result in the correct output of 3 unless B is coded to have a value of 0, or unless A is coded to have a value of

1. Personnel in the business data-processing field use a humorous, unofficial abbreviation *"G I G O,"* interpreted as "garbage in, garbage out," to emphasize the need for the presentation of accurate and logical input if accurate and meaningful output is to be expected.

The main characteristic of business data-processing applications is the performance of simple and limited amounts of computations on large amounts of data. The credit department of a large business concern, for instance, uses a computer to update each customer's account by adding to the customer's old balance all purchases made by him on account and subtracting from the sum all payments which he made during a given period, in order to arrive at a new balance for the period. This application involves basically one addition and one subtraction—functions which are extremely easy. However, the fact that thousands of customers' accounts need updating frequently means that these two simple operations must be repeated thousands of times. Thus, a great volume of data flows into and out of the computer in the process of the comparatively simple operation of updating. This makes the input and output equipment the busiest part of the system, because it has to read and print the information speedily.

Generally speaking, input and output units perform translation and communication functions. They do not do the actual processing but, rather, prepare the data so that they can be processed in the central processing unit. For this reason they are under the direct control of the central processing unit. Can you explain the meaning of the phrase: "latigid retupmoc"? Your response is an emphatic *NO!* until you are told that it is "digital computer" spelled backward. The computer finds it just as difficult to process data if the language representing the data cannot be easily interpreted by it.

The machine language is read by input devices, which then transfer the data to the computer for processing. If the output is needed immediately by management, it is put back into human language by an output device called the *printer*. If the output, on the other hand, is to be stored for future processing by the computer, this can be done by using various kinds of other output devices, that is, punched cards, punched paper tape, or magnetic tape.

To summarize, then, input equipment *translates* the machine language and transfers it to the computer. It *reads* data into the storage unit of the computer. The term to *read in* means to "put in." The data "read in" or "put in" are called "input." Output equipment *translates* machine language to human language. It provides a means of communication between the computer and the outside world. Output equipment *writes* data out of the storage unit. The term *to write out,* then, means "to put out." Thus, the data "written" or "put out" are referred to as "output." Each different type of computer has its own individual machine language and utilizes different input and output devices. It is important, then, for us to examine the different input and output media that computers use in order to comprehend more fully the implications involved in the various processing systems and to understand how "Garbage In, Garbage Out" can be prevented from occurring.

I. Input and output media and devices

A. Manual Input. One of the simplest forms of input device is the use of the keyboard of an electric typewriter. The input is fed into the computer by the depression of keys—which, in effect, is the same as typing. (See Figure 13-1.) The speed of processing the input data by

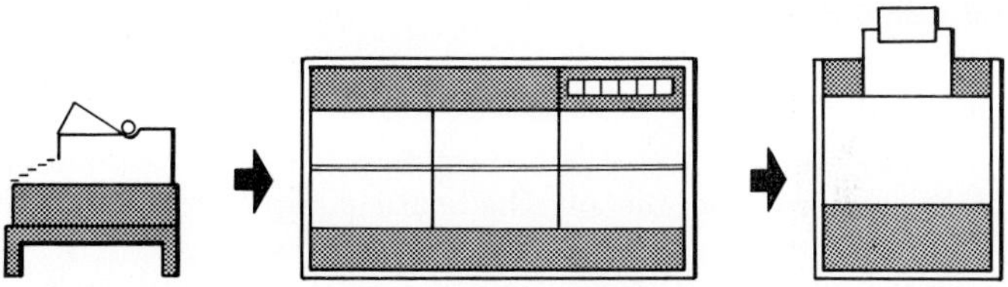

Figure 13-1

using the typewriter is dependent upon the speed of the operator in depressing each of the keys.

Although simple, the typewriter is not generally used as the chief means of input or output, except in small-size computer systems where the cost of computing time is not expensive and the question of speed is not too important. When digital computers operate at a speed measured in milliseconds (1/1,000ths of a second) and microseconds (1/1,000,000ths of a second), the typewriter, which operates at 10 characters a second, is too slow to make the best use of the computer's capabilities. In all other types of computers, especially large-size ones, the typewriter is used as an auxiliary manual method of input or output. Its most common use is as an inquiry station. The computer is interrupted during the processing of given data and inquiry is made by asking the computer to disclose the balance or other data concerning a specific account. "Asking" the computer is done by typewriting the code that tells the computer what to do and where to find the desired information. With the manipulation of certain physical switches or buttons, the inquiry takes place and accurate results are obtained.

Other uses of the typewriter as an auxiliary input device include the checking of a program, inserting missing instructions into the computer, and changing the value of a constant. The usefulness of the typewriter lies mainly in notifying the computer of these special conditions and exceptions.

B. Punched Cards as Input-Output Media. The use of punched cards as input-output media is the most familiar form of these agents, especially on small and medium-size computers. The IBM punched card is a piece of high-quality cardboard that measures 7⅜″ long by 3¼″ wide and .007″ in thickness. It is divided into 80 vertical spaces, called *columns*, and 12 horizontal spaces, called *rows*. A numeric character (*0* and *1* through *9*) is represented by a rectangular hole in a given column. An alphabetic character (*A* through *Z*) is represented by two rectangular holes: one in the numeric digit of a given column (rows 1 through 9), and another hole in the zone digit of the same column (row 0, 11 or 12).

A punched card is a "Unit Record" and may be used in different colors. It may have either a left corner cut or a right corner cut for visual identification.

1. Advantages of the use of punched cards as an input or output medium are:
   - (a) They are popular: Many business firms are familiar with the punched card and the punched-card equipment and prefer to continue their use.
   - (b) Their code is basically easy. Their popularity is also due to the ease with which they can be visually read and inspected. Their accuracy can be fairly easily checked. Further, it takes relatively little experience to learn the use and code of punched cards.
   - (c) They are versatile. As a unit record, the punched card can be easily filed and sorted, consequently becoming a part of a different file for use in various business applications.
   - (d) They are easy to store. Unlike other media, such as magnetic tape, the punched card is made of sturdy, hard paper and can withstand a reasonable change in temperature and humidity and also is unaffected by dust. Once data are punched, they are retained by the cards for storage periods of any length.
   - (e) They are inexpensive. Data previously punched in cards which become old or mutilated can be duplicated automatically without much trouble. Even duplicating a complete deck of cards involves little time and only nominal cost.

One of the main disadvantages of punched cards as direct input or output, however, is the fact that a punched card can store only 80 characters (one character in each column). Further, its physical dimensions cause files to be bulky. The fact that it can be mutilated or damaged accidentally makes it necessary for the department to keep an inventory of blank cards.

C. Punched-Card Reader as an Input Device. The punched card reader is an auxiliary machine, the purpose of which is to transfer the data punched in each card to the central processing unit for processing. (Figure 13-2.)

The data cards are placed in the feed hopper on the right (Figure

Figure 13-2. IBM 1402 brush type card reader (right) and card punch (left)

13-2). Each card is read by a sensing mechanism which interprets the holes in the card into electrical impulses which go to the central computer unit for processing. Although cards go inside the card reader to be read, they do not go inside the computer proper.

There are two types of punched-card readers: (1) the brush type and (2) the photoelectric type. Figure 13-2 is a brush-type punched-card reader. The punched-card reader reads one card at a time. A stack of cards is first placed in the read hopper 9-edge first, face down. The first card in sequence passes underneath the first set of 80 reading brushes, called the *Read Check* station. (See Figure 13-3.) The brushes take a "hole count," that is, they keep track of the number of holes in the card for checking purposes. Then the same card moves underneath the set of 80 "Read" brushes, which, after verifying the hole count made by the "Read Check" brushes, direct the data electrically into the computer unit. Then the card drops into the stacker marked "Normal Read." The second card in sequence goes through the same procedure, and so forth, until the whole file is read. They are finally dropped into the radial stacker. (Figure 13-2.)

The left side of the card reader shown in Figure 13-3 is used to punch the results of processing (output) in blank cards placed in a hopper on

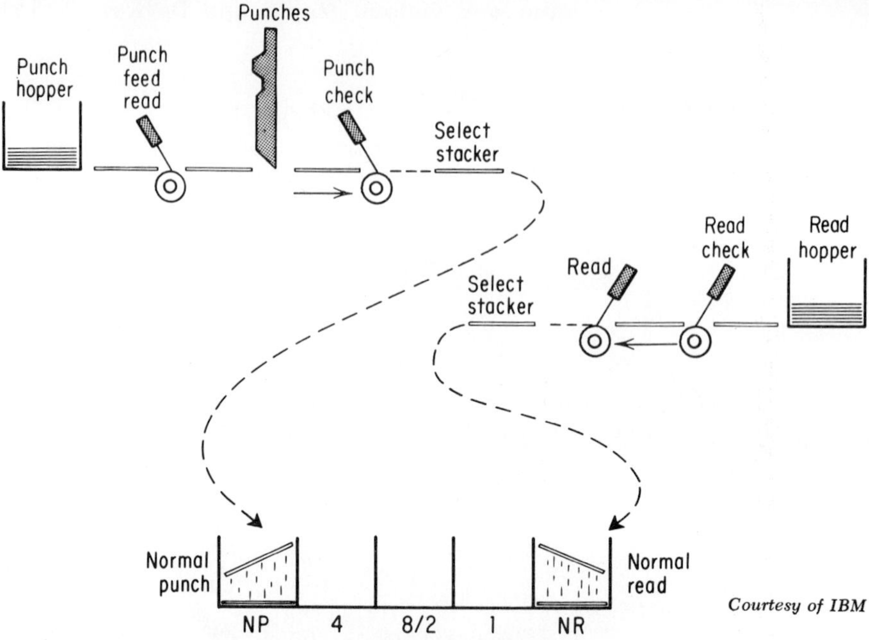

Courtesy of IBM

Figure 13-3. A 1402 punched card "read" and "punch" schematic

the left. The greatest speed of this specific card reader is 800 cards per minute. The angular device in the read hopper shown in Figure 13-2 is called a *file feed,* which facilitates the feed of as many as 3,000 cards at a time. The punched-card reader is a part of the 1401 business data-processing computer system. (See Figure 12-5 in Chapter 12.)

The photoelectric-type punched-card reader is the same as the brush type in that both machines sense holes in a card. The main difference, however, is in the method of sensing. The latter machine uses brushes to sense holes in a card, whereas in the former, 80 photoelectric cells are activated as the punched card passes over a main light source.

Other card-reader machines read cards at speeds that fluctuate between 100 and 2,000 cards per minute, depending upon the type of card reader in question.

D. Punched-Card Reader as an Output Device. The left side of the punched-card reader (Figure 13-3) is used to punch the results (output) from the central processing unit in blank cards fed into the punch hopper. A blank card moves automatically under the punch dies, and the output is punched. The punched card then moves under a set of 80 brushes to check on the accuracy of the punch dies. If they are correct, the card ejects into the radial stacker below it. Otherwise, the machine stops, indicating an error. (See Figure 13-3.) The speed of the 1402 card punch is 250 cards per minute. The speed of other machines varies, depending on the model used.

E. Magnetic Tape. Magnetic tape is another medium used for both input and output. It is preferred over the punched card primarily because of its speed, its ability to store on one inch of tape data punched in several cards, and the fact that it can be reused indefinitely by recording new data on it. It is one of the fastest forms of input or output available.

Magnetic tape is commonly made of iron oxide coated on plastic or other nonmagnetic substance. There are two types of tape: (1) The metallic type, which is the older of the two types. Its thickness reduces the number of records that can be stored on a reel of tape. (2) The acetate type, which is composed of a plastic substance coated with iron oxide.

A single computer can be used to control one or more tape units as input or output (Figure 13-4). A tape unit is a tape recorder. At the input stage, it reads the coded data to the computer. At the output stage,

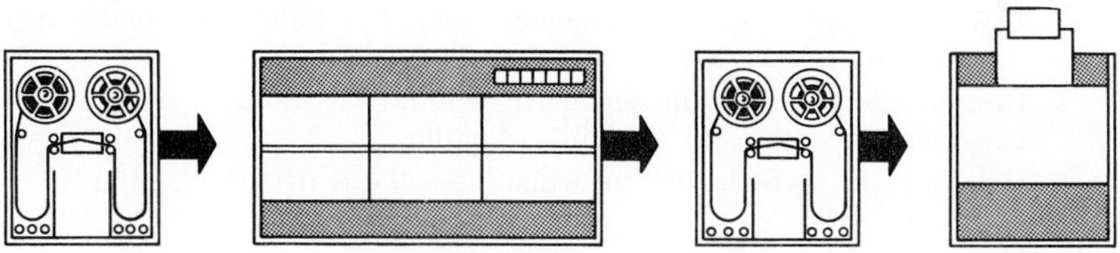

Figure 13-4

it writes (records) the results for storage and future reference. Magnetic tape and magnetic units are used most often for either secondary storage or temporary storage of data which might later be read back into the computer when needed.

F. Punched Paper Tape. Punched paper tape is used to provide direct input to a computer by means of a punched-tape reader, and also direct output from a computer, by means of a tape punch machine. (See Figure 13-5.) Data on paper tape are recorded in holes patterned along the length of the tape. The basic classification of paper tape is according

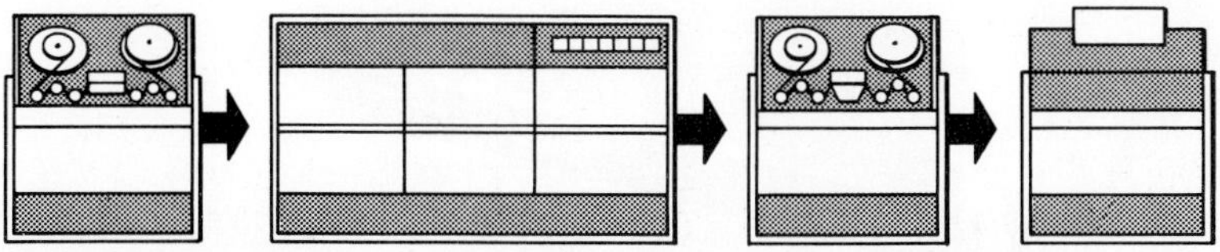

Figure 13-5

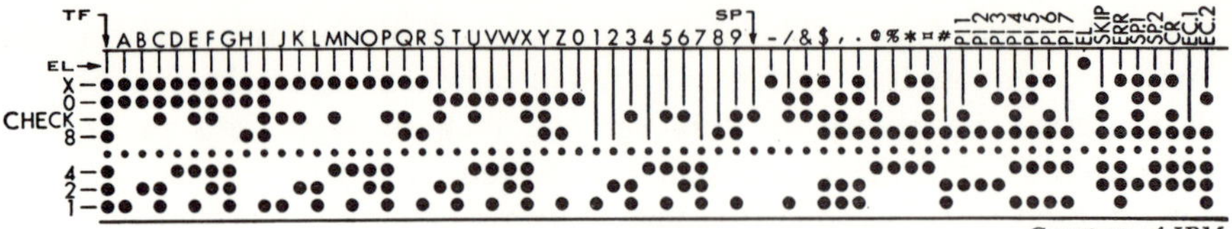

Courtesy of IBM

Figure 13-6. Paper tape 8-channel code

to the number of channels on it. Figure 13-6 shows the eight-channel tape, one of the most commonly used. A channel is an imaginary line which runs parallel to the edge of the tape. From the bottom, in an eight-channel tape, the channels are 1, 2, 4, 8, K, O, and X. A numeric, alphabetic, or special character is represented by one or a combination of holes in a given vertical column. The columns in a paper tape are similar to those in punched cards.

Disadvantages of punched paper tape are:

1. Compared to magnetic tape, it is very slow.
2. Unlike the typewriter or magnetic tape, it is difficult to make corrections or insert additional items in it.
3. Compared with the punched card, it is not as durable, neither is it as convenient to store, to file, or to handle.
4. It is difficult to reclassify information without first duplicating its contents into another form of unit record, such as the punched card.

Primary advantages of paper tape are:

1. It is used on several IBM machines. (Figure 13-7.) However, use as an input or output medium is somewhat limited in the business field.

Courtesy of IBM

Figure 13-7. IBM 382 paper tape reader

2. It is inexpensive and fairly cheap to produce (about 25 cents per 100 feet).
3. It is easier to mail than the punched card, and much lighter to handle.

G. Factors in the Preparation of a More Effective Input. It should be obvious that input must be sequenced and presented in a logical and accurate manner if we are to expect correct and meaningful results. When errors occur, they are made by the people who prepare the data for the computer's use. Because a computer can be no more accurate than its input, it is obvious that the input must be carefully and painstakingly prepared by people who have had formal training and practical experience under the supervision of "experts" in the field. Some of the common errors are: (1) A key-punch operator can punch the right information in the wrong field. (2) She can punch the wrong information in the right field. (3) She can punch the right data in the right field but omit an essential part of it. Such errors can be eliminated by the verification of each and every card before it is considered finally ready for input.

Another factor that can contribute to presenting input data more effectively is the "batching" or the accumulation of small decks into one larger file and processing it completely at one time. This will save time and money and reduce the possibility of error, because the large deck of cards is handled only once as input instead of several times, as it would be if it were in smaller batches.

II. Output devices

It is only logical to assume that all computers do process information and produce information which, when received, represent the last step in a business application. The way the result is received depends on the output device which is hooked to the system in use, and also on the specific features which it contains. Most output devices are capable of presenting the same result in various forms.

The input devices explained in this chapter are also used as output devices. The typewriter can be used as input, usually by depressing certain keys for feeding certain data into the program or by asking the computer for certain information concerning a specific account. The computer, on the other hand, can be connected to actuate the electric typewriter to print a message, showing the result or the answer to inquiry made earlier. In this function, keys are not depressed manually. The program stored in the computer directs the typewriter to print automatically.

The punched-card reader is used for input by transforming the holes in the data cards into electrical impulses upon the sensing of these holes by the wire brushes. The electrical impulses carry data into the storage section of the central processing unit. As output, the punch section of the same machine is used to receive the results of processing and to punch them in blank cards fed into the punch hopper in advance.

The magnetic-tape machine reads to the computer the data which the tape stores and also writes the results on tape for future reference. When it reads, it acts as input; when it writes, it acts as output.

The only other machine which is used exclusively in business applications as a means of output is referred to as the *printer*. The printer provides a permanent visual record of information as computer output. A printed statement is the most popular output medium to be presented to the human user—usually, to management. Depending upon the type of printer, its speed varies from 10 to 2,000 characters per second or up to 1285 lines per minute.

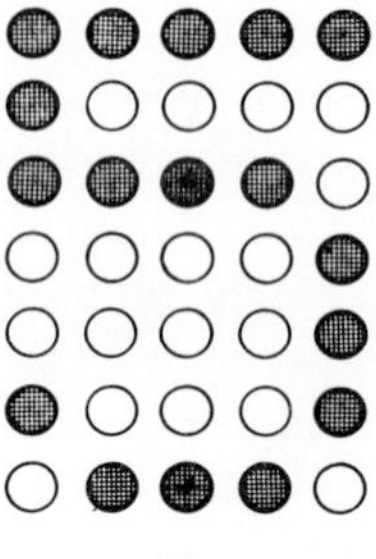

Figure 13-8

The primary printing devices used in printing computer output are the wire-matrix, the typewriter, the wheel, and the chain printer. The typewriter has been discussed previously. In the wire-matrix printer, small wires are arranged in the form of a usual 5 by 7 rectangle. (Figure 13-8.) The matrix moves along the line of the paper to print alphabetic, numeric, or special characters. The ends of the selected wires are pressed by a hammer against an inked ribbon, resulting in the printing of the data on paper.

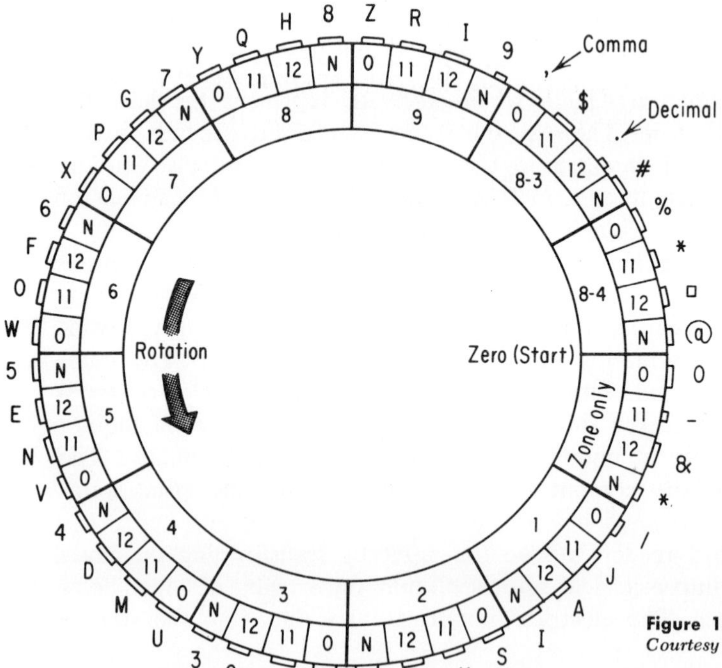

Figure 13-9. A print wheel
Courtesy of IBM

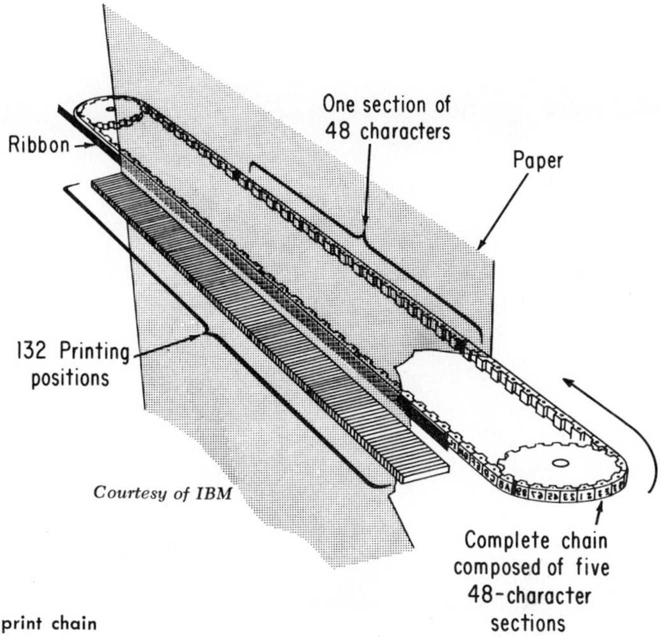

Figure 13-10. An IBM print chain

The wheel printer consists of 120 print wheels, each of which contains 10 digits, 26 letters, and 12 special characters. (Figure 13-9.) The 120 print wheels are aligned horizontally along the width of the paper and, upon printing, are positioned to print the desired information simultaneously. This means that the parallel method of printing is used and that up to 120 characters can be printed on a given line.

The chain printer is an electromechanical printer which utilizes five sections connected together to form a chain. Each of the sections contains 48 characters, to print 10 digits, 26 letters and 12 special characters. (Figure 13-10.) The chain revolves horizontally and is positioned behind the inked ribbon. The hammers, upon firing against the back of the paper, cause a character in the chain to press against the ribbon, resulting in the printing of that character on the form. Figure 13-11 shows the 1403 printer, which prints the output produced by the 1401 computer.

What Type of Output Format Is Considered the Best?

1. The output format should be usable. If a balance sheet is required, for instance, it should have the name of the company, the name of the statement, and the date. Each of these items would occupy a separate line and be centered correctly. Following this group, the assets section should be presented. Liabilities and proprietorship data follow next, after enough spacing is allowed between the total asset amount and the "Liabilities and Proprietorship" title. If the computer, instead, presented all

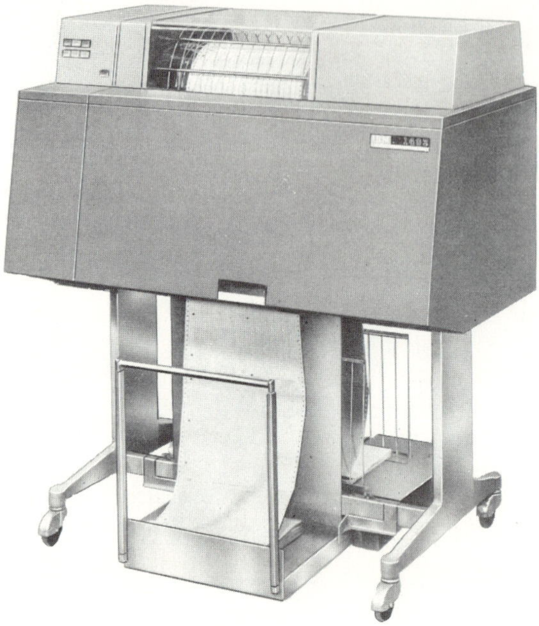

Figure 13-11. The IBM 1403 printer

these necessary facts on the same line or in the wrong order, the result would not be considered usable. In such a case, an adjustment should be made either in the output device, in the program itself by changing certain instructions, or in the presentation of the data input. The change in any of these three areas should be directed toward the improvement of the output format to meet the needs of the user.

2. The output information should be understandable to the user. This can be accomplished either by training the user to learn the machine language or to direct the computer to produce the output in simple form which can be easily understood. The latter alternative would be the more logical solution to the case, because it would be easiest for the user.

3. The output information must be relevant and complete. If, after examination of the output information, it is found that some data are lacking, the input information can be resequenced or revised in such a way as to aid in a more complete processing, leading to the attainment of more correct, more relevant, and more complete output information.

QUESTIONS FOR REVIEW

1. What are the roles of the input and output devices in a computer system? Explain.
2. What is a millisecond? A microsecond? How many microseconds are there in one millisecond?

3. What are the main uses of a typewriter as an auxiliary input device?
4. Explain the advantages of using punched cards as an input or output medium. Are there any disadvantages?
5. What are the two types of punched-card readers? What is the difference between them?
6. Explain how a punched card is read by a "brush-type" card reader. What is the function of the first read-check brushes? Why?
7. How is a punched-card reader used as an output device?
8. Describe a magnetic tape; a punched paper tape.
9. List and explain the advantages and disadvantages of paper tape.
10. Explain two main factors which contribute to preparing more effective input data.
11. What are the primary media that can be used for storing either input or output data?
12. What device is used exclusively as an output device? Describe it.
13. What is a wire matrix?
14. Describe the chain printer and tell how it operates.
15. What type of output format is considered the best? Explain.

Chapter 14

The Central Processing Unit—Primary Storage

Introduction

The central processing unit is the computer. It is the center of all data computations; without it, processing cannot be done. Its role in a computer system is analogous to the relationship of the human memory to man, or of the engine to the automobile. It is in the human memory that all computations and decisions are made affecting the daily activities of the person involved. The only difference is that the computer has to be instructed in detail by a human programmer before it *acts as* a human brain. It is, then, really more analogous to a reference book than to a human being's memory. Despite this, the term "memory" is used to describe it.

The central processing unit is the primary working mechanism in which needed data are stored as a first step in processing. Next, a decision is made about the type of computations to be performed on them. Storage of data in the central processing unit itself is referred to as internal, or *primary,* storage; storage of data anywhere else is referred to as external, or *secondary,* storage. The following example illustrates the difference between primary and secondary storage.

Every retailing firm, regardless of its size or sales volume, orders merchandise in quantities which often exceed its present needs or anticipated volume during a given period of time. Savings to be had through quantity purchasing, seasonal drop in the price of the merchandise, or price discount on quantities beyond a certain limit, say 100 items, would induce the retailer to order in large quantities. A common procedure followed is to fill the shelves on the sales floor with the merchandise they will hold and to store the rest in a stockroom. Merchandise placed on the sales floor is said to be in *primary storage,* whereas the extra merchandise stored in the stockroom is said to be in *secondary storage.* If a customer should want an item which is in secondary storage, the salesman will ask the customer to wait until the merchandise is delivered from the stockroom before the sale can be made. This process, although workable, is impractical, because it takes extra time and results in inconvenience to the customer. Therefore, to make sales efficiently, the salesman and the customer should have direct access to the merchandise.

The central processing unit, like the retail store, must have the needed information in internal storage to which it has convenient access before any decisions can be made with regard to the type of computations to be performed. It receives initial data from an input device in the same manner as the salesman on the sales floor receives merchandise from the stockroom at the beginning of the business day and more during the day, if needed. The average time it takes the computer to locate data or to recall information from any given memory location is called "Average Access Time." In primary storage, average access time is less than that in secondary storage, because data in primary storage is already within the computer, thus reducing the time it would take to recall data in secondary storage.

The "stockroom" of the central processing unit can be a punched-card reader, a magnetic-tape unit, a magnetic-disk machine, or other devices designed to transfer the information which the central processing unit might need later in the processing routine. The external-storage (or file memory) devices will be explained later.

Primary Storage

Regardless of the kinds of devices available, primary storage is any device into which business and related information can be placed which will retain information temporarily or permanently until used, and out of which the same information can be obtained any number of times. It is often referred to as "working memory," because computations and other processing routines are "worked" in it. Data stored outside the computer system are usually in a file cabinet. The external devices retaining such data are called *file storage devices.* Therefore, external storage is called *file storage* or *file memory.*

Characteristics of primary storage

1. Immediate Access to Data Stored in Memory. For the arithmetic and logic units to operate efficiently, the stored information in working memory should be accessible immediately at high speed. In other words, the access time to data in primary memory should be as close to zero as possible in order to keep the speed of delivery as high as possible.

2. Reusability. The primary-storage device, whether it is a magnetic core, magnetic drum, or other kind of device, should be capable of erasing unneeded data and storing new data in its place. In other words, it should act in the same manner as a tape recorder which is capable of erasing previous recordings every time a new recording is made on the same tape. Most of the primary-storage devices have this characteristic.

3. Permanent Recording of Data Already in Storage. In cases of electric failure, the primary-storage device should be capable of retaining any data permanently regardless of the presence or absence of electrical power. A processing unit cannot be expected to produce results unless the memory of the computer is designed to retain vital data if the electricity goes off. It should be able to retain data until they are no longer needed, at which time they may be erased purposely by the introduction and storage of other needed information by a human operator. Most primary-storage devices used in commercial computers retain data permanently.

However, some primary-storage devices lose their stored data temporarily during read out; that is, when certain information is read from storage to be used elsewhere for processing purposes. This is referred to as *destructive read out.* Since primary-storage devices are designed to retain the original data permanently and correctly, they restore the original information automatically as it is being "read out."

4. Automatic or Self-Checking Ability. In order to ascertain the accuracy of the data represented in storage, a primary-storage device should have an automatic self-checking feature. This is called "Parity Check." The computer counts the number of bits of information in storage in such a way that, upon the destruction or loss of any single bit, it signals on the console that an error has been made, thus stopping the computer. The operator can then determine the type of error and its location by manipulating certain switches.

5. Durability. Unlike a punched card, which wears out in time, primary-storage devices are built to last permanently in spite of the constant storing and restoring of data in them. It is neither convenient nor cheap to the user to replace, or frequently repair, a primary-storage device.

6. Compact Size. A primary storage device should be physically small, yet capable of storing a large amount of data, because space is always at a premium. Although it is the most expensive such device, magnetic-core memory is the most compact.

Main Types of Primary Storage

I. Magnetic-core storage

This is a very popular and practical storage medium, and one that is used in most commercial computers. A magnetic core is a doughnut-shaped ring of ferromagnetic material that measures about one-sixteenth of an inch on the outside diameter. *Ferro* hints at the presence of iron, and the word *magnetic* indicates that the material can be magnetized. A magnetic core can be magnetized fast and is highly retentive, capable of retaining its magnetism almost indefinitely, unless demagnetized.

Owing to the importance of speed, cores are made very small, because they can thus switch faster and require less magnetizing force to change their status. The magnetizing force is generated by running a heavy current through two wires, usually called *X* and *Y*, passing through the core. (Figure 14-1.)

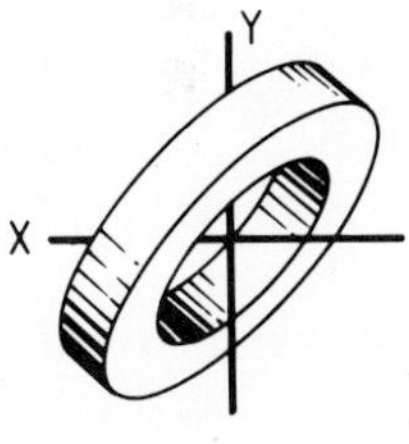

Figure 14-1. A magnetic core with two current-carrying wires

Advantages of Magnetic-Core Storage. 1. DEPENDABILITY: A magnetic core can be magnetized easily to represent data. Data stored in it are an indestructible part of the permanent memory.

2. DURABILITY: A magnetic core does not wear out or deteriorate with age because it is an immovable part which does not rely upon physical motion for its operation.

3. HIGH-SPEED ACCESS: Access time is faster in magnetic-core memory than in any of the other memory devices. In a magnetic core, the output of the desired data is not under a "read" head, as is usually the case in using a magnetic drum, for instance. Each bit of information

is stored in a separate magnetic core ready to read or write. Fast switching of a core is one of its characteristics.

4. LOW-COST OPERATION: The operating cost of a magnetic core is considered low. It does not use any power to retain the data it stores. The only time it uses power is when new data are being stored.

5. LARGE CAPACITY: Because each magnetic core measures about one-sixteenth of an inch, there are a great number of cores in the primary storage of the computer. Memories with 100,000 cores or more are not uncommon in large-size computers.

The Binary Mode. Most computers store data by using the binary mode. This is a numerical system that uses only two digits, namely, *0* and *1*. It can be compared to a light bulb which can be either energized (turned on) or de-energized (turned off). If the only values used are zero and one, how does a computer represent values greater than one? To explain this, a brief review of our decimal system will be helpful.

In the decimal system, ten digits are used. They are: *0, 1, 2, 3, 4, 5, 6, 7, 8,* and *9*. When a value greater than nine is desired, two digits are needed. The first value greater than nine is ten. *Ten* means no value of the first digit (referred to as the *units* position) plus one ten of the second digit (referred to as the *tens* position). *Forty-two* means two values of the units position plus four tens of the tens position or $(2 \times 1) + (4 \times 10) = 42$. Assume that a value greater than two digits is desired. A third digit is added on the left, referred to as the *100's* position. For example:

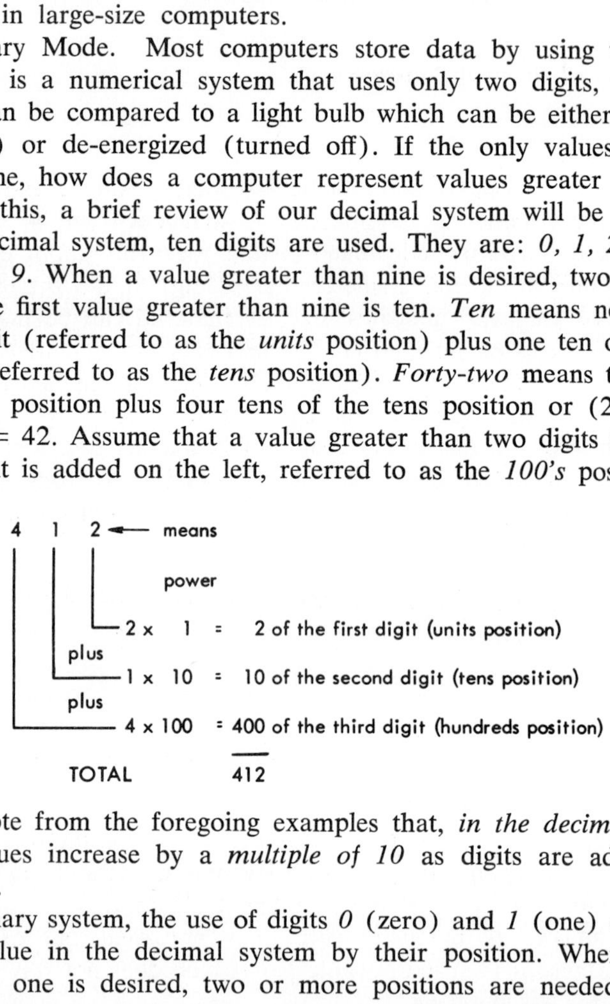

You will note from the foregoing examples that, *in the decimal system,* position values increase by a *multiple of 10* as digits are added from right to left.

In the binary system, the use of digits *0* (zero) and *1* (one) can represent any value in the decimal system by their position. When a value greater than one is desired, two or more positions are needed. For instance, *1 0* (one, zero) in binary means that the first digit position does not have any value, while a *1* in the second position designates two. The number is two, because the first digit on the right occupying the first position is equal to zero, while a *1* in second position is equal to two, because $1 \times$ the position is equal to 2.

You should remember that it is the position of a zero or a one that makes it possible for these two binary digits to represent equivalent values in the decimal system. Because 0 × the position equals zero, *1 1* (one, one) in binary means 1 × the position (1) = 1, *plus* 1 × position (2) = 2; or a total of 3. When a value greater than three is required, a third place position is added, having a value of four, because *the value of each position after the first increases in multiples of two.*

```
1  0  0  in binary means:
|  |  |
|  |  |        power
|  |  |
|  |  └─0  of  1  or  0 x 1 = 0
|  | plus
|  └────0  of  2  or  0 x 2 = 0
|   plus
└───────1  of  4  or  1 x 4 = 4
The binary number 1 0 0, then,  = 4 in decimal
```

In the binary system, values of digits increase by a *multiple of two* as they are added from right to left, instead of ten, as is true in the decimal system.

The magnetic core, used in computers as a storage device, has only two definite states: the *0* (zero) and *1* (one). A core can store either a *1*-bit or a *0*-bit of information. If values greater than one have to be stored in core, then more than one core is needed. For example, to store a decimal value of two, two cores are needed: one to represent the zero-bit and one to the left of the first to represent a one-bit, because in binary "two" means *1 0*. (Figure 14-2.) Data stored in magnetic core are referred to as "bits." The word *bit* is a condensation of the words binary digit.

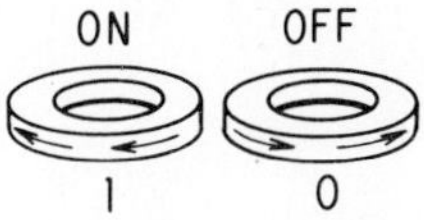

Figure 14-2. Two magnetic cores representing the decimal value 2 in the binary mode

Magnetic-Core Storage of Data. Data are stored in core by the use of magnetism. A core can be magnetized in either of two directions: clockwise or counterclockwise. When it is magnetized clockwise, it is said to be ON, as it represents a one-bit. (Figure 14-3.) When it is magnetized counterclockwise, it is said to be OFF, because it represents a zero-bit. (Figure 14-4.)

Cores are arranged in the manner of a matrix strung on a screen of wires, the horizontal ones being the *X* wires and the vertical ones, the *Y* wires. Each core has an *X* wire and a *Y* wire running through it at right angles to each other. It can be set to a *1* state by sending one-half of

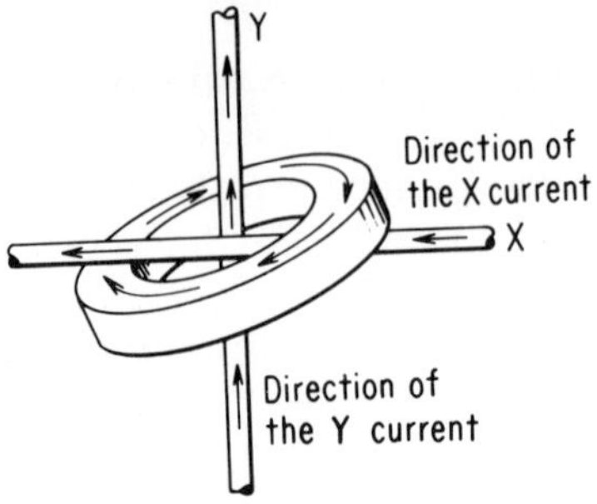

Figure 14-3. A magnetic core in a 1-bit status

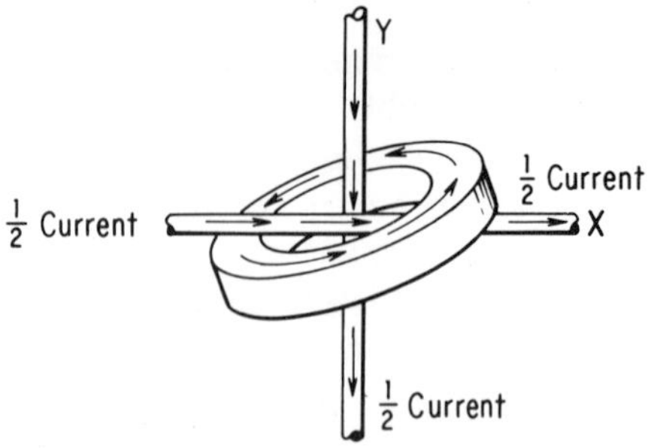

Figure 14-4. A magnetic core in a 0-bit status

the total amount of current necessary to magnetize it in that way (clockwise) through the *X* wire and the other half through the *Y* wire. To magnetize a core clockwise, current is sent through the *X* wire from right to left and through the *Y* wire from bottom to top. (Figure 14-3.) The core can be set to a zero state by sending the flow of current through the *X* and *Y* wires in the opposite directions. (Figure 14-4.) The polarity, that is, the clockwise or counterclockwise direction of magnetization, of a core depends upon the direction of the current flowing through the *X* and *Y* wires.

These bits of information (cores) are used to represent either a digit, a letter, or a special character. The CPU can be programmed to select any one of these without disturbing the others. Such an arrangement of wires is referred to as a *magnetic-core plane*. (Figure 14-6.)

Reading a Magnetic Core. When a particular core is read, one-half of the total amount of necessary current is sent through each of the *X* and *Y* wires. In Figure 14-6, one-half of the current was sent through the X^2 wire, and one-half of it through the Y^2 wire. *Only the core at the intersection of the two wires receives the full current.* That particular core is said to be *selected*. All other cores strung on the X^2 wire retain their

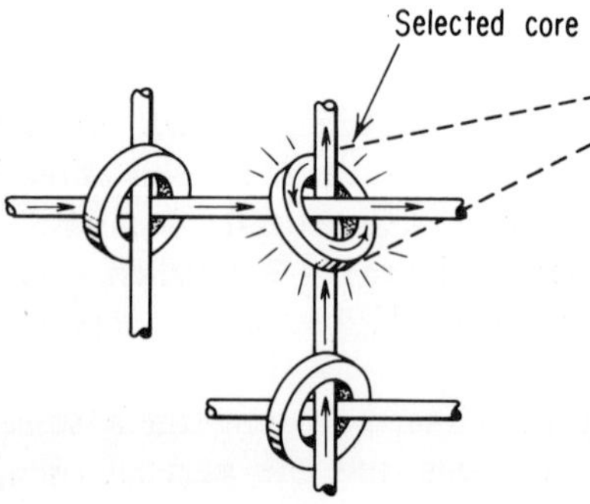

Figure 14-5. A selected core

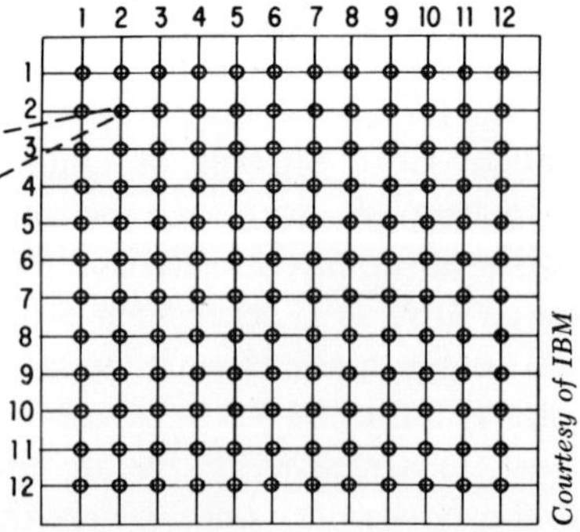

Figure 14-6. A magnetic core plane

status, because each of them receives only one-half of the current necessary to magnetize them, that is, X^2 current only. They are said to be "half-selected." Figure 14-5 shows a blown-up schematic of the "selected" core at the intersection of the X^2 and Y^2 wires.

One of the unfortunate features of the use of magnetic-core storage is the fact that it necessitates the use of a third wire, called a *sense wire,* which restores the information readout, because the readout process is destructive. After the data have been read, the cores containing the data revert to zero and, of course, no longer hold the original data put into them. Only if the core has been in the *0*-bit status originally would it remain unchanged.

In order to restore the original data to the *1*-bit status which readout has destroyed, a third wire is inserted through each core. It is called a *sense wire.* (Figure 14-7.) When a particular core representing a *1*-bit of data is read, it clears to zero. This action induces current in the sense

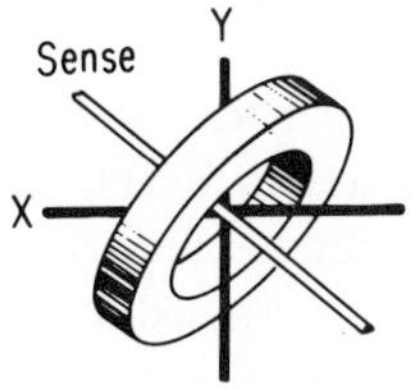

Figure 14-7. A magnetic core showing the X, Y, and sense wires

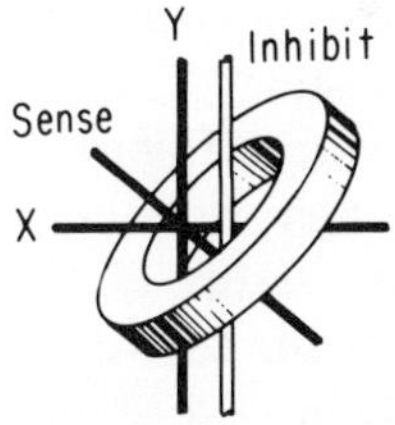

Figure 14-8. A magnetic core showing the inhibit wire

wire which signals that *1*-bit should be restored to that particular core. Then the circuitry immediately writes in the *1*-bit by reversing the current flowing through the *X* and *Y* wires of that core, so that the core is once again magnetized in a clockwise direction. However, if the selected core originally stored a zero-bit, no current enters the sense wire, and the core retains its status. The sense wire is activated only in a reading operation where a magnetic core originally representing a *1*-bit was cleared to zero as a result of readout.

Writing-in a Magnetic Core. The process of writing data in a magnetic core is somewhat more complex. Writing-in a core involves either restoring the information previously stored in it or replacing it with new information. When data are written-in a core, one-half of the necessary current is sent through each of the *X* and *Y* wires in *exactly the opposite direction of that used in readout.* That is, to write-in information, the current travels from left to right through the *X* wire and from top to bottom through the *Y* wire. To read out information, the current travels in the opposite directions through the *X* and *Y* wires.

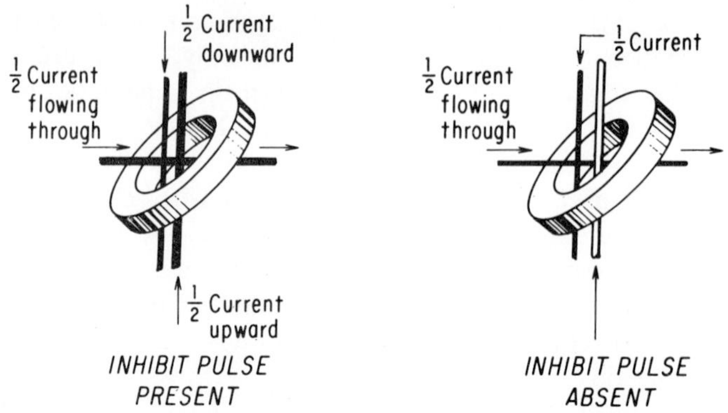

Figure 14-9. Left—the presence of an inhibit current; right—the absence of an inhibit current

The *X* and *Y* wires cannot distinguish between *0*'s and *1*'s. They merely carry current. Because at times certain cores must be coded to represent a *0*-bit, some technique is required so that these cores can be kept in this state. This necessitates the addition of a fourth wire, called the *inhibit* wire. (Figure 14-8.) It is inserted parallel to the *Y* wire and extends through every core in storage. Its main function, if activated, is to maintain the status of the *0*-bit cores by preventing *1*-bits from being written in them, as would be done normally if the procedure were not interfered with.

For example, the normal write-in procedure causes one-half of the current to flow through the *X* wire from left to right and the other half through the *Y* wire from top to bottom. To preserve the *0*-bits in their original states, only one-half of the current can be allowed to flow through them, because they would be magnetized clockwise if the full charge were permitted to pass through them. To accomplish this, the computer passes one-half of the amount of the necessary current through the inhibit wire from bottom to top. This flow neutralizes the one-half current flowing through the *X* wire, with the result that the *0*-cores have only the current from the *Y* wires flowing through them. Because this is not sufficient to disturb their original magnetization as *0*-bits, this procedure, using the inhibit wire, preserves them as *0*-bit cores. If it were not used, they would become *1*-bit cores. (Figure 14-9.)

In summary, then, the function of the four wires is:

1-2. *X* and *Y* wires are used for readout and/or writing-in magnetic cores.

3. The sense wire is used only in a read operation to determine if a given core is in a *1*-bit or a *0*-bit state.
4. The inhibit wire is used in the write operation only if it is decided that a given core is to represent a zero state.

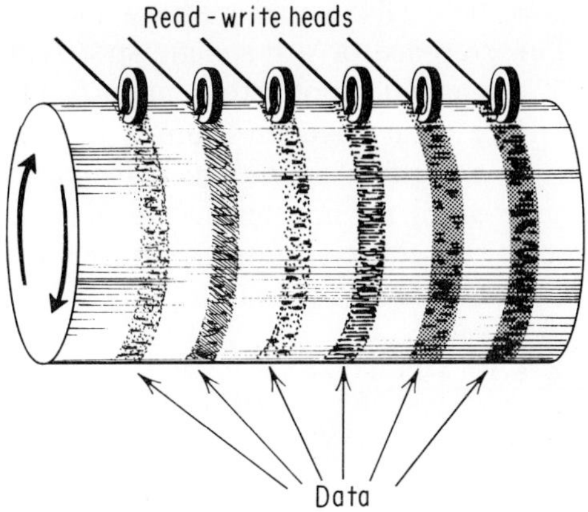

Figure 14-10. A magnetic drum schematic

II. Magnetic drum

The second type of data-storage device is the magnetic drum. A magnetic drum is a high-quality, precision steel cylinder enclosed in a copper sleeve. The copper sleeve is coated with a magnetic-material coating on which data may be written at high speed. (Figure 14-10.)

To date, drums and cores have proved to be the most practical of all the devices used for primary storage of data. Magnetic-core storage is used widely in medium-size to large-size commercial computers, because of its high speed. Magnetic drums, although not as fast as magnetic cores, are, nevertheless, used for primary storage of large amounts of data. They are also used extensively for external or secondary storage. Magnetic-drum memory is found mostly in small- to medium-size computers.

Data Storage and Processing on Magnetic Drums. Reading from and writing on a magnetic drum is accomplished by devices called *Read-Write Heads*. There are a series of parallel read-write heads, each of which is capable of reading and writing binary configuration as a result of electrical pulses received by it. Once written, the data may be read back indefinitely. Recording on magnetic drums is basically the same technique used as for the audio tape recorder, except that the latter machine records an audio signal whereas the magnetic drum records electrical pulses. (Figure 14-11.)

In a writing operation, as the drum rotates at constant speed, a current passes through the coil of a particular *write head*. This sets up a mag-

Figure 14-11. Left—home tape recording; right—magnetic drum recording

netic field (flux) and places a magnetic spot on the surface of the drum. The presence of a magnetic spot represents a *1*-bit of data. The absence of a magnetic spot represents a *0*-bit of data. Written information on the surface of a magnetic drum is in the binary mode.

In a reading operation, the magnetized spot on the surface of a magnetic drum passing under the head induces an output signal through the coil. The coil transfers the signal to the operating circuitry. In this way, reading recorded data on a drum is made possible. It is retained and read back as many times as necessary. Reading from a magnetic drum *is not destructive,* because the condition of a magnetic spot representing the *1* binary digit is not changed or erased when it passes under the *read head.* Therefore, magnetic-drum storage is permanent, and data can be so stored indefinitely even when power is turned off. The only time that data are destroyed is when new data are written in the same location.

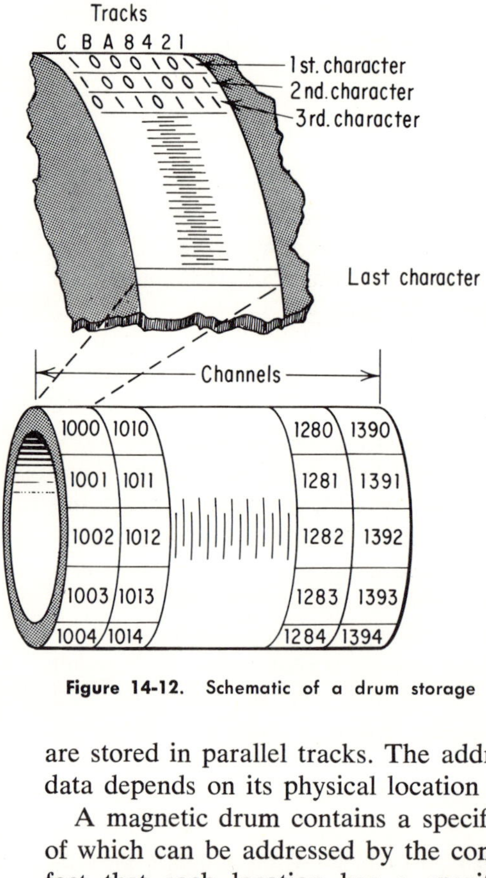

Figure 14-12. Schematic of a drum storage

A magnetic drum is divided into several channels across its length. (Figure 14-12.) Each channel has a read-write head which performs the reading and writing operations of all the storage locations in it. In other words, the binary digits representing data are stored in parallel tracks. The address (location number) of any given data depends on its physical location on the drum.

A magnetic drum contains a specific number of storage locations, each of which can be addressed by the computer. This is possible owing to the fact that each location has a specific number or an address. (Figure 14-12.) Each channel contains many characters (for storage) around the drum. If the contents of location number (address) 1004 is desired, for instance, the head designated to that particular channel which includes 1004 is activated. The time it takes to begin reading the data (access time) varies, depending upon many factors: (1) the distance to be traveled by that location to the head, (2) the physical dimensions of the magnetic drum, (3) the number and types of heads used, (4) the arrangement of data, and (5) the speed of rotation of the drum.

Some of the Advantages of a Magnetic Drum as a Storage Device.

1. HIGH STORAGE CAPACITY. A magnetic drum is a short, fat memory. Its high capacity to store data is one of its main advantages. Its speed is moderate, the most popular being 3,600 revolutions per minute (r.p.m.), although ultra-fast drums, rotating at a little less than 10,000 r.p.m., have been developed. This speed is considered adequate in small-size computers, but not as satisfactory in large computers that demand access time of a fraction of that of the magnetic drum.

2. NO ACCELERATION PROBLEM. A magnetic drum rotates at a constant speed, a fact which eliminates any acceleration problem. The latter problem is often present in other storage devices, an example of which is magnetic tape, in reading and/or writing operations.

QUESTIONS FOR REVIEW

1. Explain the difference between primary and secondary storage. Give an example to illustrate.
2. What are the characteristics of primary storage? Explain each characteristic briefly.
3. What is meant by "destructive readout"? What is "parity check"?
4. Describe a magnetic core.
5. What advantages are there in the use of a magnetic core for primary storage?
6. Explain briefly the difference between the decimal and the binary systems.
7. "A magnetic core has only two definite states." What are they? Explain.
8. Draw a magnetic core, showing clockwise magnetization.
9. What is a "magnetic-core plane"?
10. How can a given magnetic core be set to a *0*-state? To a *1*-state?
11. If the *X* and *Y* wires are used to carry current, then what is the purpose of the sense wire?
12. When is a magnetic core referred to as a "selected" core?
13. How are data read from magnetic cores?
14. How are data written in a magnetic core?
15. In what case does current flow through the inhibit wire? Explain.
16. What is a magnetic drum? Draw a schematic, showing a magnetic drum and the location of five read-write heads.
17. What is the primary difference between audio and magnetic-drum recording?
18. Explain briefly the recording and reading operations on a magnetic drum.
19. Is reading from a magnetic drum destructive? Why?
20. Describe the uses and function of a magnetic-drum channel.
21. What factors determine the access time for reading the data from a magnetic drum?
22. List and explain briefly the two main advantages of a magnetic drum.

Chapter 15

The Central Processing Unit—Secondary Storage

Why External Memory?

Business data-processing applications involve thousands of transactions and a great amount of related data. It is impossible for a large-scale computer to store all these data internally and still have enough room for processing them. Even if the computer were built large enough to accommodate them in primary storage, it would be impractical, because the computer can work on one transaction at a time only. Although access time would be much faster if all the related facts were available in primary storage, the cost of building a computer large enough to eliminate the need for secondary storage would be prohibitive. In the retail-store example, the firm could build a sales floor large enough to accommodate all available merchandise and do away with the stockroom. This would, however, be impractical, because the salesman deals with only one or two customers a day for any particular item, and unnecessary storage on the sales floor would limit the amount of efficient working space. Thus, it would be both impractical and unnecessary to attempt to eliminate the use of secondary storage, the stockroom. The same is true in the case of secondary storage in a computer system. In both cases, the advantage gained in access time would be reduced drastically, if not lost altogether, because of the new problems created by such a solution.

Why Magnetic Tape?

One of the major characteristics of a large-scale commercial data-processing computer system is its ability to process data and move any pertinent information into and out of the machine at high speed. This is accomplished by the use of a medium called *magnetic tape,* which is much faster than the punched card, paper tape, or almost any other secondary-storage medium. Magnetic tape is used as a chief source of input and output, its role being to store information until it is needed by the computer. Magnetic tape is used, then, mainly in three areas: (1) as an input medium, (2) as an output medium, and (3) as a secondary-storage medium. In any of these areas, magnetic tape is regarded as external memory, because its main function is to store information to be used later by the computer for processing.

What Is a Magnetic Tape?

Have you ever seen the plastic tape used in home tape recording? Magnetic tape used for electronic data processing is similar to the regular tape used in a home tape recorder. The only difference is that the former is much wider and is of better quality than the latter. Magnetic tape used in electronic data-processing machines is one-half to one inch wide and 1,200 to 3,000 feet long per reel of tape.

IBM magnetic tape is a plastic tape coated with a metallic oxide on one side only. It is ½″ wide and comes in two popular lengths: 1,200 and 2,400 feet.

Magnetic tape is a *sequential*-file storage medium, which means that the first record written on it must be read before the second record, the second before the third, and so forth. Assume that we have 10 records written on tape in the proper numeric sequence, that is, 01, 02, 03, 04, 05, 06, 07, 08, 09, and 10. If, for instance, record 06 is needed for processing, records 01, 02, 03, 04, and 05 must be read before record

06 moves under the reading head. Sequential-file storage is ideal where regular updating of records, such as customers' accounts, is necessary. Access time of each record to primary storage for processing purposes is faster than is the case with other secondary-storage media. Time is not wasted, because the computer does not have to search for the desired record, because each customer's account is in alphabetic or numeric sequence on the tape. In applications that require reading records scattered here and there on the tape, access time is slower than in a continuous operation such as periodic updating of every account.

How are data represented on magnetic tape?

Numeric, alphabetic, or special characters are represented on tape by means of a coding technique similar to that of the punched card. This technique is called the *seven-bit character code.* (Figure 15-1.)

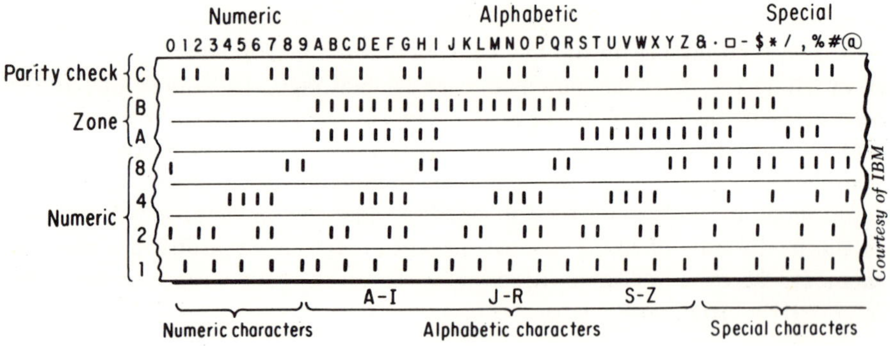

Figure 15-1. The 7-bit character code

Data are recorded on the seven parallel, horizontal channels, or tracks, along the tape. The seven recording channels are labeled *1, 2, 4, 8, A, B,* and *C*. Positions across the width of the tape represent one column of data or one character. The seven-bit positions are recorded by means of read-write heads, each of which is assigned to one of the seven channels. In Figure 15-1, a dash (|) in a given square stands for the presence of a magnetic spot, which means the same as a one-bit in the binary mode.

Numeric characters can be recorded on tape by using the lower four-bit positions; that is, bit positions 1, 2, 4, and 8. Each of these bits corresponds to a position value in the binary mode. For example, numeric character *6* is represented by the presence of two magnetic spots: one spot in 4 and another spot in 2 or a total of 6. Zero may be coded arbitrarily as *8* plus *2,* although other combinations may be used. The manner in which it is coded depends upon the make of computer under consideration. The top channel (parity check) will be discussed later.

Alphabetic characters are represented on tape in a manner similar to that used to represent them in a punched card. Each letter is represented by a combination of numeric and zero-bit positions. The alphabet is divided into three sections:

1. Each of the letters *A* through *I* is represented by zone bits A and B, in addition to the use of the numeric bits. For example, letter *A* would be represented by three magnetic spots: one each in A and B zones and one in numeric one-bit position. (See Figure 15-1.) In a punched card, letter *A* is represented by one punch in zone 12 (zone-punching position) and another punch in digit 1 (digit-punching position).

2. Each of the letters *J* through *R* is represented by zone bit B, in addition to the use of numeric bit values 1 through 9. For example, letter *J* would be represented by two magnetic spots: the B zone bit and another spot in numeric one-bit position (Figure 15-1). In a punched card, *J* is represented by two punches: one punch in zone 11 (zone punching position) and another in digit 1 (digit-punching position).

3. Each of the letters *S* through *Z* is represented by zone bit A, in addition to the use of the numeric bit positions 1, 2, 4, and 8. For instance, letter *S* is represented by means of two magnetic spots, one in zone bit A and another in the two-bit position. Letter *S* in a punched card is represented by a zero punch (zone) and a *2* punch (digit). In writing, spacing between columns is done automatically by the magnetic-tape unit. Special characters can also be coded. The code selected for each special character should be clear and entirely dissimilar to that of any other coded character.

Parity check

The six channels discussed are adequate for recording numeric, alphabetic, and/or special characters. Why, then, is there a need for the top, or seventh channel? This channel is used for checking the coding of the others. Magnetic spots on tape can be erased accidentally or obscured because of dust, dirt, or cracking of the oxide coating. To ascertain the correctness of data during tape reading or tape writing, the number of magnetized spots, or one-bits, representing each character are counted. This is called "Parity Check."

In Figure 15-1, the number of magnetized spots, or one-bits, in channels 1, 2, 4, 8, A, and B is counted vertically. If the total is odd, a magnetic spot is made in the parity check (C) channel on the top. However, if the total number of one-bits in the six channels is even, nothing is recorded in the "check" channel. This technique is called even parity check or "even parity." The goal is to have each character represented on the tape by an even number of one-bits, because the computer cannot operate if they are odd.

As an illustration, a description of the formation of digit 7 follows. Digit 7 is represented by three one-bits: one-bit of 4 plus one-bit of 2 plus one-bit of 1. The machine counts the one-bits in 4, 2, and 1. Because the total (3) is odd, it adds one more bit to the "check" position in channel 7 to make the total even. This parity check is made on both alphabetic and numeric information. If a bit is lost—for example, while data is being transferred from one device to another in the system—the signal for error appears and the machine stops, because the remaining bits equal an odd number.

A question commonly raised is what would happen if two-bits were lost for one character instead of one-bit, in which case the count would be even and the computer could not detect the loss by an even parity check. Although such an occurrence is rare, it can be avoided by using a horizontal parity check on each record. In this instance, the machine counts the number of one-bits in each of the seven channels. At the end of the record, a check character is added to each channel that contains an odd number of one-bits. Therefore, during readout, parity check is active vertically per column and horizontally per channel.

Instead of even parity check, some machines follow odd-parity check. The idea is the same, except that a check character is made in the check

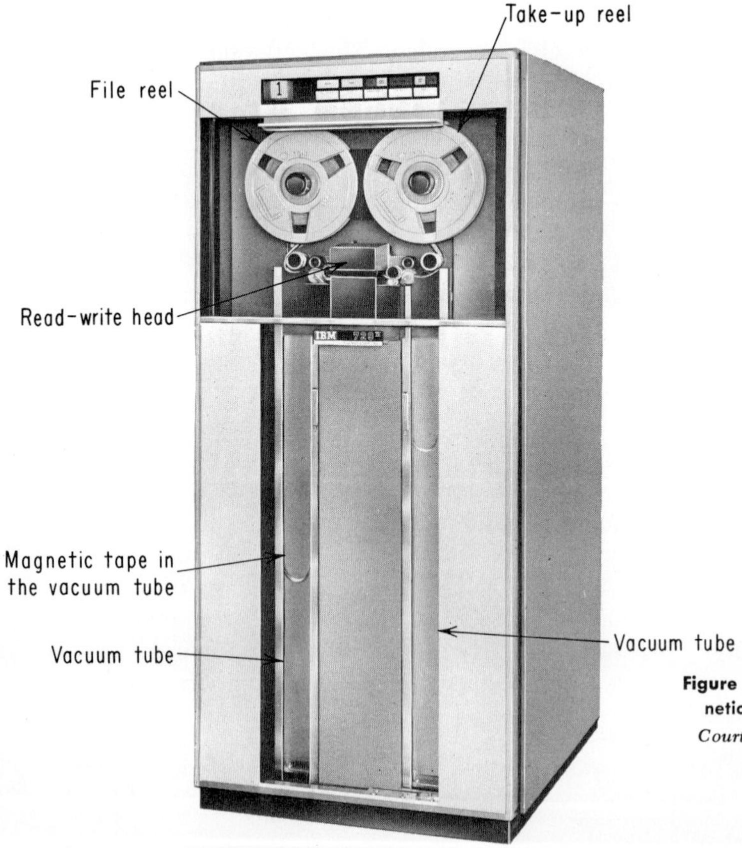

Figure 15-2. IBM 729 IV magnetic tape unit
Courtesy of IBM

channel only when the total number of one-bits representing a given character is even. In this case, an even number of bits causes the machines to signal an error and stop the operation.

The magnetic-tape unit

The magnetic-tape unit is used both as an input device and as an output device. It transports tape from one reel to another as it passes the read-write head in the actual reading or writing of information. (Figure 15-2.)

In preparing the reading or writing operation, the data tape, or file-tape reel, is mounted (loaded) on the left side and an empty reel, called *take-up reel,* is mounted on the right side. The tape from the left reel is threaded past the read-write head to the take-up reel. Because of the high speed involved in starting and stopping, a loop in the tape drops (floats) in the two vacuum tubes acting as buffers against tape breakage. The slack that this permits absorbs tension during the sudden burst of speed generated by a read instruction from the computer. As the tape in the left vacuum tube is drawn by the take-up reel, it is replenished by the file reel immediately above it. As the tape loop in the right vacuum tube begins to reach the bottom, an "electronic eye" actuates the take-up reel to take up the slack automatically.

When a reading or writing operation is completed, the data tape is wound around the take-up reel. It is important for the operator to rewind the tape and store it on the original reel, leaving the take-up reel empty for another application. The take-up reel is commonly referred to as a "machine reel."

When rewinding takes place, the tape is drawn from the vacuum tubes and fed directly from the take-up reel back to the file reel, that is, from right to left. (Figure 15-3.) During the initial part of the rewind opera-

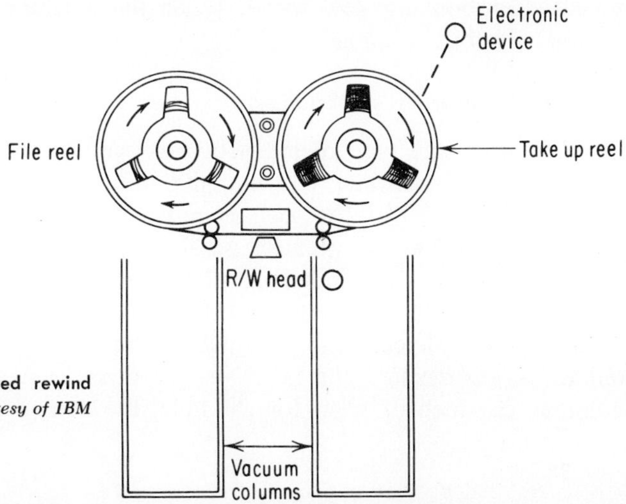

Figure 15-3. High-speed rewind
Courtesy of IBM

tions, the machine goes into a high-speed rewind until it reaches a predetermined distance from the end of the reel. At this point, the machine stops immediately and pauses for an instant. During the pause, a tape loop drops in both vacuum columns and then, at low speed, the machine rewinds the few feet of remaining tape. (Figure 15-4.) The latter part of the rewind operation is considered a safety measure which prevents

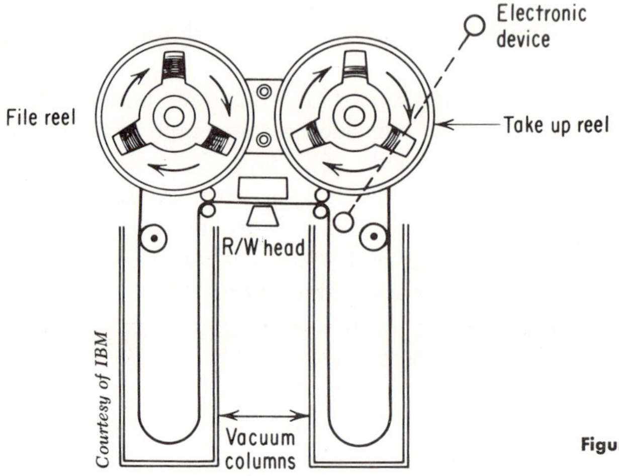

Figure 15-4. Slow-speed rewind

the machine from rewinding the entire tape at high speed, subjecting it to a possible break.

The machine is stopped just before the end of the tape by an electronic device. The device emits a beam which, at the beginning of the rewind operation, is blocked by the tape on the take-up reel (Figure 15-3). When enough tape is rewound on the file reel, the electronic beam makes contact with another device underneath the reel (Figure 15-4). This causes the tape unit to stop, forces the tape into the vacuum tubes, and throws the rewind operation into low speed. When the machine reaches the end of the tape, it stops automatically.

Density of the recorded information

Depending upon the type of magnetic-tape unit used, data may be recorded at a density between 100 and 800 bits per channel and a tape speed of from 50 to 200 inches per second.

Density is defined as the greatest possible number of columns of data that can be recorded on a unit length of tape. The unit used is usually an inch. The present densities used by IBM magnetic-tape recording units are 200 or 556 columns per inch of tape. The former density is referred to as *LO* density; the latter, as *HI* density. At a HI density of 556 columns per inch of tape, for example, the contents of about seven punched cards of 80 columns each can be stored; that is, 80 times seven equals 560. Some tape-recording units are capable of writing on tape at a super-HI density of 800 columns per inch. The faster the speed and the higher the density used, the greater is the rate at which data are read from, or written on, tape.

Format of a magnetic tape

The format of a magnetic tape is similar to the table of contents of a speech or a term paper. The first part is usually the introduction; the second part, the main body of the paper; and the third part, a summary of the report. Similarly, the contents of a magnetic tape run are typically as follows: (1) the load point, (2) the main information, and (3) the end-of-file indicator.

1. The Load Point. The load point is a reflective spot coated on one side with magnetic material and having adhesive on the other side. It measures about 1″ × 3⁄16″. It is located on the top edge of the shiny side where recording is not done. (Figure 15-5.) Photoelectric cells in the tape unit sense the label and interpret it as the beginning of the usable portion of the tape where writing or reading is to begin. A space of at least 10 feet from the beginning of the tape is recommended for the load point location. Usually, it is located between 12 and 15 feet from the beginning of the tape.

2. The End-of-file Indicator. The end-of-file indicator is also a reflective spot, or marker, coated on one side with magnetic material and having adhesive on the other side. It, too, measures 1″ × 3⁄16″. It differs from the load point in that it is used to indicate the end of the reel or when writing is to stop. It is recommended that it be placed about 18 feet from the end of the tape. It is located on the shiny side of the tape and on the side farthest from the person looking at it. (Figure 15-6.)

3. The Main Information. The data to be written on tape can be located anywhere between the load point and the end-of-file indicator. Records on tape are not restricted to fixed length, as is the case in a punched card.

Figure 15-5. Load point

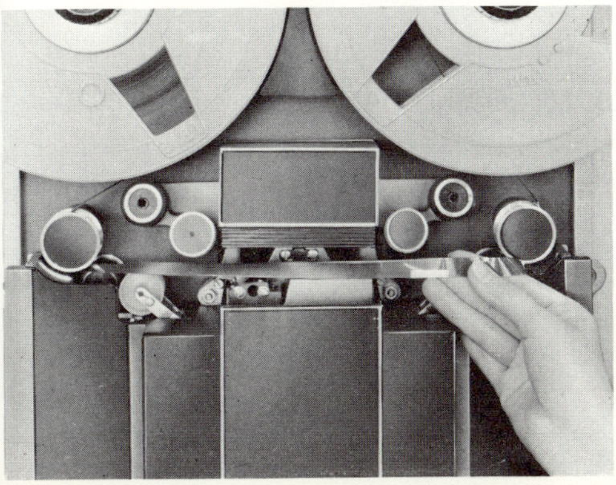

Figure 15-6. End-of-file indicator

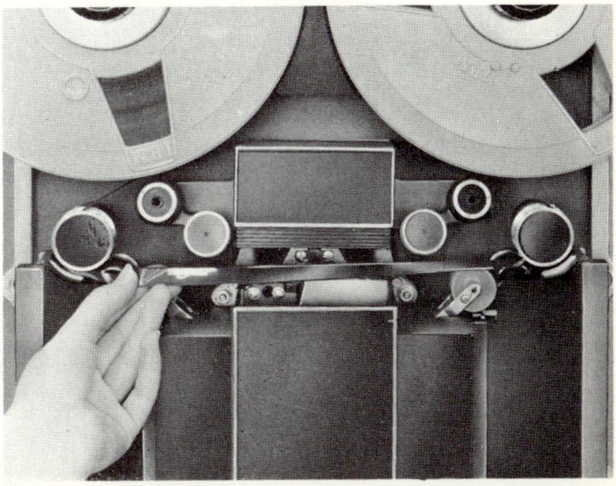

Courtesy of IBM

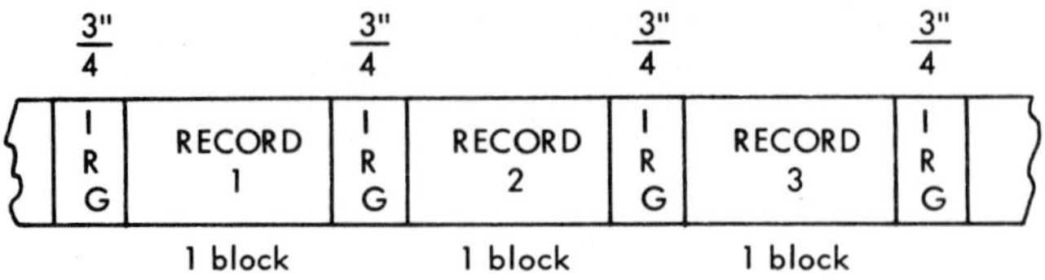

Figure 15-7. An example of interrecord gap. Also showing a single-record block

A record can be of any length within the area of the tape allowed for writing records. One record is separated from another record by a space which is referred to as an "interrecord gap," abbreviated *IRG.* (Figure 15-7.)

The interrecord gap serves two purposes: (1) to separate one logical tape record from another logical tape record; (2) to allow for the waste of tape caused by acceleration and deceleration every time a new record is read. The interrecord gap measures about three-fourths of an inch. The tape unit wastes about three-eighths of an inch every time it decelerates to a stop and also three-eighths of an inch when it accelerates to read or write the next sequential record: a total of three-fourths of an inch. The gap between records is made automatically. Each record on a tape is considered as one block and is called a *single-record block.*

Normally, a record is at least 14 characters in size. For purposes of clarity, assume that each record on a given tape averages 55 characters and can be written at a density of 556 characters per inch. This means that each record is stored on one-tenth of an inch of tape bordered by two interrecord gaps (one before and another after the record), occupying a total of 1½ inches of tape. It is clear at this point, then, that a lot of the tape consists of interrecord gaps or blanks. To solve this problem, a technique is used whereby a group of logical records is written in one block with an interrecord gap before and after the data. This technique is called *multiple-record block.* The term used is *blocking.* Compare Figure 15-8 with Figure 15-7 and note the savings in tape as a result of blocking records. There is not only a saving of tape, but also a saving in time, because the tape-recording unit will accelerate and decelerate less frequently. All the recordings in a given block are read before the machine pauses.

Group marks

In the use of multiple-record blocking, a mark is used to distinguish between the different records in each block. It is a tape character and is referred to as a "Group Mark." A group mark is part of the programming.

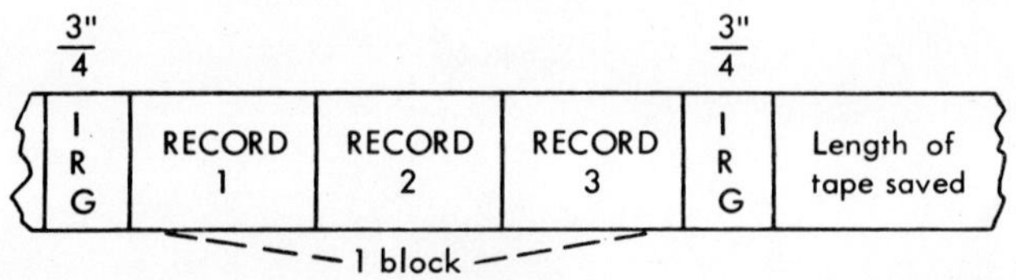

Figure 15-8. An example of a multiple-record block

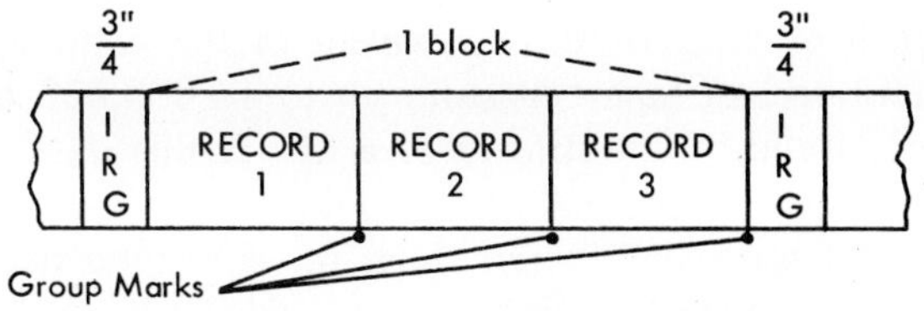

Figure 15-9. An example of a multiple-record block, showing group marks

Its purpose is to tell where one record ends and another record begins within the block. (Figure 15-9.)

One or more tape reels may be required to record a business application. A tape reel may contain one, or more than one tape record. A tape record may consist of one or more logical records. A logical record, the smallest unit on the tape reel, contains basic information and is stored for further processing by transferral to primary storage. Figure 15-10 presents a schematic of an accounts receivable application and shows the points mentioned in this paragraph.

Advantages versus Drawbacks of Magnetic Tape

Advantages of magnetic tape

(1) Saving in Storage Space. The compactness of magnetic tape permits data to be written at a common density of 556 characters per

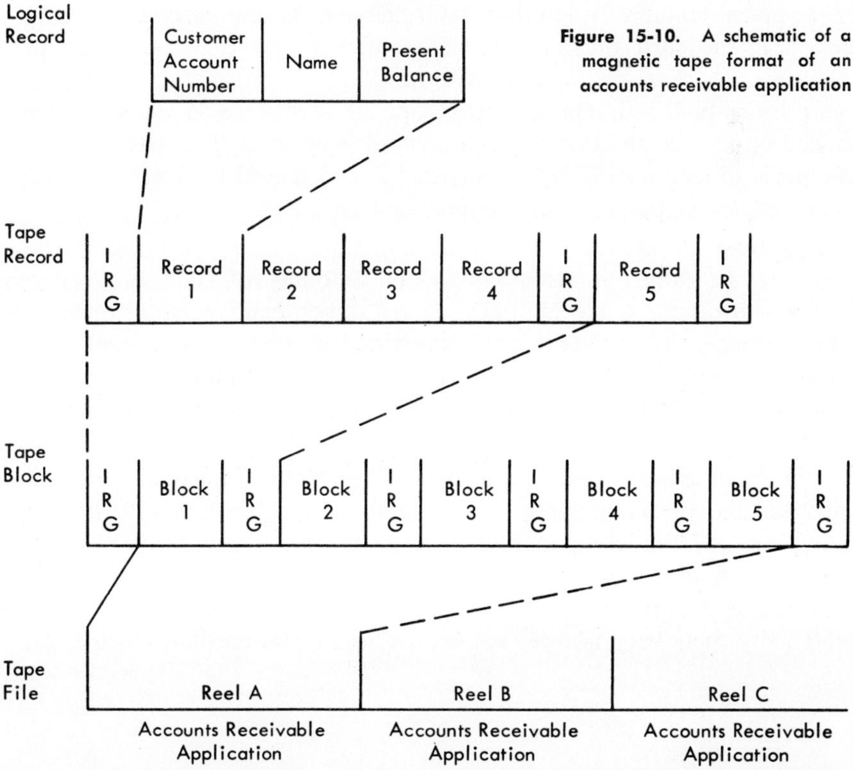

Figure 15-10. A schematic of a magnetic tape format of an accounts receivable application

inch of tape, or the equivalent of the contents of seven cards. A 2,400-foot reel of tape can store up to 14,000,000 characters, and the reel can be stored in one drawer of a file. If this data were stored permanently on punched cards, 175,000 would be required. A number of file cabinets, and floor space to put them in, would be needed. The saving in storage space gained by using tape is evident.

(2) Ease of Handling. Cards, although of convenient size, appear bulky when compared with tape. It is much easier to handle a reel of tape than thousands of cards. Too, recording on tape is much easier than recording on cards owing to the fact that each card must be handled separately either by the machine or by a human operator.

(3) More Efficient Unit Record. The use of a punched card is limited to 80 columns in which a total of 80 characters can be punched. The use of magnetic tape as a unit record is more flexible, because more freedom is gained by the fact that each record can be as long or as short as desired. The only limiting factor is the length of the tape itself.

(4) Saving in Recording Data for Storage. A punched card, once punched with certain data, cannot be used again for recording different data. In contrast, magnetic tape can be erased and used over and over again for recording any kind of data, which means considerable saving in the cost of recording data for storage.

(5) Correction of Errors. In key punching, once a hole is punched in a given column, it cannot be removed. If the wrong character is punched, the card must be destroyed and a new one use in its place. The correct character, along with any other information in the card, must be re-punched. On magnetic tape, if a mistake is made, it can be erased easily and the correct data written in instead. There is no need for rewriting or duplicating any other data in the record in which the mistake occurred, as is the case in the punched card.

(6) Cost Advantage. The density of tape makes it a low-cost storage medium. In order to store equivalent amounts of data on any other storage medium, a substantially larger investment would be required. For instance, in our previous example, the cost of one reel of tape would be about $38.00. Storing the same data in punched cards would cost about $175.00, as punched cards sell for about $1.00 per 1,000 cards.

(7) High Speed. Magnetic tape is the fastest form of direct input medium and output medium available to users of computers. It is, typically, one of the components of a large-scale computer system. High speed is attained despite the limitations imposed on all forms of input and output equipment by the mechanical parts used in their construction, which, by their very nature, are bound to be slower than electronics.

Drawbacks of magnetic tape

(1) Slow Access Time. A magnetic tape is often described as a very long, thin memory. That is, in order to find specific data on the tape, a single reading head must start scanning the tape from the beginning each time new information is desired. This takes time. The only data immediately available to the computer are those which are located under the reading head. Also, the tape itself must be started every time information stored on it needs to be read. This, too, takes time. Naturally, if a single reading head is replaced by a dozen or more reading heads, each designed to read a section of the reel of tape, the time taken to locate wanted data on tape will be considerably reduced.

(2) Physical and Environmental Factors. A. *Dust* is one of the great enemies of magnetic tape. Particles of dust can, under pressure, wipe out magnetized spots on tape or widen the gap between the tape and read-write heads. Either can cause reading or writing errors.

B. *Heat* and *humidity* can cause the separation of the oxide coating from the plastic base of the tape, destroying the data completely. For this reason, it is necessary for a computer department in which magnetic tape is used for input and output to install air-conditioning in the computer room with constant control over humidity, temperature, and freedom of air from dust or any other foreign particles that might damage the data stored on tape. A "No Smoking" sign is popular in most computer departments. Ashes can contaminate the tape with foreign matter and, in some cases, cause permanent damage if they touch the oxide coating on which data are recorded. The author observed one computer installation, in which tape was used, where the programmer was smoking. Ashes from his cigarette sprayed the tape as he was attempting to feed it through the unit. When the tape was used again the next day, trouble developed, and much time was lost in detecting and rectifying it. Needless to say, he has become a wiser supervisor of the department as a result of this experience.

(3) Sometimes Tape Breaks. When this happens, regardless of how neatly and carefully it is spliced, some data will be destroyed, because of the density at which it is recorded. Because of this fact, permanent splicing is not recommended.

(4) "Print-Through" Effect. When magnetic tape is wound on a tape reel, it is subject to "print through." That is, magnetic attractions can cause magnetic patterns on one coil to be copied on adjoining coils of tape within the reel. This distorts and obscures the data recorded on the tape, causing confusion and the processing of inaccurate data. To forestall this possibility, the operator should wind the tape loosely and

somewhat slowly. The tape should also be rewound about once a month and stored in a cool place.

Tape handling and storage

It is common for a business firm converting from punched-card or other systems to a tape system to retain its employees to operate the new equipment. Because of the special characteristics of tape, it is important for the company to give intensive retraining and constant supervision to all the personnel engaged in handling the new tape system in the computer department. This retraining includes instructions in the proper handling, control, and storage of tape. Some of the main points to consider in tape storage and tape handling are:

1. Accidental dropping or careless handling of the reel of tape can cause nicks or kinks. This, in time, will affect the quality of recording or reading the data recorded on it. A damaged tape is as inferior as a chipped or a broken phonograph disk.

2. When not in use, a magnetic-tape reel should be supported at the hub. If this is not done, especially when the reel is in storage, it may warp, thus reducing its efficiency.

3. While in operation, the door of the tape unit must always remain closed. This should be done in order to prevent any foreign particles entering and interfering with the processing of the stored data. Even when the tape is on the machine, the plastic tape container must remain closed in order to prevent dust or dirt from accumulating in it. If it becomes dirty or if dust particles collect inside the container, it should be cleaned immediately either by using a vacuum cleaner or by washing it with a regular house detergent.

4. The top of the tape unit must not be used for a working area. Doing so is inadvisable because the objects left on it might hamper the effectiveness of the cooling system, and the materials placed on the tape unit themselves would be exposed to dust and heat driven out by the blowers of the tape unit.

5. In tape control, some form of visual identification should be made. A typical computer department may have hundreds of reels of tape involved in its many processing applications. To the human operator, one reel of tape looks the same as any other reel of tape on file. Unlike the punched card, for instance, which can be read manually, the magnetic tape does not show any data that can be understood directly by an operator. It must be read by a machine.

In order to distinguish one reel from another, an external label is used to describe the data contained in the tape. The label shows the tape serial number, reel number, date of the application, type of application (payroll, accounts receivable, accounts payable, and so forth), number of times the tape has been passed through the machine, and the name of the programmer who made up the program to be stored in it. In this way, the tape can be easily identified without the need for taking it out of the container or reading the contents on the tape itself. An index can be made, by serial number or by type of application, of all the reels of tape available. When a processing run is necessary, the librarian, or the programmer, would look for the proper identification on the label in order to find the correct reel to be used.

6. In order to avoid any accidental destruction of data on tape when new information is written, each reel of tape must contain a special plastic "ring" before any recording can be performed by the tape-recording unit. The saying, "No ring—no write," among console operators simply means that the tape unit always reads data from tape unless a plastic ring is inserted in its groove which allows the tape unit to write data on tape. This precautionary feature controls the read and write operations in such a way that accidental writing is impossible. (Figure 15-11.)

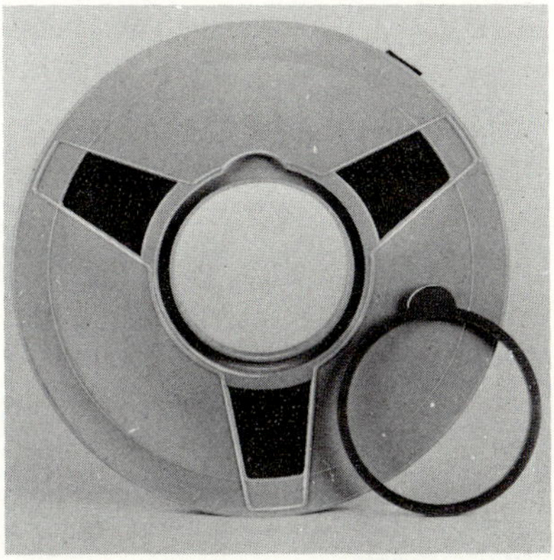

Courtesy of IBM

Figure 15-11. An IBM file protective ring

7. As a further precautionary feature in tape control, a programmer should record the description of the label to be placed in the reel at the beginning of each tape. When this is done, if the external label should be torn out, the description is always available at the beginning of the tape. When the program is loaded into the computer, the first instruction in it commands the computer to record the description of the reel of tape, to see if it is a payroll tape, for example. The tape unit causes the reel to rotate and the tape moves under the reading head, which reads the description. If the description read is the same as the one written in the program, the application continues and the data on that reel of tape will be processed. However, if it is not the same, the computer stops and the programmer will have to determine the nature of the error. If the tape used pertains to a different application, he will have to rewind the tape, take it out of the unit drive, and replace it with the correct tape.

Magnetic-Disk Storage

What is magnetic-disk storage?

In addition to punched cards and magnetic tape, magnetic disk is another medium of secondary or external storage which is used as a supplement to large quantities of data in the primary-core storage of a computer. It is usually made up of a vertical stack of magnetic metal disks similar to the musical records in a juke box. A movable selector arm moves vertically (up or down) to locate the specific disk and then moves horizontally to locate the desired record stored in one of the concentric circles, called *tracks*.

Unlike magnetic-tape storage, which is referred to as *sequential access files,* however, magnetic disk storage is referred to as *random access files*. Random access files are characterized by the ability of the system to skip around within the file and read or write specific data with no particular regard to the sequence in which the reading or writing is performed. (Figure 15-12.) The time it takes to position the read-write head over the correct location of the desired information is termed *random access time*. The operation is commonly called *RAMAC* (*R*andom *A*ccess *M*ethods of *A*ccounting and *C*ontrol).

What is a magnetic disk?

A magnetic disk is a thin metal disk coated on both sides of its flat surfaces with a ferrous oxide recording material. This material is much

Courtesy of IBM

Figure 15-12. Magnetic disk storage

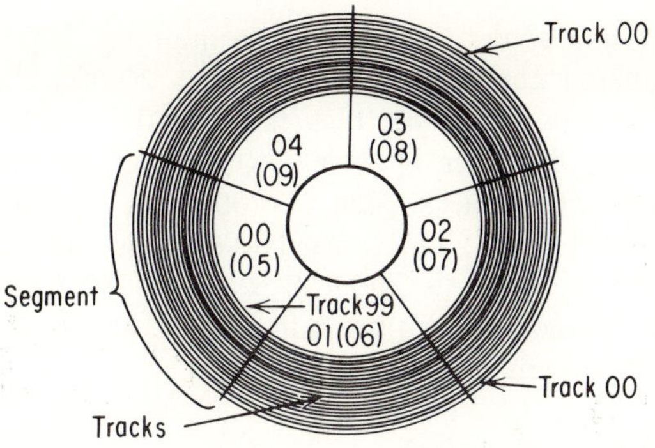

Figure 15-13. Numbers in parentheses denote the segment numbers of the bottom of the disk. Others denote the numbers of the five segments of the top side of the disk

Courtesy of IBM

the same as that used on magnetic tape. In a typical IBM RAMAC, 50 disks are positioned on a vertical shaft. Each disk is separated slightly from the adjacent ones above and below it, in order to allow the selector arm to move in and out for purposes of reading from, or writing information on, the disk. Disks are numbered from the bottom, disk No. 01, to the top, disk No. 50. (Figure 15-12.)

Each magnetic disk has flat surfaces on both sides. Data are stored in tracks on either side by means of magnetic spots caused by a read-write head which is carried by a movable selector arm. Figure 15-13 shows the appearance of the tracks on the surface of a magnetic disk. There are 100 tracks around each disk, numbered track 00 for the outer track, to track 99 for the inner track.

In order to have better control over the location of data in a specific track, the magnetic disk is also divided into five equal pie-shaped areas, called *sectors* or *segments*. The numbers of the five segments on one side are: 00, 01, 02, 03, and 04. (Figure 15-13.) The five segments of the other side of the same disk are numbered 05, 06, 07, 08, and 09.

A specific record location is normally identified by the disk number, the segment number, and the track number within the sector. The track located within a segment is of fixed length and is referred to as a "record." Each record holds 200 characters of information. How much storage, then, would a file of 100 disks hold?

To answer the question above, the following steps may be taken:

1 disk = 2 disk faces
100 disks = 200 disk faces
1 disk face = 5 segments
200 disk faces = 1,000 segments
1 segment = 100 records (track within the segment)
1,000 segments = 100,000 records
1 record = 200 characters
100,000 records = 20,000,000 characters

Another way to arrive at the storage capacity of a 100-disk file is to begin with the smallest unit and work out. That is, if each record stores

200 characters, a segment containing 100 records (tracks within the segment) can store 200 × 100 = 20,000 characters per segment. There are five segments per disk face. So the total characters that can be stored on each disk face is 20,000 × 5 = 100,000 characters. Because each disk has two disk faces, then 100,000 × 2 = 200,000 characters that can be stored per disk. There are 100 disks in the file. The total storage capacity of the file, then, is 200,000 × 100 = 20,000,000 characters. Twenty million characters is equivalent to the contents of the five telephone books of the boroughs of New York City.

Why RAMAC file?

The RAMAC system can update all accounts fast without having them in sequence. A disk file is used most commonly in business applications which require an immediate response, if the incoming data enter the system in a random manner. Updating and/or obtaining information on certain accounts in the file can be performed faster, because access to these accounts is made easier with the availability of these accounts on a number of individual disks. If, instead, the information on these disks is stored on magnetic tape, obtaining the same information would be time-consuming. The reason for this is that, when work on an account somewhere in the middle of the magnetic tape is desired, the tape has to be read and unwound until the location of the specific account is reached. Tape is, therefore, considered an efficient operation only when each and every account in the file needs to be read sequentially. However, when certain accounts in random locations must be read, the disk-file device is the better system. It is possible to go to any record in the disk file at any time, because each record is individually and directly addressable; that is, it has a separate location number.

Magnetic-disk storage accommodates the storage of a large amount of data. One disk unit has a storage capacity equal to that of two average reels of magnetic tape. Its storage can be further increased by adding additional units to the system.

Another reason for the use of RAMAC file is its lower operating cost. The fact that a magnetic disk is very durable and is manufactured to serve for a long time, along with the fact that data can be erased from it, makes it less costly in the long run to store secondary information by using this medium than by using the other secondary-storage devices available. It is one of the latest developments in automatic data-processing memory.

QUESTIONS FOR REVIEW

1. Explain why external memory is needed in business data processing.
2. What is magnetic tape? In what three areas is it used?

3. What is sequential-file storage?
4. Assume that 25 customer records are stored on magnetic tape. If only record 25 (the last record) is needed for processing, does the machine have an immediate access to it? Explain.
5. Explain the seven-bit character code.
6. Represent the following data in the seven-bit character code:
   (a) BUSINESS DATA PROCESSING
   (b) SEPTEMBER 7 1965
   (c) CATALOG NUMBER 14K1720
7. Assuming the use of even parity check, determine the status (0-bit, or one-bit) of the parity-check core in the representation of the following characters: *3, 4, 5, 6, A, C, J, L, S, T, V, X, Z.*
8. What is the purpose of the vacuum columns of a magnetic-tape unit? Explain.
9. What is meant by the term *density?* What is the difference between HI density and Super-HI density?
10. Define the following terms:
    (a) Header label
    (b) Trailer label
    (c) Interrecord gap
    (d) Single-record block
    (e) Multiple-record block
    (f) Group mark
11. List and discuss briefly the advantages and disadvantages of magnetic tape.
12. What physical and environmental factors should be considered and controlled when a tape system is used? Why?
13. What is meant by "print-through" effect?
14. List and explain briefly the steps to be taken in tape handling and storage.
15. What are the three different ways in which a data reel is distinguished? Explain.
16. When and why is a plastic ring used in the tape-recording unit?
17. What is the difference between sequential and random access files?
18. What is a magnetic disk? What advantages does RAMAC file have over magnetic tape? Explain.

Chapter 16

The Central Processing Unit—Arithmetic

Because the binary system is used in all types of computers, this chapter delves more deeply into the system and its arithmetical operations. However, before doing this, a brief review of the decimal system will be helpful in gaining an understanding of the reason(s) for the use of the binary mode in both the storage of data and in doing arithmetical computations.

The Decimal System

When man first began to count, he relied on his ten fingers. He lifted three fingers when he wanted to stress three units or three values. He added two more fingers to show a total of five units, and so forth. When he had used up his ten fingers, he found himself helpless, momentarily. However, when he needed to represent values greater than ten, a friend of his stood nearby and used his fingers, each of which was to represent a value of ten. For a value of 13, for instance, the man's friend would raise one finger to represent ten while the first man would raise three fingers to represent three units, giving a total of 13. (Figure 16-1.)

This situation resulted in the establishment of one clear fact. Whereas any finger may stand for a given unit, its position, compared to that of the other fingers raised, gives it its value. In Figure 16-1, *B* holds up one finger, representing ten units, whereas *A* holds up three fingers, each of which represents one unit. The role of *B* is to raise one finger every time *A* goes through a full count of his ten fingers. If *B* raises his ten fingers as a result of *A*'s repeated use of his fingers ten times, another friend *C*,

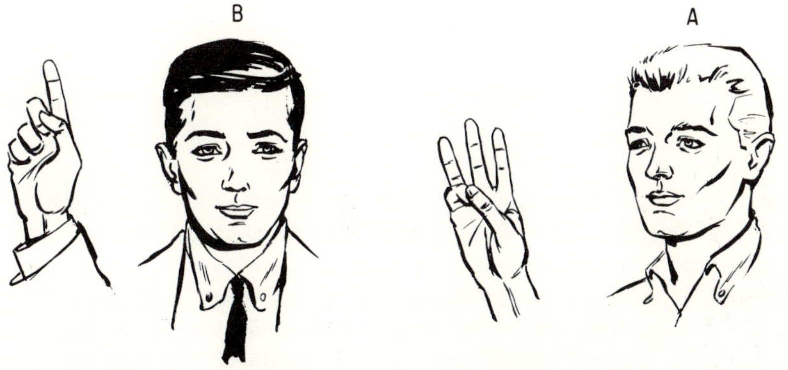

Figure 16-1

standing beside *B,* would be asked by *A* to raise one finger every time *B* went through a full count of his ten fingers, and so forth. Therefore, the value of each of *A*'s fingers is one; each of *B*'s, 10 (10 × 1); and each of *C*'s, 100 (100 × 1). *A*'s position is first to the right; *B*'s, to the left of *A,* is second; and *C*'s, to the left of *B*, is third.

This method of counting has been known ever since early days as *the decimal system of counting,* or simply, the *decimal system.* It is derived from the Latin *decem,* which means ten. When paper was invented, each man represented a position value on paper. The two men representing a value of 13 are replaced by two digits, each of which represents one of ten digits. The ten digits are: 0, 1, 2, 3, 4, 5, 6, 7, 8, and 9. When a digit is located in the first position on the right (*A*), it is said to be in the *units position.* The first man is thus in the units position. Each of his raised fingers represents a single unit. The friend, *B,* is in the *tens* (10's) *position.* Each of his fingers represents a value of ten. Therefore, in the *decimal system,* using ten digits, the *base* used is ten and the value attributed to a number is determined by its position. The first position to the right has a value of 1; the second to the left, 10; the third to the left, 100; the fourth to the left, 1,000, and so forth. As each position is added, note that it is placed to the left of the preceding one. Number 111, for example, shows the character *1* in three different positions. The decimal value of number *111* is determined as follows:

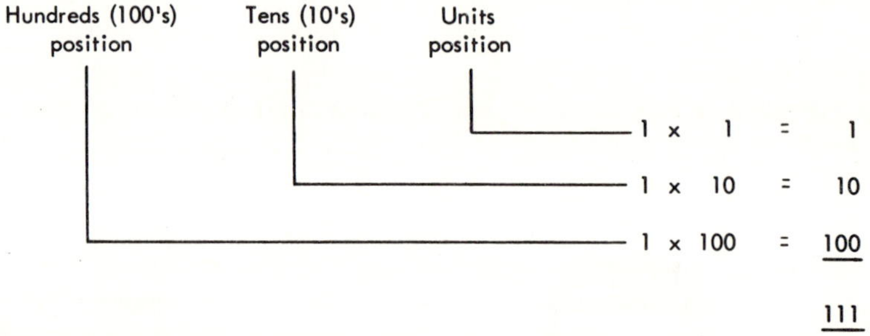

The Binary System

Because the decimal system is the most commonly used system for arithmetical operations, we have learned to add, subtract, multiply, and/or divide according to its rules. In fact, until recently, it has been the only system taught in our schools. Many call it "ten-finger arithmetic."

Unfortunately, however, "ten-finger arithmetic" is not suited to the operation of electronic digital computers in business. For one reason, the computers, being electronic, and being made up of vacuum tubes and switching devices, have two definite states. They are either energized (on) or de-energized (off). To convert these two states to numeric characters, it was decided to use the binary system so that, when the tube was on, it would represent a value of 1, and when it was off, a value of 0 (zero). Therefore, tubes would represent 1 (one) or 0 (zero), because these are the only numbers used in binary arithmetic. The binary system is sometimes referred to as "two-finger arithmetic." It is much easier and faster to use than the decimal system when it is understood clearly.

Although the decimal system uses base ten, because of its use of ten digits, the *binary system* uses *base two* because of its use of two digits. The value of each binary number is dependent upon its position, as is true of digits *0* through *9* in the decimal system. The value of each position doubles as it is added from right to left, that is, 1, 2, 4, 8, 16, 32, 64, and so forth.

It is easy to write the value of 0 or the value of 1. In the decimal system, we are not forced to add a position until we reach 9. We are forced, however, to do so in the binary system when we go past one. We add the next position to the left, which is called the *two's* (2's) position, because it is a multiple of two (2 × 1). A value of two is registered in this second position if represented by 1. (Figure 16-2.)

A *3* is recorded by placing a *1* in the second position, which has a value of 2, together with a *1* in the first position, which has a value of 1. The total of the two positions is 3. (Figure 16-3.) When *4* needs to be recorded, we have to use a third position, which has a value of 4, because numeric values increase by multiples of 2. Thus, *4* is represented by placing a *1* in the third position, 0 in the second position, and 0 in the first position. (Figure 16-4.) With these three positions, numbers up to *7* can be represented. Thus, a fourth position is added having a value of 8. To represent *8* in binary, we record *1* of position 8, 0 of position 4, 0 of position 2, and 0 of position 1. With these four positions, numbers *1* to *15* can be expressed. (See Figure 16-5.) With a fifth position, numbers *1* through *31* may be written. For numbers higher than this, additional positions must be added. Decimal equivalents of binary numbers *0 0 0 0 1* to *1 1 0 0 1* can be read from the table. To familiarize yourself with the binary mode, finish the table to the decimal equivalent of *31* in binary.

Place Value of 2	Place Value of 1
1	0

Figure 16-2. A decimal value of 2 in binary

Place Value of 2	Place Value of 1
1	1

Figure 16-3. A decimal value of 3 in binary

Place value of 4	Place value of 2	Place value of 1
1	0	0

Figure 16-4. A decimal value of 4 represented in binary

From the previous description, the method of determining the decimal equivalent of the binary number *1 1 1 0 1,* for example, is as follows:

1	in the 1's position	(or 1 × 1)	= 1
0	in the 2's position	(or 0 × 2)	= 0
1	in the 4's position	(or 1 × 4)	= 4
1	in the 8's position	(or 1 × 8)	= 8
1	in the 16's position	(or 1 × 16)	= 16

Therefore, 11101 in binary (base 2) is equal to 29 in decimal (base 10).

Decimal Equivalent	Place Value 16	Place Value 8	Place Value 4	Place Value 2	Place Value 1	Decimal Equivalent
1					1	1
2				1	0	2
3				1	1	3
4			1	0	0	4
5			1	0	1	5
6			1	1	0	6
7			1	1	1	7
8		1	0	0	0	8
9		1	0	0	1	9
10		1	0	1	0	10
11		1	0	1	1	11
12		1	1	0	0	12
13		1	1	0	1	13
14		1	1	1	0	14
15		1	1	1	1	15
16	1	0	0	0	0	16
17	1	0	0	0	1	17
18	1	0	0	1	0	18
19	1	0	0	1	1	19
20	1	0	1	0	0	20
21	1	0	1	0	1	21
22	1	0	1	1	0	22
23	1	0	1	1	1	23
24	1	1	0	0	0	24
25	1	1	0	0	1	25

Figure 16-5. A binary representation of 25 decimal values

Note, from the above values, that it requires two digits in the decimal system (base ten) to express a value of 29, whereas it requires five digits in the binary system (base two) to express the same value. The use of more digits in binary does not present any problem to the computer because of the speed with which its electronic switches operate. The electronic switch can go on and off (two states) hundreds of thousands of times in one second. Thus, a great number of binary digits is immaterial to the computer.

One method of converting a number from decimal to binary is to divide the decimal number by 2 successively. Take 39, for example:

$$39 \div 2 = 19 + \boxed{1}$$
$$19 \div 2 = 9 + \boxed{1}$$
$$9 \div 2 = 4 + \boxed{1}$$
$$4 \div 2 = 2 + \boxed{0}$$
$$2 \div 2 = \boxed{1} + \boxed{0}$$

1 0 0 1 1 1

Therefore, decimal number 39 is equivalent to *1 0 0 1 1 1* in binary: that is, the sixth position, having a value of 32, plus the first three positions totalling a value of 7. Zeros in the fourth and fifth positions, having values of 8 and 16, respectively, of course, signify 0.

Binary versus Decimal Arithmetic

Because arithmetical operations, in most computers, are performed in binary, the data in the decimal system to be worked on (input) are converted automatically into the binary system when they enter the computer. The results (output) are then made available to us in the decimal system by a conversion process from binary to decimal within the computer. It would be embarrassing, indeed, if, for example, an employee's pay check of $8.00 for one day were written by the computer in the binary, which is $1,000.00. The employer could not expect the bank to read the amount and pay the employee in binary, because the decimal system is the accepted form of communication. The binary combination 1 0 0 0 is converted to the decimal 8, so that the 8 appears on the pay check as the result.

Unfortunately, however, the conversion process in a binary computer is both awkward and complex, and is performed at the sacrifice of considerable time. There are computers, on the other hand, that are considered decimal computers which do not use binary arithmetic. Their primary advantage is that they are not involved in the complex conversion problems. One of the drawbacks, however, is their comparatively slow processing of decimal data. Additional circuitry and related parts can be integrated to speed up the arithmetic operation, but this creates additional cost to an already expensive machine. For this reason, the remainder of this chapter presents the methods of addition, subtraction, multiplication, and division used in the arithmetical units of both decimal and binary computers.

Types of arithmetic

Depending on the type of computer, arithmetic is performed by one of two methods: (1) Serial or (2) Parallel operation.

In *serial* addition, one position in a decimal number is added at a time. This procedure follows the manner in which addition is performed manually with pencil and paper. For example, adding 113 and 177 would involve the following steps:

	Step 1	*Step 2*	*Step 3*
Augend	113	113	113
	+	+	+
Addend	177	177	177
Carry	1	1	
Sum	0	90	290

In step 1, the figures in the units position are added. In step 2, those in the 10's position plus the carry from step 1 are added. In step 3, the figures in the 100's position are added.

In *parallel* addition, all the decimal positions of a decimal number are added in one step at the same time. Using the example presented for serial addition, the step involved in adding 113 and 177 in parallel is as follows:

	One step
Augend	113
	+
Addend	177
Carry	1
Sum	290

Serial addition takes more time than parallel addition. The total time involved depends primarily upon the number of places used. If the numbers are six places long, it would take the serial adder about twice as much time as it would take adding numbers three places long. In serial addition, a computer has lower speed but less equipment; whereas in parallel addition, a computer has greater speed but more equipment. To add two three-place numbers, for example, like the above, would require the use of three one-position adders in parallel addition which operate simultaneously. The serial addition of the two three-place numbers would require the use of one adder which goes through three consecutive steps to add the units, 10's, and the 100's digits of the two numbers.

Binary and decimal addition

Nearly all arithmetical operations are performed by computers through addition. One number is placed under another number and the two are added. In decimal addition, we carry a number from one column to the next, if the sum of the first column exceeds 9. In binary addition, we carry a number from one column to the next, if the sum of the first column exceeds 1. Let us add two numbers together (in decimal and binary) and see how each works:

	Binary Numbers		*Decimal Numbers*
Addend	1 1 1 0	=	1 4
	+		+
Augend	0 1 0 1		5
Carry	1		
Sum	+ 1 0 0 1 1		+ 1 9

Note that in binary, two *1*'s added together equal *0* with a carry of *1*.

Starting from the right bit:

Right bit		0 + 1 equals *1*
2nd	bit	1 + 0 equals *1*
3rd	bit	1 + 1 equals *0* and carry 1
4th	bit	1 + carry 1 equals *0* and carry *1*

Therefore, the sum is *1 0 0 1 1* or 19 in decimal. As you can see, the addition rules in binary are few and simple. They are summarized as follows:

$$\begin{array}{cccc} 0 & 1 & 0 & 1 \\ + & + & + & + \\ \underline{1} & \underline{0} & \underline{0} & \underline{1} \\ 1 & 1 & 0 & 10 \end{array} \quad \text{(zero and carry 1)}$$

Take a larger binary number to apply the binary addition table further:

	Binary Addition	Decimal Addition
Addend	1 1 1 0 1	2 9
	+	+
Augend	1 0 0 1 1	1 9
Carry	1 1 1 1	1
Sum	1 1 0 0 0 0	4 8

In Binary:

1st bit	1 + 1 = 0	and carry 1
2nd bit	0 + 1 = 1	1 + carry 1 = 0 and carry 1
3rd bit	1 + 0 = 1	1 + carry 1 = 0 and carry 1
4th bit	1 + 0 = 1	1 + carry 1 = 0 and carry 1
5th bit	1 + 1 + 1 = 1 and carry 1	

Note that three *1*'s added equal 1 + a carry of 1. Therefore, the sum is 1 1 0 0 0 0, or 48 in decimal.

Binary and decimal subtraction

A popular method of subtraction by computers is performed by complementing the subtrahend (the lower number) and then adding that complement to the minuend (the upper number) to arrive at the remainder. In the decimal system, the 10's or the 9's complement is used. In the binary system, the same method is referred to as the "2's complement" or "1's complement," respectively.

The decimal 10's complement method of subtraction

In using the 10's complement, the complement of a number is the amount that must be added to that number to make a total of the appropriate power of 10. For example, the complement of 4 is 6 (10 − 4 = 6). The complement of 19 is 81 (100 − 19); of 10, 90 (100 − 10); and so forth. Let us take two decimal numbers and subtract one number from another by the use of the 10's complement.

Minuend	9
Subtrahend	− 3
Difference	+ 6

Step 1: Complement the subtrahend. The 10's complement of 3 is 7.

Step 2: Then add the minuend, 9, and the complement 7. If the sum results in a carry in the high-order position, replace the carry by a plus sign.

Therefore:

```
    9
 +
    7
 ①  6    The difference of 9 − 3, then, is equal to + 6.
 +  6
```

If no carry develops in step 2 above, this means that the remainder is in complement form, and that the final answer will be negative. If the remainder is in complement form, this means that it is not the true remainder. To get the true remainder, it must be complemented. For example:

Minuend	4
Subtrahend	− 7
Difference	− 3

Step 1: Complement the subtrahend 7. The 10's complement of 7 is 3.

Step 2: Then add 4 plus the complement 3.

```
    4
 +
    3
 +  7
```

Step 3: Since there is no carry in the high-order position in step 2, 7 is the complement remainder. The 10's complement of 7 is 3, and its sign is negative, since a carry is absent. The answer, then, is equal to − 3.

The decimal 9's complement method of subtraction

The 9's complement method of subtraction is similar to that of the 10's complement, except that the complement of the subtrahend is the amount that must be added to that number to make a total of 9. That is, the complement of 5 is 4, the complement of 3 is 6, that of 62 is 37

(99 − 62), that of 621 is 378 (999 − 621), and so forth. Let us take the following two numbers:

Minuend		61
	−	
Subtrahend		32
Difference	+	29

Step 1: Take the 9's complement of the subtrahend:

The appropriate power of 9 is:		99	
	−		
Minus the subtrahend		32	
The difference	+	67	is the 9's complement of the subtrahend.

Step 2: Add the complement to the minuend:

Minuend		61
	+	
9's Complement		67
The Sum	(1)	28
		(1)
	+	29

Step 3: If a carry in the high-order position of the sum develops in step 2 above, add it to the units digit and give the total value a plus sign. Therefore, the remainder of 61 − 32 is + 29.

However, if no carry develops in step 2 above, it means that the sum developed is not a true remainder. It is, instead, in complement form. It must be re-complemented and a negative sign given the difference. For example:

Minuend		64
	−	
Subtrahend		78
Difference	−	14

Step 1: Take the 9's complement of the subtrahend:

The appropriate power of 9 is		99
	−	
Minus the subtrahend		78
The difference	+	21

Step 2: Add the complement to the minuend:

Minuend		64
	+	
9's complement		21
The sum	+	85

Step 3: If no carry develops, as is the case in step 2 above, re-complement the sum and add a − sign to the true remainder. The 9's complement of 85 is 14. The true remainder is, then, − 14.

Binary subtraction

Like decimal subtraction, which is performed by the use of the 10's complement, binary subtraction is done by the use of the 1's complement. The subtrahend is complemented simply by changing all zeros (*0*'s) to ones (*1*'s) and all *1*'s to *0*'s, and then adding. For example:

Minuend	1 0 0 1	9
	−	−
Subtrahend	0 1 1 0	6
Difference	+ 0 0 1 1	+ 3

Step 1: Complement the subtrahend by reversing its numbers, and then add:

Minuend	1 0 0 1
Plus Subtrahend in complement form	+ 1 0 0 1
	1 0 0 1 0

Step 2: If a carry in the high-order position develops, add it to the units position and give the result a plus sign.

```
   1 0 0 1
+
   1 0 0 1
(1) 0 0 1 0
 \______→
         1
+  0 0 1 1
```

The difference, then, is 1 1 in binary, or a decimal value of + 3.

However, if no carry develops, it means that the result is a remainder in a complement form, and that it is a negative remainder. It must be re-complemented and a negative sign added to get the right answer. For example:

Minuend	0 1 1 1	7
	−	−
Subtrahend	1 0 1 1	11
Difference	− 0 1 0 0	− 04

Step 1: Complement the subtrahend by reversing its bits, and then add:

```
  0 1 1 1
+
  0 1 0 0
  -------
  1 0 1 1
```

Step 2: If no carry develops, re-complement the result in step 1 and give it a negative sign.

1 0 1 1 in complement form becomes 0 1 0 0.

The true difference, then, is – 1 0 0, or the decimal equivalent of – 4. Note that, in binary subtraction, both the minuend and the subtrahend must have equal length.

9 in binary is 1 0 0 1
3 in binary is   1 1

Before complementing the subtrahend and subsequently performing subtraction, the subtrahend must be filled with zeros to equal the number of bits of the minuend.

```
Therefore, 1 0 0 1                 1 0 0 1
           –             becomes
               1 1                 0 0 1 1
           -------                 -------
After complement, it becomes       1 0 0 1
                               +                Step 1
                                   1 1 0 0
                                   -------
                               (1) 0 1 0 1
                                         1      Step 2
                                   -------
                                   0 1 1 0      or 6 in decimal
```

Binary and decimal multiplication

In the decimal system, multiplication by *ten* can be done by placing a zero to the right of the number. For example,

$$21 \times 10 = 210$$

Likewise, in the binary system, multiplication by *two* can be done by placing a zero to the right of the number. For example,

$$11 \times 10 = 110$$

The binary multiplication table involves four basic steps:

$$0 \times 0 = 0$$
$$0 \times 1 = 0$$
$$1 \times 0 = 0$$
$$1 \times 1 = 1$$

In the binary mode, multiplication is done by either of two methods: (1) the decimal-system method or (2) the shift method.

The decimal system of binary multiplication

The decimal method simply utilizes the technique which we follow when we multiply manually, using pencil and paper. That is, we multiply by each bit of the multiplier and then add. Note the similarity in the following illustration:

	Decimal System	*Binary System*
Multiplicand	5	1 0 1
	×	×
Multiplier	3	1 1
Product	+ 15	1 0 1
		1 0 1
		1 1 1 1 = 15
Multiplicand	7	1 1 1
	×	×
	5	1 0 1
	+ 35	1 1 1
		0 0 0
		1 1 1
		1 0 0 0 1 1 = 35

The shift method of binary multiplication

Multiplication is performed, using the shifting method, by multiplying the multiplicand by the first left-hand bit of the multiplier and then shifting left one position and adding 0. The same procedure follows on the second-position bit of the multiplier, and so on until the operation is complete. For example:

Multiplicand	3	1 1
	×	
Multiplier	3	1 1
Product	+ 9	1 0 0 1

Step 1: Multiply the multiplicand by the first left bit of the multiplier:

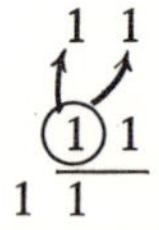

Product of the first multiplier

Step 2: Shift left one by adding zero (0) to the right: The product (1 1) of step 1 becomes 1 1 0.

Step 3: Multiply the multiplicand by the next bit of the multiplier.

Product of the second multiplier

Step 4: Add the product attained in step 3 to the shifted product in step 2. Or:

```
   1 1 0
     1 1
 -------
 1 0 0 1   The final product
```

Multiplication on a computer is performed in a similar way. A device called an *accumulator* is used to record the steps illustrated above.

Binary and decimal division

In either the decimal or the binary system, division is performed by successive subtraction. It is, in fact, the opposite of multiplication, which is a series of successive additions. When we divide, the quotient is the number of times subtraction of the divisor is made from the dividend. For example:

$15 \div 3 = 5$

$15 - 3 = 12$	Result of 1 subtraction
$12 - 3 = 9$	Result of 1 subtraction
$9 - 3 = 6$	Result of 1 subtraction
$6 - 3 = 3$	Result of 1 subtraction
$3 - 3 = 0$	Result of 1 subtraction
The quotient, then, is $=$	5

In binary, the same procedure is followed. For example:

```
          1 0 1  (5) the quotient
     1 1/1 1 1 1
         1 1
         -----
         0 0 1 1
             1 1
         -------
             0 0
```

How does the computer detect a remainder?

As mentioned, division is performed by successive subtractions. A computer does not know when to stop subtracting until it has gone too far. In fact, one step too far. This takes place in an operation when the dividend does not go an even number of times into the divisor, as is the case in $14 \div 4 = 3$ and remainder 2. When a remainder of 2 is arrived at by the computer, the computer keeps on subtracting until it encounters a negative remainder, at which time it restores the last subtraction and considers the result as a true remainder. This method is referred to as the *restoring* method. For illustration, assume the decimal division of $14 \div 4$:

Step 1:	14		
	– 04	1 subtraction	Total number of subtractions is equal to 3—the quotient.
	+ 10		
Step 2:	04	1 subtraction	
	+ 06		
Step 3:	04	1 subtraction	
	+ 02	True Remainder	
Step 4:	– 04	Unnecessary under our manual method	
	– 02	Negative remainder	
Step 5:	+ 04	Reversing step 4	
	+ 02	Restored remainder	

The last step which is taken unnecessarily by the computer can be avoided if the remainder of each subtraction is compared with the divisor for equality. The operation can be programmed to halt any further subtraction when the first unequal compare is detected. However, this would involve complex controls and the aid of auxiliary equipment.

QUESTIONS AND PROBLEMS FOR REVIEW

1. Convert the following values from decimal to binary:

(a) 4	(c) 11	(e) 25	(g) 126
(b) 9	(d) 17	(f) 64	

Convert these values again, using the division method.

2. Convert the following values from binary to decimal:

(a) 101	(d) 10001	(g) 111001
(b) 111	(e) 11101	(h) 1001100
(c) 1001	(f) 10111	

3. "The decimal system uses base ten, whereas the binary system uses base two." Explain this statement in detail. Give an example to illustrate.
4. What are the two methods used in arithmetic addition? Demonstrate by giving an example of each method.
5. Add the following values in binary. Check by converting to decimal:

(a) 100	(b) 011	(c) 101	(d) 101	(e) 111
011	101	011	110	110
(f) 111	(g) 10111	(h) 11011	(i) 10111	(j) 11111
111	11011	11110	11011	11111

6. Subtract the following problems in binary. Check by converting to decimal:

(a) 10	(b) 11	(c) 11	(d) 01	(e) 101
01	10	01	10	100
(f) 010	(g) 1011	(h) 0100	(i) 1111	
101	0100	1101	1000	

7. Multiply the following problems in binary. Check also by converting to decimal:

(a)	(b)	(c)	(d)	(e)
100	101	111	111	1011
11	11	11	111	1101

8. Multiply each of the problems in No. 7, using the shift method.
9. Perform the following divisions:

(a) 100 ÷ 10 (c) 111 ÷ 10 (e) 10010 ÷ 11 (g) 11101 ÷ 101
(b) 110 ÷ 10 (d) 1001 ÷ 11 (f) 11110 ÷ 110

Chapter 17

The Central Processing Unit—The Coding System

Chapter 16 presented the primary mathematical language associated with computers used in data processing. The most commonly used mathematical languages (the binary and decimal systems) were explained in detail. Their roles as symbols in representing various quantities for performing arithmetic have also been discussed. The binary and decimal systems are the most commonly used numbering systems used for representing various quantities for arithmetical computation and storage purposes. The specific numbering system in use depends upon the type and design of the computer.

The coding system is a technique which utilizes a set of different symbols to represent (code) all the incoming data (input data), whether they are numeric, alphabetic, or special characters. The symbols are not the data but represent data by one-bits in a fixed number of binary combinations determining the code of the data. As described in Chapter 16, numeric, alphabetic, and special characters can be stored (written) on magnetic tape by the presence or absence of magnetic spots in a given column. The presence of a magnetic spot symbolizes a one-bit. Its absence symbolizes a zero-bit. However, regardless of the number of one- or zero-bits representing any given character, the total is limited to seven binary bits per character.

This chapter describes some of the most commonly used computer codes. They are: (1) the binary coded decimal; (2) the seven-bit alphameric code, (3) the two-out-of-five code, (4) the excess-3 code, and (5) the bi-quinary code.

I. The Binary Coded Decimal (BCD Code)

Even though most computers operate in the binary mode, some of them use straight binary representation as a coding system. Straight binary representation ranks second in popularity among computer codes used within an automatic digital data-processing machine. It represents data by translating a decimal number, regardless of its size, into one binary combination. For example, a decimal value of 954 is symbolized by the following straight binary representation:

Place Value	512	256	128	64	32	16	8	4	2	1	
Binary Equivalent	1	1	1	0	1	1	1	0	1	0	= 954

For purposes of facilitating arithmetical computations, straight binary representation is more suited to scientific calculations than to commercial data processing. In business data-processing computer systems, each code digit should be instantly recognizable. Therefore, a special coding technique is required. For easy representation of decimal digits, coded-decimal techniques are more popular. The most popular coded-decimal technique is referred to as "the binary coded decimal."

Decimal equivalent	Binary coded decimal
0	0 0 0 0
1	0 0 0 1
2	0 0 1 0
3	0 0 1 1
4	0 1 0 0
5	0 1 0 1
6	0 1 1 0
7	0 1 1 1
8	1 0 0 0
9	1 0 0 1

Figure 17-1

The binary coded decimal is used in computers which are a compromise between pure binary and pure decimal computers. The technique simply takes each decimal digit and codes it in a fixed number of binary bits. We have 10 digits in the decimal system. A combination of two one-binary bits (1 1) will represent only a maximum equivalent of 3 in decimal. A combination of three one-binary bits (1 1 1) will represent a maximum equivalent of 7 in decimal. Therefore, four one-binary bits (1 1 1 1) are needed to represent any of the one-decimal digits (0 through 9). The BCD code of the ten decimal digits is shown in Figure 17-1.

From Figure 17-1, a fixed number of four binary bits, or digits, are needed every time a decimal digit is represented. The decimal value 954 is represented in BCD as follows:

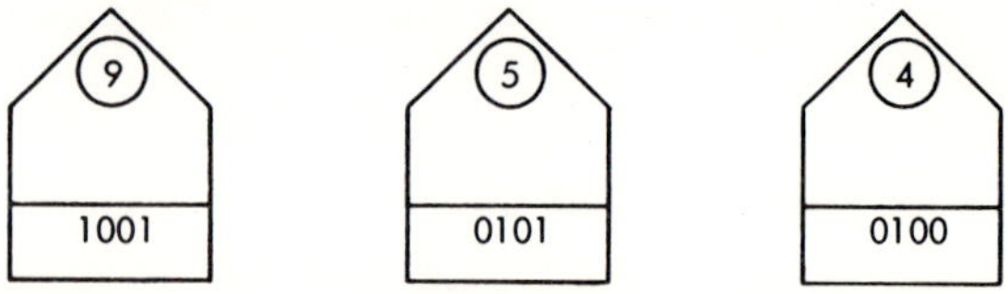

Figure 17-2

The main advantage of the binary coded-decimal technique is that the binary coding of decimal digits is easily and clearly understood. Anyone who has an understanding of the binary values of the 10 decimal digits can recognize and interpret the decimal equivalent of any specific binary coded-decimal number. (Figure 17-2.)

The primary disadvantages of the BCD are: (1) its inefficiency; (2) the difficulty in doing arithmetic when compared with the binary system; and (3) two types of arithmetic are performed in each arithmetical operation.

1. The BCD system is inefficient because, although the four fixed binary digits (8 4 2 1) can represent up to the decimal equivalent of 15, they, however, are employed to represent only the first ten decimal digits.

2. In arithmetical operations, the BCD encounters difficulty with regard to the decimal carry. When an addition requiring a carry is made, it does not provide a carry. Instead, it represents the sum of two or more decimal digits in one binary combination. For example: 9 + 4 = 13. In binary:

Decimal	*BCD*
9	1 0 0 1
+	+
4	0 1 0 0
13	1 1 0 1

3. The arithmetic section must perform the double function of binary and decimal arithmetic. In other words, binary addition within those

binary digits being added, and decimal addition when the number of decimal digits added exceeds two.

It can be seen that the binary coded decimal does not provide for the required decimal carry. In 13, the sum 3 (0 0 1 1) and a carry should be obtained. Instead, the system represents the whole sum (13) in one decimal digit. Computers which use the BCD code need some corrective techniques of representing the desired carry.

Where no carry is required, however, addition in the BCD is very easy and convenient. For example, add 6 + 3 = 9.

Decimal	*BCD*
6	0 1 1 0
+	+
3	0 0 1 1
9	1 0 0 1

The decimal sum in this example does not require a carry. The sum is one digit. The BCD system works well, because the sum represents one decimal digit only.

II. The Seven-Bit Alphameric Code

From the presentation of the BCD code, it can be concluded that only numeric information (essentially, decimal digits *0* and *1* through *9*) can be represented. Some mention was made, however, in Chapter 15, of how nonnumeric data is written on magnetic tape. The seven-bit alphameric code used to write numeric and alphabetic data on tape follows the same pattern as that used by automatic commercial computers in storing the same information internally.

The seven-bit alphameric code is, in fact, an outgrowth of the BCD. That is, for alphabetic data coding, two additional digits, called *A* and *B*, are added to the four fixed binary combinations (8 4 2 1), with a seventh bit for parity check. (Figure 17-3(a).) The two additional digits (*A* and *B*) are equivalent to the zone punching positions (0 and 11) in punched-card alphabetic coding. The third card zone punching position is represented by combining *A* and *B*.

The check bit in the seven-bit alphameric code system stands for *even parity check*. Each coded character must have an even number of one-bits when they are added in the alphabetic and numeric zones. If the sum of one-bits in the alphabetic and numeric zones representing a given

Figure 17-3 (a)

C	B	A	8	4	2	1
parity check bit	zone bits		numeric bits			

Decimal digit	Check bit C	Zone bits B A	Numeric bits 8 4 2 1
0	0	00	1010
1	1	00	0001
2	1	00	0010
3	0	00	0011
4	1	00	0100
5	0	00	0101
6	0	00	0110
7	1	00	0111
8	1	00	1000
9	0	00	1001

Figure 17-3 (b). The 7-bit alphameric code system, showing the coding of decimal digits 0, and 1-9

character is odd, the check bit is turned on or one check bit is added to make it even. Otherwise, the check bit is always zero. If, during processing or the transfer of data, a one-bit is destroyed, remaining one-bits become odd. The computer signals an error, which prevents further processing until it is corrected.

Numeric representation uses the four binary combinations of the BCD code (8 4 2 1). (Figure 17-3(b).) Note that zero is coded as 1010. This is done in order to make possible the coding of a blank, which is coded as 0000. Also note that, for coding numeric characters, bits A and B are always zero.

Like the punched-card code, when alphabetic characters are coded, they are divided into the following three categories: letters *A* through *I* are coded by the presence of two one-bits in A and B alphabetic zones, in addition to numeric values 1 through 9, respectively. (Figure 17-4.) The second category involves the coding of letters *J* through *R*. Letters *J*

Alpha. char.	Check bits C	Zone bits B A	Numeric bits 8 4 2 1
A	1	11	0001
B	1	11	0010
C	0	11	0011
D	1	11	0100
E	0	11	0101
F	0	11	0110
G	1	11	0111
H	1	11	1000
I	0	11	1001

Figure 17-4. The IBM 7-bit alphanumeric code system, showing the coding of letters A through I

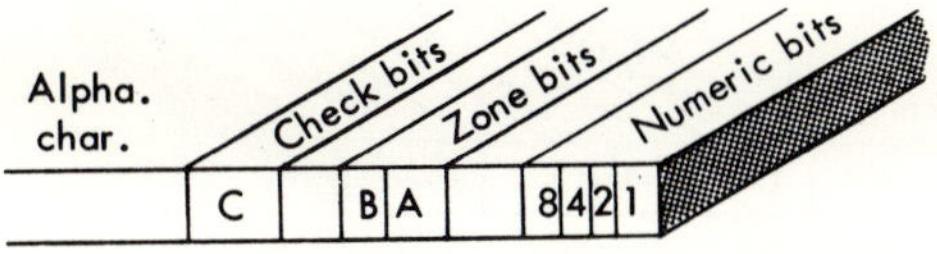

J	0	10	0001
K	0	10	0010
L	1	10	0011
M	0	10	0100
N	1	10	0101
O	1	10	0110
P	0	10	0111
Q	0	10	1000
R	1	10	1001

Figure 17-5. The 7-bit alphameric code system, showing the coding of letters J through R

through *R* are coded by the presence of one B-bit in the alphabetic zone bits, in addition to numeric values 1 through 9. The A-bit in the alphabetic zone in this category is always zero. (Figure 17-5.)

The third category involves the coding of letters *S* through *Z*. These last eight letters are coded by the presence of one A-bit in the alphabetic zone, in addition to numeric values 2 through 9. The B-bit in the alphabetic zone in this category remains zero. Note that letter *S* has a numeric value of 2, based on the coding used in the punched cards. (Figure 17-6.)

Special characters are usually represented by a combination of alphabetic and numeric bits other than those already representing numeric and alphabetic characters. The special characters presented in Figure 17-7 pertain to the IBM 705 Data-Processing System.

III. The Two-Out-of-Five Code

Another coded decimal system which is used to symbolize data is

Figure 17-6. The 7-bit alphameric code system, showing the coding of letters S through Z

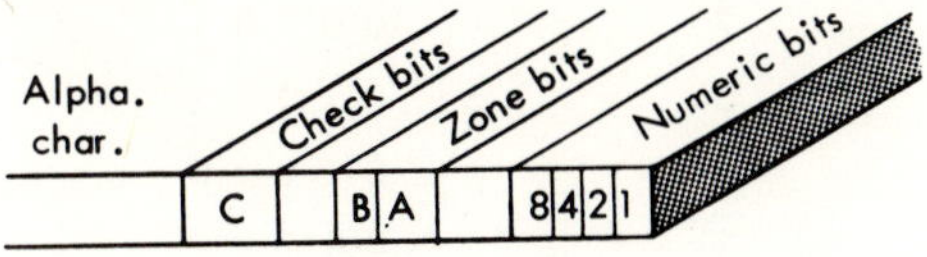

S	0	01	0010
T	1	01	0011
U	0	01	0100
V	1	01	0101
W	1	01	0110
X	0	01	0111
Y	0	01	1000
Z	1	01	1001

Special char.	Check bits C	Zone bits B A	Numeric bits 8 4 2 1
+0	0	11	1010
-0	1	10	1010
.	1	11	1011
$	0	10	1011
*	1	10	1100
,	0	01	1011
%	1	01	1100
@	0	00	1100
#	1	00	1011

Figure 17-7. The IBM 705 special character code

referred to as the *two-out-of-five code*. It uses five binary combinations with assigned values of 6, 3, 2, 1, and 0. Two one-bits must be present in the fixed number of five binary bits representing a given decimal digit. (Figure 17-8.) It is highly regarded for its special checking feature. Note that the coding of zero is arbitrary. The checking feature makes use of the fact that two one-bits are always found in each of the five binary combinations representing a decimal digit. If, for example, one of them is destroyed, only one one-bit remains. The computer, therefore, signals an error and stops.

One disadvantage of this system is that it is not so easy to use for arithmetical operations as the BCD is, for instance. Further, it is not so simple to learn, primarily because of the apparent irregular pattern of its

Decimal Equivalent	2 out of 5 binary code (6 3 2 1 0)
0	0 0 1 1 0
1	0 0 0 1 1
2	0 0 1 0 1
3	0 1 0 0 1
4	0 1 0 1 0
5	0 1 1 0 0
6	1 0 0 0 1
7	1 0 0 1 0
8	1 0 1 0 0
9	1 1 0 0 0

Decimal value 35, for example, is written:

3	5
0 1 0 0 1	0 1 1 0 0

Decimal value 714 is written as:

7	1	4
1 0 0 1 0	0 0 0 1 1	0 1 0 1 0

Figure 17-8. The 2 out of 5 code system

five binary combinations (6 3 2 1 0) and the representation of decimal digit *0,* which is arbitrary.

IV. The Excess-3 Code

The excess-3 code is a unique derivation of the binary coded-decimal system. Like the BCD code, it uses a fixed number of four-binary combinations. The four-binary combinations can be arranged to represent a maximum of 16 combinations. (Figure 17-9.) Because only 10 decimal

	Decimal equivalent	Excess–3 code	Number of combinations
First 3 combinations		0 0 0 0	1
		0 0 0 1	2
		0 0 1 0	3
Middle 10 combinations	0	0 0 1 1	4
	1	0 1 0 0	5
	2	0 1 0 1	6
	3	0 1 1 0	7
	4	0 1 1 1	8
	5	1 0 0 0	9
	6	1 0 0 1	10
	7	1 0 1 0	11
	8	1 0 1 1	12
	9	1 1 0 0	13
Last 3 combinations		1 1 0 1	14
		1 1 1 0	15
		1 1 1 1	16

Figure 17-9. The excess-3 code

digits are represented, the six unused combinations are the first three and the last three, leaving the middle combinations to represent the 10 decimal digits.

In Figure 17-9, the first three combinations (0000, 0001, and 0010) and the last three combinations (1101, 1110, and 1111) are not used. Each decimal is symbolized by its binary equivalent plus 3. Thus digits 5 through 9 are complements of digits 4 through 0, a feature which can be a useful computational aid. Like the BCD code, odd digits end in 0 and even digits end in 1, a useful feature in code check. The main drawback of the excess-3 code is that it is harder to understand than the

BCD code. Further, it is inefficient, because every time the computer adds two digits it performs two additions; the second of which is done as a correction factor. That is, 3 is added to any sums resulting in a decimal carry, or a subtraction of 3 from that sum not resulting in a decimal carry in the high order position.

V. The Bi-Quinary Code

The bi-quinary code requires seven binary positions to symbolize each of the 10 decimal digits. In the name of this code, the *BI*nary part stands for two bits *with arbitrarily assigned values* (0 and 5) and the *QUI*nary * part stands for five bits with arbitrarily assigned values of (0, 1, 2, 3, and 4)—a total of seven bits. Two of these seven bits must be one-bits, one binary bit and one quinary bit. The remaining bits must be zero-bits. The position values of the bi-quinary code is, then, from left to right, 0, 5, 0, 1, 2, 3, 4. (Figure 17-10.)

The primary advantage of this code is that it is easy to understand. It is also convenient as a code check because of the constant presence of two one-bits out of seven making up each bi-quinary combination. The absence of a one-bit from any such combination is immediately detected. The system is considered inefficient, however, because each combination uses seven positions, which, in binary, could be used to represent 127 different decimal numbers, to represent in bi-quinary only ten of them.

---

* It will be remembered that in the decimal system, *quin* means 5. A well-known popular version of this meaning is used in the word *QUINtuplets* to mean five children born at the same time.

Decimal Digit	Bi-Quinary code system: Bi (0 5)	Quinary (0 1 2 3 4)
0	10	10000
1	10	01000
2	10	00100
3	10	00010
4	10	00001
5	01	10000
6	01	01000
7	01	00100
8	01	00010
9	01	00001

A decimal value 35, for example, is represented in the bi-quinary code as follows:

3			5	
10	00010		01	10000

Figure 17-10. The bi-quinary code system

QUESTIONS AND PROBLEMS FOR REVIEW

1. What is a "coding system"?
2. What is the difference between straight binary and binary coded-decimal representation?
3. Why are four binary bits used to represent the decimal digits?
4. Explain some of the disadvantages of the BCD code.
5. Describe the seven-bit alphameric code. How does it differ from the BCD code?
6. Using the seven-bit alphameric code, code the following data:
   (a) 14728
   (b) BUSINESS EDUCATION
   (c) PRODUCT NUMBER 6K4821
7. Explain the two-out-of-five code.
8. What is the excess-3 code? In what respect is it similar to the BCD code?
9. Show how the following values are represented in: (1) pure binary, (2) BCD, (3) two-out-of-five, and (4) the excess-3 code.

(a) 3	(d) 13	(g) 106
(b) 4	(e) 89	(h) 890
(c) 8	(f) 98	

Chapter 18

The Block Diagram

An electronic computer is dependent on man. Although it aids his work, it cannot replace him. The degree of its aid is limited to the degree of experience and knowledge of the human programmer. To follow an old adage, "The stream can be no greater than its source." A program is a part of a problem-solving cycle which, when done carefully, saves time as well as money for the user. In order to provide an over-all understanding of the problem-solving process, we shall explain in this chapter the steps involved in preparing to program the problem. These steps must be properly planned and carried out before any program can be written. Like the links in a bicycle chain, each step represents a link which, if detached or weakened, can ruin the effectiveness of the other links.

Steps in the Problem-Solving Process

Working out a solution to a business problem follows the same steps as those used in working out a solution to a scientific problem. The "scientific" method includes: (1) defining the problem, (2) organizing the required data, (3) devising a procedure for a desired solution, (4) testing the procedure, and (5) carrying out the program.

1. Problem definition

The goal of a computer system is the realization of meaningful information as output. Problem definition involves the advance determination of what is needed as input to obtain the information desired as output. The first necessary step in problem solving, then, is a clear, detailed definition of the type of information needed. The objective of each step must be determined. No procedure can be deemed pertinent that will not lead directly to the attainment of a predetermined goal. The following quotation from *Alice in Wonderland* brings out the basic idea that the objective must be set before effective action can be taken:

> "Cheshire Puss, would you tell me, please, which way I ought to go from here?"
>
> "That depends a good deal on where you want to get to," said the cat.
>
> "I don't much care where—," said Alice.
>
> "Then it doesn't matter which way you go," said the cat.

Such aimless wandering cannot be condoned in problem solving because it wastes time and costs money. A sufficient amount of time must be allowed for defining the specific problem as well as for gathering together the specific information to be used in its solution. If the objective is not clearly defined, or if the goal is determined too hurriedly, the steps followed will lead to meaningless results.

When the goal has been determined, the personnel responsible for its achievement should keep in mind the capabilities and limitations of their particular computer system. The type of output information expected must be within the capabilities of the system. Through experience and observation on the job, it is possible to determine the details of what the computer installation can and cannot do. If such an installation is the result of status seeking by the firm without regard for the value of the computer in helping to do repetitive work, or if the wrong type is installed, the firm has an expensive layout which cannot be justified. It becomes entirely purposeless when management does not receive the hoped-for information. The blame cannot be put on the computer, because this is the result of bad judgment on the part of humans. The computer is the "victim," not the "villain," in such a case. System design, the degree of experience of the programmers, and other factors involved in the planning, such as the way in which data are received and produced, are all related closely to the success or failure of a computer data-processing system. The failure of a computer installation to be of value to a business organization is either the result of the inability of humans to recognize precisely the organization's need for it or the failure of those in charge to utilize fully the capabilities of the system.

II. Data organization

After the problem is defined, the next logical step involves the organization of the proper source data to be used in the application and the preparation of the program for the computer system so that the data can be processed. The term *organize* is synonymous with the terms *arrange, institute,* and *bring into being*. It involves the preparation of the basic component parts and their relationships to each other in such a way that they contribute effectively toward the realization of the predetermined goal.

In a payroll application, for instance, the problem can be defined as the determination of the employee's pay for the period covered, including the computation of taxes to be withheld and the preparation of pertinent statements to support such computations. Problem organization, in this respect, involves the preparation of the time cards (the source data), the employee's regular base rate and his overtime, his number of withholding exemptions, and other related factors which would affect the amount of his pay check for the period covered. The results of data organization begin with recording the source data by punching them into cards and verifying them to ascertain their accuracy. In order to do this, the systematic recording of specific data in a given location in the card is a "must." Next, the file must be sorted and classified in a given order before processing can take place effectively and correctly.

The above example stresses the importance of the punched card for temporary data storage. It is important to bear in mind that the punched card is neither necessarily the best type of direct input in a computer data-processing application nor the only means used in business-computer installation.* It is generally agreed that it was the technique used originally in the past and that it is still in popular use today. However, regardless of the exact input medium used, data must be punched into a card originally so that the human language in the source documents can be converted into the machine language that an input device can understand.

* The comparatively limited use of optical scanners at present, and their likely popular use in the future would make the need for punching data in a card for input a matter of choice.

III. The development stage

The steps presented thus far can be properly labeled the "collection stage." The source data must be accurately recorded, properly classified, and be checked out as the proper data for accomplishing the objective for which an application is being run.

The next stage in problem solving is referred to as the *development* stage. Although general, the term nevertheless includes the remaining steps leading to the output results. Those who are responsible for the results to be procured compare these results with the objective in a "trial run" in order to satisfy themselves concerning the accuracy and reliability of the future computer output. In fact, it is a corrective step for a better output in future applications.

One of the main steps in the development stage is devising a procedure which will convert the input data into meaningful results. A *procedure* is defined as "a specific way of doing something." For its success in helping to accomplish the objective, it is important to bear in mind the information needed on the final reports, the form which the report should take, the sequence leading to its preparation, and the extent of detail it should contain. To illustrate, the procedure involved in admission to college follows a specific series of steps. When you decided to go to college, you followed a procedure which involved certain steps, that is, writing a letter to the registrar or an admissions officer, mailing a transcript of your high school grades, asking one or more of your teachers for a recommendation, possibly visiting the college or meeting a representative of the college for a personal interview, and taking a series of entrance examinations. Finally, if everything was considered acceptable, you were notified of your acceptance to commence college work at that particular institution. This procedure was constructed after the objectives of the institution were determined—which, in their turn, were based on the college's knowledge of your aims with regard to a college education. The objective must be in harmony with that of the prospective student, because he cannot expect to learn something that is not available to him in the college of his choice.

What is a block diagram?

In preparing a program, a procedure is devised by the technique of the block diagram, consisting of a number of blocks each containing an instruction which the computer must execute, in proper sequence. A block diagram is essential in that it makes it possible to write the program in an orderly manner.

Either the technique of a block diagram or a flow diagram or a program flow chart can be used. Whichever is chosen, it is in effect an outline in detail of the steps which must be performed by the computer

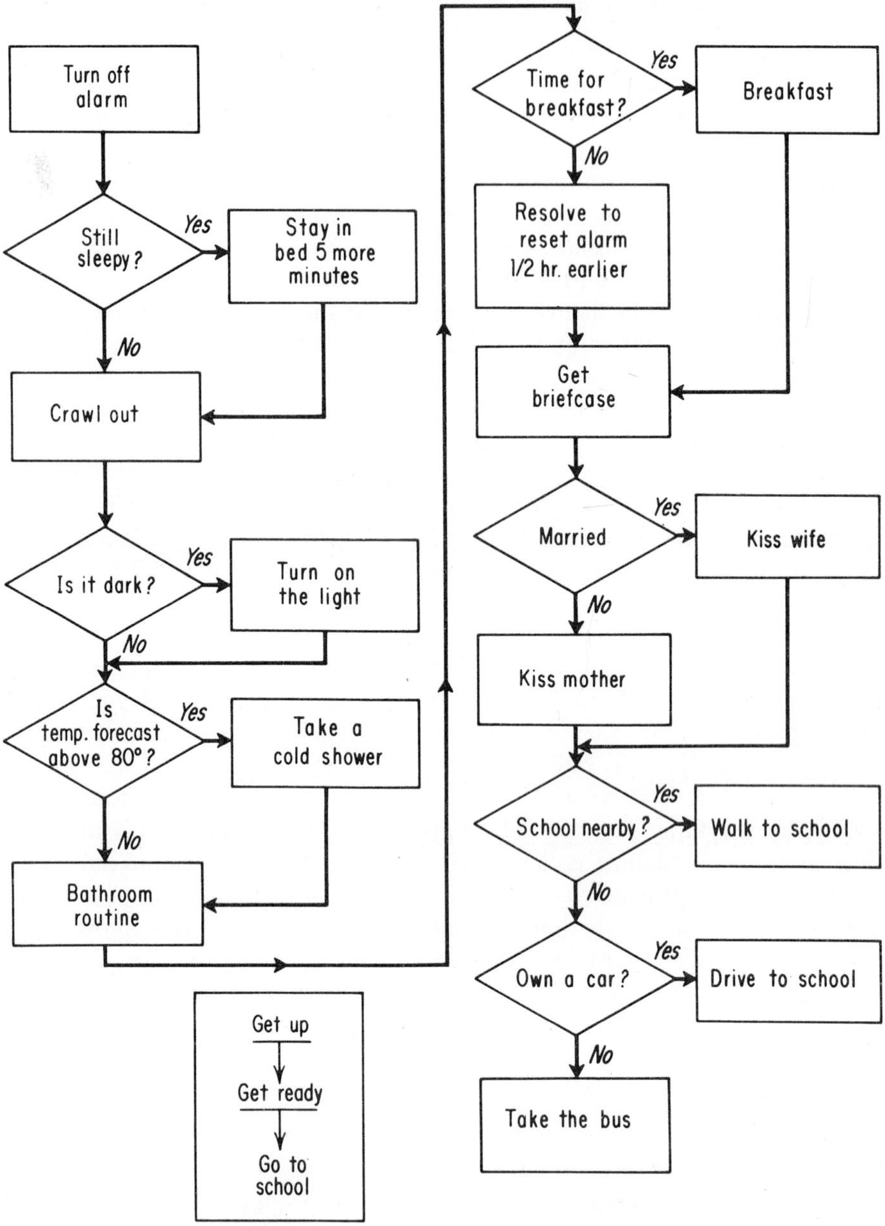

Figure 18-1. A block diagram of "How to Get to School in the Morning." Bottom—a general diagram

for the accurate processing of the data involved. The diagram or chart places emphasis upon "how" the computer is to go about solving a problem. It is a graphic representation of operations, decisions, and the order in which they are to be made. This aids the programmer in visualizing the sequence of the necessary operations. The diagram acts not only as a visual aid, but also as a guide to coding the symbolic language which it contains into machine language. The programmer's main interest is to mechanize a specific application. He uses various blocks and builds a diagram which he feels would be the best approach to an efficient solution of the application. Once the program is "debugged" and proved workable, it is kept on file for future reference either to be used as is or to be modified if experience with it shows that this should be done.

A block diagram, then, is a means of outlining a given problem. The author recalls how his speech instructor outlined on the board the steps involved in delivering a speech: that is, (1) "Stand up," (2) "Speak up," and (3) "Shut up." Each of these steps can be expanded to show other detailed sub-steps leading to a complete speech. A term paper follows a similar basic series of steps: namely, the introduction, the main body, and conclusions. Many ideas can be presented under each of these three headings, particularly the middle one. These three headings constitute a "general" flow diagram. When the details are included, it is called a detailed flow diagram or *block diagram*. An example of a block diagram, "How to Get to School in the Morning," is presented in Figure 18-1. This will serve to illustrate that plans of action for our daily routines are really "block diagrams" which are repeated so often that they are "written" in our memory. We are likely to become upset if anything interferes with any step in the routine, because we know that the objective will be interfered with.

Although various symbols are used by different manufacturers for representing ideas in a block diagram, each has as its purpose the representation of a specific action. Figure 18-2 presents the IBM flowcharting template X20-8020. It contains the symbols used in the various IBM

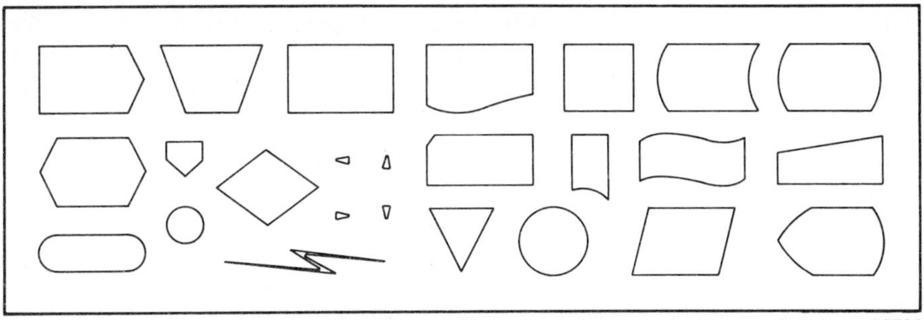

Courtesy of IBM

Figure 18-2. The IBM flowcharting template X20-8020

systems available on the market. For the sake of presenting a bird's-eye view of basic block-diagramming techniques, only the main symbols used in outlining any program will be explained.

The basic symbols of a block diagram

1. Direction of Flow. The direction-of-flow symbols constitute simple but basic elements in a block diagram and are indicated by a line and an arrow. (Figure 18-3.) They connect any two symbols so that all the symbols in the diagram flow in a related pattern in meaningful relationships to each other. A block diagram is usually constructed to read from top to bottom and from left to right, to conform to the manner in which

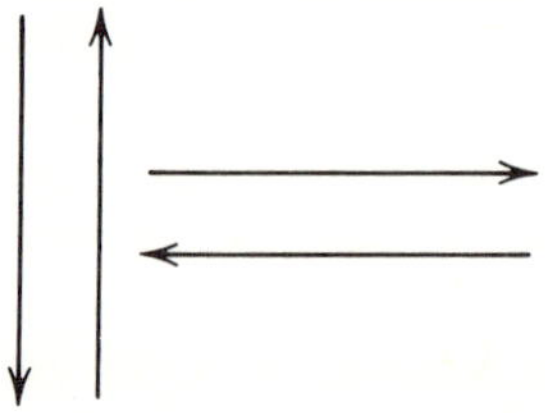

Figure 18-3. A direction of flow symbol used in block diagrams

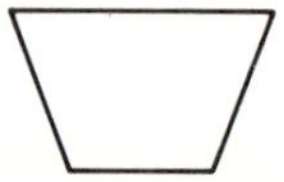

Figure 18-4. The IBM input/output symbol

English is read or written. When a block diagram is being written, the programmer begins at the top left column of the sheet. As he reaches the bottom of the sheet, he goes to the top of the next column, and so on until he is finished. However, if the whole diagram can be completed in one column of symbols, the middle part of the sheet is used. The main factors to keep in mind in block diagramming are neatness and consistency. Because the top-to-bottom rule is familiar, the use of the direction-of-flow arrow at the end of a column is not always used in its construction.

2. The Input, or Output, Symbol. The input, or output, symbol stands for an instruction to an input, or an output, device. (Figure 18-4.) The input device transfers the input data to the computer for processing. The output device prepares the result of the processed information for the user. These symbols are usually shown on either end of a complete block diagram. At times, other symbols are shown before the input symbol to instruct the computer to form what is referred to in programming as "housekeeping," or the preparation of the system for a new application. Some examples of input/output steps are:

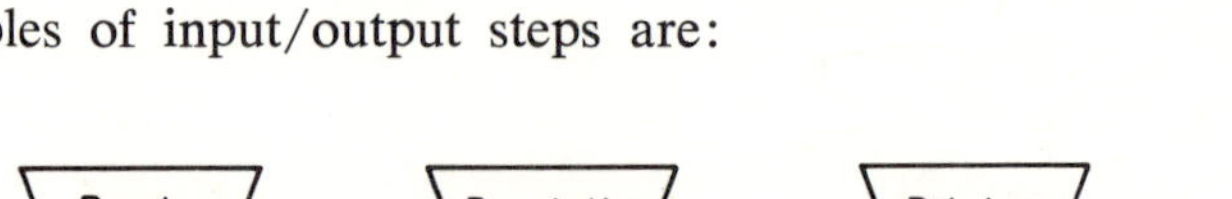

The "Read a card" instruction simply tells the card reader to read the first card in sequence and to transfer its contents to the central processing unit. Without this step, it would be impossible for the computer to do any work, unless other means were used to move the data into primary storage in it.

The "Punch the results" instruction is an output instruction and is usually the last step before the computer stops or loops (branches) back to the beginning of the program to repeat the steps on another account. This instruction causes the punching unit of an output device, that is, an auxiliary machine connected by a cable to the computer, to punch in a card the results of the processing routine.

The "Print a line" instruction is another output step. The printer receives the output data from the computer and prints them on a form. Output can be presented to the user either in printed or in punched form. The former method is the one used when management wants the results immediately; the latter, when the data are to be stored for future use in the processing cycle.

Both punching in a card and printing the same data on a line can be performed simultaneously in the machine run if desired. The only exception is that the printer has preference (in terms of timing) over the punching unit.

3. The Processing Symbol. The processing symbol denotes an operation involved in the actual processing of data. It is represented by the symbol  Some examples of processing are:

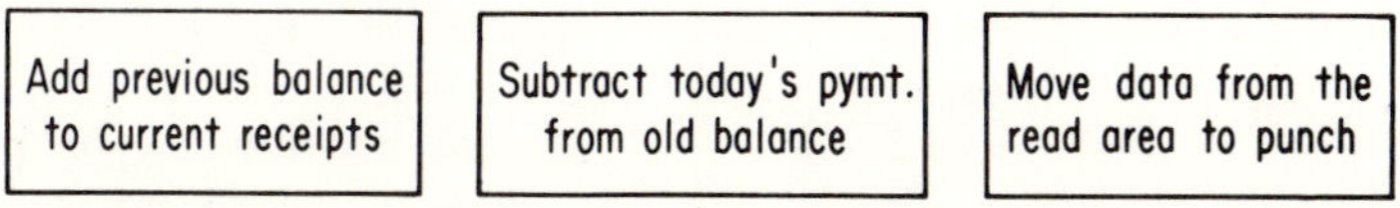

These steps are carried out in the central processing unit. The symbol is referred to, then, as the "stored program" symbol.

To illustrate the use of the symbols discussed thus far, assume the following:

The Problem: Assume the use of a computer system which utilizes card input and card output. Block-diagram the following steps for solving an accounts receivable problem: Previous balance − Cash received + Additional sales on account = Present balance.

The construction of a block diagram follows the same reasoning, obviously, as if the application were to be done manually.

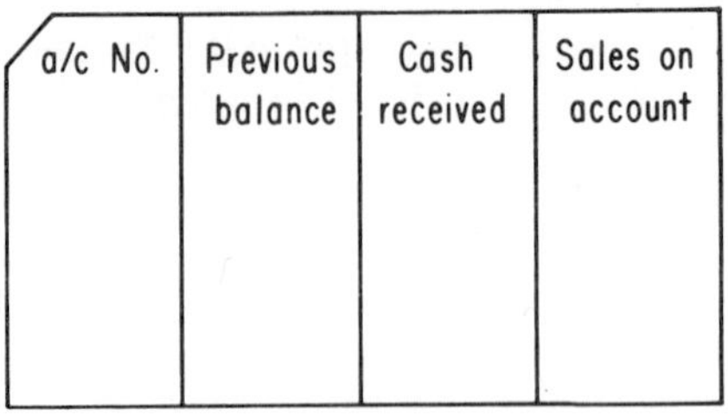

Because a number of accounts, all following the same repetitive procedure, are to be processed, it is necessary to design the program in such a way that the computer can go through the same necessary procedures for each of the accounts to be processed without stopping after each has been completed. To do this, a technique is used called "looping." In Figure 18-5, after the computer executes the last instruction of the program, "Punch the new balance," on the first account card, it loops back to the first instruction, "Read a card," which causes the second account card to be read and the same procedure applied to it. One and only one program for the whole file of accounts receivable cards has to be prepared. If it were not possible to *loop,* the only other alternative would be to store as many complete programs as there are accounts to be processed, which would not be practical in updating the accounts because the programs might occupy most of the primary storage unnecessarily.

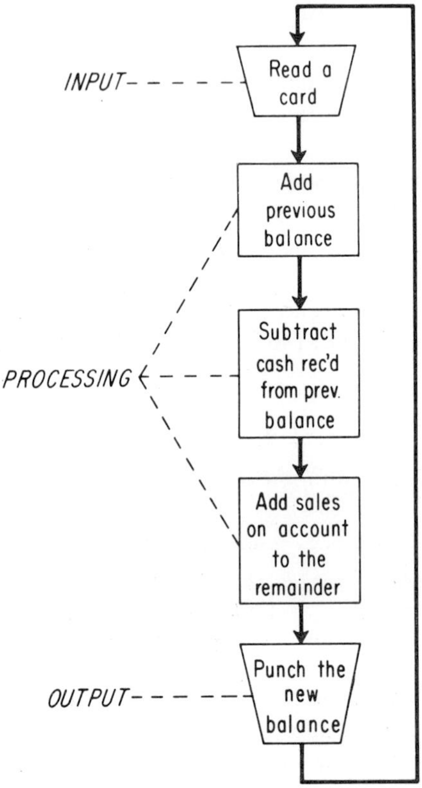

Figure 18-5

4. The Decision Symbol. One of the more important capabilities of an electronic computer is its ability to choose among several alternatives, when programmed to do so. This is done by comparing two values and consequently following an instruction which tells it to use a certain routine in a specific case. The decision, or *logic,* symbol is represented by 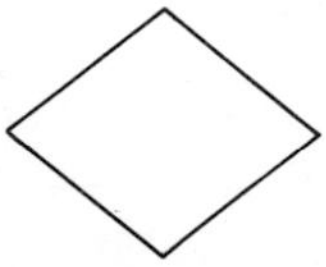 . Some examples of decision functions are:

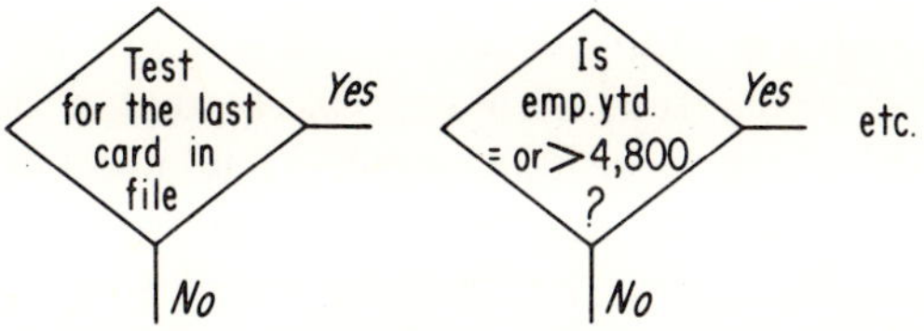

Although in a computer system utilizing punched cards as input the card reader stops the operation automatically at the end of the program, the computer would check to see if the card processed is the last card. Two alternatives exist: If it is the last card, the operation should halt. Otherwise, it would loop back and start from the beginning in order to process the next card in sequence. (Figure 18-5.) When this decision symbol is added to the example in Figure 18-5, it would be as follows:

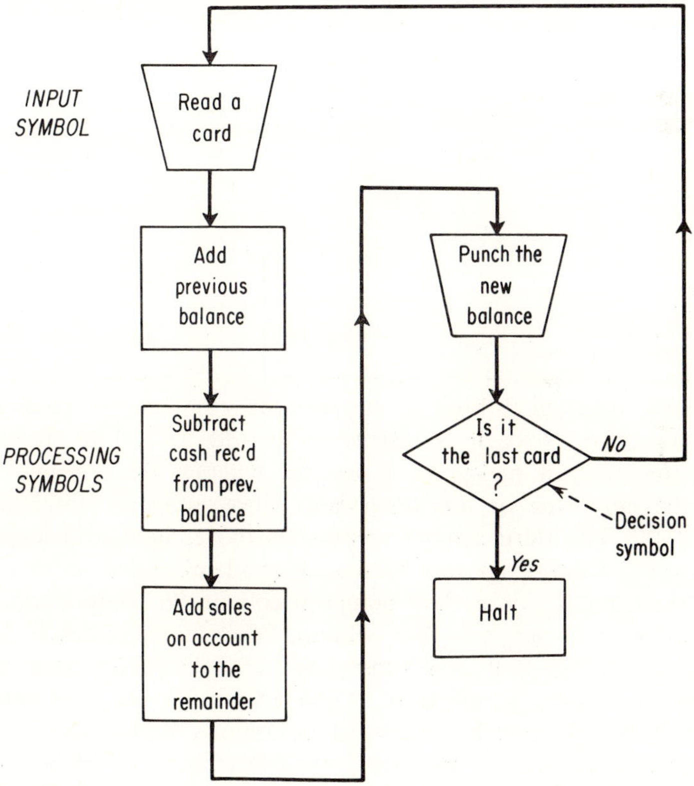

Figure 18-6. A block diagram showing the use of a decision symbol

A decision symbol does not have to be in any specific location in the block diagram. In the case of Figure 18-6, it is located toward the end, because its purpose is to check for a last card and to cause the system to halt if it is the last card. A decision symbol is usually located somewhere between the input and the output symbols, depending on the type of decision that must be made. It is also very likely that a block diagram will contain more than one decision symbol. The number of decision symbols desired depends on the number of alternative courses of action demanded by the program. For the purpose of illustrating the use of decision in a block diagram, other than testing for a last card, assume the following problem:

Problem: A group of cards in a file representing both employees and their supervisors are to be processed. Fifty ($50.00) dollars are to be added to each of the employees' current pay. In the event that the card represents a supervisor, an additional $40.00 is to be added. The output is to be printed. In order to distinguish an employee's card from that of a supervisor's, an "X" punch is made in column 76 of the supervisor's card. The input card is divided into the following fields:

Employee clock no.	Employee name	Employee's net earnings	Blank
1-4	5-36	37-43	44-80

The block diagram is built to instruct the computer to read the first card in sequence. Next, it is instructed to add $50.00 to the earnings field. In this case, it makes no difference whether the earnings field is that of the employee or the supervisor, since either is entitled to the initial $50.00. The third symbol commands the computer to identify the card to which $50.00 has just been added. Identification in this case is done by the detection of an "X" punch in column 76. Only a supervisor's card contains an X punch in that column. When an X punch is detected, the computer interprets it as a supervisor's card and then takes the next instruction in sequence, which is, "Add $40.00 to the earnings field." However, if no "X" punch is detected in column 76, the card is an employee card. In this case, the computer "branches" to block 5 of the program and moves the data in the card to the print area, where the results are printed. (Figure 18-7.)

Branching is like a road detour. It bypasses the regular route for a logical reason. The computer branches by bypassing block 4 only when the card is an employee card. Otherwise, it follows the program from top to bottom as presented, one instruction at a time. The last decision symbol tests for a last card. If the answer is *No,* it loops the program back to the beginning for the processing of the remaining card(s) in the hopper. If the answer is *Yes,* it halts.

General block-diagramming hints

Some of the points considered helpful in constructing a block diagram are:

1. The steps constituting the diagram should start at the top of the sheet and flow down and toward the right to the lower right-hand section.

2. Each page should be numbered sequentially, and enough space should be allowed for the title of the business application, the name of the programmer, and the data from which it was constructed. The title should be short and clear.

3. The language used in describing each of the steps in the block diagram should be in English, not machine, language. This is desirable because it contributes to a better understanding of the instructions by people other than the programmer, who may not know the system used in working the machine language.

4. In each instruction, all the writing should be clearly written within the symbol. If too many words are in the symbol, it tends to be confusing, especially if abbreviations are used. When you construct a block diagram, put yourself in the position of an uninformed reader. This will help you to see the problems involved.

5. Use a standardized template with clearly recognizable symbols, because the diagram will then look neater and more presentable than if a hand-drawn diagram is employed.

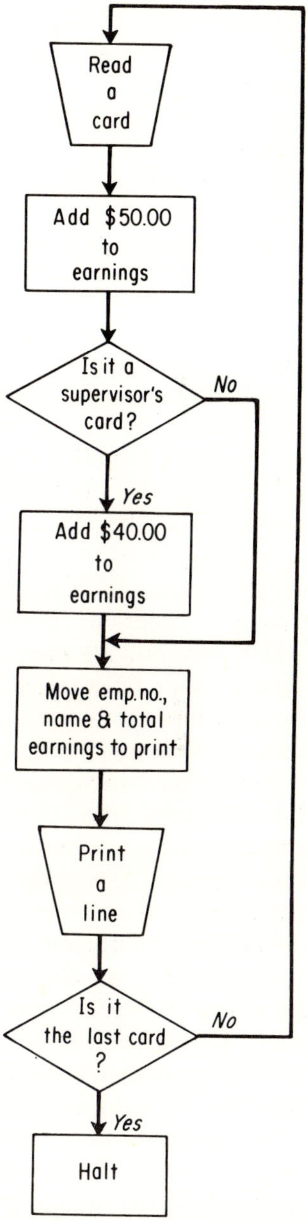

Figure 18-7

The coding stage

As was explained in Chapter 17, after the block diagram is constructed and debugged, the next step leading to the solution of a given problem is *coding.* Coding simply involves the translation or conversion of each of the instructions in the block diagram into language understandable to the computer. At this point in the developmental stage, the coding process contributes to the processing of data by preparing a guide to the precise location of various fields of data in memory so as to make it possible to address them when necessary. Coding does not take a great amount of time if the block diagram, methods of input and output, and the location of various fields in memory are determined in advance. In most cases, coding can be done automatically. Automatic programming involves utilization of the computer itself to aid in coding the instructions written by a programmer. The utilization of the computer to do the clerical part of the coding reduces coding time and is much faster than doing it manually.

The "debugging" stage

The term *debug* means to locate and then correct any errors that may have been made in preparing the program. It is important that a program be debugged to the extent that it is certain to attain the results for which it was constructed. Debugging should take place as each of the major steps in writing the program is completed. The more frequently the problem-definition stage and data-organization stage are worked over, or "debugged," the fewer are the errors that are likely to occur when debugging of the block diagram and its coding are done. The problem of debugging increases geometrically as the size of the program increases arithmetically. In other words, it would take considerably more time to debug a program consisting of several hundred instructions than one which contains 30 instructions. In some cases, a complex program can take days or even weeks to debug thoroughly. Delays in processing will be kept to a minimum if the program is written as accurately as possible in the first place. Thus, valuable time, and money, will be saved.

There are two major types of errors that are likely to be detected in the debugging stage: (1) logical errors and (2) clerical errors. A logical error occurs as a result of poor interpretation of a phase of a problem or of lack of knowledge of some part of the data-processing setup. For example, the failure to take into consideration the fact that no employee should be paid for more than a maximum 45 hours a week is considered a logical error. In the absence of instructions to control this factor in the program, the computer will go ahead and multiply an employee's reported 65 hours worked for the week by the rate per hour to arrive at his gross pay. The result of this calculation is obviously inaccurate, owing to the fact that the man who wrote the program was not accurate enough.

A clerical error is another type of error that occurs in programming and, especially, in the coding stage. A programmer, for instance, may assign, by error, two unrelated values to the same memory location, or he may assign the wrong address of the data needed in processing a certain application. An example of the latter case is assigning address 7128 instead of 7218. The use of automatic programming aids in reducing the error of assigning more than one character to a given address. When assignment of addresses to data is made manually, it is especially important that the debugging technique be utilized to locate and correct all types of errors within the shortest time possible. Again, in this case, the cost factor is of importance. If debugging of a given program causes too great a delay before the final program can be made ready to be stored in the computer, the processing job may be delayed so long that the results obtained may not be delivered in time for the knowledge to be effectively used by management.

IV. The testing stage

Once the program is debugged and errors eliminated, the next logical step is to test its effectiveness. The program is loaded into the computer. Input data are loaded into the input device. The computer is started and the program begins to process the data. Answers to data being processed for testing purposes must have been worked out in advance by the programmer or his supervisor so as to compare them with those arrived at by the computer. If these results match, with a reasonable allowance for deviation, the program is considered clear of errors. The rest of the input data can then be processed with a high degree of confidence. However, if the answers seem to deviate greatly, the program must be analyzed and worked on further. The overlooking of one factor, however minor it may be, at any stage of working out the problem will be greatly amplified at the programming stage or the coding stage. The purpose is to locate the error that is preventing the program from processing data correctly. In a complex program, which includes hundreds of instructions, the search for an error or errors is as difficult and time-consuming as searching for a needle in a haystack. Great patience, experience, and technical knowhow are necessary before a program of this size can be put to use in a reasonable length of time. It should be kept in mind that debugging is considered ineffectual in eliminating logical errors. The programmer should review the program for the correction of any logical errors first, and then for the correction of clerical errors.

The program, when completed, is stored for future use. If future input data pose exceptions for which the program is unprepared, it should be modified or changed sufficiently to handle the "new" input data.

QUESTIONS FOR REVIEW

1. Why is the problem-definition stage important in problem solving? Explain.
2. What is involved in data organization? Discuss.

3. What is meant by the "development" stage? How is it different from the collection stage?
4. What is a block diagram? Explain in detail. Give an example.
5. Block-diagram a project or a routine of interest to you. Explain the steps which you have included.
6. Explain briefly the following block-diagramming symbols:
   (a) Direction of flow
   (b) Input/output
   (c) Processing
   (d) Decision or logic
7. What is *branching?* When and why is it used in a block diagram?
8. Explain the debugging stage and the testing stage.
9. What is the difference between a logical error and a clerical error? Give an example of each.

Chapter 19

The Central Processing Unit— The Control Unit and the Stored Program

By now you have learned the various primary steps through which data must go in the electronic processing cycle ending in the attainment of the desired reports as a form of output. Input and output media or devices have been discussed. The primary- and secondary-storage devices and concepts have also been explained. In Chapters 16 and 17, some of the computer coding systems have been presented with emphasis upon their role in arithmetic operations. The previous chapter brought out block diagramming and its basic techniques. The study of electronic business data-processing concepts will be complete only when the heart of the matter has been discussed, that is, the control unit and the stored program.

The Control Unit

The control unit of a computer determines the path through which given data must move in order to participate in the successful performance of the various operations that take place within it. To do this, the control unit must first select the specific data related to a given operation before it determines the path along which the selected data must move. The control unit is similar to a railroad-switchyard control tower. The operator of the control tower decides which train should be routed where and then determines the track (path) over which it should travel. Once these decisions are made, he throws a switch which allows the train to make the desired transfer to the proper track safely.

The control unit of a computer can also be compared to a chief cook in a large restaurant. The cook supervises the number and kinds of ingredients that are to be mixed in a recipe. He directs his assistants to select the right temperature and the use of the proper utensils for the successful preparation of a pie or an exotic meal. His job is vital in that his knowledge of what goes on in his department makes it possible for the restaurant to render service and to offer the meals listed on the menu.

Like the cook, the control unit of the computer tells the input device *when* and *what* information to transfer to the memory section of the computer and when to do it. Once the selected data reach memory, it tells the memory where to store them. The control unit also tells the computer what arithmetic operation to do, where in memory to locate the data, and what to do with the results after the arithmetic is performed. Further, the control unit tells the output device *what* to print and *when* to stop printing. If output is in punched form, it tells the punch device *what* to punch and *when* to stop punching.

Not only does the control unit select the data and properly connect the units that work on them so that the procedure is self-operating, but it also constantly watches over the operation as a whole to ascertain that every step is done according to schedule and on time. This "traffic director" is one of the most significant parts of a commercial electronic digital computer. For it to do its job, however, it in turn gets its "briefing" from what is called the *stored program.*

The Stored Program

What is a stored program?

Do you still recall the series of events that took place during your high school commencement? The main activities on that day very likely went something like this:

1. Processional—*Pomp and Circumstance*
2. National Anthem—Audience please stand.
3. Prayer—Remain standing.
4. Opening Remarks—Audience seated.
5. Main Speaker.
6. Speeches of those awarded honors.
7. Awarding of diplomas—Audience will hold applause until all diplomas are awarded.
8. Recessional—Audience will remain seated until graduating class has exited.

These steps, including pertinent details, were printed and copies distributed to students, parents, and guests. They were called the commencement *programs.*

A program, then, is a series of acts, or a set of instructions, on how to carry out a particular operation or event. It presents the necessary instructions in a sequential, clear, and detailed manner. The term *sequential* means that the instructions are to be followed in the exact order in which they are presented. In the example of the commencement program, the diplomas could not have been awarded without the speeches of the honors graduates. Their speeches, in turn, could not be delivered before that of the main speaker. The main speaker could not deliver his speech until after the national anthem, the prayer, and the opening remarks had been completed. None of these things could be done until the completion of the processional which set the stage for their occurrence. In this example, the program began with the processional and ended with the awarding of the diplomas. The seniors to be graduated can be thought of as "input," and the awarding of the diplomas, as "output." The processional can be considered the "input device." The activities in between "input" and "output" represented the "processing" steps that led the audience and the speakers (the "computer") through the exercises ("operation"), in an orderly manner, so that a successful commencement was conducted.

Computer programming demands skill and knowledge of the subject matter, as was true of the people responsible for the conduct of your commencement. The required skill is related to the aptitude level and degree of experience of the human programmer. The more experience and talent a given programmer possesses, the more likely he will be to succeed in presenting a factual, informative, clear, and otherwise well-prepared program. Although it is highly desirable for his educational background to include the fundamental fields of business administration, that is, finance, production, accounting, marketing, and management, this is not absolutely necessary. Many successful programmers do not have a college education but have gained their knowledge in those fields by experience. However, knowledge of the principles of management, and experience in dealing with the field of human relations, will brighten his prospects for becoming the manager of the department in which he works as a computer programmer, should the opportunity present itself.

Features of a program

If a computer control unit is to direct the various processing steps correctly, plans must be made in advance. In successful planning, the following steps are necessary:

1. Define Input and Procedures. The meeting place of all the graduating seniors for the starting of the procession, the doors through which they will pass, the hallways they will march through, the side of the auditorium they will enter and exit, the specific seats they will sit in, and the side of the stage they will approach upon receiving their diplomas are all a part of what is known, in the language of computers, as the *procedure*. The graduating seniors are considered as input. No program can be worked out satisfactorily without someone knowing what the input is to be and then preparing the "input" to act immediately upon the beginning of the strains of *Pomp and Circumstance* and instructing "it" what specific procedure is to be used so that the result may be a dignified and orderly "output"—in this case, the awarding of diplomas.

2. Use Suitable Language. Because English is the language understandable to the members of a graduating class in this country, if the program were communicated in Spanish, for example, translation into English would have to be completed before any activity of the commencement exercises could be initiated properly. In data processing, a program must also be written in language understandable to the computer before the computer can follow instructions successfully. This language is referred to as "machine" language. Because programs are outlined in human language, translation into suitable machine language has to be completed before any processing can be conducted.

3. A Program Must Be Accurate. An accurately produced program is the result of the way in which a computer operates as well as of the job the computer is to be directed to process. By analogy, a vacationing motorist would need to know where he wants to go before a local resident could give him accurate directions as to how to get there. Also, the preparation of accurate instructions demands that the programmer have basic understanding and sound knowledge of the particular computer to be programmed, because computers differ from one another. Again, by analogy, the directions given to a vacationing motorist are likely to be different from those given to a truck driver, even though each of them is heading for the same destination.

4. A Program Must Be Precisely Prepared and Produced. Computers require that programs be precisely directed and contain clear,

definite, detailed instructions. The kind of precision differs because of differences in computers and also because of the types of applications.

5. A Program Must Offer Complete Sequential Directions to the Computer. A computer must have access to a program which offers complete instructions in the proper order and yet is brief enough to be considered efficient. The brevity of a complete program depends on the type of application.

6. Self-Operation. Once the computer is provided with a program containing clear, accurate, detailed, sequential instructions written in machine language, it is up to it to execute those instructions well. The control unit takes orders on the basis of the program. It takes one instruction at a time from the program and executes it, until it reaches the last instruction. It executes the last instruction and stops automatically, unless the last instruction tells it to start again from the beginning. If the latter is the case, the control unit starts from the beginning of the program and follows its instruction for "traffic directing" in the same manner as it did previously.

Program storage and computer memory

Before a computer can process a problem, it must have direct access to the program which contains the necessary instructions. The instructions tell it *what* to do and *how* to do it. Each instruction represents a command to the computer. The program is read into, or loaded into, the memory of the machine. As soon as it is stored, the execution of instructions and the primary processing of the data can begin.

Because of its popularity in business data-processing applications, the IBM 1401, a 4,000-storage-position computer, will be used to explain further the memory characteristics of a computer and, later, the program cycle. The understanding of one digital computer aids greatly in learning the workings of other computers, because most electronic digital computers operate in the same way. The memory section of the 1401 IBM computer has different storage capacities. Some are built to store 1,400 characters; others, to store 2,000, 4,000, 8,000, 12,000, or 16,000 characters.

Storage Address. The memory of a medium-size 1401 computer is divided into 4,000 storage locations. Each of these storage locations has a location number, called an *address*. They are arranged in a regular order ranging from location number (address) 0000 to 3999. This arrangement is similar to a coat checkroom which can store a certain number of coats. The coat checkroom contains several racks, each of which has a separate number. The racks are arranged in regular order, for example, from 01 to 99. Each of these numbers is called an *address,* which is printed on a card to be given to the owner of the coat. Without this means of identification, it would be difficult for the coat-check girl to return the proper coat to its rightful owner. After all, who would want to have a $29.95-quality coat substituted for a $189.00 tailor-made imported coat!

The programmer, too, should be able to keep track of the program instructions and other related data which he loads into the memory section of the computer. When he needs to process certain data or to tell the computer where to find them, he would simply give it (the computer) the address (location number) of the data. The same is done with the coat-check girl. When a particular owner demands his coat, he hands the girl the ticket number, which represents the address of his coat in the coat checkroom. She, in this case, occupies the role of a computer which stores the data and later on fetches them for the programmer whenever they are needed.

The memory of the IBM 1401 under discussion is composed of a number of planes stacked vertically in such a way that they are capable of storing a total of 4,000 characters. (Figure 19-1.) Each character position contains eight magnetic cores. The top seven cores are the seven-bit alphameric code system. The BCD (1,2,4,8) can be used to store numeric digits. The BCD bits and the A and B zone bits can be coded to store alphabetic and special characters. The top bit is used for parity check. (Figure 19-1.)

The Word Mark. The bottom, or eighth, bit available in each of the 4,000 storage locations in the memory of this particular computer is referred to as the *word mark*. As you will recall from the section on punched cards, a punched card can be divided into different areas, each of which

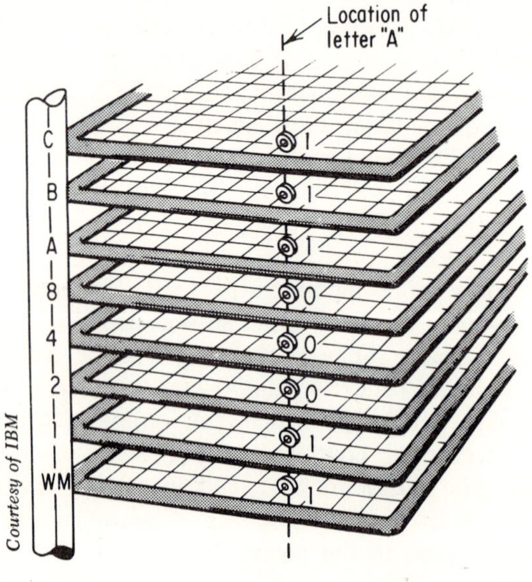

Figure 19-1. The location of letter A in the IBM internal storage

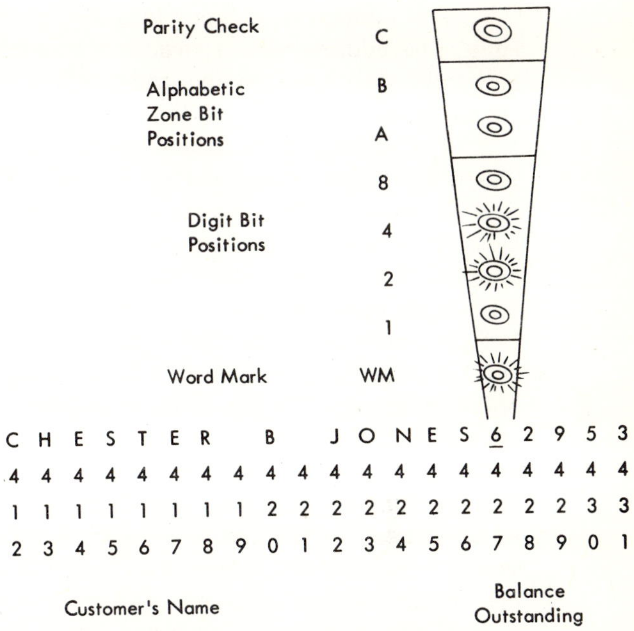

Figure 19-2. A schematic showing a word mark set in the high-order position of the balance outstanding field

may be used for representing a specific type of information and each of which is called a *field.*

Once the contents of a given punched card are read into memory, the data should be stored by *fields.* In the event that only a part of the data needs processing, the identification of each particular field by the computer becomes necessary. The *word mark* is used as a "field definer." The term *word* is synonymous with *field.* A *word* is a group of characters which are treated or handled as a complete unit. A customer account number is an example. The term *field* is usually used in the punched-card processing routine, whereas the term *word* is used in the electronic-computer programming routine. However, either term can be applied. A *mark* is a sign which defines the limit of the word. The eighth bit in Figure 19-1 is a magnetic core which is turned on to represent a one-bit every time the programmer finds it necessary to define the limit of a given word. For example, assume that a customer's name is in storage location 412-426 and that the balance outstanding is stored in location 427-431. If during processing we wish to take the balance from storage to the arithmetic unit to be added to or subtracted from a different number, it is necessary to have a word mark which will separate the "balance outstanding" word from that of the customer's name. Therefore, a word mark is "set" in the high-order position (left) address. (Figure 19-2.)

From Figure 19-2, the following points stand out:

1. The address of a word identifies its location only and *not* its contents. The address tells us *where* a character is stored. It does not give any indication whether the character is a digit, a letter, or a special character.

2. The address of a data word is always identified or located in the low-order (right) position. In Figure 19-2, the "balance outstanding" field is located at the address 431. The reasons for this will be explained later. The location to the far right in a word is referred to as the *low-order* position. The location to the far left in a word is referred to as the *high-order* position.

3. Whereas the *address* of a data word is in the *low-order* position, the word mark separating it from another word is always located in the high-order position. In Figure 19-2, it was necessary to separate the "balance outstanding" field from the "customer's name" field. Therefore, a word mark (represented on paper as a dash) is set in 427. If, for some reason, a word mark should be set anywhere else in memory, it can be done by an instruction to the computer, containing the address and the code for setting a word mark. Clearing a word mark can also be done by giving the appropriate instruction to the computer.

4. Either data to be processed, or instructions, can be stored in the memory of a computer. Both are stored in the same manner. It is not necessary that processing data be stored in one section of memory while instructions are stored somewhere else in memory. As long as the programmer keeps track of the addresses of both the data to be processed and the instructions, any storage location can be used. It is customary, however, for instructions to be stored in sequential ascending locations in an available gap in memory large enough to store the whole program. This is primarily a matter of convenience to the programmer.

The two primary activities related to the stored program

Before a program is written, a programmer takes two basic steps. They are: (1) block diagramming, and (2) coding.

The Block Diagram (Review). A block diagram is one means of outlining the steps in the problem. It presents in graphic form the steps which the computer is expected to take before a proper solution can be achieved. It is a technique used in outlining a plan for action by which data are to be processed by a computer. Each of the steps shown in a block diagram is an instruction, which, when coded in machine language, tells the computer how a given job is to be done. A more complete explanation of the block diagram has been presented in the previous chapter. For purposes of illustrating stored-program concepts and the functional units of a computer memory, familiarity with and emphasis upon the following symbols are desirable:

1. Input and Output Symbol. The beginning of any block diagram has an input symbol, which means that data must be read first from an external source into the internal memory of the machine before any processing is possible. The symbol for input is also used to represent output, after processing has been performed on the input data. Therefore, each block diagram should necessarily begin with an input symbol and end with an output symbol. The use of magnetic tape or other media of input and output would, at times, change the symbols.

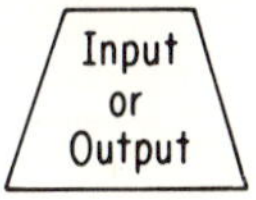

2. The Processing Symbol. After the input data are received into storage, processing can be done on them. This includes moving data from one place to another in storage and doing arithmetical operations, such as adding, subtracting, multiplying, or dividing. The symbol used for processing is rectangular in shape.

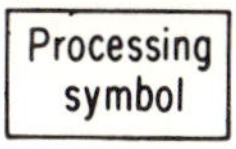

3. The Logic or Decision Symbol. The logic symbol is a decision function which involves a comparison between two values to determine whether one value is greater than, equal to, or less than another value. The result of a comparison is a selection between two alternatives, referred to as *branching.*

In conclusion, therefore, each block diagram includes an input symbol, a processing symbol, a logic or decision symbol if necessary, and an output symbol.

Coding. After the block diagram is completed and "debugged," or checked out, the next step in the preparation of a program is coding. Coding involves translating, or converting, each of the steps in the block diagram into an instruction coded in language understandable to the computer. Programs can be written in two different languages:

1. Symbolic Language. Symbolic language is using symbols or mnemonics. The term *mnemonic* means any code that aids memory. Mnemonic, or symbolic, language uses codes that aid the memory of the programmer. For example, letter *A* stands for *Add, S* for *Subtract, M* for *Multiply, D* for *Divide, P* for *Punch, W* for *Print* or *Write, R* for *Read,* and so forth. The program in this chapter will be written in symbolic language, because the purpose of this presentation is to show how a program is developed and, later, executed by a computer, and not to teach coding language.

2. Machine Language. When a program is initially written in symbolic language, it must be converted into machine language before it can be loaded into computer memory to be used satisfactorily when needed. For example, in the 1401 computer, the equivalent machine-language codes for a few of the symbolic codes are shown in Figure 19-3.

It is evident that symbolic language is easier for the programmer to use than machine language, because it is more similar to the English

English Term	Symbolic Term	Machine Language
Read	R	1
Punch	P	4
Print (write)	W	2
Set Word Mark	SW	,

Figure 19-3. A presentation of some symbolic and machine language codes used in the IBM 1401 computer programming

language than is machine language. The majority of programmers, therefore, write their programs first in symbolic language. An assembler is used to translate the symbolic instructions into machine language automatically. A few gifted programmers, however, write their programs directly in machine language and claim that it is just as fast and easy as symbolic language. In this event, translation is not necessary.

The rest of the chapter presents a simplified program and shows, step by step, the method of loading the program and of executing the instructions it contains.

The problem

The program to be presented is for an accounts receivable application. The idea is to instruct the computer to update each customer's record, using the formula: "Previous balance, less today's payments, equals balance outstanding." A punched card is used as an input device for the input, "Previous balance." Its details are as follows:

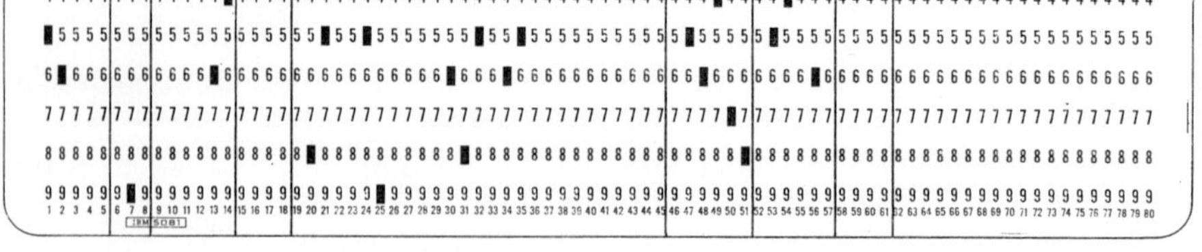

Figure 19-4

"Balance outstanding" is the output. The steps to be considered are:

1. *Input*. The program begins with an instruction to the card reader to read a card and transfer its contents to the computer.

2. *Processing*. Another instruction tells the control unit that today's payment is to be subtracted from the "Balance to Date," and that the answer is to be moved from its location to the punch area so that it can be punched in a blank IBM card.

3. *Output*. The last instruction tells the unit to see that the answer in the punch area is punched in a new card.

A block diagram showing all these steps in graphic form is presented in Figure 19-5. Once a block diagram is prepared and "debugged," the next step is to convert each of the steps into more definite instructions to the computer. In order to understand this, it is necessary to have basic knowledge about the instruction format.

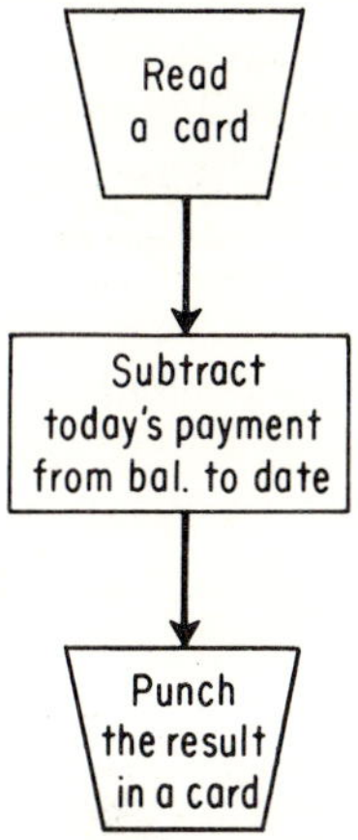

Figure 19-5. A block diagram showing three major symbols

The instruction format

Generally, each instruction consists of two parts: (1) the operation code, and (2) the operand. The operation code is the first character of a written instruction read by the computer, as it specifies what is to be done. For example, in our accounts receivable example, we need to use instructions containing operation codes to tell the computer to *read* (R) a customer card, to *subtract* (S) today's payment from the previous balance, to *move* (MCW) the answer to the punch area, and lastly to *punch* (P) the results in a new card. Each of the italicized words is a separate instruction for a different operation. The letters in parenthesis represent the operation code for each of these instructions in symbolic language. In preparing a program for the 1401, the operation code consists of one character only for each instruction. The symbolic language describing the instruction can be up to three characters in length.

The operand is the remaining part of the instruction. It designates the address of the data needed for a given operation. In programming the 1401 computer, the operand section consists of two addresses, that is, the A-address and the B-address, both of which are referred to as *data addresses*.

The A-address represents the location of the word in storage *from which* it is to be moved.

The B-address represents the location of the area *to which* the word is to be moved. Each of the addresses is three characters in length in machine language or four characters in length in symbolic language. For example, 0 1 7 is a three-character address in machine language whereas in symbolic language it is four-characters, that is, 0 0 1 7. When a programmer writes his program in symbolic language, he uses a four-character data address. In the final conversion to machine language, all four-character addresses are coded as three-character ones.

The last part of an instruction format is referred to as the *digit modifier* (D-modifier). In the present connection, its role of strengthening the operation code is the significant one. The presence of the D-modifier in an instruction adds more power and flexibility to the type of operation to be performed by a computer. It is always a one-character code.

An instruction, then, may contain up to four different parts:

1. The Operation Code.
2. The A-Address.
3. The B-Address.
4. The D-Modifier.

OPERATION CODE	A-ADDRESS	B-ADDRESS	D-MODIFIER
X	X X X	X X X	X

Figure 19-6. The IBM 1401 instruction format

The computer being programmed can handle instructions of varying lengths. For example, a "Read" instruction consists of operation code "R" only. This code causes the contents of a given punched card to be read

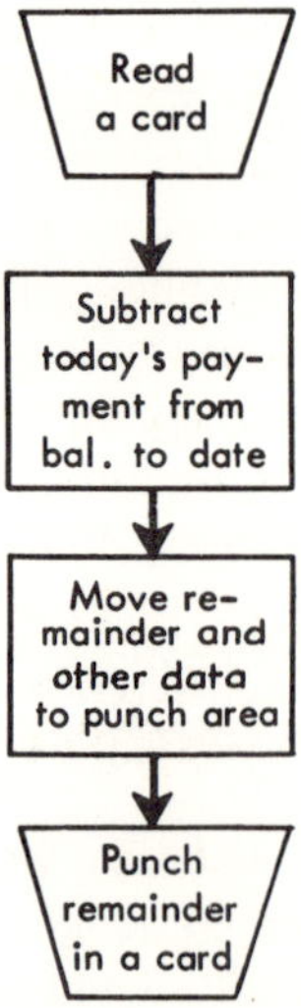

	Operation Code	A-Address	B-Address	D-Modifier
1.	R			
2.	S	0 0 5 7	0 0 5 1	
3.	M	0 0 6 1	0 1 6 1	
4.	P			

Figure 19-7. Program instructions in symbolic language

into memory in one step. Other instructions contain more than one character code as we shall see later.

An example of a symbolic program

Having developed essential knowledge about block-diagramming and the instruction format, our analysis of the accounts receivable application program can be continued.

The block diagram shown in Figure 19-5 is amplified in Figure 19-7.

Before the program can be loaded in the memory of the computer, the symbolic language must be converted to machine language to replace the "human" program with a "machine" program. The conversion is as follows:

	Op. Code	A-Address	B-Address	D-Modifier
1.	1			
2.	S	0 5 7	0 5 1	
3.	M	0 6 1	1 6 1	
4.	4			

Figure 19-8. Program instructions of Figure 19-7 converted into machine language

"Loading the program into memory" means that the instructions have to be read or put in. The four instructions are punched in four separate cards and fed into the card-reader input device which, upon the depression of a "load" button, will load the program (contents of four cards) in the first available positions in memory. The number of positions that it occupies are 16 positions. They are determined as follows:

Instruction

1. One position for the operation code "1," which stands for "read" a card.
2. Seven positions: one for the operation code "S" for "Subtract" plus three for the address of the payment word (A-address) plus three for the address of the "previous balance" word (B-address).
3. Seven positions: one for the operation code "M" for "Move" plus three for the address of the move word (A-address) plus three for the address of where to move it—punch area (B-address).
4. One position for the operation code "4" meaning "Punch" (what to do in the punching area).

Reserved areas in memory

The IBM 1401 computer memory reserves certain areas at the beginning of storage for making input and output easier. In the processing of data, input information is held temporarily in an area called the *Read* area. The "read" area consists of the first 80 positions in storage; thus, it can store the maximum number of characters in any given punched card numbered 001-080. Every time data are received from an external source as input, they enter the "read" area and await further instruction. If a program, for example, includes two consecutive read instructions, the input data from the first "Read" instruction are automatically destroyed upon storage of data from the second card as a result of the execution of the second "Read" instruction. Therefore, it is important that data from one card only be dealt with at a time while they are held in the "read" area. No other information should be allowed to enter the "read" area until the present information is either moved to a permanent storage location or processed satisfactorily. (Figure 19-9.)

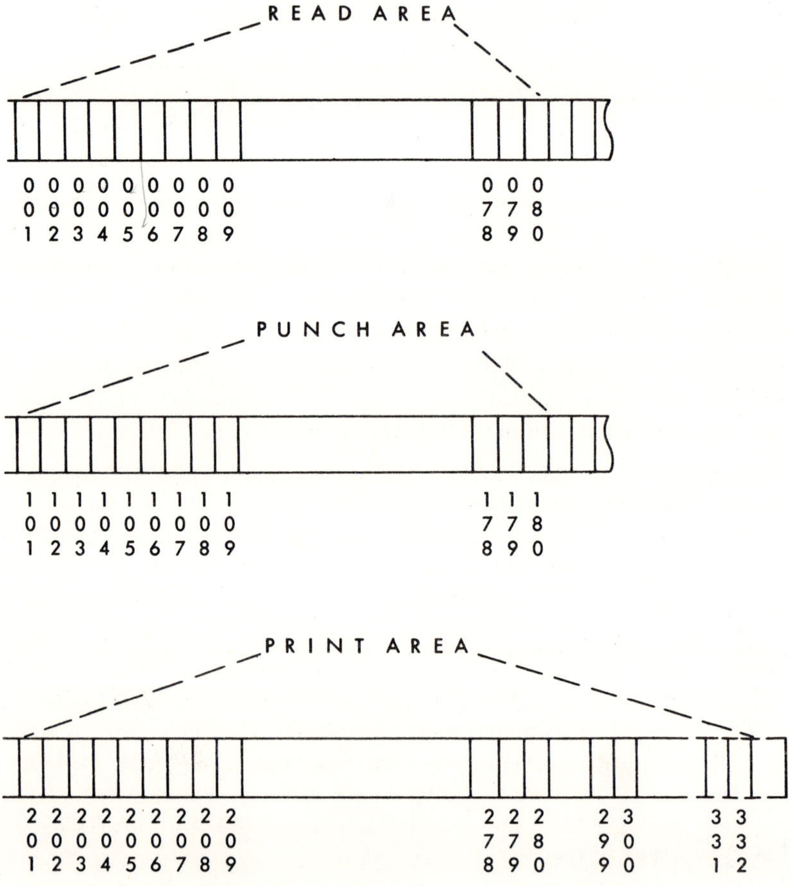

Figure 19-9. A schematic of the IBM 1401 read, punch, and print areas

Another 80-character area is reserved in storage for output numbered 101-180. It is called the *Punch* area. (Figure 19-9.)

If the output is to be in the form of punched results, results must be moved to the punched area. A "Punch" instruction ("P" symbolic, "4" machine language) tells the control unit that the data in the "punch" area are to be transferred electronically to the punched card.

A third reserved area is called the *Print* area. In order that the results of a given problem can be printed, they must be moved to it. Then, by means of a print instruction (symbolic "W," machine language "2"), the data in the print area are printed. The print area occupies position numbers 201-300, but in some printers they go as high as 332. The reason for the latter capacity is that the printer is able to print up to 132 characters on a line. If this is to be done, however, the print area must be larger to accommodate the storage of the additional 32 characters.

Storage of instructions

Assuming that we wish to store our program, which consists of four instructions, in the first available storage positions, instruction 1 will be stored in position number 333, instruction 2 in position numbers 334-340, instruction 3 in position numbers 341-347, and instruction 4 in position number 348. (See Figure 19-10.)

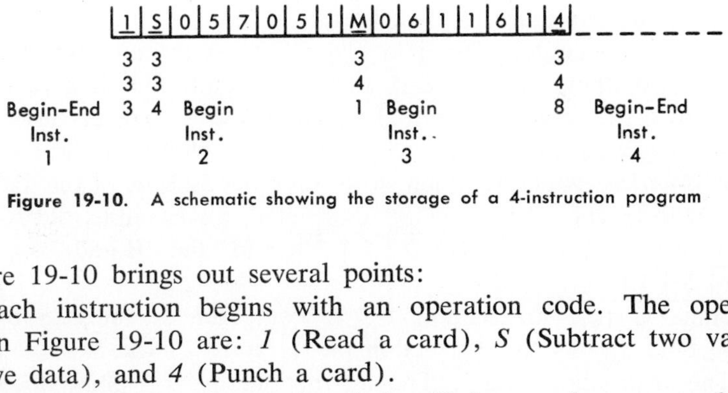

Figure 19-10. A schematic showing the storage of a 4-instruction program

Figure 19-10 brings out several points:

1. Each instruction begins with an operation code. The operation codes in Figure 19-10 are: *1* (Read a card), *S* (Subtract two values), *M* (Move data), and *4* (Punch a card).

2. Because only one instruction is handled at a time, a word mark must be used to separate each instruction. Therefore, a word mark (represented on paper by a dash) is set in the high-order (the left) position in the instruction word. Figure 19-10 shows word marks denoting the presence of four different and separate instructions in storage positions 333 to 348.

3. The address of an instruction word is opposite to that of data words. The address of the operation code of each instruction is in the instruction's high-order position, because it identifies the instruction. An in-

struction word is read in storage from left to right, whereas a data word is read from right to left.

4. The location number of an instruction is referred to as an *instruction address.* For example, in Figure 19-10,

333 is the address of instruction 1
334 is the address of instruction 2
341 is the address of instruction 3
348 is the address of instruction 4

Interpretation and execution of program instructions

The Internal Registers. The computer goes about its work of interpreting and executing instructions by the use of registers. A register is a storage-unit device. Depending on its size, it can receive information, retain it, and later transfer it to a designated location. A register is named after the operation it performs. There are two types of registers: that is, the instruction register and the data register.

1. The Instruction Register. It holds the address of the instruction to be executed. For example, if instruction 1 pertaining to reading a card into memory is desired, the computer consults the contents of the instruction register (abbreviated "I-register") to locate it. The I-register would contain | 0 | 3 | 3 | 3 |. Unused positions are filled with zeros. Because it has the capacity of storing up to a four-digit address, it is referred to as a four-character I-register.

2. The Data Register. The data register stores the address of the data to be worked upon. In the IBM 1401 computer, the data register can store up to a four-digit address. The principal data registers used are the *A-address register,* which stores only the address of the data in the A-field, and the *B-address register,* which stores only the address of the data in the B-field. If instruction 2 were being interpreted, for example, the A-address register would contain | 0 | 0 | 5 | 7 | and the B-address register, | 0 | 0 | 5 | 1 |.

Machine Cycles—Instruction 1. A computer operates in two consecutive phases: (1) the instruction phase, and (2) the execution phase.

1. The Instruction Phase: The instruction, or "I," phase locates and interprets an instruction. Using the prepared program (Figure 19-10), the machine is started and the address of the first instruction is shown in the instruction register (0333). The computer goes to storage location 333 and finds "1" with a word mark. The machine language "1" is an operation code and, therefore, it is loaded in the operation register. (Figure 19-11.) It will remain there until the instruction is completely executed.

The presence of a word mark in 334 tells the computer that instruction 1 is a one-character instruction. After operation code 1 is loaded in

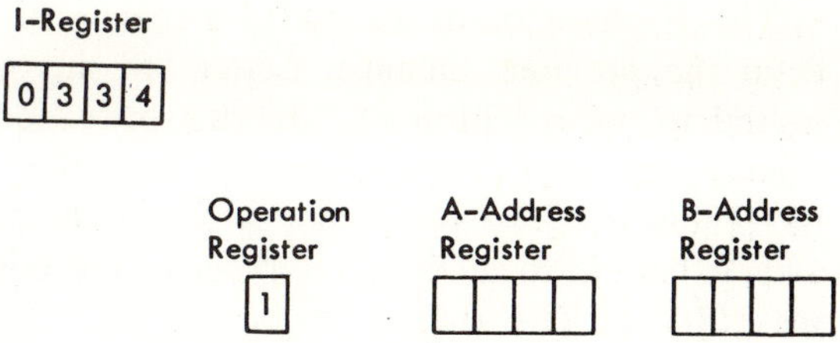

Figure 19-11. A schematic of the I-phase, pertaining to a read instruction in Figure 19-10

the "op-register," the instruction phase is ended. No data have been moved yet. Only the instruction has been loaded in the proper registers to prepare for its execution.

2. The Execution Phase: The execution, or "E," phase carries out the instruction. When Operation code 1 enters the op-register, it is interpreted to mean "Read a card." The card reader containing the data cards reads the first card and transfers its contents to the "read" area of the computer memory. The customer's account number, *56013,* punched in columns 1, 2, 3, 4, and 5, is stored in position numbers 001, 002, 003, 004, and 005 of the "read" area. Other data columns in the card, if any, are transferred to their corresponding locations in the "read" area also.

After the card is read, and its contents stored in the "read" area, the machine cycle pertaining to instruction 1 is ended. It starts again by loading instruction 2 into the registers.

Machine Cycles—Instruction 2. During the I-phase of instruction 1, the I-register was automatically incremented by 1, thus holding the address of the operation code of the second instruction. The I-phase of instruction 2 begins by referring to the contents of the I-register | 0 | 3 | 3 | 4 |. The computer goes to storage location 0334 and finds letter "S." Being the first character in instruction 2, it is interpreted to be the operation code. Therefore, it is loaded in its register, the Op-register. Next, the computer takes the following three characters and automatically loads them in the A-address register. It checks for the presence of a word mark, and, finding none, it loads the next three characters into the B-address register. The computer is built so that it will interpret the first three characters as the A-address and the next three characters as the B-address.

Next, the computer attempts to load letter "M," but, detecting a word mark, it considers the letter "M" as a part of the third instruction. This ends the I-phase of instruction 2. No data have been processed yet. (Figure 19-12.)

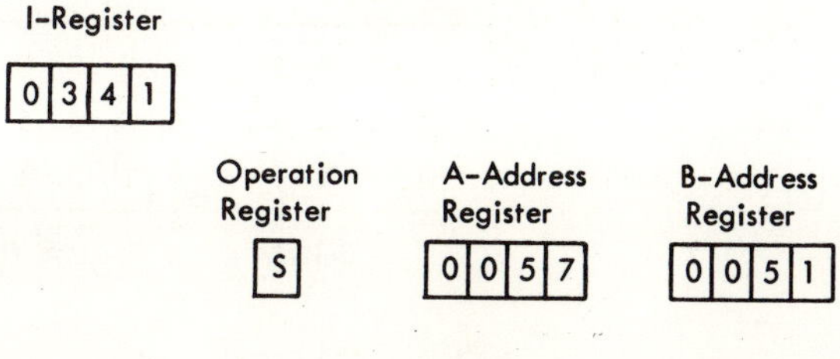

Figure 19-12. A schematic showing the I-phase of instruction 2 loaded in the registers

The E-phase of instruction 2 begins with subtracting today's payment from the previous balance. Letter "S" in the operation register is interpreted to mean "Subtract." In this operation, the contents of the A-field (today's payments) are subtracted from the contents of the B-field (previous balance). The remainder is stored in place of the previous balance. The A-field is located by referring to the contents of the A-address register (0057). The B-field is located by reference to the contents of the B-address register (0051). (Figure 19-13.)

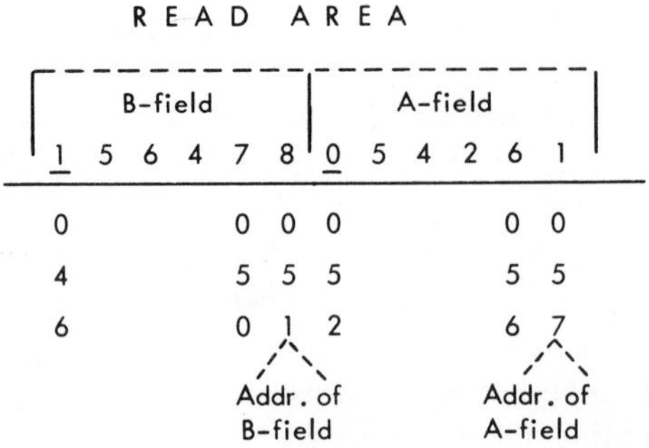

Figure 19-13. A schematic showing the A and B fields in the read area

Subtraction is performed in the same manner as it is manually, that is, one digit at a time from right to left. The steps taken by a computer to subtract the two values are:

Step 1. The data in address 057, (1), is subtracted from the data in 051, (8). The remainder (7) is stored in the place of *8* in the B-field. The result:

1	5	6	4	7	**7**	0	5	4	2	6	1
0	0	0	0	0	0	0	0	0	0	0	0
4	4	4	4	5	5	5	5	5	5	5	5
6	7	8	9	0	1	2	3	4	5	6	7
B-field						A-field					

Step 2. During the subtraction in step 1, the contents of the A- and B-address registers are decremented by one. This is done automatically so as to prepare the computer for the next subtraction. In the absence of a word mark, subtraction continues.

The computer subtracts the data in 056, (6), from the data in 050, (7). The remainder (1) is stored in the place of *7* in the B-field. The result:

1	5	6	4	**1**	**7**	0	5	4	2	6	1
0	0	0	0	0	0	0	0	0	0	0	0
4	4	4	4	5	5	5	5	5	5	5	5
6	7	8	9	0	1	2	3	4	5	6	7
B-field						A-field					

Step 3. During the subtraction in step 2, the A- and B-address registers are decremented by one; that is, 0055 and 0049, respectively. The computer subtracts the character in 0055, (2), from the character in 0049, (4). The remainder (2) is stored in the place of *4* in the B-field. The result:

1	5	6	**2**	1	7	0	5	4	2	6	1
0	0	0	0	0	0	0	0	0	0	0	0
4	4	4	4	5	5	5	5	5	5	5	5
6	7	8	9	0	1	2	3	4	5	6	7
B-field						A-field					

Step 4. No word mark has been detected as yet. Thus, subtraction continues. The A- and B-address registers are decremented by one. They now contain 0054 and 0048, respectively. The character in 0054, (4), is subtracted from the character in 0048, (6). The remainder (2) replaces digit *6* in the B-field. The result:

1	5	**2**	**2**	1	7	0	5	4	2	6	1
0	0	0	0	0	0	0	0	0	0	0	0
4	4	4	4	5	5	5	5	5	5	5	5
6	7	8	9	0	1	2	3	4	5	6	7
B-field						A-field					

Step 5. No word mark is detected, so subtraction continues. The A- and B-address registers are decremented by one. They now contain 0053 and 0047, respectively. The computer uses the address 0053 in the A-field to locate digit *5*. It uses address 0047 in the B-field to locate *5*. It subtracts the first 5 from the next 5. The remainder (0) replaces the *5* in the B-field. The result:

1	**0**	**2**	**2**	1	7	0	5	4	2	6	1
0	0	0	0	0	0	0	0	0	0	0	0
4	4	4	4	5	5	5	5	5	5	5	5
6	7	8	9	0	1	2	3	4	5	6	7
B-field						A-field					

Step 6. Because no word mark has been detected yet, subtraction continues. The A- and B-address registers are decremented by one each. They now contain 0052 and 0046, respectively. The character is 0052, (0) is subtracted from the content of 0046, (1). The remainder (1) replaces *1* (actually it remains the same) in the B-field. The result:

1	0	2	2	1	7	0	5	4	2	6	1
0	0	0	0	0	0	0	0	0	0	0	0
4	4	4	4	5	5	5	5	5	5	5	5
6	7	8	9	0	1	2	3	4	5	6	7
B-field						A-field					

The detection of a word mark in the B-field indicates to the computer that the end of each of the A- and B-fields has been reached. This ends the E-phase of instruction 2. The new balance (1,022.17) is now available in the B-field, which previously contained the old balance of 1,564.78. You will have noted by now that *data words* are *processed* or picked up from storage *one character at a time from right to left* in the same manner as is done manually. You will have noted also that *instruction words,* on the other hand, *are picked up* from storage (one character at a time) *from left to right.* (Figure 19-10.)

The "read" area of the computer memory after instruction 2 is executed would be as follows:

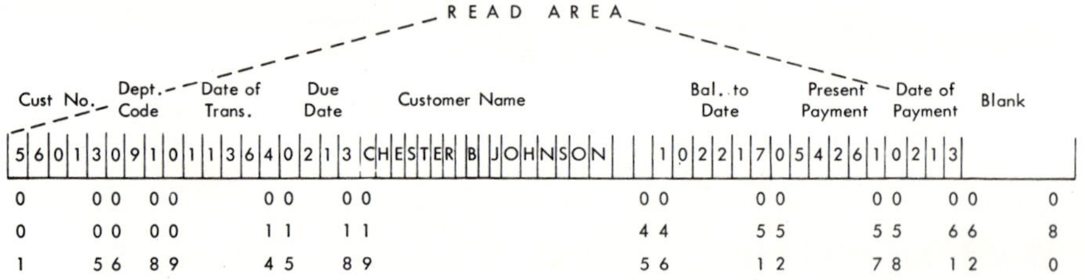

Figure 19-14. The contents of the read area after subtraction of payments from previous balance is performed

Machine Cycles—Instruction 3. Like the first two instructions, instruction 3 goes through an I-phase and an E-phase. During the E-phase of instruction 2, the I-address register was incremented by 7, the length of instruction 2, showing address 0341, the address of instruction 3. The computer finds letter "M" in 0341 which is loaded in the Op-register. The next three characters (061) are loaded in the A-address register, and address 161 in the B-address register.

Assuming that the two word marks have been cleared, the computer begins moving the entire contents of the "read" area one digit at a time, beginning at address 061, to the "punch" area. That is, data in 061 are moved to 161 ("punch" area), data in 060 to 160, data in 059 to 159, and so forth, until every character stored in the "read" area is moved to its corresponding position in the "punch" area. (Figure 19-15.)

Machine Cycles—Instruction 4. The computer loads machine code "4," meaning "Punch a card," from its address, 0348, into the Op-register. This instruction causes all the characters moved into the "punch"

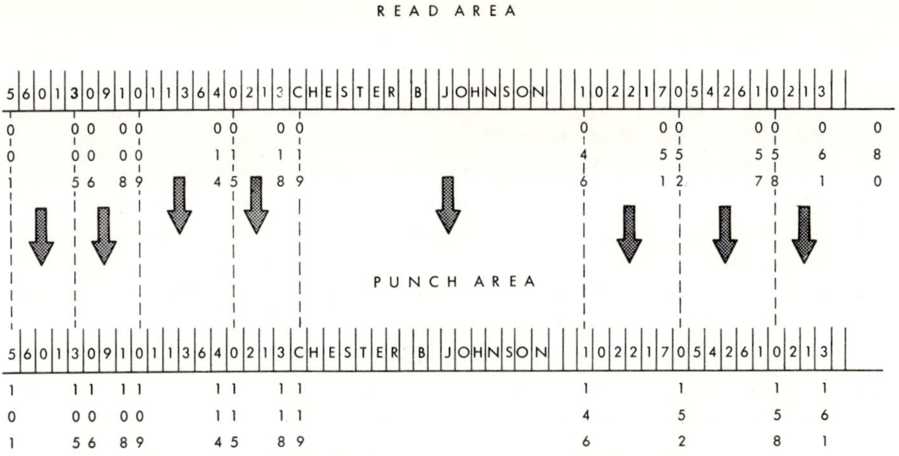

Figure 19-15. Instruction 3 transfers contents of the read area to the corresponding number in the punch area before punching takes place in instruction 4

area to be punched in a blank card by the punch end of the card reader. The machine stops automatically upon the detection of the last card.

Looping. The program presented in this chapter illustrates the cycle completed by the computer on each customer's account in an accounts receivable application. The computer is programmed to continue until the last account has been processed. This is done by instructing it to go back (loop or branch back) to the beginning of the program and execute each of the four instructions over again. This cycle is followed in processing the rest of the accounts. The instruction to branch the program is:

Op. Code	I-Address
B	333

"B" stands for "branch." 333 is the address of the first instruction of the program. It is written in the A-field, because the A-field can be used to store *either* the data address, as we have seen in the "move" instruction, or the instruction address, as shown in the branch instruction above. Like the first four instructions, the branch instruction must also be programmed and stored in memory. Usually, its storage location will be next to the fourth instruction. In the illustration, it would then occupy position numbers 349 to 352.

Branching causes continuous processing until all the cards are read. The cycle described above is repeated as many times as there are accounts. In this way, an entire accounts receivable file containing thousands of accounts can be updated frequently, quickly, and inexpensively.

QUESTIONS AND PROBLEMS FOR REVIEW

1. What is the function of the control unit? Explain how it manipulates the operation of the complete system.

2. What is a stored program? Explain the difference between the control unit and the stored program.
3. List and explain the necessary steps for program planning.
4. What is the importance of the self-operational feature of a computer?
5. Why is it necessary for the programmer to keep track of the location of data in storage?
6. What is a word mark? Why is it used in programming? When present in a field, in which position is it located?
7. Distinguish the difference between an address and data.
8. Set a word mark where required in order to define the "customer number," "customer name," and "amount due" fields:

0	5	2	S	T	E	V	E		W	A	L	L	S	1	7	4	9
2	2	2	2	2	2	2	2	2	2	2	2	2	2	2	2	2	2
1	1	1	1	1	1	1	1	2	2	2	2	2	2	2	2	2	2
2	3	4	5	6	7	8	9	0	1	2	3	4	5	6	7	8	9

Cust. No. — Customer Name — Amt. Due

9. In Problem 8 above, what is the address of the "customer number" field? The "customer name" field? The "amount due" field?
10. What is a block diagram? Why do we use a block diagram?
11. Explain the input/output symbol, the processing symbol, and the logic symbol.
12. What is meant by the term *branching?* The term *debugging?*
13. Differentiate between symbolic language and machine language. Which language is usually written first?
14. Block-diagram the following problem:

    Read a card. Add A + B = T.
    If *T* is more than 1, add it to *R*.
    If *T* is less than 1, subtract it from *S*.
    Punch the results in a card and then branch back to the beginning of the program.
15. Block-diagram the following problem:

    Read an employee's earnings card.
    Compare the year-to-date gross pay to $4,800.00.
    If it is equal to or greater than $4,800.00, branch to net pay calculations.
    Otherwise, compute for FICA. Assume 3⅝ per cent for FICA withholding tax.
16. What is an operation code? An operand? Give an example on each.
17. What are the A- and B-fields used for? Which field is also used to hold an instruction address?
18. What are the three reserved areas in a 1401 computer? What are they reserved for? Briefly explain each area.
19. If card output is desired, to which area in the central processing unit must the data be moved first?
20. What is the difference between a data address and an instruction address?

21. Assume the following program:

$\underline{1}$	$\underline{A}$	0	1	2	0	2	6	$\underline{M}$	0	2	6	3	2	6	$\underline{2}$	$\underline{B}$	5	0	0
5	5	5	5	5	5	5	5	5	5	5	5	5	5	5	5	5	5	5	5
0	0	0	0	0	0	0	0	0	0	1	1	1	1	1	1	1	1	1	1
0	1	2	3	4	5	6	7	8	9	0	1	2	3	4	5	6	7	8	9

Questions:

(a) How many instructions are there in the program?
(b) How many operation codes are there?
(c) What is the address of the second instruction?
(d) What is the address of the fifth instruction?
(e) Is the address of the last instruction a data address? If the answer is *No,* what is it called?
(f) When the program begins, which instruction is handled first? What is its address?

22. Explain in detail the instruction phase. When does the execution (E) phase start?

Chapter 20

Banking Application—Proof of Irregular-Payment Loans

Although the coverage of the basic ideas explained in Part III of this text is generally comprehensive, it would be helpful at this point to conclude by presenting the steps leading to the development of a program in a banking application, using a 1401 computer system. Because most programs written for business applications were found to be lengthy and to include advanced programming techniques, the selection of the brief application presented in this chapter was made with little choice.

One of the chief services of a commercial bank is the extension of loans of various types. Loans are ordinarily paid in a given number of equal monthly installments. For example, a loan for $1,800 extended to customer *A* can be paid back in six installments at $300.00 each installment,

12 payments at $150.00 each payment, 18 payments at $100.00 each payment, and so forth. It is no longer considered unusual, however, for a customer to dictate his own terms with regard to the method and amount of payment of the loan. A bank finds it only practical, and in some cases profitable, to arrange for "irregular" payments of loans by certain customers.

The following is a step-by-step description of the development of a program constructed for the purpose of verifying payment coupons (the total of which equals the amount of the loan) before they are mailed to the customer to accompany his future payments.

Background Information

On January 1 Mr. Julius Wilson, a senior programmer at a local firm, walked into the main office of a commercial bank and applied for a personal loan of $950.00. His 18-year-old daughter, Caroline, has recently been accepted by a Midwestern university to begin her undergraduate study in the department of Business Administration. Because her application for a scholarship was not favorably considered, her father decided to secure enough funds toward payment of her expenses during the first year.

When the application for the loan was approved the next day, Mr. Wilson asked the bank to arrange the payments in 11 monthly installments, beginning in February, as follows:

The interest on the loan plus other charges increased the amount due from $950.00 to $1,000.00. (Figure 20-1.) The loan card is shown in Figure 20-2. Mr. Wilson's method of payment is irregular, in that he wishes to repay the loan in 11 installments of unequal amounts, instead of the regular method of repaying in 6, 12, 18, 24, 30, or 36 monthly installments of equal amounts.

There are various reasons for the irregular payment of a loan. In the case of Mr. Wilson, his living expenses in March go up slightly on account of the Easter holiday. This makes it necessary

Payment No.	Due Date	Amount Due
01	Feb. 28	$ 90.00
02	Mar. 31	50.00
03	Apr. 30	90.00
04	May 31	90.00
05	June 30	90.00
06	July 31	90.00
07	Aug. 31	90.00
08	Sept. 30	90.00
09	Oct. 31	90.00
10	Nov. 30	90.00
11	Dec. 31	140.00
Total amount due		$1,000.00

Figure 20-1. Mr. Wilson's payment schedule

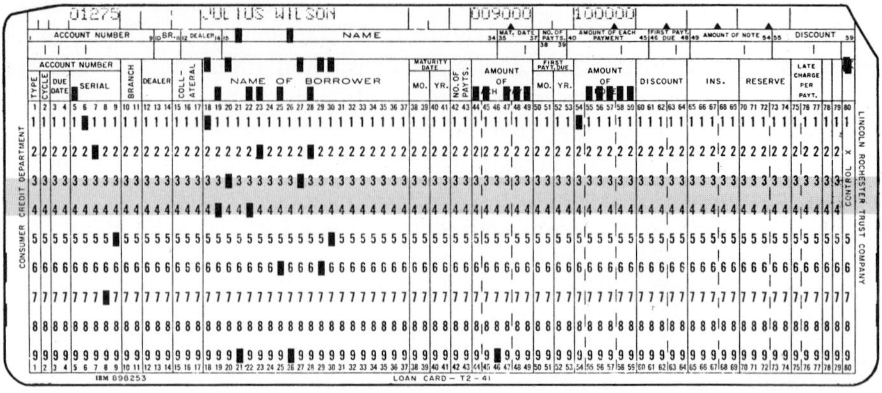

Figure 20-2. Mr. Wilson's loan card (Courtesy of Lincoln Rochester Trust Company)

for him to be permitted to pay only $50.00 at the end of that month. However, he would be in a good position to pay the balance of the loan ($140.00) on December 31, because his firm pays its usual yearly Christmas bonus to its employees during that month. The bank approved Mr. Wilson's terms and sent the necessary data to the consumer credit department for processing.

The first step required in the processing of Mr. Wilson's loan is the conversion of loan detail from the form which he signed to a punched card, called the "loan card." (Figure 20-2.) The loan card is punched with a serial number assigned to the specific loan, the name of the customer, the amount of each payment, and the amount of the loan (including interest and service charge). The $50.00 payment in March and the $140.00 payment in December are treated as exceptions in comparison to the majority of the payments represented by $90.00 each payment. These exceptions are dealt with in a different program when the "balance outstanding" on the loan is determined.

Next, the key-punch operator punches 11 payment coupons with Mr. Wilson's account number (01275) and the amount due ($90.00). The coupons are fed into an interpreter which is wired to read the holes in the coupon card and to print their meaning in the proper boxes on the top of it. Figure 20-3 shows the payment No. 01 coupon with the account number and the amount due.

The Problem

Before the coupons are stapled together to form a book and later mailed to the customer, the bank first makes sure that the sum of the

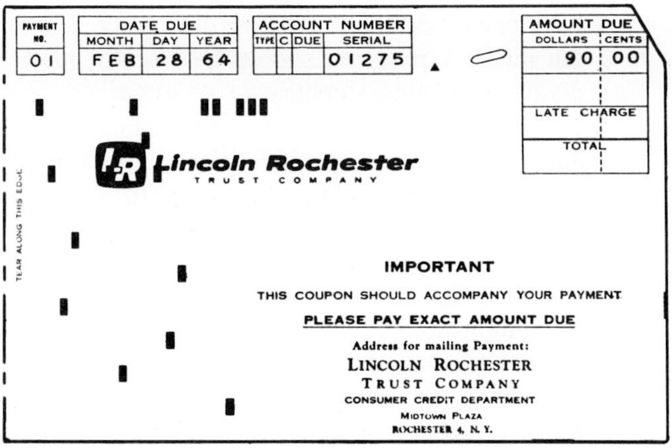

Figure 20-3. Mr. Wilson's payment No. 01 coupon card (Courtesy of Lincoln Rochester Trust Company)

amounts due on all of the coupons is equal to the amount of the loan. Considering the fact that Mr. Wilson's loan is only one of many other irregular loans, the computer is programmed to do the verifying on each of them. The following steps involve the organization of the input data, the construction of a program to "proof" the irregular-payment loans, and debugging and testing the program.

Data Organization

In order to prepare the input data for verification by the computer, the collator is used to merge behind each loan card all the coupons belonging to it. The loan cards are fed into the primary hopper and the coupon cards are fed into the secondary hopper. The control panel of the collator is wired so that a comparison is made between the account number of the loan card and that of the coupon. The result, in the case of Mr. Wilson's loan, is shown in Figure 20-4.

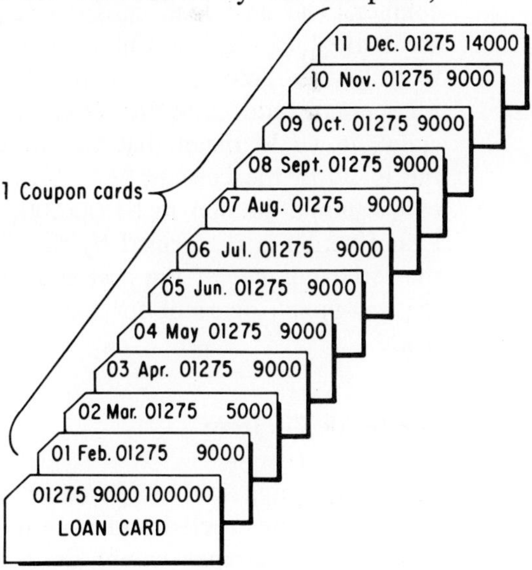

Figure 20-4. A loan card and coupon cards merged in proper sequence

The Development Stage

Up to this point, the key punch, the interpreter, and the collator have been used for the preparation of the data for input for a computer application. A program should be written, next, to instruct the computer to do the following steps:

1. To read the first card (the loan card). Each loan card should have an *X* punch in a specific column to distinguish it (being a loan card) from the coupon cards following it. An *X* in column 80 is arbitrarily chosen in this application. The coupon cards should not have an *X* punched in column 80. The program should include an instruction which would cause the computer to halt in the event an *X* punch is not detected in column 80.

2. Assuming that the first card is read and an *X* punch is detected in column 80, the computer is to move the amount of the note field (columns 54-59) to a storage area. It will remain there until the subsequent payment-coupon cards pertaining to the loan are read and the sum of the amount due on them is compared for equality with the amount of the loan. The serial number of the loan (columns 5-9) is also placed in a specific location for comparison with the serial number on the coupon card to make sure that the coupon card is related to the loan card.

3. Next, coupon payment number 01 is read. The account number is compared with that of the loan card serial number. If they are equal, it means that the coupon is a payment coupon for the loan card placed in storage. The amount due is added to a counter. The amount due from all other coupon cards is also added to the same counter.

4. All coupons belonging to a specific loan card are added to the counter. The next loan card, having a different serial number, will cause the computer to ignore it momentarily. It compares the sum of the counter, to which the amount due from all coupon cards bearing the same serial number are added, to the amount of the loan. If they are the same or equal, it would mean that the coupons contain a total equal to that of the loan. In the case of Mr. Wilson, the amount due in his 11 coupon cards should add up to $1,000.00. However, if they are not equal, then a subtraction is performed by the computer. The discrepancy, along with the serial number of the customer, is printed. This can be shown later to the key-punch operator for the purpose of alerting her to the mistake(s) made.

The Block Diagram

The foregoing four steps can be performed by a computer if a suitable program is constructed and eventually coded into machine language. But first the programmer would draw a block diagram in order to have a visual means of expressing a solution to the problem of "proofing the irregular-payment loans." It is shown in Figure 20-5.

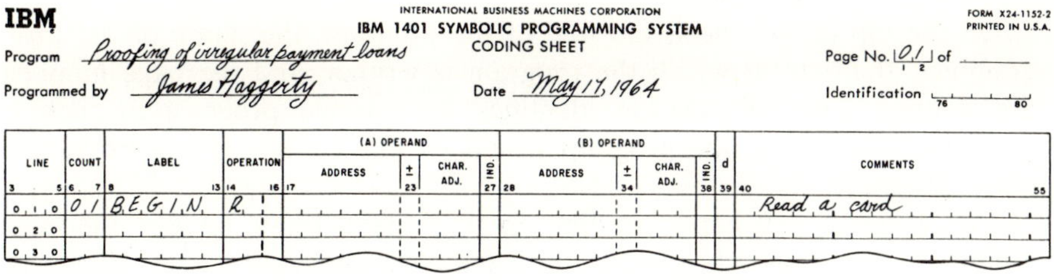

IBM

INTERNATIONAL BUSINESS MACHINES CORPORATION
IBM 1401 SYMBOLIC PROGRAMMING SYSTEM
CODING SHEET

FORM X24-1152-2
PRINTED IN U.S.A.

Program *Proofing of irregular payment loans*

Programmed by *James Haggerty*

Date *May 17, 1964*

Page No. *01* of

Identification

LINE (3–5)	COUNT (6–7)	LABEL (8–13)	OPERATION (14–16)	(A) OPERAND ADDRESS (17–)	± (23)	CHAR. ADJ.	IND. (27)	(B) OPERAND ADDRESS (28–)	± (34)	CHAR. ADJ.	IND. (38)	d (39)	COMMENTS (40–55)
010	01	BEGIN	R										Read a card
020													
030													

Figure 20-5. The IBM 1401 SPS coding sheet

The block diagram shows all the input, processing, and output details pertaining to the application in question. The programmer should, at the block-diagramming stage, attempt to modify and otherwise prepare the steps as correctly as possible. Any logical errors should be eliminated, because by doing so less time would need to be spent in debugging the program at the remaining stages before it becomes workable.

The Coding Stage

The common procedure followed by most programmers is to write the program instructions in language other than the machine (absolute) language. The language used in the preparation of this program is referred to as the *Symbolic Programming System* (SPS). As was explained in Chapter 18, the use of mnemonics or letters or codes that aid the memory constitute the approach followed in the use of the symbolic language. For example, letter "R" stands for *R*ead, "A" for *A*dd, "W" for *P*rint, and so forth. It is easier for most programmers to prepare a program first in language such as the symbolic language and next to use an automatic program coder (or a compiler) where all the instructions are converted into machine language.

Standard forms are used in writing instructions in symbolic language. Figure 20-5 is an IBM 1401 Symbolic Programming System Coding Sheet. It is divided into various vertical areas making up the necessary parts of a complete instruction. Horizontally, the SPS coding sheet contains 26 lines, each of which is used to write one instruction which will be punched in a single card. Therefore, the maximum number of instructions which can be written on any given coding sheet is 26. If the program consists of 30 instructions, for instance, another sheet (marked page *02*) would be used for writing the last four instructions. Figure 20-5 is a coding sheet showing the standard headings and the first three lines of the SPS sheet. Instruction 1 of the symbolic program (Figure 20-6) is also shown.

In an attempt to explain the subsequent steps in this computer application, a brief description of the parts of the SPS coding sheet pertaining to the application should be helpful.

On the top of the sheet, the title of the program, the name of the programmer, the date at which the program is written, and the page number are written. This information identifies the specific program in such a way that, when filed, the program would be unique in relationship to the other programs.

The extreme left-hand heading in the main frame shows the line number. Each line when filled in represents one instruction. The line number occupies three columns when punched in a punched card. They are columns 3-5. The rest of the vertical columns on the sheet correspond to the card columns to be punched.

The *count* columns (columns 6 and 7) are filled with the number of characters that the instruction on that line will occupy. For example, in Figure 20-5, the first instruction shown consists of an operation code R ("Read a card") only. Because letter "R" occupies only one address, the count stands for 01.

The *label* section (columns 8-13) is used for the purpose of writing a word description of the instructions on that line. Because, in symbolic programming, addresses are used to specify the location of any given instruction, the label becomes useful in that it stands for the address of that instruction. When an assembly program converts the instruction from symbolic to machine language, it replaces the label with an address (called "instruction address") which will identify the instruction in the program. In the case of the first instruction, its operation codes were stored in location number 333 in the primary storage, for instance. In this case, then, the word *BEGIN* is replaced by that address (333) in the machine-language deck. If the word *BEGIN* is used elsewhere in the program, it is also replaced by 333. To clarify this point, assume the following symbolic instructions:

Label	*Op. Code*	*A/I Address*	*B-Address*	*d*
BEGIN	R			
	B	BEGIN		

The first instruction simply means "Read a card." The second instruction is interpreted as "Branch" to an instruction that has a word *Begin,* or back to the first instruction. When these two instructions are converted into machine language, assuming that program storage begins in 333, they are converted as follows:

Instruction Location	*Op. Code*	*A/I Address*	*B-Address*	*d*
333	1			
334	B	333		

Because the word *begin* in the symbolic program identified the location of the first instruction, and because the letter "R" (converted to *1* in machine language) is stored in memory location 333, the word *BEGIN* in the A/I address of the second instruction is automatically converted to 333. The second instruction means: "Branch to 333 or to the first instruction to read another card."

The *A-Operand* section (columns 17-27) contains the A-address information. For the purposes of the application, it would suffice to say that columns 17-22 of the A-operand are used for writing the A-address of the instruction. The *B-operand* section (columns 28-38) contains the B-address information. Columns 28-33 are used for writing the B-address of the instruction.

Column 39 is reserved for a digit modifier code which, when present, can strengthen the operation of code by causing the computer to branch, halt, or do other required functions. In this application, we want the computer to halt if an *X* is not detected when a loan card is read. This conditional storage, when coded properly, constitutes the d-modifier; and in the above example, upon the failure of the computer to detect the presence of *X* in column 80 in the loan card, it halts immediately.

The *comments* section (columns 40-55) can be used for writing any informative comments which would tend to clarify an instruction. The programmer should comment on the instructions which seem clear only to him. If another programmer continues this operation or tries to complete the program begun by the first programmer, the absence of comments can make the job difficult to complete or to process. The author heard of an unfortunate incident in a case which involved the preparation of a complex program for a large business application. Two programmers spent several weeks constructing the program and finally succeeded in applying it to process the desired data according to the plan. A week later, they accepted a more attractive position with a competitor. Much to the surprise of management, they left behind a program with no comments, explanation, or any indication of how it was constructed. When the program needed modification as a result of some changes in the input data, the newly hired programmer preferred to rewrite the program from the beginning. This, naturally, duplicated the work of the former programmers unnecessarily, not to mention the delay in data processing and the expense incurred as a result of such an avoidable mistake.

Before the program is converted from a symbolic to machine language, each of the instructions on the SPS coding sheet is punched in a card. Figure 20-6 shows instruction 1 punched in an IBM card. Therefore, the number of cards representing a symbolic deck should be equal to the number of instructions written on the coding sheet.

Coding a symbolic deck into machine language involves the use of a

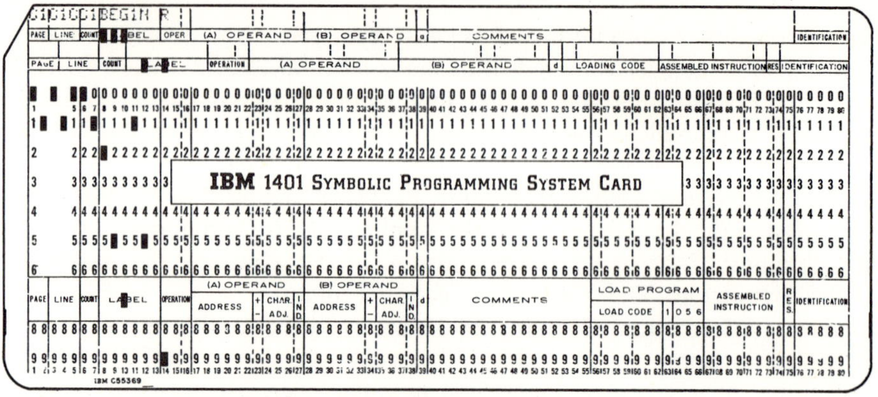

Figure 20-6. An IBM symbolic programming system card

converter, called the *assembly program* or more commonly referred to as "the assembler." The symbolic deck providing the source for a machine-language deck is called the *source program.* Because the object is to arrive at a deck of cards containing the instructions in a machine language, the latter deck is referred to as the "Object Program." (Figure 20-7.)

The assembly deck is placed in the card reader first, and behind it is fed the symbolic deck. In the punched end, a number of blank cards is fed into the punch hopper. The assembly program is not a machine. It is a deck of cards which are coded in such a way that the instructions they contain tell the computer, with machine language, how to convert a symbolic instruction. When the card reader is started by the depression of the LOAD button, the assembly-program instructions are transferred and loaded into the computer. Next, the symbolic deck is read, one card (one instruction) at a time. The result is the punching of a blank card with the symbolic instruction on the left side and the machine-language equivalent on the right side. (See Figure 20-8.)

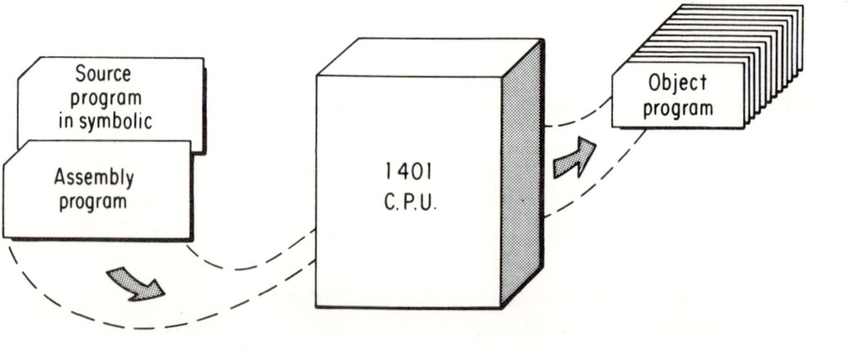

Figure 20-7. A schematic showing the steps in the coding process

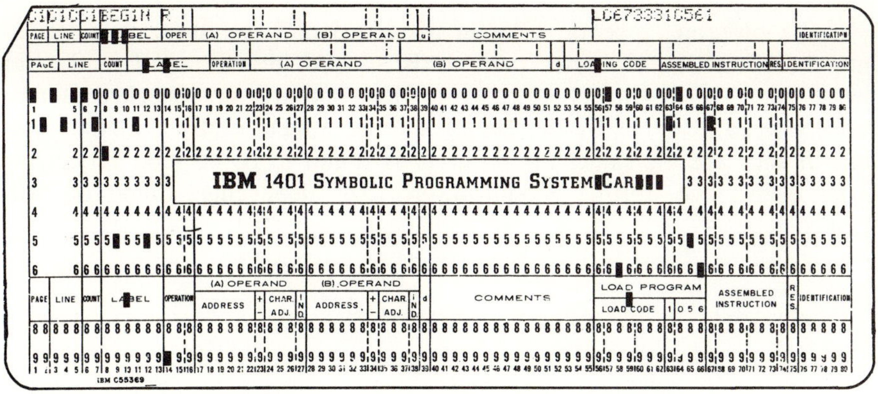

Figure 20-8. A program card in absolute language

Post-Listing

When all the cards are finally punched with machine language, they are fed behind a special assembler for the purpose of post-listing them through the use of the printer. For the purpose of convenience, it is felt more practical to interpret and check the program in printed form rather than from punched cards. (Figure 20-9.) At this stage, the programmer can make any necessary modifications or check on any phase of the program.

PG	L/N	CT	LABEL	OP	A OPERAND	B OPERAND	D	LOC	/NSTRUCT/ON COMMENTS
1	010	1	BEGIN	R				0333	1
1	011	8		BWZ	GOON	C080	K	0334	V 349 080 K
1	012	7		H	0001	C001		0342	. 001 001
1	020	4	GCCN	SW	0005			0349	, 005
1	030	7		MCW	0009	STR		0353	M 009 512
1	040	4		SW	0054			0360	, 054
1	050	7		MCW	0059	ACCUM		0364	M 059 501
1	060	1	START	R				0371	1
1	070	8		BWZ	TOTAL	C080	K	0372	V 410 080 K
1	080	7		SW	0038	C044		0380	, 038 044
1	090	7		C	0042	STR		0387	C 042 512
1	100	5		B	TOTAL		/	0394	B 410 /
1	110	7		A	0049	CTR		0399	A 049 507
1	130	4		B	START			0406	B 371
1	140	7	TCTAL	S	CTR	ACCUM		0410	S 507 501
1	142	4		S	CTR			0417	S 507
1	145	7		MZ	0081	CTR		0421	Y 081 507
1	150	7		MZ	0081	ACCUM		0428	Y 081 501
1	160	7		C	ACCUM	ZERO		0435	C 501 518
1	170	5		B	GOON		S	0442	B 349 S
1	180	7		MCW	ACCUM	C220		0447	M 501 220
1	190	7		MCW	STR	C208		0454	M 512 208
2	010	1		W				0461	2
2	020	4		CS	0280			0462	/ 280
2	022	4		S	ACCUM			0466	S 501
2	024	7		MZ	0081	ACCUM		0470	Y 081 501
2	025	8		BWZ	GOON	CC80	K	0477	V 349 080 K
2	040	7	ERROR	H	0002	C002		0489	. 002 002
2	060	6	ACCUM	DCW	*			0501	
2	070	6	CTR	DCW	*			0507	
2	080	5	STR	DCW	*			0512	
2	090	6	ZERO	DCW	*		000000	0518	
2	100			ENC	BEGIN				/ 333 080

33 CARCS

Figure 20-9. Post-listing of the program from the machine language cards

If the program appears to be in good order, it is tested: it is loaded into the computer, and then data cards are fed into the card reader for processing. The results obtained from the computer are checked against those arrived at either by the use of another system or by a manual system. If they are the same, the program is found to be in good processing order. Otherwise, further modification(s) or debugging should be performed.

PART 4

MANAGEMENT OF DATA PROCESSING

Chapter 21

Management Problems Involved in The Introduction of a Data-Processing System

Status-Seeking Firms

It is common knowledge that the majority of people in the United States constantly strive to reach a class level higher and more refined than any other level their associates have been able to attain. Whether this objective can be realized actually or not is not so important as the desire to aim in that direction. Most of us surround ourselves with symbols which represent a rank or a position, namely, a status higher than what we really have or are able to afford. It is like the case of the Japanese specialty-shop owner who purchased a modern calculator and placed it in the shop window while instructing his bookkeeper to continue using the abacus for calculating purposes. He wanted to impress his customers that he was using modern equipment as a tool in preparing his financial matters.

A business firm is in no way different from other members of the community. It is made up of people, who also aim toward achieving a status higher than that of their competitors. Whether or not they are able to maintain that status seems, in many cases, less important than attaining it, regardless of the expenses incurred. Some business firms (both large and small) seem to be hypnotized by the glamor and prestige of a data-processing installation—especially, a computer installation. They hear about and believe in stories told about the fantastic potentials of computers in business. Some envision a computer which can solve all their problems, meet their needs and expectations, make decisions in major areas, and eliminate all the worries and frustrations that a manager often encounters. Such firms are said to have "computeritis."

Whereas a data-processing system appears to be a sign of progress and prestige resulting from the apparent ability of a company to purchase or rent the equipment, it does not necessarily hold true that the introduction of the system itself is the best approach to solving a given problem. The major part of the gain realized by the use of the equipment can be achieved under the manual or the presently used semimechanized methods if they are changed periodically to meet the needs of the business. Many firms neglect to modify or revamp their system, however old it is, as long as they realize a reasonable return on their investment. They grow in size and expand their operation over a number of years with a realization of a high margin of income. They thus reach a stage where they realize suddenly that their manual method of data processing is no longer adequate to do the job well. Some panic and conduct a hurried, and brief, feasibility study resulting in the installation of a punched-card, or an electronic, data-processing system. Experience shows that most of those firms who awakened a bit too late to their need for improvement and alignment with the competitive business surrounding, after their hurriedly installed system is put into operation, begin to realize less than desirable results. In order to adjust the equipment to the procedures used by the various departments, additional auxiliaries are added. They find the system so unfit to do the work that must be done that they decide to revert to the previously used manual system.

What Type of Firms Buy Computers, and Why?

In order for a company to survive the competitive pressure and continue to make a profit large enough to remain in business and provide for expansion in the future, methods other than the manual techniques of information flow appear to be desirable. Companies are becoming more complex in their structure, organizational framework and relationships, and diversity of products and in the voluminous amounts of data to be worked on and rearranged daily. To a firm, production of quality products at a competitive price means a need for equally efficient and modern data-processing equipment to aid in the realization of that goal by processing the data needed for analysis quickly and cheaply.

Naturally, it is not an easy task to decide on the installation of a computer in business. Risks are involved which cannot be determined accurately. The unforeseen future makes many firms feel helpless if they do not have any way to use the tools of business forecasting or market research. When costly equipment is introduced, whether purchased or leased, the firm should make sure that such equipment has the capacity to handle present business needs, and also that it can be modified conveniently in the event that unexpected developments, such as a rise in production or sales or general expansion, should take place, making alterations necessary.

What should a business firm do with regard to the introduction of data-processing equipment? Can it afford to stand still and learn from the experiences of other firms, or should it initiate a complete and detailed survey of the available equipment with regard to the existing data-processing problems that need to be solved? The former alternative has merit in that a company can learn from the experimentation of other companies of similar size in the use of specific equipment. However, it is unlikely that the firm experimenting with its new computer will divulge any information which would put it at a competitive disadvantage. The second alternative promises results if a thorough feasibility study is made and if enough time is allowed for research so that the right equipment to do the job for which such assistance is needed is obtained.

If top management is to take advantage of the advances in the field of data processing, decisions must be made relating to: (1) the overhauling of procedures used in order to discover exactly what they are and where they need correction; (2) the feasibility of using an installation in its operation; (3) acceptance of the installation by operative members of the firm, including its employees as well as its stockholders; (4) the willingness of all concerned to cooperate in the operation of the data-processing system after it is installed; and (5) the problem of retraining those of its employees affected by such an installation.

The procedure should be really "block-diagrammed" in the minds of top-management members so that important details will not be overlooked in the transition from thinking in terms of the manual performance of any of its applications. If each step is worked out carefully and painstakingly, time will be saved in the long run, because many of the problems incident to the installation of a computer system will have been foreseen and allowances will be made for them.

The types of firms that purchase computers are typically:

(1) Those which can well afford to pay for them. The cost of the installation usually comes from funds which are not earmarked for any other particular or preplanned project. Such firms are usually medium-size to large-size ones that can use a computer to maximum capacity. The exception in this case is the small firm which cooperates with a neighboring firm or firms to purchase the computer, a charge being made by the contracting firm for its use. This approach is widely used also by educational institutions which reserve a certain amount of time per week for sale to local firms for the processing of their data.

(2) Another factor which characterizes the firm that is likely to buy a computer is the employment of a large amount of clerical help for purposes of computation. The larger the firm, the larger is the clerical staff. Computations performed in business range from simple addition or subtraction in updating customer accounts in the credit department to more complex computations involving mathematical formulas used in research or the production-control area.

(3) Not only is the type of computation a factor, but also the number of computations and the time it takes to complete them are significant in inducing a firm to install a computer system. Simple computations may take a few minutes each. By contrast, a complex scientific or mathematical computation may take hours to complete.

From the foregoing discussion, it can be inferred that some of the major objectives of an electronic data-processing installation would be:

(1) To process progressively increasing volumes of data resulting from a company's expansion over the years which are not efficiently handled by the presently used system.

(2) To deal with more complex computational problems which cannot be processed efficiently by manual methods.

(3) To attempt to reduce the cost of computing complex applications, as well as that of processing voluminous amounts of data involving simple computations. Cost is important in that its reduction will result in a greater increase in the profit figure, assuming that all other factors remain fairly constant.

(4) To provide a framework for decision making by management based on the facts processed and produced by the installation. These facts play an important role in that an increase in their accuracy, along with a reduction in the time it takes to process and prepare them in report form, will help management arrive at better conclusions in planning future courses of action for the firm.

The Feasibility Study

A feasibility study involves the survey and evaluation of the advantages of using a computer to work out a set of given applications for a firm.

In deciding whether a computer system should be installed, the character of a firm's operations, its present operational procedures, and its general objectives should be carefully reviewed in the light of the purposes that the processing machines are designed to serve. Management must formulate a sharply defined picture of its data-processing needs and of how a computer can fit into the organization to serve its various departments in this respect. *It should be plainly understood that a computer is intended only as an aid to men.* Without this understanding, the whole character of the system when installed is likely to be misconstrued and frustrations caused by its failure to live up to expectations.

The steps involved in conducting a feasibility study are similar to those used in solving many of our personal daily problems.

To illustrate: After graduating from college, Ralph Bender, a business management major, accepted a position with a manufacturing concern. Considering the limited income of a management trainee, his new job, and the need to have a mode of transportation, Ralph purchased a used car for $95.00 from a friend who was answering the call from his local draft board. In time, Ralph advanced within the firm. He gained recognition and promotions steadily. A year and a half later he married and, during the same month, he was promoted to head a department in the manufacturing division of the main plant.

With a substantial increase in salary and a relocation to a suburban area, Ralph felt the old "jalopy" to be unsuited to his new status. The upkeep proved to be exorbitant because repairs had to be made frequently. It was *unreliable,* in that mechanical failure happened at inopportune times, often resulting in his late arrival at the plant. It was also *inefficient* with respect to the excessive gasoline and oil it consumed. It had a *shabby appearance,* and also was *hazardous* to drive at high speeds.

Knowing that his present car no longer met his needs, Ralph conducted a "feasibility study." He spent his free evenings shopping for a new automobile. He contacted dealers who sold various makes and models. He drove a few demonstration cars and obtained literature about the various models. To supplement his general knowledge about the merchandise, he contacted friends and associates to learn what their experience had been with the new automobiles they had purchased. He also read articles in independent magazines about the results of tests made on various makes.

After two weeks of survey and evaluation, Ralph considered his present position and his chances for further advancement with the firm. The chances looked good. He also considered the expenses involved with regard to his home mortgage, his living and other expenses, the amount of cash he had available, and the amount he needed to borrow to pay for a new car. He weighed the price of the car against the savings in gasoline and oil and the car's known reliability, efficiency, and speed. When his analysis was complete, to his wife's very apparent pleasure, he placed an order for the purchase of a specific make, size, power rating, and price range. He selected the dealer to whom he gave the order because of his reputation for guaranteed prompt delivery, courteous service, and extension of reasonable credit terms.

The feasibility study conducted by a business firm for determining whether to use a computer to serve its needs is similar to that conducted by Ralph in the determination, and the eventual purchase, of his automobile. The remaining part of this chapter explains the steps involved and the factors which should be considered in the installation of a computer system.

Impetus for a feasibility study

For a feasibility study to succeed, it is necessary that: (1) the survey and evaluation be made by competent, qualified personnel; (2) the study must guarantee savings in clerical and other related costs; and, most importantly, (3) it must be approved by top management, especially when the need for it is being recognized and supported by members of the lower ranks in the management organization. When top management initiates a feasibility study, their motive is generally a desire for experimentation, with less emphasis upon cost or the obtaining of funds. Their aim is to use a computer for producing information, such as sales analyses or business forecasting, which is useful to management and which is unobtainable under the present system. When interest in this is generated at the top level, the project gets under way fairly easily, because top-management people are already sold on the need for and the desirability of having a computer. More often lower management initiates the interest because of a known need for the use of faster methods in the processing of data in their departments. Regardless who conceives the idea, top management must be sold on the need for its implementation. In the latter case, communications flow upward first, and all data pertinent to the problem which would be helpful in gaining the approval of superiors must be presented. Success in gaining the approval of top management is related, to a great extent, to their attitudes and personalities as shown in their dealings with lower management men. If the members of top management are young, aggressive, willing to risk investment of money in new ideas, in new ways of doing things, and in applying the latest methods available for the purpose of meeting competition head on, then there is no great problem in gaining their support. On the other hand, if top management are conservative, unimaginative, insisting on the presentation of all the facts regardless of their value, and spending an unreasonable amount of time deliberating on the matter, then the job of selling them the idea of introducing a new computer would be difficult. It is assumed in this discussion, however, that management is interested in knowing in some detail about the specific problems at hand, a description of the proposal, and the basic facts which would support the contention of the person presenting the need for the new system. That person would find it helpful if a survey were conducted to show the cost of the new system in comparison with the anticipated saving resulting from its installation and use.

The mystery period

At this stage, little is known of the uses and capabilities of, and the real need for, a computer to serve the needs of the company and, particularly, to solve the specific data-processing problem(s) in which a need is felt. An electronic computer is mysterious primarily because of the ignorance of the layman in understanding its real potentials and the ways in which it can be useful to him and his firm. In order to start the project, assuming that management approves, a preliminary survey is usually the first step.

The project team

Before any survey is made, whether preliminary or detailed, personnel from the various levels of the organization are appointed to assume responsibility for the project. They are referred to as the *project team.* The team usually consists of the various department heads, whose main job is to find out whether or not a data-processing system can perform various applications for the firm. The group is to keep in mind, not only the immediate problems and applications, but also the long-range applications. The new system must be capable of meeting an expanding business situation and, with the addition of the necessary components, process those applications the information from which is used to keep the firm in good competitive standing. Further, questions such as the following should be borne in mind: What is the basic objective of the computer? Is it feasible to centralize operations and reduce costs? What application(s) appear to be economical to run as a start, and what applications are economical to run after a computer is installed? Is it possible to have the cooperation of the responsible people in the firm, as well as of the employees? How flexible is a specific computer with regard to adding more components for faster processing or more storage capacity? Attempting to answer these questions is not an easy task. The job becomes similar to that of an architect who must use all his resources and blend various facts in such a way as to bring about a good plan for the construction of a house or other type of building.

The desirability of forming a project team to initiate a feasibility study is based on the belief that man's background and know-how are limited to the favorable performance of certain duties and that he is a less competent judge in regard to those about which he is unfamiliar. When a few men from various departments, encompassing vast knowledge in different areas, are grouped as a team, the benefit of their combined knowledge and experience should aid in bringing about better results.

Authority and Responsibility of the Project Team. The project team should have authority commensurate with the responsibility which it agrees to assume. Its members should be authorized to contact line managers, as well as to seek information through the staff personnel for data-collection purposes. This cannot be done successfully unless top management are in full agreement about what the team is doing. Top management should be willing to be used to gain the cooperation of the operating units at lower levels so that the work of the team may be done with minimum loss of time. By the same token, all report findings, and other important information, should be reported to top management—preferably, to the chief executive of the firm. In the case of a very large firm, an executive vice-president in charge of manufacturing or finance would be a good substitute.

The Project Director. Regardless of the background and knowledge of the project team investigating the feasibility of introducing a new computer, their job can be done well only after someone has been appointed to supervise the study and synchronize the work of the team as it is related to the duties and functions of other people in the organization. He is referred to as the *project director*. To "direct" means to issue directives, orders, and commands, and to supervise the work of his staff group so that it works within the plan set in advance toward the goal for which it was created. A project director is a management man with special abilities and above-average intelligence. He is imaginative and able to size up a problem quickly and to arrive at the alternatives, adapting the one that can provide a solution. He should have a wide background in business and specific knowledge in accounting and finance, because most business applications involve knowledge based on these two fields. A knowledge of accounting will help him to understand the accounting implications pertaining to an application and to communicate more effectively with those personnel who are engaged in payroll, accounting, and other related departments. His finance background should help him to consider more seriously the matter of costs versus savings. Cost justification has to be made to management before a new installation can be approved. It may be that a firm's vice-president in charge of finance becomes the project director, because he already possesses such knowledge. He is unlikely to have financial bias, because his work and position are independent of any department or division of the organization. His function is simply to determine the goals of the company and find out how to introduce an electronic data-processing system to meet these goals.

Senior Management Committee. Personnel selection is usually headed by a *senior management committee* whose job it is to disseminate information and maintain communications among the various executives about the findings of the project team, the members of which it is responsible for selecting. The senior management committee is used to level off any misunderstanding about the automatic data-processing system and to promote enthusiasm and interest for the use of the computer by the departments. Without that, the project may collapse. Therefore, the cooperation of all departments is necessary. The committee transmits all information it receives (feedback) to the project team and keeps it informed about other matters of concern to its members.

What are the desired personal qualifications of each of the project-team members? A team member is expected to be knowledgeable in and guided by the concepts and policies that management uses in operating the company. He should seek whatever information is necessary to understand how these policies and concepts are worked out. A knowledge of company procedures will provide the basis for an analysis and evaluation of the flow and transformation of data through the organization by the use of the current system. Without this knowledge, it would be difficult to select a computer that is tailored to solve the specific problem(s) for which purpose the study is conducted.

Above all, a project-team member must be experienced in human relations, because he will be dealing with other people at all times. His experience must guide him in communicating effectively to gain their cooperation and help in matters related to the study. Further, he must be creative, because data-processing systems demand new ways of doing things, owing to their flexibility. It takes imagination, hard work, and patience to do detailed charts and to construct useful programs.

Part of the work of the project team involves the collection of cost figures on the present system. A team member should be unbiased, impartial, and able to evaluate clerical and other related costs and to utilize any other information which would help him to arrive at a true and clear survey and evaluation report.

When asked to serve on the team, some men may be reluctant to do so. The interest and attitude of the team members are also very important because they may not wish to learn a new and different field unrelated directly to their own. The sign of a mathematical formula, however basic or elementary it is, discourages some personnel from pursuing the field any further. Lack of knowledge is ignorance in a given area. Ignorance generates fear. Some personnel fear that the introduction of an electronic data-processing system, once installed, may fail to render the desired results. They feel fully responsible in view of the thousands of dollars that may be invested. That is where the project director, a leader with confidence and hope, can "water down," if not suppress, those fears and reservations in the minds of the members of the team. This can be accomplished by: (1) reducing as much as possible the amount of work that team members have to do on their regular jobs. Preferably, they would be in a better position if all of their regular duties were assigned temporarily to someone else, thus allowing them to concentrate freely on the project. (2) To ease the deadline pressure, the director can emphasize a deadline of presenting their findings to management after the team has had a chance to become familiar with the new computer field.

Also, the team members may not wish to put in the time and effort necessary, especially when the person in question is reaching retirement age or has in mind a transfer to a better position within the company or elsewhere. For these reasons, it is desirable to select for the project team men between the ages of 30 and 45. Generally speaking, those under 30 probably have not been with the firm long enough to understand it well or to have had experience in dealing with people effectively. By the same token, some of the men over 45 years of age may have decided already to concentrate on a specific field and may have planned to use their talent and time in developing it further. Their hopes lie in moving ahead in an area with which they are already familiar. There are, of course, exceptions to these generalities. Many of those exceptions have proved invaluable to the more effective survey and evaluation of the project.

Technical Qualifications of the Project Team. In addition to the personal qualifications described above, members of the project team should possess the proper technical knowledge needed in the job. A knowledge of accounting and a background in electronics are desirable. Problems are bound to arise when the project team is too heavily weighted in either direction. Personnel with a background in electronics tend to put more emphasis upon the aspects of a computer from the electronics viewpoint, such as speed, access time, and so forth, with too little emphasis upon the procedures used by the firm. On the other hand, personnel with an accounting background stress the procedures but put little emphasis upon electronics. The result of either extreme can only be the introduction of an inadequate computer system. Hence, the need for balance in the team's make-up between these two kinds of "experts" is obvious.

Members who have combined a broad background in the accounting system used by the firm and basic knowledge of electronics or electronic data processing appear to be ideal. If such men are not available in the firm, and a choice has to be made, those with the accounting background are preferred, because it is felt that it is easier to teach an accountant how to program a machine and how its parts work than it is to teach an expert electronics man accounting systems.

Companies have tried to solve the problem by pirating personnel with the desired background from other firms, luring them with attractive salaries and fringe benefits. Although this is done repeatedly, it is not considered exactly ethical and is not too productive. After all, a newcomer will have to acquaint himself with the procedures, the policies, objectives, and needs, and the data-processing problems of a firm with which he is unfamiliar. Because he has worked in the same field elsewhere, however, his learning period is bound to be shorter than that of a person who starts "from scratch."

The preliminary survey stage

The foregoing discussion involved the selecting of personnel to form a project team headed by a director for the purpose of investigating the feasibility of introducing an electronic data-processing system to the organization. Once this stage is completed and management approves the project, the first stage to be carried out is a preliminary survey. Like Ralph Bender, the college graduate, after a need is felt for a new system in solving an existing processing problem, the members of the team should begin to contact and visit various computer manufacturers in order (1) to acquaint themselves with the computer field, (2) to have a visual view of the components on display, (3) to get a general orientation to the over-all capabilities of electronic data-processing systems, and (4) to gain impressions about the possibility of using one of the systems in their firm. Throughout the survey stage, it would be important for the members to keep in mind the particular problem(s) of their firm as they learn more about the various systems. They are also to remember that there is no "cookbook" to guide them as to what to tell management in regard to which computer will solve their problem(s) satisfactorily.

The team members should contact more than one computer manufacturer. Like Ralph in his contacting of several dealers selling different makes of automobiles, the members of the team are interested in educating and exposing themselves to what is available on the market. This eliminates the bias factor for a specific computer manufacturer. However, it is contended that, if a project team concentrates on one set of equipment put out by a given manufacturer, the members would learn to program well and do an application for testing purposes. In this case, less time would be wasted, especially because they would not run the danger of becoming confused by viewing too much of essentially the same equipment.

Although concentration on one manufacturer's equipment appears advantageous and time-saving, the disadvantages might outweigh the advantages. Like any other manufacturer, a computer manufacturer is a sales-minded person. Occasionally a customer can be "high-pressured" to purchase a computer system just as is true in buying other items. The team should, therefore, spend a reasonable amount of time looking at each offering in the market before they concentrate on any one model.

More intensive survey and evaluation stage

When the "acquaintanceship" stage is well under way, the project team should make frequent contacts with computer manufacturers and consult them with regard to whether the company's problem(s) can be processed electronically. Whatever type of computer system is recommended, the team should obtain cost data as well as a description of the specific types of application(s) that can be done on it. Pressures brought on the team members, whatever their source, should not be allowed to "hurry" the decision unduly.

In addition to consultation with computer manufacturers, a check on the success of other firms which have had experience with the same or a similar system would be helpful. As mentioned earlier in this chapter, obtaining such data may not be possible.

Small and medium-size firms and, less frequently, large firms seek the aid of a management consultant for gaining information, advice, and direction in a feasibility study. Even though consultants' fees are high, smaller firms do use them, primarily because they (the firms) do not have skilled men within their organization to do the survey well. A consultant's chief duty is to guide a project team in planning and supervising the survey. Many consultants have little knowledge of electronic data processing, but they are experienced in analyzing and solving problems. They have leadership qualities and the ability to "size up" the situation well. No matter how well they may be able to "size up" the situation themselves, many organizations seek the aid of a consultant so as to have a third party's independent and unbiased views with regard to the recommendations presented by the project team. The idea of having outlined the solution to a problem based on a procedure supervised by a consultant commands respect, and often consent, by the operating heads and other levels within the organization. Organizations should be quite selective in hiring a consultant. When a project involves thousands of dollars of investment, care and caution, with efficiency, should be exercised continuously throughout the study.

Other services of a consultant who is a specialist in electronic data processing include training in programming and education in how computers work. Some consultants also have a reliable background in systems design. They can be of great help in formulating a system tailored to the company's needs. A consultant can also provide technicians, programmers, and other temporary help to operate the new computer installation until the company trains or hires someone on a more permanent basis. Many computer manufacturers offer these services also, once their particular systems are chosen for installation.

Personnel training

Acquaintanceship alone is insufficient either for arriving at a decision or preparing a valid recommendation to be considered and approved by management. It is important, then, that the project team undertakes to learn more about the uses of data-processing equipment in solving processing problems generally and those that are prevalent in their own organization specifically. This education is available either in academic institutions or in educational training centers directed by computer manufacturers.

Many academic institutions of higher learning have already introduced courses at the undergraduate and graduate levels in electronic data processing. For the past few years, colleges and universities have felt the impact of the electronic computer upon industry. In a number of forward-looking educational institutions, programs in the business and science fields were tailored to include courses in data processing and programming. Members of the project team can benefit immensely from the computer facilities of nearby universities that have an installation.

The other alternative open for a prospective customer is attending a computer manufacturer's educational center. Most manufacturers of necessity believe in the "sale through education" approach. Courses ranging from "the basics of key punching" to those in advanced programming techniques for large-scale computers are available. In most cases, this education is rendered free to prospective customers. The project team should utilize this privilege and take a series of courses suitable for their needs. One popular series of courses progresses from the history of data processing through machine functions, flowcharting and block-diagramming, programming basics and techniques, and coding to the role of management in the field of electronic data processing.

When basic knowledge has been acquired and the team has learned some programming techniques, it would be a good idea to program a typical application of the firm. After the program has been written, it should be tested in order to judge whether a specific computer produces the desired results. This brings up the question: what application should be selected? Should it be a brief and easy application, with the purpose of speeding up the process of selecting a computer, once a specific computer has passed the test by processing the application successfully? Or should the application be a major, detailed company application to see if it can be processed properly, because it would occupy a substantial part of the computer time when the computer is installed? The latter alternative is preferred in most cases, provided that the steps in the application are systemized and well presented. Such preparation makes the job of programming the steps and testing the application as a whole less difficult.

Others argue that the application to be selected should involve the development of data which it is not feasible to process by the presently used methods. This would test the capability of a computer in producing results important to management for making better decisions. However, most of those who have had experience in undergoing a feasibility study will agree that an application from the "brute force area" where a large number of personnel and much clerical work are involved would be the best to use. Economy and cost reduction are factors which are constantly stressed and are most likely to be the major factors which make many firms feel a need for conversion to an electronic data-processing system. In manufacturing, such "bread-and-butter" applications include inventory control, product control, factory scheduling, and so forth. In a bank, consumer credit loans and loan accounting are popular examples.

Electronic data processing versus the employees of the firm

During the survey and evaluation stage, the employees should be informed of the possibility of introducing electronic data-processing equipment into the plant. Although the employees should not share in decision making with regard to the installation itself, before any installation is considered seriously, the project team should investigate its effect upon them. Because of their lack of knowledge in the electronic data-processing field, they fear being replaced by a computer. They worry about their job security. Some begin to have a "mental inferiority complex" because of their apprehensiveness about working in a new and strange environment and expect the computer "to tell them what to do." If left unchecked, the net effect would be the employees' refusal to cooperate. Information begins to be withheld deliberately, and soon the system has been sabotaged altogether. For these reasons, management cannot afford to ignore the feelings and attitudes of its employees. The matter becomes worse in a unionized firm where the union can cause inconvenience and fight for the security of its employees. Management should publicize, educate, and distribute materials on electronic data processing to quiet replacement fears. The suggestion box is a useful safety valve which employees should be encouraged to use to air their grievances and suggestions with regard to the installation. It should be kept in mind that the grapevine is a great, though unofficial, line of communication. No executive can stop its use. It should be utilized to the best advantage of the firm by feeding needed information to the rank-and-file employees, especially those whose jobs may be affected. All that can be done should be done, in terms of instilling confidence and hope in the minds of the employees as far as job security is concerned. It is understandable that all people resist change, especially older employees. They dislike any innovation which they do not understand. If the majority of the firm's employees are older men and women, the job of selling them the advantages of a computer installation becomes more difficult.

Employees can be sold on the fact that (1) the use of a computer means less physical as well as less mental effort, (2) that it is a tool to aid them in doing their jobs with greater efficiency, (3) that more opportunities are bound to arise of which they can avail themselves. The use of a second, and possibly a third, shift will open a new set of jobs for women, and especially housewives who do not find it convenient to hold a job during the day. (4) There will be no unannounced overtime because of the speed at which routine data are processed within the regular shift.

What makes more difficult the job of selling the employees on the value of a computer system is the poor publicity which constantly frightens and threatens the layman. It is not uncommon to find cartoons in newspapers and magazines depicting a computer as superior intellectually to man. Employees take this to heart and add it to their fears and frustrations. This tends to cast suspicion on the real situation and makes it more difficult for management to sell the advantages of electronic data processing and to get the cooperation and willingness of employees to be educated and adjusted to the real meaning of the proposed installation.

Cost-analysis stage

Although the educational program is being carried out and an application is being programmed to test the effective use of a computer system, the project director should see that a cost estimate of the computer is made. A comparison should then be made between this cost and that of the presently used system to see if any saving can be realized. Cost estimates are helpful in that they aid the project team in determining the amount and degree of savings from an automatic data-processing installation.

The estimated annual savings can be presented in the following condensed form (all figures and data are hypothetical):

Estimated cost of operating the present system	$1,250,000
Estimated cost of operating the new system (when installed)	500,000
Estimated gross saving	$ 750,000
Less estimated computer rental	420,000
Estimated net saving per year	$ 330,000

Costs incidental to a computer installation:

(1) The cost of investing cash in the equipment and related factors in addition to the price of the equipment. Included in it are also the costs of remodeling, purchase of furniture and fixtures, personnel training, systems design, installation of air conditioning, and the feasibility study.

(2) The operation cost. This includes the cost of employing technical personnel, programmers, console operators, and coding and maintenance employees. Because the jobs of most of these employees are skilled, such personnel command higher salaries than those hired under the previous system. This can increase the cost of operating the new system to the extent that savings become negligible. Also included in the operation cost is the cost of input and output preparation. Data must be punched in cards or recorded on tape from punched cards for input. In the former case, a key punch is needed and a card inventory must be available for input preparation. In addition, the need arises for a sorter or a collator for classifying the data in a form suitable for the computer as input. In the latter case, data must be punched in a card or paper tape and, by the use of a converter, recorded on tape for input preparation.

The cost of output involves primarily the use of punched cards, if the results are to be punched, or statement forms, if they are to be printed. Stocking cards and statement forms might cause confusion in the stockroom. In the event that a computer installation is decided upon, the stockroom should be cleared of any and all forms pertaining to the old system in order to avoid confusion and delay in finding the desired materials.

(3) Physical and technical obsolescence can be costly. In the case of companies that purchase the computer, an allowance for depreciation is made because of the gradual reduction in the value of the system. The depreciation range is generally between 5 and 10 years. There are situations, however, where this range reaches 15 years. Technical obsolescence is inherent in the field of electronic data processing. Computer design, speed, and so forth, change constantly. A computer that appeared to be ideal two years ago may not be as efficient today. Again, in this case, the firm needs to look at its procedures, its short- and long-range objectives, its needs and requirements with regard to the data, and the way they must be processed. If the computer still serves these needs, it can be concluded that, as far as the firm is concerned, the computer is still efficient.

In many cases, the discovery may be made that present manual methods are equal to, or superior to, the proposed method of mechanization. Unless there are large enough applications which require detailed repetitive treatment (that can be done easily once the procedure is outlined), management had better think twice about spending money on a proposed electronic data-processing system. If the volume of data surrounding any one application is not large enough and requires too many exceptions in its treatment—which involve judgment—it may take so long to program on a computer that this type of installation would be out of the question. On the other hand, it might be adaptable to a punched-card system. In examining procedures used to accomplish its objectives, management may find that these will have to be changed in some way if the processing is to be most rewarding. It has been the experience of some executives that, when they got their procedures really straightened out, they found there was no need for conversion to a better system as the presently used methods, once brought up to date, were quite adequate.

Another question that arises in this connection involves a value judgment: that is, whether the information to be provided by a computer system is really needed as quickly as it can be procured. This depends a great deal upon the type of decisions that management men are faced with making. Unless they demand information quickly in order that action on decisions may be speeded up, the rapidity of procuring data under a manual system of processing is probably adequate. If, on the other hand, the length of the waiting time for data is of paramount importance to the decision-making process, a mechanized system will probably be welcome. A good amount of thought should be given to this question of the real need for speed in the procurement of basic information, in justifying the acquisition of a data-processing system.

In summary, then, if the savings and the frequency of use of a computer system are not great, the adoption of a less expensive system, perhaps a punched-card system, would be a suitable substitute. Consideration will be directed, then, to the preparation of plans for consideration of the punched-card equipment.

Concluding the feasibility study

At this stage, the team has learned much about computers. After the results of processing the application which the project team has worked out are known, a specific system should be recommended. However, before the team report is finally written, key men of the organization should attend a seminar, the purpose of which would be to educate them in the use of electronic data processing as it is done by a specific computer. After the principles have been explained, the computer demonstration should be presented. The old adage, "Seeing is believing," is especially applicable in this case. A familiar company application should be used in the demonstration to show that the computer can, and does, process data better than is the case with presently used processing methods. Theory alone is not sufficient to sell the product. It is sold more easily when the customer observes its operation. That is one reason why Ralph Bender drove demonstration models before he finally chose his particular automobile.

When the seminar and demonstration are over, a question-and-answer period should be conducted. Personnel should be encouraged to ask questions with regard to the installation. Normally questions are asked without any prompting from those demonstrating the equipment. Each key manager is likely to be interested in utilizing the computer, especially if his department is in need of help in the processing of its data. His suggestions as to how the computer can be used successfully to help him solve his problems could contribute greatly to the success of the system when installed.

The decision-making stage

Decision making involves the formulation of an opinion and the arrival at a course of action for solving a given problem. After the project-team members have had an opportunity to survey the need for a computer, and have compared the results obtained by processing the same application on different computers, their next logical step is evaluation of their findings.

They must recommend a system which in their opinion, based on the facts available to them, will do the best job for their firm. Despite what the team has learned from the claims of various computer manufacturer(s), or from other companies' experience with a specific system, the final responsibility for the choice lies with the team members alone.

All pertinent facts are studied and weighed. The team's recommendation is the only step lacking before a final decision can be made by top management either to approve or to reject the computer installation.

In arriving at a recommendation, the team must consider: (1) the actual results desired from an electronic installation, (2) the proper size and type of system to be ordered, and (3) whether to purchase or rent.

1. The Actual Benefits Desired From an Electronic Data-Processing Installation. Most firms, whether large or small, hope that, when a computer is installed, they will realize benefits abbreviated in a four-letter word, *PEAS,* which stands for *P*ublicity, *E*conomy, *A*ccuracy, and *S*peed. Like the Japanese specialty-shop owner, a forward-looking, progressive company wants to identify itself with the latest equipment, thus impressing both its customers and its competitors. The installation is usually, but not always, a sign of efficiency, progress, and prosperity. It is not uncommon, then, for "computerized" organizations to make their equipment available to others, for a price, and to encourage local citizens to visit the installation. This is considered free advertisement for the firm. On the other hand, it can be costly, because one or more company

representatives will have to be around to show and explain the system to the visiting group(s). Some companies hire guides whose sole job is to take groups on tours to explain the system and the applications it processes. Not only does this make a good impression on the local citizenry, but it is likely to have a favorable effect on the company's employees as well. If the company employees are aware of the uses of, and the benefits derived from, the system, they tend to take pride in it and consequently publicize it in their community to the best advantage of the firm.

When a project team reviews the reasons why a computer installation is being considered, economy in space and cost reduction are usually stressed. A business firm using manual methods of data processing may be using a large room or rooms, where many clerical employees, bookkeepers, and other aides work behind desks, using calculators, adding machines, typewriters, pencils, and paper. Such a system can be costly with regard to the amount of space allowed for this purpose, if a satisfactory amount of space is allowed for each employee. A fraction of this space might be satisfactory for an average-size computer installation designed to do the same job. With regard to economy through cost reduction, there can be a significant saving in time, thus reducing the marginal cost of data processing, especially in the "bread-and-butter" type applications.

With a computer installation, *accuracy* mounts, owing to minimum human intervention during processing and, also, because of the self-checking features which are built into the equipment. The project team should consider the *speed* factor with relation to the saving in time, which can be of great importance to certain departments within the firm. For example, in a retail store, the credit department can use the computer to process customer accounts, keeping special track of delinquent accounts. The credit department can hope to collect more quickly, when statements are prepared and mailed promptly, than can be expected under slower manual methods.

2. The Size and Type of Computer System To Be Used. The project team should choose either a "special-purpose" or a "general-purpose" computer, whichever more nearly fits its particular needs. Briefly, a special-purpose computer is less flexible in running different applications than a general-purpose computer. In ordering a "special-purpose" computer, the firm placing the order bears the total cost of design. This makes it quite costly. The team should be able to justify the need for its use in detail, considering the higher cost. A "general-purpose" computer is more widely advertised, more widely used, and much more flexible than a "special-purpose" computer. It can be used for several different kinds of applications. It is less costly, because it is a "standard" item and the cost of its design is spread among all of the firms which decide to use it.

Computers are classified under three general sizes: (1) small-size, (2) medium-size, and (3) large-size. When considering size, the team should think in terms of the applications to be processed at present as well as those anticipated in the future. In other words, the computer system under consideration should be capable of handling the present problems of the firm as well as those anticipated from future expansion.

The price that a company pays for a computer is based on the size it orders and the number of auxiliary components that come with it. In purchasing an automobile, for example, a low-priced, fully equipped automobile can be as costly as a high-priced, luxury, stripped model. In considering ordering a computer, the project team should determine whether a small-size computer with additional auxiliary components is more suitable than a medium-size or a large-scale installation with the basic components only. Size has a bearing on cost. The larger the computer, the more primary storage capacity it is likely to contain, and its speed is usually greater than that of smaller computers. Speed and the amount of storage space are two chief factors that determine the cost of the basic computer. Also, the need for input and output equipment and the speed with which they operate help to determine the total cost of the system.

Another important consideration is the "compatibility" of the computer system. *Compatibility* means a system the components of which operate in harmony with one another. If the central processing unit has access time at the microsecond speed, for instance, the use of a punched paper tape for input is considered incompatible, because the speed with which data are read from punched paper tape is not great enough to use the central processing unit to its best capacity. Some companies put stress upon speed and accuracy with less emphasis upon economy. Others stress processing of data accurately and economically, with speed being a minor point. Still other firms stress accuracy only, with little consideration for speed or economy. A project team must weigh these factors in the light of what its firm needs and can afford.

3. Purchase versus Rental. Should a given firm purchase or should it rent a computer? What factors determine the choice between these two alternatives? After the project team has decided upon the type and size of computer that will satisfy its data-processing needs, the next step would be a decision on whether the equipment should be purchased or leased. Many firms rent a computer chiefly because of the technological obsolescence factor. New computers are put on the market every year. Manufacturers improve and modify the equipment constantly and offer it in better form periodically. Renting permits flexibility in adapting a new system to the firm's particular problems, whereas the purchase of a computer may mean that revising the problems to be processable for the computer may be necessary.

Leasing usually includes maintenance and repair. The computer manufacturer prefers to provide his own personnel to service the equipment, in order to ascertain whether it is in good operating condition. This relieves the company which is using the computer of any responsibility in this regard. Rent usually includes the cost of servicing the equipment. If the system is purchased, however, the firm may need to train and provide its own maintenance personnel to service the machinery. If such personnel are not available, the manufacturer can be called upon to do so for a reasonable charge. In any event, maintenance can be expensive to a firm that is responsible for servicing its own equipment.

The decision to rent a computer is easier to make, because it puts less responsibility on the project team in deciding on the installation than might be the case in purchasing it. When a computer is rented and later proves unsatisfactory, it can be returned to the manufacturer without costly investment. This, however, depends largely upon the terms of the lease agreement. A company which is bound by a five-year lease policy, for example, may not find it as convenient to return a computer as would be the case under a one-year lease contract. Not only the terms of the lease, but also the cost of the computer rented, should be considered. A company with a good cash position, expecting to use a particular computer for a long time, might find it more profitable to purchase than to rent the equipment. Finally, the project team should consider this problem from the standpoint of the initial cost of acquisition as well as from that of the costs involved in operation after the acquisition has been made. As complete a cost picture as possible should be procured. Because many data-processing installations are on a lease basis, the rent paid each month must be considered as a capital investment over and above any operating costs incident to using the machines involved. The rent is a fixed cost which will have to be paid whether the system is in constant use or not. This, plus the daily operating costs, constitutes the firm's cost of processing data electronically. If this cost on a daily, weekly, or monthly basis amounts to more than that involved in the manual system in use, it would appear that the firm's management should discontinue thinking about procuring any type of mechanized system. If, on the other hand, it is lower, there is every argument for procurement on a cost basis. If the two equal each other, arguments other than that of cost will have to be presented to justify an installation. If possible, cost should be put on a per-unit basis rather than on the basis of total cost, because the former in many cases is more revealing than the latter.

Assuming that top management decides to approve the installation, a budget is approved and an order is placed with one particular computer manufacturer. Once a computer is placed on order, the company begins a pre-installation phase, during which time some employees go through training programs in how to operate the equipment to be installed. Usually there is a waiting period of six months to two years after the order is placed, depending upon the type and size of computer ordered and the demand-supply situation at that time. The waiting period should not present any particular problem to the firm, because it would normally take approximately that much time to get ready to use the system efficiently.

One of the questions often asked is, "How long does it normally take to conduct a feasibility study for the introduction of a computer installation?" The answer differs with the firm. Some of the factors that have an effect on the time limit are:

1. The competency of the projection-team members and the extent of their knowledge about the problems and policies of their firms, as well as their general understanding of the computers available on the market.
2. The speed with which the team collects cost and other needed data for the preparation of its final report and for the forming of an opinion as to whether a computer system should be installed. If cost data, for example, are not available because of present inefficient methods, or because of a deliberate attempt on the part of employees to withhold such vital information, it would take a great deal more time for the project team to form an opinion than it would if these conditions did not exist.
3. The size of the firm doing the study. The larger the firm, the more complex its operations are likely to be. These operations include systems, procedures, and people. In order for a project team to understand the systems and procedures that will be affected by a computer installation, detailed studies have to be made which would be time-consuming. The people consulted during the procedure can reduce this time by cooperating in promptly producing the data sought by the team.
4. The size of the computer installation under study. Regardless of the size of a given computer, it takes time for a firm to become familiar with it and to learn about the techniques which cause it to produce results. However, it takes less time to select a desk-size computer, for instance, than a large-scale computer. In the first place, a desk-size computer is easier to operate than a large-scale one. A large-scale system can be very complex, and it is a challenge to learn its maze of peripheries and the ways it can be programmed. Determining the need for a computer of this size would involve lengthy surveys and an equal amount of time to evaluate its usefulness in the particular processing applications for which it is being considered.

In conclusion, it would, generally, take a large firm needing a large-scale computer more time than it would take a small firm needing a smaller size to arrive at a satisfactory conclusion. The range is, roughly, between four months and five years. This generality is not meant to imply that there is any necessary connection between size of the firm and the size of the computer needed. That depends solely on processing needs rather than firm size.

QUESTIONS FOR REVIEW

1. What is meant by the term *computeritis?*
2. What alternatives can a business firm select from when confronted with the installation of data-processing equipment? Explain.
3. What problems must top management decide on before data processing is introduced?
4. What factors characterize the firm which is likely to purchase a computer? Explain.
5. What major objectives can be realized from an electronic data-processing installation?
6. What factors determine the success of a feasibility study? Explain.
7. Who stimulates interest for a feasibility study? Why?
8. Who is usually appointed as a project-team member? What is the project team's main function? Explain.
9. What qualifications (personal and technical) should a project director have? Explain.
10. What are the desired qualifications of each of the project-team members? Explain in detail.
11. Why are some team members reluctant to be on the team or unlikely to do a satisfactory job?
12. What is your opinion with respect to companies pirating personnel from other firms?
13. Explain fully the preliminary survey stage.
14. Discuss the advantages and the drawbacks of a project team's concentration on one manufacturer's equipment.
15. What types of firms are likely to hire a consultant? Why?
16. Present and describe some of the services which are offered by a consultant.
17. What two main areas are open for training a project team? Explain these areas in detail.
18. What application should be selected for the purpose of programming and testing a given computer? Why?
19. How should the company employees be informed about and educated on electronic data processing? Explain.
20. What factors are included in the preparation of an estimated annual savings statement?
21. List and explain briefly the incidental costs of a computer installation.
22. Who and what is involved in the decision-making stage? Explain.
23. Explain in detail the actual benefits desired from an electronic data-processing installation.
24. Discuss the advantages and disadvantages of a special-purpose computer and a general-purpose computer.
25. What determines the price of a computer? Explain.
26. Expound on a firm's purchasing versus renting a computer.
27. What factors determine the time it takes to conduct a feasibility study?

Chapter 22

The Data-Processing Department

Transition Problems

Chapter 21 introduced the problems faced by management in the introduction of a data-processing system and the manner in which they may be solved. This chapter presents briefly the problems which are likely to occur when a data-processing department is added to the organization, as well as a discussion of the services rendered by it.

When a company is changing from a manual system to a punched-card or electronic data-processing system, problems are bound to occur. These problems stem mainly from the conversion stage and affect employees as well as data.

The Effect of the New System on Employees

Many firms feel morally obligated not to lay off (at least for a while) employees who are not likely to "fit in" with the new system, especially those who may be too old to learn but not ready to retire. Their replacement, or displacement, would seem to be a step in the right direction, because the goal of the new installation is to maximize efficiency and minimize costs. However, it is very difficult for a company, regardless of its size, to lay off those employees, either gradually or abruptly, without suffering undesirable effects. These may result in the reduction of morale in the remaining employees, poor community-company relations, or, in the case of a unionized firm, harassment, if not a costly legal battle. Mindful of these factors, many firms which choose to install a computer system conveniently neglect to take any action. In fact, the manager of the new data-processing department may choose "the lesser of two evils" by assigning trifling duties to "unfit" employees, thus retaining them on the company payroll. This move is sometimes taken to show the employee that the company is acting in good faith, although its real motive is to discourage him from remaining with the firm. The net effect in this case would be one of two alternatives: (1) The employee would eventually find his job so meaningless and himself so unwanted that he would resign and find a more suitable position elsewhere. (2) The employee would decide to stay on the job, a course which results in frustration for all concerned. If the first alternative is chosen, the company hopes that the assumed result will take place. The second alternative leaves much to be desired: both the company and the employee are unhappy about the *status quo*. The employee's morale suffers, as he expects the worst and hopes for the best continually. His presence in the department affects the morale of the other employees as well.

Can a company realize any significant savings if it is to retain many of its employees who do not contribute adequate service to their employer because of the new data-processing system? The answer depends on the circumstances resulting in the decision to retain or displace them. Generally speaking, the answer is *No*. No company can or should retain employees who were formerly engaged in the operation of the manual system and whose background now makes them no longer needed. The exceptions include: (1) Those who are willing and qualified to be retrained for a new position. For example, a typist whose job previously was to type statements can be retrained to operate a key-punch machine and thus fill a useful position in a punched-card installation. The attitude and ability of the employee are very important. In one case, a 42-year-old production-scheduling clerk was asked by his supervisor to improve his academic background by taking courses in mathematics at night school to prepare himself for helping to program the new installation. He refused on the basis that he could no longer compete with younger students because he had not been to school for a number of years. Math was his weakest subject, and he felt that he could not possibly take the computer math course which his supervisor recommended. (2) Those who can be transferred to another department where, with a brief orientation, they would be able to render service in that department. This is possible especially when the work of one department is similar to that of another department. When this is the case, the possibility of employee transfer is worth looking into.

The Effects of the New System on Data

A new installation, punched-card or electronic, requires standardization of input data and its preparation in a manner acceptable to the system for processing. Problems in this regard are bound to occur. When an error is not detected in the planning stage, it is bound to reappear at a later stage as the new system becomes more complete. Whenever errors occur, they should be corrected immediately. This is not meant to imply that the system itself is inadequate or ineffective. It should be remembered that a system can be no more effective than the accuracy of the input data allows it to be. To help achieve effectiveness from the new system, it is desirable to "debug" all errors from the source documents and to present the latter in a standardized, clear manner. Such presentation relieves the key-punch operator and other personnel responsible for the preparation of data from the need for verifying the accuracy of the source documents or the sequence in which they are presented for key punching.

It has been said that the fewer the people, the greater the department's accuracy. However, because it would be difficult for a data-processing department to be completely automated, people will always be needed to perform key tasks. This fact emphasizes the vital role of effective and clear communications. Communication is the act of transferring information either orally or in writing. Clear instructions should be communicated to those employees preparing the source documents as well as to those who convert the documents into input. In the case of the latter employees, they must know exactly what is to be done and how they are to proceed in converting the source documents into the specified form. Naturally, when anything goes wrong, poor communication may not always be the reason. The reason may be the incompetence of those doing a job which requires some degree of skill. The inadequate knowledge of an employee doing a given job can usually be easily detected. It should be solved immediately, either by further training or by replacement. Before any hurried replacement is made, however, the supervisor should analyze the situation thoroughly to find out whether the problem arises from poor presentation of the source documents, from the complex nature of the job, or from the incompetence of the person performing the work. In the first possibility, a contact should be made with the proper personnel, the purpose of which would be to call attention to the need for better presentation of the source document. If, however, the source document is presented properly but its contents are too involved, allowance should be made for its conversion into punched cards or any other medium. For instance, it would take a key-punch operator more time to punch alphameric data in a given field such as product number 1AK27 than to punch either alphabetic (CABLE) or numeric (5604) data separately, especially when automatic shifting into alphabetic or numeric mode is not programmed into the key punch. Therefore, if input data are to be punched and processed successfully, the cooperation of the departments preparing the source documents is necessary.

The Data-Processing Department

Location

The exact location of a data-processing center differs in different firms. Some firms believe that the computer facility should be under the "department of most use" or in the department where clerical costs are the highest and savings to be achieved are greatest. Others believe that it should be an independent department not tied directly to any other department. The "department of most use" approach is likely to be a better choice when most of the applications processed belong to a given department. As far as the manager of the computer center is concerned, his responsibility ends in satisfying the head of that department. However, when the computer installation is made an independent center, the manager must have a broader knowledge about company procedures and systems, because he will be serving the company in general. The independent organizational status of a computer center is most likely to reflect management's view that it is a tool to aid in controlling the organization. Consequently, it should have an independent position where its manager reports directly to a top key officer.

Organization

Generally, a data-processing center is manned by systems analysts, programmers, console operators, key-punch operators, and others to aid in the preparation of data. These personnel are headed by an experienced data-processing man referred to as the "Manager" of the Data-Processing Department or Center. (Figure 22-1.)

The Data-Processing Manager. The highest position in the data-

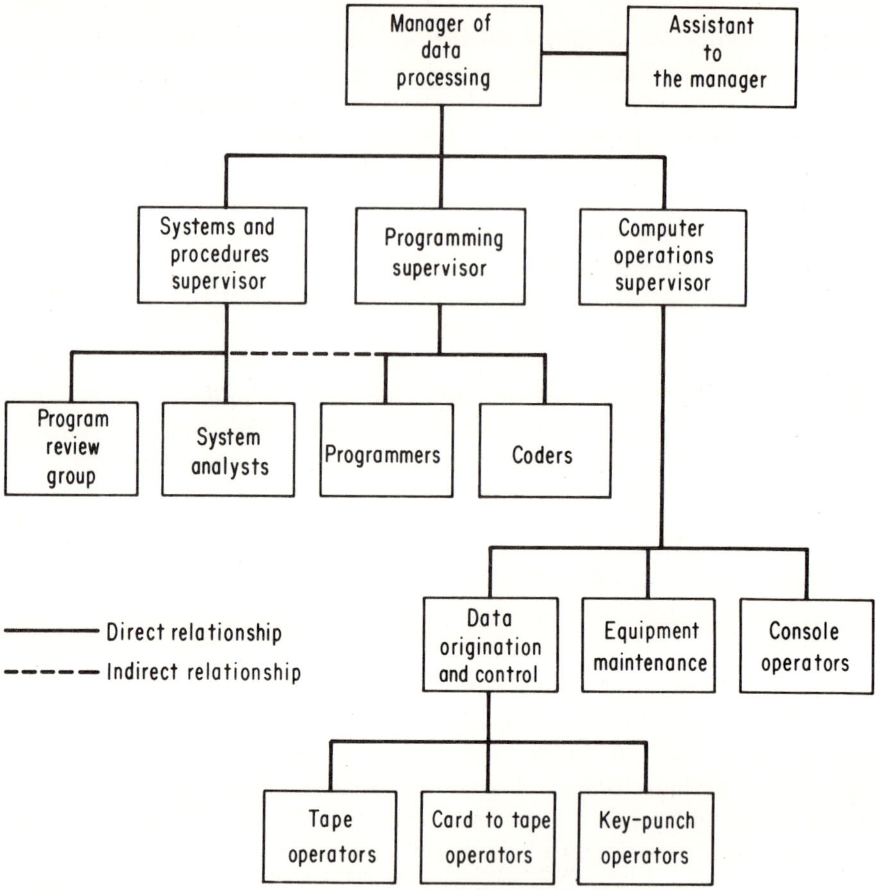

Figure 22-1. General organizational structure of a data-processing center

processing center is that of the manager. *Management* is described as a social process. It is social because it deals with people. It is a process because it involves a specific way of doing things. The manager's job involves dealing with people in achieving an integrated data-processing system to accomplish certain goals. He is fully responsible to his superiors for the work of his employees and for the results of the processing. His position as a manager should command respect from without his department as well as from within. If used effectively, the manager's knowledge about data processing and his ability to sell to other department heads what his department has to offer them will have a great influence on his effectiveness within the organization. If the services received are satisfactory, it is very likely that his status and recognition of him by top and middle management will become firmly established. Most people respect a man who can prove his worth by the knowledge he possesses and by the actions which he takes. If the result of what he offers is a sincere reflection of his personality and ability, the "old-timers" will accord him due respect. On the other hand, if a manager tries to "bluff his way through," he will find it equally as difficult to gain the respect and cooperation of his colleagues.

Leadership and Human Relations. A manager can gain respect within his organization by the way he manages his subordinates. In the management and human relations areas, a manager must develop skills and qualities to lead people at all levels within his department, and especially those with whom he copes daily. Coping with people requires understanding of their needs and wants. Human needs are highly individualized and change constantly. That is, what an employee needs today may change tomorrow. These needs and wants can generally be satisfied by: (1) praising the employee for good work, (2) showing appreciation for work, (3) instilling in his mind the fact of job security and the opportunity for promotion and advancement within the department, (4) payment of competitive wages and building hopes for regular salary increases, (5) offering work that sustains interest and motivation, and (6) good working conditions. In brief, an employee's main goal is the attainment of personal job satisfactions, recognition of his status, and the respect of his fellows. Once he is convinced of the possibility of attaining this goal, his morale and attitude will be such that the problem of motivating him solves itself.

The foregoing discussion suggests that a manager's real authority be granted and recognized by the group which he heads, because it is what they think of him as a leader that makes him respected and effective, and not solely the authority which he receives from his superior. In other words, the effectiveness of a manager comes from below upward, not from the top downward. When his employees report to work on time, are self-directed, self-motivated, and anxious to do their job assignments, he is considered a good "boss," because people work *with* him rather than *for* him. If the opposite occurs, the result usually leads to confusion in the department, which certainly does not promote maximum effectiveness in performance.

This discussion brings us to the question of the type of leadership that a data-processing manager should possess. There are three main types of leaders, namely, democratic, authoritarian, and free-reign type.

Democratic leadership emphasizes informal group participation and the desire to satisfy its members. A data-processing manager will get much done if he allows his subordinate supervisors, and, indirectly, his system analysts and programmers, to participate in evaluating a project and to suggest solutions to it. Naturally, the final decision rests with the manager. It is assumed that, for a democratic type leadership to succeed, the employees must be competent and be briefed on the details of the project under discussion.

Authoritarian leadership implies that leadership is a right given and approved from above and one that should be exercised. In this approach, the manager assigns jobs to his subordinates, and there is only one-way communication with regard to commands and the delegation of work assignments. This type of leadership can accomplish results fast, because it does not allow undue delays in consultations or group participation. On the other hand, if the individual employees do not feel as though they are a part of the group as a result of this approach, they can make the manager's job unpleasant.

The free-reign approach regards the employees as competent, well-qualified members of the department. They are asked to make decisions on problems which affect them as long as they accomplish results in a satisfactory manner. This is advantageous in that it gives each employee a chance to think and to help arrive at decisions in problem solving. However, the lack of supervision may cause unnecessary confusion in the department if the employees involved abuse their freedom. In this approach, the manager must be willing to take the final responsibility for the actions of his subordinates.

In conclusion, an ideal manager is a person who has knowledge of his employees' needs and wants, who allows his subordinates to participate in discussing and evaluating a given project but reserves to himself final authority in the matter, and who is a leader who *earns* rather than *demands* support and respect.

Technical Background of the Manager. An elementary but significant qualification of a data-processing manager is the possession of a broad knowledge of data processing generally and an expert knowledge of the particular system with which he must deal. He is considered an expert in his field, and other department heads within the organization will rely on his judgment and technical knowledge to plan and process their data on the computer.

Being an expert in data processing means that the manager will find it important to evaluate the results achieved with the present installation and to keep abreast of the technical developments in other systems available in the market. He should make sure that the company is not lagging behind because of either obsolescence in its equipment or his failure to suggest modifications or introduce new ideas which would help in improving the efficiency of the present installation.

A manager's technical knowledge is necessary for handling internal problems. Programmers, for instance, who are working on a problem where they are not sure of the proper procedure or who are uncertain about some phase of the procedure, should feel free to consult the manager for help in solving such technical problems. If he is unable to do so, his prestige as the top man of the department in the eyes of his subordinates suffers a blow. Although it would be desirable for him to be so, this does not mean to imply that a manager should be an expert in all phases of the technical work, nor that he should take over the completion of each job which cannot be completed by his subordinates. The manager is not necessarily a machine operator or a specialist in programming, although, with limited training in management, some men with a natural bent for it have risen from a position as a programmer or systems analyst to head of the department. In management, stress is more upon the synchronization of team efforts in such a way that they work harmoniously toward the accomplishment of the goal than on the specialized technical knowledge in any one of the areas delegated to other men.

Where can a business firm find a manager for its data-processing department who has both managerial and technical background? In the first place, a man of this caliber is not easy to find. Firms have a tendency to recruit from without the organization. This is done in the hope that an outsider may inject impetus and introduce new ideas to the department.

Another approach is to promote from within the organization. It may be that a qualified person is already available who can be replaced in his present position with greater ease than an "outsider" can be found to manage the data-processing department. A third approach is to select a well-trained technician from the ranks of the firm and train him in the fields of management and human relations before he is assigned to his new post.

Subordinate Groups. Immediately under the data-processing manager there are three main groups, each of which is headed by a section head or a supervisor: (1) the systems and procedures group, (2) the programming group, and (3) the computer operations group.

(1) Systems and procedures:

Systems and procedures discover what information must be provided to management and the ways in which it can be obtained. In other words, after an order has been received with regard to "what is required," the systems and procedures group devise a data-processing procedure which produces the results most efficiently. They are also concerned with designing a system which makes possible the use of manual, mechanical, and electronic machines sequenced in such a way that each application can be processed successfully. This requires thorough knowledge of the capabilities and limitations of the installation. (Figure 22-1.)

To qualify as a systems and procedures analyst, a college background in one of the business areas—that is, production, finance, accounting, management, or marketing—as well as a basic background in mathematics and statistics, is desirable. Some business firms find that experience in the operation of a computer, in addition to systems analysis, is desirable. People with the "ideal" background, however, are difficult to find. The average business graduate may have an excellent background in production, finance, marketing, accounting, or management but a poor one in mathematics and data processing. The demand for this background varies with the firm. Because mathematics is related intimately to the workings of a commercial electronic computer, it is highly desirable for a business student to take courses in numerical analysis or computer mathematics if he is interested in entering this field.

The program review group consists of systems analysts and selected senior programmers whose jobs are evaluating and revising proposed data-processing procedures. In small installations, they may also be required to develop mechanized procedures in addition to their regular assignments. The combined background of the group helps to ascertain that all procedures and/or programs being evaluated are workable and efficient.

(2) Programming:

Generally, programming involves determination of the results expected of the computer, block-diagramming, preparation of a set of instructions for the computer, coding the program, and debugging. Programming in itself includes the first three steps. In large organizations, programmers concentrate on the construction of block diagrams and writing instructions in symbolic language. The coder carries out the rest by converting the symbolic instructions into machine language to be used directly by the computer.

Programmers are often expected to do coding as well as block diagramming and writing the program. Coders do not have to know how to program in order to retain their positions as coders. In fact, their duties, in some cases, are performed by the use of auto-coders or other devices that translate directly from symbolic into machine language.

(3) Computer operations:

Any duties involved in the preparation of the data for input, in maintenance, and in actual operation of the equipment are parts of the computer operations area. The bulk of the employees of the data-processing department are employed here. The group consists of console operators, tape operators (if any), maintenance employees, and key-punch operators. This is an area which requires close attention to details. The supervisor should check on the flow of data from the input stage to the processing stage to make sure that it is completed satisfactorily. This will minimize any machine "downtime" or "idle time." He should also make sure that employees are cooperating with one another. For instance, the console operator must rely on the key-punch operator for the initial punching of the source data in cards before he is able to process them on the computer. If any delay occurs, his job will be delayed also. The required training for operative employees differs with the position. The key-punch operator normally is expected to have had some experience in the use of the key punch, either from a former employer, through courses taken in a private educational institution, or on the job. However, in the event that a firm is interested in retraining its own employees, they are sent to a manufacturer's training center for the purpose of learning the concepts and operation of the key punch. When they return, an on-the-job-training program should supplement their formal training and give them practice in operating the key punch.

Console operators follow the same procedure as key-punch operators except for the time limit. It takes more time for a complete orientation in the operation of a computer than it does for orientation in key punching. A computer console consists of a number of buttons and switches which have to be manipulated and used in a given sequence if processing is to be done correctly. The depression of a button at the wrong time may foul up the loading of the program or the processing of data. Manual dexterity and alertness on the job are required of a console operator. Alertness on the job means being able to detect and correct any machine malfunctioning or to handle emergencies during processing. It is desirable for a console operator to have some programming background, so as to correct any minor errors on his own. Some programmers begin as console operators and then gradually advance to the job of a programmer.

The jobs of the employees who operate the equipment become monotonous. Because employees usually produce better results if the type of work they perform differs occasionally, it is desirable to rotate them on different jobs. For instance, the programmer can operate the console on one application and act as a coder on another application. A console operator with a programming background can develop a program in one application and code a program in another application. This will not only allow employees to gain broad experience, but will also act as a back-up system in the event of an emergency such as illness, vacation, or the like. Employees can substitute for one another temporarily or as needed. This gives flexibility to the operation of the data-processing department.

Key punching can become routine and boring, especially when a large volume of data is to be punched in the same location in each card. This monotony often results in high labor turnover. The author is familiar with an installation which employs 11 key-punch operators. Within one year, only two of the original 11 operators were left. The other nine were new and semi-experienced. Some of the reasons given by those leaving were: (1) little incentive, (2) no challenge, (3) monotony and boredom on the job, (4) too much like a factory job, (5) no opportunity for advancement, (6) low pay and heavy work load, (7) irregular and unsatisfactory raises, (8) limited social opportunity, and (9) little brainwork.

In order to avoid the drudgery of the job, it would be helpful for the supervisor to assign to key-punch employees duties which involve some decision making and a variety of tasks. For example, a key-punch operator could be asked to prepare a program card for the key punch or to make suggestions as to better ways of designing a data card. A key-punch operator can also operate the sorter or the collator in the routine of preparing punched data for processing by the computer. Many key-punch operators have been found to be excellent in operating such machines. Management can be instrumental in reducing labor turnover by developing a balance to cut monotony and by introducing creativity, thus improving morale through motivation.

Responsibilities of the data-processing center

The data-processing center should be regarded as a service department the purpose of which is to make the job of the other departments easier through the preparation of reports based on data which they supply for processing. If this attitude prevails throughout the organizational structure, it will make the job of data processing easier. The issuance of accurate and meaningful reports is the primary responsibility of the data-processing center.

Before the data-processing department can assume the responsibility of serving other departments and producing reports and statements for them, it is necessary that the source documents it receives be accurate. Accurate input data depend, to a large extent, upon three factors:

(1) Correct procedures must be followed in other departments. Managers at different levels in the organization must first know what information they want. To illustrate, the general manager of the production department is responsible to the president for the application of the over-all broad policies adopted by the board of directors. He would not be interested in the voluminous details which are generated in the departments of his subordinate supervisors. Unless exceptions occur, his way of managing is through the reports and other condensed statements which he receives concerning their activities and operations. Likewise, the department head is responsible to the general manager for efficient operation of his department within the budget appropriated for that purpose. He, too, would not generally be concerned with routine matters occurring at the lower level unless exceptions to the formulated policies and procedures occur. What each manager requires for managing his department determines the types of reports which must be prepared by the data-processing department. Unless the department managers are specific on this matter, the data-processing department is in no position to act on the data it receives from them.

(2) The data to be processed must be forwarded by someone in each department who has the authority directly to request the work from the

data-processing department. If a given department head, for instance, has complete autonomy over what goes on in his department, he should request the service of the data-processing center directly. If, on the other hand, his authority in this matter is limited, he should have the approval of his immediate superior, who would be in reality the one requesting the services. In the latter case, the data-processing manager should be so informed.

(3) There must be standardization of procedures in those departments that are authorized to use the service. For instance, before a payroll application can begin, the exact regular and overtime pay for each class of employees must be determined and exceptions, such as sickness and vacations, with or without pay, systematized. Also, the time and frequency of payment of bonuses, commissions, and dividends should be determined. The data-processing department cannot process the payroll unless the amount and frequency of payments of the elements included in it are outlined by the particular department heads involved.

Once the type and number of reports are determined, the authority of each person requesting service clarified, and procedures with regard to basic input data are systematized, the data-processing department is ready for effective operation. It can obtain accurate and timely results, however, only if its manager devises proper procedures to systematize the service. The procedure begins with a request form and ends in the presentation of the finished results.

The Request Form. Before any service is rendered, it is necessary for authorized personnel first to contact the data-processing manager, requesting service. This *can* be done on the phone. However, to eliminate any misunderstanding or misinterpretation of the facts, the request should be in writing. Employees in the data-processing department should not accept or authorize the rendering of service for any other department without the approval of their manager. When a request is presented, the data-processing manager is the proper person to approve or disapprove it. The form should include spaces for information such as: (1) the name of the department requesting service, (2) the names and titles of the persons filling out the form, (3) the type of data to be processed, (4) the form in which the results are to be presented, that is, summary form or detailed form, (5) the sequence of the results to be presented, (6) the number of copies needed, (7) the frequency of the processing of the reports, that is, whether the application needs to be processed daily, weekly, or monthly, (8) the party who should receive the results, and (9) the signature of the party authorized to request the service.

In requesting a new application, the department requesting the service should arrange a meeting with the data-processing manager to discuss the problem from the standpoints of economy and workability of the application on the computer system. Once a procedure is devised and the application prepared, further meetings are not necessary, as it can be run at the regular intervals requested.

Some of the advantages of a request form are: The data provided on the form help the data-processing manager to estimate the time that the application would take, permitting him to promise delivery of the results on a certain date. The use of the data-processing equipment is limited to the number of hours in a given shift. Considering other jobs to be done, it would be necessary for the manager to check as to whether the application can fit into the schedule without disrupting it. Without the request form, confusion in scheduling could result very easily.

Also, the request form serves as an historical record of the completed application or of the services rendered. The manager can tell how much time is spent on each machine, the frequency of usage, and, consequently, the cost of each application. This machine cost, plus the portion of the employees' salaries charged to the completion of the application, would constitute the cost of the application. This cost can be reported to the proper department so that it can absorb its share of the cost of operating the data-processing center. In a small firm, this procedure may not be necessary. If emergency requests for service are made, the data-processing department should have enough flexibility to handle them immediately. Effective communications in this regard are important. When they are verbal, the manager should "listen" and not just "hear." A story is told of a general manager who called the data-processing manager and inquired about the time when the regular trial balance would be ready. The processing manager answered, "Immediately," thinking that the general manager telephoned because the trial balance had priority. This resulted in running the trial balance ahead of other equally important applications and causing complaints from other departments.

Scheduling. Once the request form is evaluated, a schedule should be set up for running the application. The manager or his subordinate in charge of scheduling should promise a realistic delivery date, making proper allowance for the processing of other applications, machine breakdown, and unforeseeable problems. It is commendable of the manager to promise a deadline earlier than usual if he is sure it can be met. However, it would not be fair for him to do all or part of the work just to please the department requesting the service, although at times it is considered a good gesture for him to participate in operating the machines as a last resort and when no other help is available. In the event of emergencies, an overtime shift should be arranged. In this case cost is a factor which should be weighed to see whether the emergency processing of the application is justified.

In small installations, it is not uncommon for a manager to spend approximately 40 per cent of his time operating the equipment and the remainder of his time managing the department. He performs the functions which should be assigned to a machine operator. Some managers have limited authority, are overworked, and are underpaid as well as understaffed. Their authority is so limited in some cases that even the purchase of a professional book would require a superior's approval. This limited authority appears to be unfortunate in that ideally a manager should spend his time planning the work of those in his department so as to get things done through them. Final responsibility for the accuracy of the results and for their delivery to the proper party rests in the manager of the data-processing department.

QUESTIONS FOR REVIEW

1. Discuss the effect of the new system on the firm's employees.
2. Discuss the effects of the new system on data.
3. "The fewer the people, the greater the department's accuracy." Do you agree with this statement? Defend your answer.
4. Where should the computer be located? Under whose direction should it be? Why?
5. What are the qualifications of a data-processing manager? What are his duties and responsibilities?
6. What can a manager do in order to satisfy the needs and wants of his subordinates?
7. List and explain the three types of leaders. Which type do you prefer? Why?
8. What three main groups are under the manager's direct supervision?
9. What technical background should a manager possess? Explain.
10. What is the main function of a systems and procedures analyst? What qualifications should he have?
11. What steps are involved in programming? Which of these steps are considered the most pertinent to programming?
12. What types of positions are available in the area of computer operations? Explain each position briefly.
13. Name seven reasons why key-punch operators leave their jobs.
14. Discuss the responsibilities of the data-processing center.
15. What purpose does a request form serve? What type of information does it contain?
16. Do you believe that a manager should spend a reasonable amount of his time operating equipment? Explain.

Bibliography

American Management Association, *Electronic Data Processing in Industry* (New York: The Association, 1955).

Bakst, Aaron, *Mathematical Puzzles and Pastimes* (Princeton, N.J.: D. Van Nostrand Co., Inc., 1941).

Becker, Esther R. and Eugene F. Murphy, *The Office in Transition* (New York: Harper & Row, Publishers, 1957).

Berkeley, Edmund Callis, *The Computer Revolution* (Garden City, N.Y.: Doubleday & Company, Inc., 1962).

——— and Lawrence Wainwright, *Computers, Their Operations and Applications* (New York: Reinhold Publishing Corporation, 1962).

Bibby, Dause L., *Your Future in the Electronic Computer Field* (New York: Richards Rosen Associates, Inc., 1962).

Bowden, B. V., *Faster than Thought* (Middlesex, England: Penguin Books, 1954).

Brandon, Dick H., *Management Standards for Data Processing* (Princeton, N.J.: D. Van Nostrand Co., Inc., 1963).

Bukstein, Edward J., *Digital Counters and Computers* (New York: Holt, Rinehart, & Winston, Inc., 1960).

Canning, Richard G., *Electronic Data Processing for Business and Industry* (New York: John Wiley & Sons, Inc., 1956).

Chapin, Ned, *An Introduction to Automatic Computers,* 2nd ed. (Princeton, N.J.: D. Van Nostrand Co., Inc., 1955-63).

———, *Programming Computers for Business Applications* (New York: McGraw-Hill Book Company, 1961).

Crowder, Norman A., *The Arithmetic of Computers* (Garden City, New York: Doubleday & Company, 1960).

Eckert, W. J., *Punched Card Methods in Scientific Computation* (New York: T. J. Watson Astronomical Computing Bureau, Columbia University, 1940).

Falmestock, James D., *Computers and How They Work* (New York: Ziff-Davis Publishing Company, 1959).

Flores, Ivan, *Computer Logic* (Englewood Cliffs, N.J.: Prentice-Hall, Inc., 1962).

Friedman, Burton Dean, *Punched Card Primer* (Chicago: Public Administration Service, 1955).

Gibbons, Conway J. and D. E. Watts, *Business Experience with Electronic Computers, A Synthesis of What Has Been Learned from Electronic Data Processing Installations. A Research Study and Report Prepared for Controller Institute Research Foundation, Inc. New York, 1959.*

Gotlieb, C. and J. N. P. Hum, *High-Speed Data Processing* (New York: McGraw-Hill Book Company, 1958).

Halacy, D., *Computers, the Machines We Think With,* 1st ed. (New York: Harper & Row, Publishers, 1962).

Haskins & Sells, *Data Processing by Electronics* (New York: 1955).

———, *Introduction to Data Processing* (New York: 1957).

Hein, Leonard W., *An Introduction to Electronic Data Processing for Business* (Princeton, N.J.: D. Van Nostrand Co., Inc., 1961).

Hoos, Ida R., *Automation in the Office* (Washington, D.C.: Public Affairs Press, 1961).

Jacobowitz, Henry, *Computer Arithmetic* (New York: Hayden Book Companies, 1962).

———, *Electronic Computers,* 1st ed. (Garden City, New York: Doubleday & Company, 1963).

Kaufman, Felix, *Electronic Data Processing and Auditing* (New York: The Ronald Press Company, 1961).

Laurie, Edward J., *Computers and How They Work* (Cincinnati, Ohio: Southwestern Publishing Company, 1963).

Leeds, Herbert D. and Gerald M. Weinberg, *Computer Programming Fundamentals* (New York: McGraw-Hill Book Company, 1961).

Levin, Howard S., *Office Work and Automation* (New York: John Wiley & Sons, Inc., 1956).

Martin, Edley Wainwright, *Electronic Data Processing, an Introduction* (Homewood, Ill.: Richard D. Irwin, 1961).

McCracken, Daniel D., *Digital Computer Programming* (New York: John Wiley & Sons, Inc., 1957).

———, Harold Weiss and Tsai-hwa Lee, *Programming Business Computers* (New York: John Wiley & Sons, Inc., 1959).

McGill, Donald, *Punched Card Data Processing for Profit Improvement* (New York: McGraw-Hill Book Company, 1962).

Nett, Roger and Stanley A. Hetzler, *An Introduction to Electronic Data Processing* (New York: Free Press of Glencoe, Inc., 1959).

Oakford, Robert V., *Introduction to Electronic Data Processing Equipment*—Its Operation and Control (New York: McGraw-Hill Book Company, 1962).

Postley, John A., *Computers and People* (New York: McGraw-Hill Book Company, 1960).

Salmon, Lawrence J., *IBM Machine Operation and Wiring* (Belmont, Calif.: Wadsworth Publishing Company, 1962).

Scott, Theodore G., *Basic Computer Programming,* 1st ed. (Garden City, New York: Doubleday & Company, Inc., 1962).

Siegel, Paul, *Understanding Digital Computers* (New York: John Wiley & Sons, Inc., 1961).

Sprague, Richard E., *Electronic Business Systems* (New York: The Ronald Press Company, 1962).

Van Horn, Gregory, *Automatic Data Processing Systems* (Belmont, Calif.: Wadsworth Publishing Company, 1960).

Van Ness, Robert G., *Principles of Punched Card Data Processing* (Elmhurst, Ill.: Business Press, 1962).

Wilkes, M. V., D. J. Wheeler and Stanley Gill, *Programs for an Electronic Digital Computer* (Reading, Mass.: Addison-Wesley Publishing Co., Inc., 1957).

Williams, Samuel B., *Digital Computing Systems* (New York: McGraw-Hill Book Company, 1959).

Index